Infidels and the Damn Churches

Infidels and the Damn Churches

Irreligion and Religion in Settler British Columbia

LYNNE MARKS

26 25 24 23 22 21 20 19 18 17 5 4 3 2 1

Printed in Canada on FSC-certified ancient-forest-free paper (100% post-consumer recycled) that is processed chlorine- and acid-free.

Library and Archives Canada Cataloguing in Publication

Marks, Lynne Sorrel, author
Infidels and the damn churches : irreligion and religion in settler British Columbia / Lynne Marks.

Includes bibliographical references and index.
Issued in print and electronic formats.
ISBN 978-0-7748-3344-8 (hardcover). – ISBN 978-0-7748-3345-5 (pbk.). – ISBN 978-0-7748-3346-2 (PDF). –ISBN 978-0-7748-3347-9 (EPUB). – ISBN 978-0-7748-3348-6 (Kindle)

1. Irreligion –British Columbia –History. 2. Secularism –British Columbia – History. 3. Religion –British Columbia –History. 4. British Columbia –Religion. I. Title.

BL2530.C3M327 2017 200.9711 C2016-907468-4
C2016-907469-2

Canada

UBC Press gratefully acknowledges the financial support for our publishing program of the Government of Canada (through the Canada Book Fund), the Canada Council for the Arts, and the British Columbia Arts Council.

This book has been published with the help of a grant from the Canadian Federation for the Humanities and Social Sciences, through the Awards to Scholarly Publications Program, using funds provided by the Social Sciences and Humanities Research Council of Canada.

Printed and bound in Canada by Friesens
Set in Garamond by Artegraphica Design Co. Ltd.
Copy editor: Deborah Kerr
Proofreader: Caitlin Gordon-Walker
Indexer: Cameron Duder
Cover designer: George Kirkpatrick

UBC Press
The University of British Columbia
2029 West Mall
Vancouver, BC V6T 1Z2
www.ubcpress.ca

To John Hale Blakely,
Dori Benjamin Marks Blakely, and
Mira Rachel Marks Blakely

Contents

List of Illustrations / ix

Acknowledgments / xi

Introduction: Leaving God Behind? / 3

1 A Godless Province? Counting the Infidels and the Indifferent / 29

2 Pie in the Sky When You Die: Political and Cultural Challenges to Religion / 55

3 Manly White Men, Fuzzy Fidelity, and Practical Christians: Blurred Boundaries of Belief and Chasms of Racialized Difference / 78

4 Sundays Are So Different Here: Communities in British Columbia, Ontario, and Nova Scotia / 100

5 Could Sodom Be Worse? Christianity, Moral Reform, and the Godless of Vancouver and Victoria / 134

6 Under Siege: Non-Christians, Racialized Groups, and White Women's Rights / 161

7 Subtler and More Dangerous Forms of Error: Metaphysical Religions / 186

Conclusion: Godless Past and Present / 213

Appendix: Tables / 222

Notes / 234

Bibliography / 291

Index / 311

Illustrations

British Columbia, 1915 / xiv
Silverton miners, Standard Silver Mine, Kootenays, 190- / 47
Columbia Avenue, Rossland, 1896 / 48
Coal miners at Ladysmith, Vancouver Island, 191– / 50
Colonel Robert Thornton Lowery, 189– / 57
Hotel saloon, Nelson, 1899 / 70
John Houston, c. 1900 / 75
Father Pat (Henry Irwin), c. 1909 / 80
Wellington Hotel, Wellington, Vancouver Island, c. 189- / 85
Sunday School picnic, Nelson, n.d. / 89
St. George's Church, Rossland, 1905 / 90
Nelson Oddfellows in regalia, c. 1900 / 91
Orange Parade, Revelstoke, 1900 / 95
Funeral at Atlin, 1899 / 97
Nelson, c. 1900 / 104
First Anglican church in Rossland, c. 1905 / 105
Trinity Methodist Church, Nelson, c. 1911 / 109
Jimmy White, panning on the Wild Horse River, Fort Steele / 113
Annie McQueen Gordon wedding photo, 1889 / 114

Jessie McQueen, 1885 / 116
Kaslo Methodist Ladies Aid Society, 1898 / 118
Church of England, All Saints, Vernon, c. 191– / 127
Reverend J.C. Speer, n.d. / 139
Vancouver, looking west to Gastown, 1911 / 150
Temple Emmanu-El, Victoria Synagogue, 190– / 163
Palace of the Saints, Victoria Chinatown, c. 1899 / 169
Chinese Rescue Home, Victoria, May 1906 / 173
Indigenous people and Catholic missionaries at Fort Fraser, 1900–01 / 177
Delegates to the Women's Missionary Society conference, Victoria, 1912 / 183
Hannah Maynard and her grandson, c. 1893 / 195
Spiritualists' picnic at Cordova Bay, near Victoria, 1890 / 196

Figures

1 Atheists and those of no religion, BC and Canada, 1901–2011 / 5
2 BC population by racial and ethnic origin, 1901 and 1911 / 10
3 Canadian population by racial and ethnic origin, 1901 and 1911 / 10
4 Protestant church involvement by census districts, 1901 / 34
5 Catholic church involvement by census districts, 1901 / 35
6 Atheists, agnostics, and no religion, Rossland, Slocan, and BC, 1901 / 46

Acknowledgments

This book has taken more years than I care to remember – although I think that my nineteen-year-old son may have come into the world at least a few years before it began. Given the length of this process, I have many people whom I am very pleased to thank.

Infidels and the Damn Churches began as a part of the Canadian Families Project (CFP), and I owe a debt of gratitude to Peter Baskerville and Eric Sager, who brought me into the project and provided support, advice, and encouragement. I am also thankful for their willingness to share databases from the Canadian Century Infrastructure Project with me. I would like to thank SSHRC, which funded the CFP. The CFP enabled me to hire a range of impressive research assistants and to develop the databases that were essential to this project. Work study funding and internal research grants from the University of Victoria provided further support. This project has been in the works for so long that I'm bound to omit some of the hard-working research assistants who participated in it, but I would like to thank Donna Mandeville, Tina Block (who has just produced a book of her own on this subject), Lorraine O'Donnell, Sean Mattys, Christie Shaw, Lana Castleman, Linda LeDrew, Cameron Duder, Georgia Sitara, Nick Matte, Nancy Newlove, Judith Gibbard, Tim Noddings, Bonnie Sawyer, Sarah Lebel Van Vugt, Noah Miller, Paige Fehr, Liang Han, and Drew Koehn. Marc Trottier, many years ago, provided a great deal of assistance with computer programming. I am very grateful to Theresa Gallant for her exceptional ability to rescue me (as she has so many times before), cheerfully and incredibly efficiently, in this case by putting all of the chapters and tables together in the right places, at lightning speed. Thanks also to Dori Blakely for his work on the graphs and the tables.

Like all historians, I owe a major debt of gratitude to many archivists. All the archivists at the BC Archives were very helpful, but I am particularly grateful to Lucky Budd, who organized the invaluable Imbert Orchard Collection of oral histories at the archives. Archivists at a range of religious archives in British Columbia, Ontario, and Nova Scotia were also very helpful. I want to particularly remember the late Bob Stewart at the United Church Archives in Vancouver, who helped me find a range of crucial documents and took an interest in this project during its early stages. The archivists in the Anglican Diocesan Archives in Kelowna and the Catholic Archdiocesan Archives in Vancouver were also particularly helpful, as was Walter Meyer Zu Erpen, who generously provided me with access to the records of the Survival Research Institute of Canada. I am also grateful for the assistance of archivists in a range of small local BC archives, including those at Rossland, Revelstoke, and Kelowna. Over the course of researching and writing this book, the nature of historical research has been transformed through the digitization of so many primary sources. Historical newspapers, which would once have required laborious microfilm research, are increasingly available (and searchable) from one's computer. The accessibility of census databases online is also most useful, and I am particularly grateful to Patrick Dunae for his work on the ViHistory database. All of this has made a huge difference in the latter stages of this project, and I am very appreciative of the many historians, librarians, and archivists who have made, and continue to make, historical records increasingly available online.

I am grateful to the University of Victoria's Centre for Studies in Religion and Society. Two fellowships from the centre – one near the beginning of this project and the other right at the end – provided the time I needed to focus on research and writing. Some of this book was written at the centre, and over the years much of it was written in days (and more commonly, nights) in a small collectively owned house at the very edge of the ocean, where the generosity of my partner gave me the uninterrupted hours that can be so crucial to one's ability to write and think, and where the sound of the waves and the beauty of the moon on the water provided further inspiration.

I also want to thank my friends and colleagues who read all or part of the manuscript and provided crucial feedback: John Blakely, Ruth Frager, Elliot Hanowski, Kari Jones, Patricia Roy, and Elizabeth Vibert. I am particularly grateful for the generosity of Eric Sager, who not only read and commented on the manuscript, but also ran many logistic regression analyses for me, as well as patiently explaining how to understand and utilize them in my analysis. A special thank you is also owed to Nancy Forestell, who read the manuscript and gently but firmly pushed me to do further thinking about race and racialization, integrating this theme more into my analysis than had originally been the case. Pat Roy, Patrick Dunae, Zhongping Chen, and Jeremy Mouat generously shared insights and/or elements of their own research. Two anonymous readers also provided very helpful comments that I hope have improved the book. Darcy Cullen and Lesley Erickson of UBC Press have been most patient and helpful in shepherding the book to publication, Deborah Kerr was a careful and meticulous copy editor whose work has improved it, and Cam Duder did an excellent job on the index. My graduate and undergraduate students have also taught me a great deal, some of which I hope is reflected in these pages.

My parents didn't live to see this book published, but they would have been very proud, as they always were. The subject matter would have resonated with them: my mother, Marion "Burn the Bibles" Marks, as she was known in her fierce battles for gay rights and against the religious roots of homophobia, and my father, Gerry Marks, a rationalist atheist scientist who felt most at home in Jewish contexts, leading seders, reciting blessings, and reading from the Torah – and relishing the irony of it all.

This book is dedicated to my beloved children, Dori Benjamin Marks Blakely and Mira Rachel Marks Blakely, the first Canadian- and BC-born members of my family – proud Jews and proud atheists – and to John Hale Blakely, who as a very lapsed Anglican was never that interested in religion to begin with, but whose generosity, love, on-the-ground feminism, endless patience, support, and sense of humour made this book possible and have illuminated my life and sustained me.

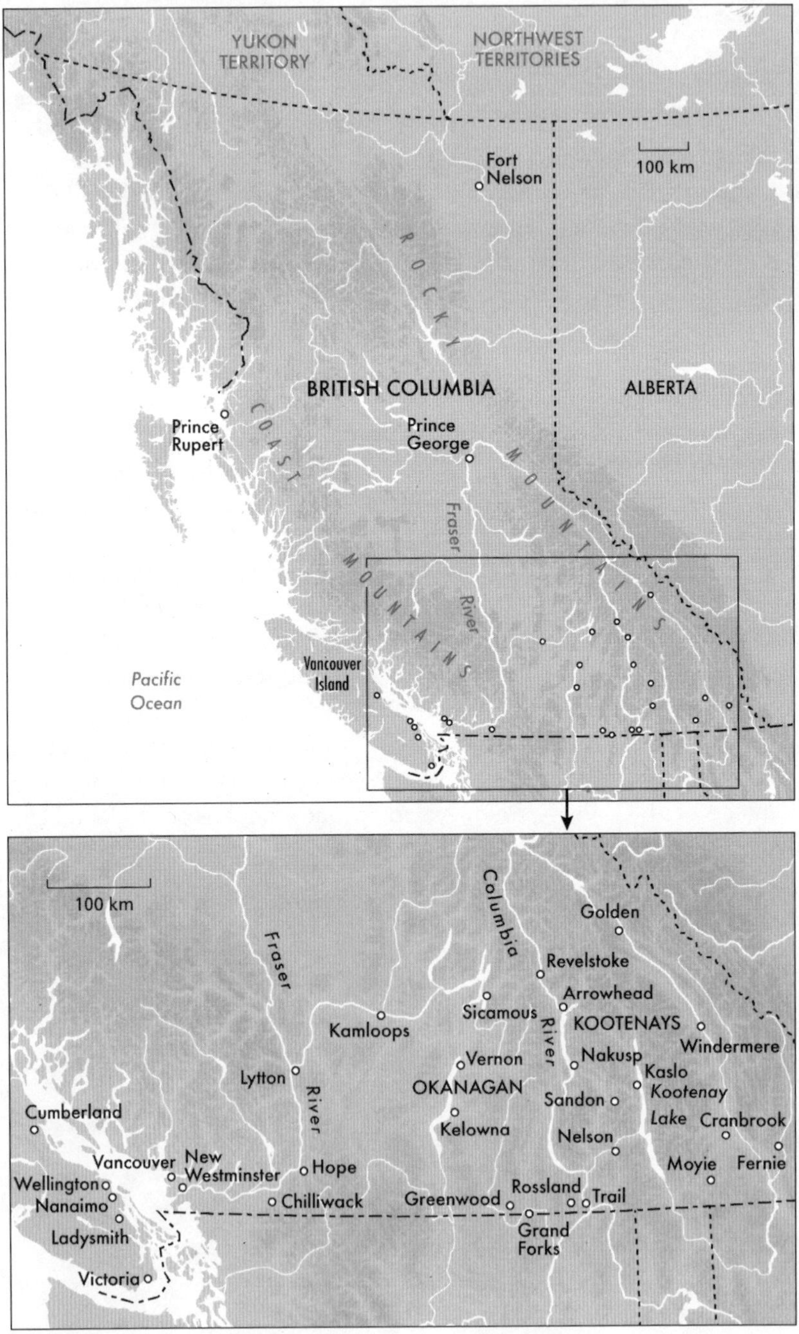

British Columbia, 1915

Infidels and the Damn Churches

Introduction

Leaving God Behind?

When I left Toronto and moved to British Columbia during the early 1990s, I had just completed a study of religion in late-nineteenth-century small-town Ontario. I left a province and a city that prided themselves on being cosmopolitan, but where the moralistic Protestant values of an earlier era were not far below the surface. The ugly demonstrations against gay adoption that I witnessed were a reminder – if I needed one – of Ontario's Christian past and its long cultural shadow. In many ways, British Columbia felt like a very different place. On my drive from the airport to Victoria, I marvelled at the ocean and the mountains, but the rundown housing on the Indigenous reserves that I passed and the blatant anti-Indigenous racism and somewhat more subtle anti-Asian racism I saw in Victoria itself created uncomfortable echoes of my white South African heritage.[1] There were other differences as well. After the "mushy middle" of Ontario politics, I found the explicitly class-polarized nature of BC politics a source of fascination.

The province's more secular nature was a surprising and refreshing change. Rather than dealing with the dregs of anti-Catholicism that still existed in the subconscious even of many enlightened Ontarians, here I taught many students who were totally unaware of the differences between Catholics and Protestants, and who saw religion as a fascinating, exotic, and unknown subject. As a Jew who deeply values her religious culture and heritage, but who defines herself as agnostic in personal religious faith, and is hostile towards the dogmatism and moralism sometimes associated with such faith, this more secular environment was a welcome one.

A few years after arriving in Victoria, I found myself beginning a new project on irreligion and religion in my new home. As I dug deeper in the historical sources, I uncovered some of the roots of what I found distinctive – both positively and negatively – about current BC society entwined in the story I tell in this book.

A common late-nineteenth-century saying declared that men left God behind when they crossed the Rocky Mountains into British Columbia.[2] This may have been an exaggeration, but it did reflect considerable truth, particularly among white settler men, many of whom came to British Columbia alone to make their fortunes on the resource frontier. Some of these men, who toiled for many hours and low pay in dangerous mines or logging camps, found socialism and loudly and proudly rejected God. Others who toiled beside them did not completely reject God but had little interest in attending church, where ministers bitterly attacked the kinds of fun they enjoyed in their limited leisure time and often supported the economic system that oppressed them. In late-nineteenth- and early-twentieth-century British Columbia, many of these white men found a unique freedom to be actively irreligious, whether by abandoning the churches, Christianity, or God himself. This freedom was much less available to, or less sought out by, the white settler women who also made their way to British Columbia in these decades. The many Asian men who came to work in the province's mines and on the railroad enjoyed leisure activities that were similar to those of their white counterparts and were even more roundly condemned by Christian ministers. These men may not have abandoned the religious traditions they brought with them from Asia, but they certainly had no interest in accepting the Christianity offered by a profoundly racist society. As we'll see, ministers had a challenging time in turn-of-the-century British Columbia, trying to impose Christian norms that were taken for granted elsewhere in Canada on the many Euro-Canadians and racialized non-Christian immigrants who had no interest in Christianity.

This book explores the nature of these challenges and thus the origins of British Columbia's greater openness to irreligion. From the 1880s to 1914, the period that is the focus of this book, British Columbia was a less religious place than the rest of the country, a pattern that has remained remarkably consistent over time. BC church involvement rates have been the lowest in Canada for over a century. In the 1901 census, although total numbers were small, British Columbians were ten times more likely than the average Canadian to call themselves atheists or agnostics, or to state that they had no religion. Over the last 110 years, the province has always

FIGURE 1 Atheists and those of no religion as percentage of total population, BC and Canada, 1901–2011

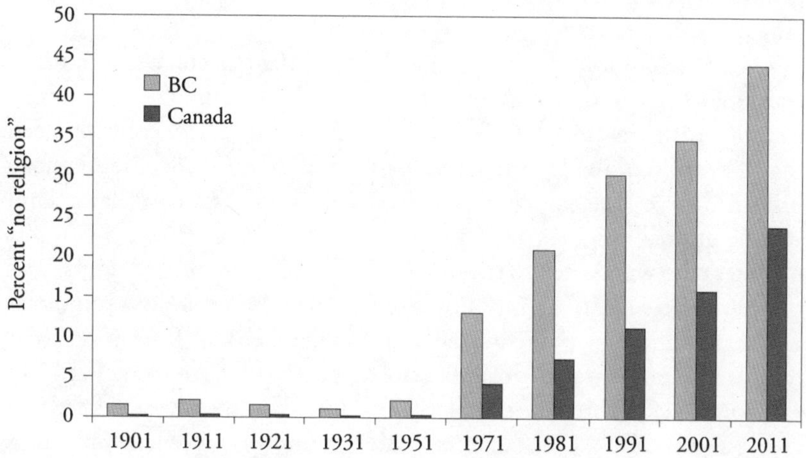

Source: See note 3 for detailed references.

had the highest proportion of Canadians of "no religion" of any province. In 2011, over 44 percent claimed to have no religion, as compared to less than 24 percent of the total Canadian population (see Figure 1).[3] A 1996 Angus Reid poll indicated that they were the least likely North Americans to think of themselves as Christian and the least likely to pray regularly; a 2015 poll noted that they were most likely to reject religion entirely.[4]

British Columbia is part of the "unchurched belt" of the West Coast of North America, as church involvement rates in Alaska, Washington, Oregon, and California have been consistently lower than in states farther to the east. As we'll see, a hundred years ago "godless" Americans from these and other Western states contributed to the development of the irreligious culture explored in this book. At the present time, however, the proportion of those who claim "no religion" is far higher in British Columbia than in the West Coast states, at 44 percent versus 26 percent, although these states have the highest proportion of the non-religiously affiliated in the United States.[5] It is also easier in British Columbia to say that one doesn't believe in God than it is in the Western United States. Samuel Reimer notes that many Americans have not attended church in recent decades, particularly on the West Coast, but still define themselves as believers. In explaining this, he cites the hegemonic power of the American culture of religious belief, or "culture-religion," whereby belief is strongly assumed to be the norm. This ideological context makes it difficult for people to state that they are not believers, even if they have no interest in religious institutions.[6]

A similar "culture-religion" of Christianity was extremely powerful in late-nineteenth- and early-twentieth-century Canada, though it was much less influential in British Columbia. BC church leaders were convinced that they lived in the least religious part of Canada. In 1881, the Anglican bishop George Hills lamented the province's "non-Christian" nature and "constitutional religious apathy."[7] Reverend J.W. Winslow, a Methodist minister who was posted to the Nicola Valley in the late 1880s, complained that there were far too many "heads of families whose religious principles are elastic" and who valued "gold and popular freedom from moral and religious restraints far above more noble 'goods' that are to be found in the homes left behind in the places from whence they have come."[8] In 1899, Reverend E.D. McLaren, pastor of St. Andrew's Church in Vancouver, observed that in British Columbia there was "a good deal of theoretical infidelity and a great deal of practical infidelity."[9] McLaren was not talking about sexual unfaithfulness, but about unfaithfulness to God.

The clergymen who were appalled by the irreligious nature of many British Columbians came from cultures, primarily in Central and Eastern Canada and England, where Christianity was almost universally accepted and was very much a hegemonic discourse. Hegemonic discourses construct systems of meaning that become the common sense "taken for granted" ideas and beliefs through which people in a particular society understand their worlds.[10] This does not mean that everyone in Central and Eastern Canada attended church regularly. Many did not. Many men, particularly single men, did not fully live up to Christian moral ideals, and some individuals and small groups did challenge orthodox Christianity, or even Christianity itself. Nonetheless, as Nancy Christie and Michael Gauvreau argue, as does Peter Beyer, Christianity in late-nineteenth- and early-twentieth-century Canada was the dominant cultural and ideological system.[11] Although this was true for most of Canada, it was less true in British Columbia, where irreligion was a much more accepted option.

What exactly is meant by irreligion in this context? This is a very slippery concept, much debated by scholars.[12] The irreligious people who are the focus of this book span a continuum, ranging from those who told the census-taker that they were atheists or "infidels," thus actively rejecting God, to those who were not involved with a religious institution, generally a church. The broad definition of irreligion used here entails "beliefs and activities that are expressive of attitudes of hostility or indifference towards prevailing religion." This includes either religion in general or "any of its more specific organized forms." This definition does not assume that all irreligious people rejected God or gods, although many may have, but it recognizes that they were at a minimum indifferent to organized religion.[13]

Irreligion in some form was accepted by a significant component of the BC population during this period, but it did not have the kind of influence it was to gain by the early twenty-first century. Christianity still held considerable social and cultural power, although its hegemony was challenged by a range of forces. Many of these were rooted in the province's unique demographic and economic makeup.

Gender, Race, Class, and the Economy in Settler British Columbia

From the beginning of European settlement to well into the twentieth century, non-Indigenous men outnumbered non-Indigenous women in what eventually became British Columbia. An economy based on natural resources drew far more settler men than it did women, even as the nature of the resources shifted. In the early days, furs were the main focus, and the Hudson's Bay Company controlled British trade with Indigenous people in the region. It also founded Fort Victoria, later Victoria, on the southern tip of Vancouver Island in 1843. In 1858, with the discovery of gold on the Fraser River, thousands of men (and some women) poured into Victoria en route to the gold fields to seek their fortunes, leading the British government to create the new colony of British Columbia on the Mainland during that year. A year later, Vancouver Island was removed from direct Hudson's Bay control, becoming a separate British colony. In 1866, the two colonies were united as British Columbia, and in 1871 the colony entered Confederation with Canada. For the rest of the nineteenth century, resource extraction remained the basis of the economy. In the early 1860s, the Cariboo gold rush attracted many men from around the world to the BC Interior. Coal mining around Nanaimo on Vancouver Island, and fishing and logging along the coast, also drew many men and some families to British Columbia. Less than 4 percent of the province was suitable for agriculture, so the family farm was much less central to the BC economy than in most of Canada, although agricultural areas certainly existed, particularly on southern Vancouver Island and in the

Fraser Valley; in the Interior, the Okanagan Valley and later the Cariboo and Chilcotin regions became cattle-ranching centres.[14] By the late 1880s and 1890s, silver and other metals had been discovered in the Kootenay mountains of the Interior, leading to an economic boom with the development of major mines and mining centres; and coal mining began farther east, around the Crowsnest Pass.

Vancouver and Victoria were the largest urban centres in the province. In 1901, Victoria was almost as large as its rival, at 20,919 to Vancouver's 26,386, but it lost ground after that. By 1911, though its population had increased to more than 30,000, Vancouver had almost quadrupled in size, growing to over 100,000 people. The next-largest communities were all mining towns: coal-mining Nanaimo had a population of 6,130 in 1901 and more than 8,000 ten years later; the new hard-rock mining communities of Nelson and Rossland in the Kootenays boasted just over 5,000 and 6,000 people respectively in 1901, although a productivity decline in the mines had led to some loss of population by 1911, particularly in Rossland (see map on page xiv).[15] The mining regions of the province, both on Vancouver Island and in the Interior, saw the development of very class-polarized communities, as employers sought to extract resources while maximizing profits. In response to unsafe conditions, low pay, and long working hours, employees organized into militant unions, and significant numbers were attracted to socialist political solutions.[16]

The continued focus on resource development meant that among the non-Indigenous inhabitants of the province, men remained in the majority, composing almost 75 percent of the adult non-Indigenous population in 1891, 71 percent in 1901, and 70 percent in 1911.[17] Many were very transient, moving from one opportunity to the next in the boom-and-bust economy, both within British Columbia and beyond. Beginning with the gold rush of 1858, the BC resource frontier attracted a diverse population of men from around the world, and this continued to be true in the late nineteenth century, as the number of settlers grew rapidly. Indigenous people, who had composed the majority of the population into the early 1880s, made up only 16.2 percent of it in 1901 and just over 5.0 percent in 1911.[18] The total population of the province increased from 98,173 in 1891 to 392,480 in 1911. The majority of settlers came from the United States, Britain, and Central and Eastern Canada, as well as in increasing numbers from Continental Europe.[19] Most were defined as white by the racial categories of the time. As today, these categories were socially constructed and subject to change, which is why scholars tend to speak of racialized people, as opposed to people of a particular race, since groups can be racialized differently in different times and places. In this period, southern and eastern Europeans, especially the Italians and Slavs who emigrated to British Columbia in growing numbers after 1900, were racialized as "not white" and were therefore not as acceptable as their "white" northern European counterparts. Although they encountered prejudice, they (or at least their children) were viewed as potentially assimilable because they were European and Christian. This was not the case for Asian immigrants.[20]

Chinese men had begun to migrate to British Columbia in significant numbers with the 1858 gold rush, seeking prosperity for themselves and their families back home. Increasing numbers of Japanese people began coming to the province during the 1890s, although the Chinese remained the majority of Asian migrants. A smaller South Asian migration, largely of Sikhs, began in the early twentieth century. Asian migrants, primarily male, composed almost 11 percent of the BC population in 1901 and close to 8 percent in 1911. Most Asian immigrants who came to Canada during this period lived in British Columbia.[21] British Columbians of Euro-Canadian origin responded to their presence with virulent racism. Asian workers were seen as an economic threat to the jobs of "white" workers and tended to be racialized as completely foreign and unassimilable. The fact that they were "heathens" who espoused non-Christian religions and showed little interest in converting to Christianity exacerbated the racism and othering that they faced. In British Columbia, they experienced both official and everyday racism, including violence and restrictions on the jobs they could hold and their right to immigrate. By the early twentieth century, all those of Asian origin had lost the right to vote.[22]

In the early twentieth century, British Columbia was the most racially and religiously diverse province in Canada (see Figures 2 and 3). By 1911, groups that were racialized as non-white (those of Asian, southern and eastern European origin, and Indigenous people) together composed over 19 percent of its population (Figure 2).[23] The Prairie provinces were the next most diverse, but the largest racialized group on the Prairies by 1911 consisted of (potentially assimilable) southern and eastern Europeans.[24] Other than in British Columbia, provincial populations were almost exclusively Christian, except for a small minority of Jews.[25]

As we will see, the predominance and transience of men among the non-Indigenous population, the class-polarized nature of the workforce, and the racial and religious diversity of the province all help to explain the less hegemonic and more contested place of religion, particularly Christianity, in British Columbia. At the same time, it is important to recognize that the vast majority of British Columbians who defined themselves as

Figure 2 BC population by racial and ethnic origin, 1901 and 1911

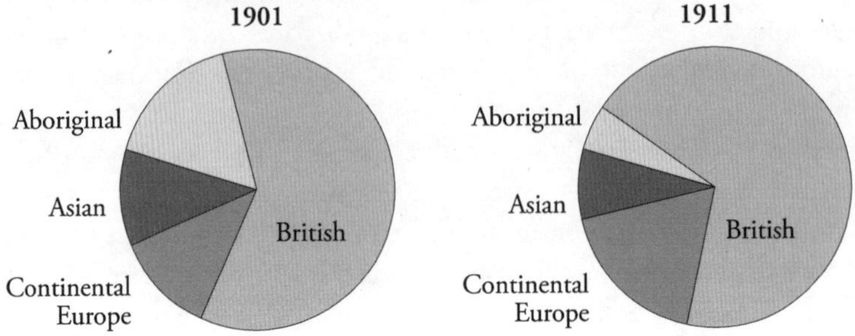

Source: Data taken from Dominion Bureau of Statistics (DBS), *Census of Canada, 1901* (Ottawa: Census Office, 1902), vol. 1, Table 11; DBS, *Census of Canada, 1911* (Ottawa: C.H. Parmelee, 1913), vol. 1, Table 9.

Figure 3 Canadian population by racial and ethnic origin, 1901 and 1911

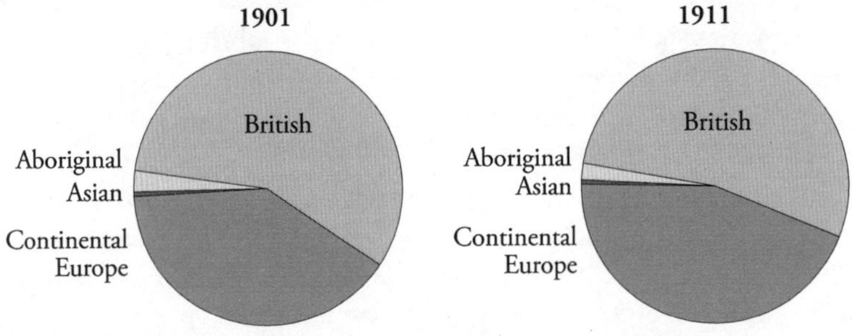

Source: Data taken from Dominion Bureau of Statistics (DBS), *Census of Canada, 1901* (Ottawa: Census Office, 1902), vol. 1, Table 11; DBS, *Census of Canada, 1911* (Ottawa: C.H. Parmelee, 1913), vol. 1, Table 9.

irreligious, or who demonstrated their irreligion by staying away from religious institutions, did not come from non-Christian racialized groups: they were Euro-Canadians. Elsewhere in the country, they would be expected to define themselves as Christian. As noted by scholars of other national contexts, it is perhaps not surprising that the irreligious came from a Christian background, as in defining themselves as irreligious they were reacting directly against, as well as in relation to, Christian norms.[26] And as will be discussed below, though many completely rejected these norms, the irreligion of many others was not entirely devoid of echoes or fragments of Christian practice or belief.

Secularization and the Secular

Definitions of secularization are much contested but generally refer to a process in which religious institutions lose cultural and social authority in a society, moving gradually from the centre to the periphery of power and influence. At the same time, secularization is also reflected in an increasing abandonment of mainstream religious participation, adherence, and ultimately belief.[27] This book explores and analyzes the lower levels of religious belief and participation in British Columbia as compared to the rest of Canada, examining a society in which the churches had relatively less power and influence than elsewhere in the country.

A secularization approach may not be ideal here, however. To become secularized, a culture must first be religious. Was this ever true of settler British Columbia? This book focuses on the late nineteenth and early twentieth centuries, but the limited work on the earlier colonial period suggests that though the province may not have been "born secular," as a few scholars have claimed, it was never as religious as Central Canada.[28] It seems appropriate to talk about the secularization of British Columbia in the latter decades of the twentieth century and into the twenty-first century, when Christian affiliation declined dramatically. However, for the decades covered in this volume, when levels of irreligion remained fairly stable, it may be more useful to speak of the secularization of many of those who migrated to British Columbia (particularly the men who came from more eastern parts of Canada), than of the secularization of the province. To apply a Canada-wide lens, one could say that the largely hegemonic Christian culture of late-nineteenth- and early-twentieth-century Canada showed its first signs of secularization in the most westerly province.

The timing, causes, and indeed existence of secularization have been hotly contested in the international context. Some of the best scholarly studies have concentrated on the United States and Europe. Robert Orsi views the many ways in which people adopt and transform various elements of official religious practices, making them their own, as "lived religion" and sees lived religion as having potentially powerful sustaining and transgressive force. Sarah Williams similarly explores the ways in which working-class Londoners used a mix of official practices and folk magic to construct their own popular religion.[29] Whereas Orsi and Williams perceive such popular practices and beliefs as valuable resources in their own right, other scholars, both historians and sociologists, see them as way stations on the route to a more secular culture.[30] Orsi and other American scholars are particularly resistant to models of secularization, preferring to speak of religious change rather than any clear pattern of decline. Certainly, the American religious trajectory of recent years has provided much justification for this position.[31] A more global perspective can also serve to challenge overarching theories of secularization.[32]

Scholars of Britain and other parts of Europe, however, have recently seen striking shifts away from the churches, prompting them to explore some form of secularization analysis, although earlier models of secularization, in which it was seen as a process of modernity, an inevitable by-product of industrialization and urbanization, have fallen out of favour.[33] These scholars look into the past for signposts of secularization. Some examine religious and intellectual developments of the seventeenth and eighteenth centuries, others find evidence in nineteenth-century working-class shifts away from the churches, and increasing numbers focus on the 1960s as the key decade of secularization. Still others, though recognizing patterns of both religious change and decline, prefer to analyze and seek to explain these phenomena within specific local and regional contexts rather than accepting any overarching model of secularization.[34] Canada's own trajectory in the latter decades of the twentieth century does rather confirm the legitimacy of a concept of secularization, but the unique religious and irreligious patterns of British Columbia also demonstrate the value of studying these questions in local and regional contexts. All of this fine work, whether accepting, contesting, or seeking to complicate concepts of secularization, informs my efforts to scrutinize the complex boundaries between religion and irreligion in late-nineteenth- and early-twentieth-century British Columbia.

This topic has thus far received very little attention from historians of British Columbia. Most literature on the social history of religion in Canada focuses on Ontario, Quebec, and the Maritimes. A few historians of these regions have discussed popular religious involvement and belief but have said little about irreligion itself.[35] Recently, important new work has explored the relationship between irreligion and the left, primarily in interwar Canada.[36] Most Canadian work that touches on irreligion in the late nineteenth and early twentieth centuries deals with the "secularization debates," in which scholars contest the timing of secularization in English Canada. Some suggest that Canadian secularization originated during the late nineteenth and early twentieth centuries, whereas others argue for the continued hegemony of Christianity in Canada during the first half of the twentieth century. This literature tends to be Ontario-centred, with some attention paid to the Prairies, and often has a more intellectual than social history bent. Gender is only occasionally a focus of analysis.[37]

In recent years, scholars have begun to discuss issues of Canadian secularization and secularity in the post–Second World War period. Some have studied Central Canada, but important new work moves the focus westward, concentrating as much on regional secular cultures as on secularization over time.[38] Tina Block compares the secular context of post-war British Columbia with that of Washington State, and American scholars of the West Coast unchurched belt also provide a North American framework for the analysis of BC secularism. In *Religion and the Demographic Revolution,* a broadly comparative study of secularization, Callum Brown traces the rapid secularization of Canadian society during the final decades of the twentieth century, suggesting that gender was key to this development and that British Columbia was in the forefront of the change, not only in Canada but in the English-speaking world.[39]

Other scholars have made pioneering contributions regarding the particularly secular nature of British Columbia. The late Bob Stewart wrote an important article on this subject in the early 1980s. Norman Knowles and Stuart Barnard have written valuable local studies of religion and irreligion among BC miners in the Interior.[40] Vincent McNally has studied the secular nature of the BC school system, noting that British Columbia is the only Canadian province that (until the late twentieth century) never provided funding for separate Catholic schools and that has generally tried to keep religion out of public schools.[41] As early as 1872, the Public School Act ruled that the schools were to be "strictly non-sectarian." They were to teach "the highest morality" and "no religious dogma or creed." McNally argues that significant American influence among early BC settlers explains popular pressure regarding the "separation of church and state" in the school system. The religious diversity of the population was also cited as an issue, as was the not-unrelated fact that "British Columbia is unique among Canadian provinces in that it has always been and remains the most unchurched region of the country." NcNally mentions many and various complaints by Catholic bishops, from before Confederation to the late nineteenth century, who challenged the lack of funding for separate Catholic schools and the "Godlessness" of the public schools, which they blamed on the power of the "sect of irreligionists" in the province.[42]

Other scholars argue that BC schools were more non-denominationally Protestant than they were secular, but in the late nineteenth and early twentieth centuries church leaders of all denominations decried the province's "godless" educational system, which permitted no explicit religious instruction other than the Lord's Prayer in schools.[43] In August 1900, three clergymen, two Protestant and one Catholic, wrote to the *Vancouver*

Province, complaining bitterly about the absence of Bible readings in BC schools. The Presbyterian minister, Reverend E.D. McLaren, argued against justifications for this policy, which had been based on the religious diversity of the BC population, stating that "the fact that Jews, Turks, and infidels are citizens of Canada has never been suggested as a reason for doing away with the oath [on the Bible] in courts of law." These ministers were very gratified that the Vancouver School Board was attempting to permit Bible readings in the schools, although a number of people who wrote to the local papers, styling themselves "Agnostic" and "Freethinker," were appalled. Despite the efforts of the school board, the "sect of irreligionists" still seemed to retain considerable political influence. Throughout the following three decades, ministers continued to complain about the absence of Bible readings or other religious instruction in BC schools.[44]

As we will see, the clergy did not limit their complaints to the public school system. Protestant church leaders bemoaned their lack of influence over government policy on a variety of social and moral reform issues, such as Sabbath observance, prohibition of the sale of alcohol, and control over gambling and the sex trade. As discussed in Chapter 5, church leaders were well aware that their lack of influence over legislation was linked to government perceptions that the bulk of voters were not dedicated, moral Christians. Church leaders were very unhappy about this, and as will be evident throughout this volume, the irreligion or religious indifference of British Columbians was a major and frequent cause of lamentation.

In examining other Canadian contexts, some scholars have contended that church leaders' rhetoric about godlessness had much more to do with their distaste for popular religion and their need to justify their labours to funding organizations, than with actual irreligion.[45] Such arguments may rely overmuch on discourse analysis, but they do have some relevance for our understanding of clerical whining in turn-of-the-century British Columbia. Certainly, as Chapter 3 reveals, some British Columbians practised varieties of popular religion, straying far – often very far indeed – from the ideal of disciplined, moral, and pious churchgoers. And in the early twentieth century, some BC churches remained at least partially reliant on financial support from Eastern Canadian church organizations, motivating leaders to justify their labours to religious superiors and funders. At the same time, a broad range of empirical evidence provides clear corroboration of many of the church leaders' concerns about irreligion. A number of lay people, particularly women, also reported being shocked by the irreligion of many British Columbians (as will be discussed more fully in Chapter 4). Quantitative analysis of census records establishes that

British Columbians were much more likely than other Canadians to identify themselves as atheists or as having "no religion." And various church and government sources clearly demonstrate that they were the least likely of Canadians to be involved in a church.

Nonetheless, one must be careful not to take church leaders' lamentations at face value, as doing so could lead to the impression that British Columbia was an almost entirely godless place. Levels of hostility or simple indifference to religion were certainly much higher than what church leaders would have experienced elsewhere in Canada at this time. Non-Christian racialized communities and alternative spiritualities were also much more present in British Columbia - further challenging the Christian hegemony that ministers took for granted in Central and Eastern Canada. Given these realities, a little hyperbole is perhaps not surprising.

Gender, Family, and the Resource Frontier

There were, however, many strong Christian congregations in the province. They may have felt more embattled than their counterparts in Ontario, Nova Scotia, and other eastern provinces, but they had much in common with them. For example, they consisted largely of women.

Dominant gender ideologies identified women as more moral and pious than men. Women who desired to be respectable had few alternatives beyond the churches, which also offered them both sociability with other women and the consolation of faith. Faith in troubled times could be particularly important for mothers, who were expected to be caring nurturers in a world of high infant and child mortality.[46] Men could also be found in BC churches, but the majority were married and were inspired to attend, in British Columbia as elsewhere, by a combination of personal faith, wifely piety, at least some acceptance of norms of domestic masculinity, and a wish to display respectability as heads of Christian families who were raising their children on the proper Christian path.[47]

The predominance of women in BC churches, though similar to patterns elsewhere in Canada, is perhaps surprising in light of the province's skewed gender ratio, with non-Indigenous men far outnumbering non-Indigenous women. It points to the fact that men, especially the many single transient working-class men on the BC resource frontier, were very unlikely to set foot in a church. Although they were the most likely to abandon traditional Christian practices, or to challenge them, they were not alone. Some married middle- and working-class men, particularly those who were far from their families, were also willing to do so. And together, these men created a provincial culture in which Christian hegemony could be defied in a range of ways: by declaring oneself an atheist on the census, attacking the churches as tools of the employing classes, shunning Sunday services, and/or embracing the "rough" male leisure options of drinking, gambling, and frequenting red light districts.

Men were in the forefront of challenging Christian hegemony in British Columbia. But in some contexts, particularly in centres of labour radicalism, working-class atheist husbands and fathers were joined by their wives and daughters, sharing a class-conscious irreligious culture. Scholars have also noted that, in Britain and the United States, most irreligious people during this period were men, but they have identified a few outspoken activist atheist women who were not necessarily linked to male unbelievers.[48] In British Columbia, a few women defined themselves as irreligious without being linked to men, but they were not outspoken unbelievers in any forums. However, some were willing to play an active role in more heterodox religious milieus. For women who were not comfortable with a complete abandonment of faith, the challenges to the dominance of Christianity in British Columbia made it more possible for them to embrace, or at least dabble in, a range of alternative spiritualities. Rejecting mainstream religion did not automatically translate to espousing a purely material or rational world view, and thus they sought transcendence in other forms. As a result, alternative creeds have been particularly popular in British Columbia, from the spiritualism, Theosophy, and Christian Science of the late nineteenth and early twentieth centuries to the New Age religions of the present day.

For many other Euro-Canadian settler women, church involvement remained a vital anchor, providing faith, familiarity, and female sociability in a new society where they were very much in the minority. Many participated in women's church-based organizations, as they had in their previous environments. Through these groups, they became key allies of clerical leaders in the social and moral reform movements that attempted to transform British Columbia into something that more closely resembled the Christian and "civilized" societies of Central and Eastern Canada.

Historians have studied the impact of British Columbia's skewed gender ratio on both Indigenous and settler women. Adele Perry has done important work on this subject in connection with colonial British Columbia and has provided crucial insights into the rough homosocial culture of settler men during this period. Scholars have also explored what the predominance of men may have meant for BC labour activism and socialist radicalism.[49] How these men may have helped to shape the religious, or irreligious, fabric of the province has received much less attention.

International literature on gender, religion, and resource frontiers provides useful insights and a broader context for this study.[50] Laurie Maffly-Kipp's work demonstrates that California's transient, predominately male, and racially diverse mid-nineteenth-century gold-rush society lacked an interest in organized religion, particularly Protestantism, whereas Sandra Frankiel has examined the social factors that explain why many Californians were attracted to alternative spiritualities in the latter half of the nineteenth century.[51] Scholars Marilyn Lake and Patricia Grimshaw have explored the "civilizing" political activism of white Christian settler women, who were a minority in Australia's rough white male culture.[52]

Other scholars have done important work on the nature of frontier settler masculinity, although most have paid little attention to men's relationship with religion.[53] Irreligious BC men were very creative in using masculine norms to oppose Christianity. Some of their challenges were not dissimilar to those of less pious men in other parts of Canada and in Britain, but they took on a particular edge in British Columbia.[54] Irreligious men regularly questioned the manliness of the clergy, deriding their inability to cope on the frontier, while defining themselves as "real men" – through either their rational atheist socialism or their rough leisure pursuits. They fiercely attacked Christian efforts to enforce temperance and other forms of moral regulation as feminized and effete Eastern affectations. Throughout this book, we see the range of ways in which gender is used as a rhetorical tool, both to shore up and to challenge various religious, irreligious, and heterodox positions, defining them as either manly and rational or as feminine, effete, irrational, and hysterical.

Both internationally and in Canada, historians have examined the role of religion in the family, exploring how Christianity was nurtured in the nineteenth-century domestic sphere.[55] *Infidels and the Damn Churches* reinforces the perception that transient men who were living apart from their families were likely to abandon their religious practices, particularly in contexts, such as pre–First World War British Columbia, in which being irreligious was a legitimate cultural option. This book also contributes to our understanding of the relationships among religion, gender, and family by scrutinizing families in which one member, generally the husband, defined himself as having no religion; it examines the responses of other family members, particularly wives, for whom irreligion was less culturally acceptable. It explores the fluidity of religious affiliation among family members over time, looking, for example, at what happened to irreligious men when they married and to widowed women who had associated themselves with their husband's agnostic identity.

Religion, the Working Class, Labour, and the Left

There have been a number of debates, in Canada and internationally, about the importance, or lack thereof, of Christianity to the nineteenth-century working class.[56] Focusing on Ontario, some scholars have argued that workers were well integrated into the Christian churches. They have suggested that Christianity was as central to the working-class world view as it was to that of other classes, and indeed more central than identity categories such as class. Others have either ignored the role that religion may have played in the lives of workers or claimed that many workers moved away from the churches as they developed a distinct and oppositional working-class consciousness.[57] In *Revivals and Roller Rinks,* I took a more middle ground in studying religion in small-town Ontario – noting that Christianity could sometimes serve as a resource for working people in generating an oppositional working-class consciousness, whereas at other times they were active, but generally not equal, participants in broader church communities. Gender, marital status, and local context also made a difference to levels of working-class participation. Young men rarely went to church, although the vast majority still told census-takers that they were Christians. This reflected what I found to be the complex, diverse, sometimes oppositional, but primarily Christian perspective of the Ontario working class.[58]

The relationship between religion and the BC working class was quite different. Although many BC workers did remain pious Christians, many others did not, with significant numbers adopting the socialist critique of religion as the "opium of the masses" and the churches as implements of capitalist exploiters. Early Canadian histories of labour and the left in British Columbia argued that the brutal conditions in the resource towns fostered a particularly radical form of unionism and socialism that was less common elsewhere in Canada. More recent scholars have downplayed this image of BC "exceptionalism," maintaining both that much of the BC labour movement was less radical and that there was more radicalism elsewhere in Canada than was previously recognized.[59] *Infidels and the Damn Churches* provides a partial refutation of this scholarship. The relatively high proportion of those who called themselves atheists or said they were of "no religion" in certain strongholds of labour activism, particularly in the Kootenays, suggests a level of adherence to the radical atheism espoused by the Socialist Party of British Columbia that was much less accepted elsewhere in the country, where left-wing attacks on Christianity had to be soft-pedalled to avoid alienating potential working-class supporters.[60] The class-conscious atheism of certain popular journalists in the Kootenays further suggests that the BC working class was perhaps more exceptional than we previously believed.

Racism, Racialization, Class, and Religion

In the 1980s, a battle raged among scholars as to whether race or class was more significant in BC history.[61] Religion was nowhere to be found, as is true in much of BC historiography. Although race and racialization might seem to have won the debate, given their predominance in the literature, I argue here that race, class, and religion all need to be analyzed together. I further speculate that the centrality of both race and class concerns in British Columbia may have helped to establish irreligion as a normalized option in the province, in a way that did not occur elsewhere in Canada. Working-class consciousness fuelled a rejection of the churches and of Christianity for many BC workers. The opposition of at least some clergymen to the exclusion of Asians, when many white workers saw exclusion as crucial to safeguarding their jobs, simply exacerbated this alienation. Virulent prejudice against the province's racialized populations may also have made it easier for working-class white men to see themselves as part of the respectable community, primarily on the basis of their racialized and class identities, regardless of religious affiliations or lack thereof. This book breaks new ground in exploring the relationship between racialization, racism, and irreligion, as it is a subject that is only beginning to be explored in the international literature.[62]

Although this book suggests that the significance of religion as a marker of inclusion may have been diminished in British Columbia in the face of a deeply racist culture, it also argues that religion and irreligion must be integrated with the other significant categories of analysis used by historians, if we wish to understand the complexity of BC society. This integration already exists in the rich literature on missionary work among Indigenous communities and the Indigenous response to missionization. Religion does make brief appearances in the literature on race and racialization in British Columbia: for example, Patricia Roy and Peter Ward identify the varying positions of Christian ministers on Asian exclusion, and Renisa Mawani states that Christian beliefs, or their lack, helped to define both the civilized norm and the racialized "other."[63] The present study builds on this work but focuses on new questions, including how the presence of large non-Christian racialized communities helped to undermine the Christian churches' cultural reach and power in the province.

This book explores the range of religious and irreligious practice and belief in British Columbia, from outright atheism to active church involvement, as gendered, classed, and racialized phenomena. Marital status, transiency, immigration, and ethnic differences are also crucial categories in understanding the province's religious and secular fabric during this period. This book concentrates largely on British Columbians of Euro-Canadian, and Christian, backgrounds, many of whom discarded their faith, or at least church involvement, upon arrival in the province. These (primarily male) individuals helped to lay the secular foundations of British Columbia by making challenges to Christianity more acceptable and more normalized than elsewhere in Canada. Protestants (or former Protestants) are central to this story. Although many Catholics also jettisoned their faith, or at least their religious practice, others, particularly from certain ethnic groups, found the Catholic Church a source of ethno-religious comfort and community.

Euro-Canadians of previously Christian affiliation are central to the story of irreligion in British Columbia, but the fact that the province was the most racially diverse in Canada also played a role. British Columbians of Chinese, Japanese, and South Asian origin largely rejected Christian proselytism, thus constituting a major obstacle to the hegemony of the mainstream churches. Most Indigenous groups were at least nominally Christian by the turn of the century, but the churches remained anxious about the depth of their conversion. They knew they had a major task in maintaining and enhancing Christian belief and practice among Indigenous people and in eradicating "pagan" elements such as the potlatch.[64] Indigenous people thus posed another challenge to Christian hegemony in the province, despite the apparent success of late-nineteenth-century missionization. The "godless" and sinful white men who feature prominently in these pages are also very visible in missionary accounts, where they are often cited as major impediments to the full Christianization of the Indigenous peoples.

The complexity of Indigenous people's relationship to Christianity has been the focus of much impressive scholarship.[65] However, very little has been said about the complex interplay between religion and irreligion among settler groups in British Columbia. As traced in this book, some parts of the story are clear: those who occupied the extremes of the religiosity-irreligiosity continuum are readily identified. There were significant numbers of atheist Marxists in the province who fiercely denounced the churches and Christianity as tools of the capitalist classes. And there were many pious Methodists and Presbyterians who regularly attended church, kept the Sabbath, and supported the creation of legislation that would impose Protestant morality on other British Columbians. But many people did not fit either mould. Some might occasionally have gone to church, or at least baptized their children or sent them to Sunday School. Others who never entered a church prided themselves on being "practical Christians" who followed certain Christian moral precepts, and yet others spent their leisure time drinking and gambling but happily joined in a hymn sing led by a travelling missionary in a local bar. Some of these people told the census-taker that they were of "no religion," whereas others called themselves Methodists, Presbyterians, or Anglicans. In this book, we will explore how they fit into British Columbia's more irreligious but not totally secular culture.

Sources and Methods

Infidels and the Damn Churches uses a range of sources and methods. The manuscript census was a key document, and this book would not have been possible without the large national, regional, and city- and town-specific census databases for 1901 and 1911 that have been constructed through the Canadian Families Project and the Canadian Century Research Infrastructure Project, as well as through the ViHistory online database, which includes the entire Vancouver Island manuscript census from 1881 to 1901 and the 1911 manuscript census for Victoria.[66] Early historical studies that used the manuscript census as a major source were quite uncritical of it, but later scholars have recognized that it is very much a biased and constructed document. As Bruce Curtis shows, census categories reflect far more than a search for the "facts" about particular populations. They also reveal the ideologies, interests, and agendas of the politicians and civil servants who created them. In addition, Curtis demonstrates that we need to look closely at how censuses are actually taken. Who asks the questions, and who answers them? Where should people who are temporarily absent from their permanent homes on census day be enumerated?[67]

The very existence of a question about religion on the Canadian census tells us something about the political dimensions of the country that conducted the census. American censuses do not, and never have, asked any questions about religion, as the US Constitution decrees that church and state must be separate. No such separation has existed in Canada. In Canada, the religious nature of Canadians was seen as closely tied to the moral standing of the country, and data about the numbers and locations of francophone Catholics and anglophone Protestants were crucial political tools.[68]

The enumerators of the 1901 census were told to enter religion of an individual "according as he or she professes, specifying the church or denomination to which the person belongs or adhere, or which he or she favour." They were told that "if a person is not a member of or does not adhere to or favour any one church or denomination he must not be classed with one or another ... If he is an agnostic, or a non-believer, or a pagan, or a reincarnationist, or whatever his relationship to religion may be, he should be so classed." They were also instructed not to make inferences, but only to record information as stated by the individuals themselves.[69] As a result, though most people said that they were Methodists, Presbyterians, and so on, this instruction meant that people were at liberty to tell the enumerator that they were atheists, agnostics, socialists, infidels, skeptics, humanitarians, and a range of other labels. When the census was compiled for publication, many of these idiosyncrasies were collapsed into constructed categories and thus rendered invisible, though the categories of atheist, agnostic, and "no religion" remained. An analysis of the manuscript census reveals the range of choices that individuals made in describing their belief, or non-belief. At the same time, as in the case of mother tongue and other categories that were not always simple in practice, people were required to indicate that they adhered to only one religion.[70] Thus, people who attended both a Methodist church and spiritualist seances had to choose one or the other, and we should not be surprised if they opted for the more socially acceptable alternative, given that enumerators were usually members of their local community. In other cases, individuals may have felt that they belonged in a certain category, but social pressures may have stopped them from saying so. For example, those who didn't believe in God but were part of a pious Methodist family might be reluctant to disclose their atheism to a local enumerator, particularly in certain social contexts, such as small-town Ontario.[71] As we will see, at least some British Columbians could be more open about their unbelief than was the case elsewhere in Canada.

The question of who spoke to the enumerator is also important. Enumerators were instructed to talk to every adult in a family, but the "head" of the family was ultimately responsible for ensuring that they received all requested information.[72] In cases when enumerators spoke only to the family head, would he (or she) always divulge the actual beliefs or adherence of everyone in the house, which could include both servants and boarders? In many instances, male household heads would have been at work when the enumerators called, and thus the census information would have been supplied by the wife and mother, who was more likely to be at home. If religious ambiguity or conflict existed in her family, the information she provided might differ somewhat from that disclosed by her husband, particularly if she was a church member and he was not.

In some cases, census-takers seem not to have spoken to those whom they enumerated, or if they did, language barriers and racism severely limited the value of the information they transcribed. For instance, in the 1901 census for Victoria, one enumerator, a Mr. Phipps, recorded that fifty-four of the fifty-nine Chinese people in his district were "agnostics," although the Chinese in other Victorian polls were defined by a range of religious categories. This example tells us more about the racism and ignorance of the census-taker than about the religious beliefs of those whom he enumerated. This and other serious problems with the enumeration of racialized groups mean that it is almost impossible to use the census to draw meaningful conclusions about the religious affiliation of racialized groups in British Columbia at this time.

In addition to using the manuscript census (with care) as a stand-alone source, I linked the names of individuals in the manuscript census to identical names in church records for a range of BC communities and, for comparative purposes, for Ontario and Nova Scotia as well. Here, I employed church membership lists, which provide a fairly complete record of the most active participants in most Protestant churches (see Chapter 4 for further discussion of this topic).[73] Either because of inadequate detail about certain individuals in church records or the fact that some church members may have lived outside of town and thus did not appear on the local census, not everyone could be linked between census and church list.[74] Nonetheless, the linkages that could be made furnish valuable information about the social backgrounds of church members.

Oral history was also an important source for this book. Because *Infidels and the Damn Churches* spans the 1880s to 1914, I obviously could not conduct oral history interviews myself, but I benefitted from the foresight of those who did so during the 1960s, 1970s, and early 1980s. In certain cases, some context for the interviews and the projects that undertook them was provided, but in other instances little was available. None of these oral history projects focused specifically on irreligion, and many asked no questions about religion, perhaps reflecting the secular nature of this province in the latter decades of the twentieth century. The few projects that did ask about religion were framed by explicit assumptions from interviewers that "we were all more religious in the past." This may have prompted some interviewees to provide answers that would not disappoint the interviewers. And, of course, as scholars have noted in recent years, oral history interviews, particularly on topics as subjective as religion, tell us at least as much about the nature of memory as they do about "what actually happened" in the past.[75] Nonetheless, even interview collections with either religious or secular lenses furnish some valuable insights regarding religious and irreligious practices and perceptions. Two collections were particularly helpful. The first was the Coal Tyee Society Oral History Collection, which consists of interviews with people who lived in and around the coal-mining area of Nanaimo. Interviewees were asked directly about religious practice and belief, without any clear agenda on the part of the interviewer, and both religious and irreligious beliefs and practices were clearly articulated. The Imbert Orchard Collection was also very useful; it includes over nine hundred interviews, conducted during the 1960s, primarily with people who lived in British Columbia before the First World War. A number of Orchard's interviews dealt with religion and irreligion, and although Orchard sometimes seemed to share the "people were more religious then" perspective, some of his interviewees nonetheless provided fascinating information regarding religion and irreligion in early British Columbia.

Although oral history supplied valuable material for this project, written qualitative sources were most central. These included a range of local newspapers, religious papers, and labour and socialist papers from Vancouver, Victoria, and smaller towns across the province.[76] They also encompassed published and unpublished church reports from various denominations, as well as letters from ministers and missionaries to their superiors. Naturally, these records have a certain bias, but they provide valuable insights about the nature of religious and irreligious behaviour and about clerical attitudes. Finally, I also used published and unpublished reminiscences from people who lived in British Columbia or who visited it between the 1880s and 1914, and a smaller number of letters and diaries. I cannot claim that my selection of these sources was exhaustive, but they were written by a number of individuals, both religious and irreligious, who made important observations.

THE FIRST CHAPTER OF this volume gives a quantitative overview of the nature of religion and irreligion across British Columbia. It explores both the minority who identified as atheist or as having "no religion" on the 1901 and 1911 censuses, and the far larger group that claimed a religious affiliation but did not belong to a church. This chapter examines the class, gender, ethnicity, and birthplace of those who defined themselves as irreligious, and it looks at their family status, immigrant status, levels of transiency, and regional representation in the province. It also addresses the question of why the racism of census enumerators makes it very difficult to use the census to assess the racialized status of the irreligious.

Chapter 2 undertakes a more qualitative cultural analysis of irreligion in British Columbia, highlighting certain popular and colourful journalists who helped to normalize irreligious discourse in the Kootenays. The chapter also discusses the trenchant and bitter critiques that socialists, syndicalists, and other radical labour activists levelled at Christianity and the churches. The gendered and often racist language that these irreligious opinion leaders employed in their attacks is also analyzed. Some of the most rancorous gendered attacks by the Kootenay journalists focused on Christian efforts to control or shut down elements of "rough culture," such as drinking, gambling, and the sex trade, which were central to the leisure of most male workers and many middle-class men. This chapter also notes how the strong anti-Asian sentiment in the province made whiteness a key part of most male workers' sense of respectable social identity, helping more men to discard the Christianity that had once been integral to that identity.

Chapter 3 teases apart the complex and fuzzy religious and irreligious realities of many British Columbians, particularly the transient working-class men who were central to the province's secular nature. Some were "hardcore" atheists, but many others retained some religious connection, even if it was no more than the desire to have a minister officiate at their funeral. This chapter also explores involvement in fraternal orders as a way of demonstrating that the combined forces of a less religious culture and a deep anti-Asian racism appeared to reduce certain sectarian tensions among the white population, particularly between Catholics and Protestants, which remained acrimonious in the rest of Canada.

Chapter 4 looks closely at church involvement and non-involvement by analyzing case studies of four relatively small BC towns, all in the Interior, and comparing them to two communities in Ontario and two in Nova Scotia. This chapter further discusses the significance of gender, marital status, class, and transiency to the particular nature of church involvement and non-involvement. Women and family are central to the analysis; though women constituted a minority in the province's population, they were a majority in the churches, often, but not always, drawing their husbands and families with them.

Chapter 5 puts the spotlight on Victoria and Vancouver, looking at both distinctive and shared patterns of religion and irreligion in the urban context. Like the smaller towns examined in Chapter 4, both cities had vibrant church communities. Their evangelical Protestant churches were closely associated with active Christian social and moral reform organizations. At the same time, many more people remained outside the churches than in Eastern Canada. Although local ministers identified Victoria as a non-churchgoing city, it was fast-growing Vancouver that had a significant and concentrated Euro-Canadian low-income irreligious population, primarily of men. This chapter analyzes the churches' less than successful efforts to convert these men on the streets of Vancouver and identifies other struggles between the religious and the irreligious that occurred on the streets of both cities.

Chapter 6 looks at non-Christian communities, primarily in the larger cities. Not all non-Christians were seen as equally threatening – Jews were far more accepted than non-Christian Asians – which points to the complex intersection of religion and race in constructing the "other" in the BC context. This chapter also identifies some possible similarities and differences between Euro-Canadian irreligious men and the province's non-Christian and often racialized communities, also largely male. Rough leisure culture seems to have been a common feature of these groups, but for the non-Christian minorities living in a hostile and racist environment, religious institutions played a range of diverse ethno-cultural roles for the religious and the irreligious alike.

The chapter also explores Christian attitudes toward racialized Asian non-Christian communities and church efforts to convert them. These attempts were relatively unsuccessful, with such failures further weakening the hegemony of the churches.

In seeking to convert the many racialized "heathen" and Euro-Canadian infidels, and to regulate the leisure culture of both racialized and Euro-Canadian men, churchmen needed all the allies they could get. This chapter concludes by scrutinizing their alliances with Euro-Canadian Christian women, who sought, and received, their support for suffrage rights; churchmen understood that the support – and the votes – of white Christian women were crucial in the struggle to Christianize a racially diverse and not very Christian province.

Chapter 6 identifies some of the rich religious diversity of British Columbia, whereas Chapter 7 examines a particular and significant strand of this diversity. Adherents of "alternative" metaphysical religions such as spiritualism, Theosophy, and Christian Science were a small minority of British Columbians in these years, but they were nonetheless very much over-represented in the province compared to elsewhere in Canada. For some British Columbians, especially women who were uncomfortable with mainstream Christianity, these forms of spirituality provided a more appealing option than outright atheism. Some of these religions, particularly Theosophy, attracted politically activist British Columbians, nurturing their commitment to feminism, class struggle, or anti-racism, and though they claimed links to Christianity, church leaders rejected them as outrages that were as deplorable as unbelief. These New Age spiritualities further undermined the cultural dominance of the Christian churches in the province.

British Columbia – the "Left Coast," or "Lotusland" – is often seen as "out there" in the popular imagination of the rest of Canada. Historians have been less keen on the idea of BC exceptionalism, although chroniclers of the province's history of racism and racialization have recognized it to some extent. This book argues that the roots of British Columbia's more secular "exceptionalism" are very evident in the pre–First World War period and were not restricted to any given part of the province. Although it does not claim to be exhaustive, it traces issues of religion and irreligion across the province. In the late nineteenth and early twentieth centuries, the Kootenays may have furnished some of the most colourful and class-conscious examples of irreligion, but working-class Gastown in Vancouver was not far behind, and according to local ministers, Victorians of all classes would rather work in their gardens than attend Sunday service. The coal-mining towns on Vancouver Island had their own versions of godlessness, as well as the highest number of spiritualists (the New Agers of their day). And as we'll see, many towns also boasted strong church communities, with white settler women playing key roles, as they sought to re-create traditions of faith and female sociability in a foreign and very male context. This book seeks to identify and understand both these average Christians and their irreligious (and sometimes heterodox) counterparts, finding traces of their lives and beliefs (or non-beliefs) in a range of sources. In this book, we also hear from more high-profile Christian moral reformers and feminists as they battled with atheist journalists, socialists, and "New Agers" for the social and religious salvation of British Columbians in newspapers, streets, churches, and meeting halls across the province. And we'll see how Chinese, Japanese, and South Asian immigrant groups, in both large cities and smaller towns, more quietly but very clearly rejected the missionaries' message of Christian salvation, and that the depth of Indigenous conversions remained a source of anxiety for missionaries. Throughout this book and across the province, I trace how a combined assault on Christian hegemony from many directions created a mutually reinforcing cultural space in which irreligion and heterodoxy were far more accepted than elsewhere in Canada.

1
A Godless Province?
Counting the Infidels and the Indifferent

In 1899, a Presbyterian missionary declared that in British Columbia "the great mass of the people care nothing for the gospel and treat all church organizations with supreme indifference."[1] In the same year, another Presbyterian noted that "positive and aggressive infidelity" existed in most regions of the province.[2] Ministers were concerned that British Columbians often stayed away from the churches and that many took the extra step of "aggressive infidelity," proudly identifying themselves as atheists. This chapter will explore the empirical basis of such clerical anxieties, using the 1901 and 1911 manuscript censuses to look at those who defined themselves as atheists or as having no religion, as well as those who might have identified with a Christian denomination for the census-taker but who nonetheless "treat[ed] all church organizations with supreme indifference."

Census records demonstrate that ministerial concerns were not groundless: the irreligious were far more common in British Columbia than elsewhere in Canada. In 1901, the gap between the proportion of British Columbians who told the enumerator that they were agnostics or had no religion (2,674 people) and the proportion of all Canadians who did the same was the largest it has ever been. These irreligious British Columbians made up 1.5 percent of the BC population, as compared to the 0.16 percent of irreligious among all Canadians. To put it another way, about 30 percent of all non-religious Canadians lived in British Columbia, at a time when the province was home to about 3 percent of Canada's total population. During the first decade of the century, their numbers more than kept pace with the province's population growth: in 1911, there were 8,198 non-religious British Columbians. At that point, they constituted 2.1 percent of the BC population, as compared to the still tiny 0.4 percent across Canada.[3]

In late-nineteenth and early-twentieth-century Canada, calling oneself an atheist, agnostic, or freethinker was a major challenge to dominant cultural norms. Stating that one had no religion was an only slightly less blatant challenge. Claiming at least a nominal adherence to a religious denomination was an integral part of Canada's cultural framework.[4] There is evidence that at least some Ontarians who saw themselves as atheists or freethinkers told the census-taker that they were Methodists or Presbyterians. Most of the small minority who held irreligious beliefs remained discreet for fear of social and economic consequences.[5] Canadians were certainly not uniformly pious: many did not attend church on a regular basis, and by the late nineteenth century many opinion leaders, both clerical and lay, were expressing fears of secularization.[6]

Nonetheless, the dominant discourses of the time were imbued with Christian values and beliefs. Many people who were not churchgoers sent their children to Sunday School, and most provinces exposed students to Christian teachings in both the public and separate schools.[7]

Public language, public institutions, and public and private practices assumed a common belief in God and in the basic tenets of Christianity. Personal faith and regular church attendance were central to the lives of many Canadians. For others, adherence to a particular denomination was as much about ethnic belonging, family traditions, and a sense of respectability as it was about belief, but that made it no less socially and culturally significant.[8]

In late-nineteenth- and early-twentieth-century Canada, being an atheist was no longer literally "unthinkable," as some scholars have suggested it was in earlier centuries.[9] However, it was very far from culturally or socially acceptable. Some or many of those who said they had no religion may have been rejecting the Christian Church rather than God, but in the context of the time, the willingness to publicly identify as having no religion put one beyond the pale. Stating that one had no religion could have dire social and economic consequences, including the loss of friends, jobs, or customers. In the public mind, such people would have been lumped in with atheists and agnostics as "infidels," a pejorative term that had deeply racialized overtones.[10]

Were there in fact any significant differences between those who defined themselves as atheists or agnostics or simply as having no religion on the

1901 and 1911 manuscript censuses? Enumerators were instructed to record exactly what individuals said, so we can assume that a census listing of "no religion" reflects their words, or something very similar. Those lumped under the category of agnostic for the published census, however, encompassed a range of self-reported options, including atheists and freethinkers, as described in the Introduction.[11] In 1901, this cohort made up 40 percent of the non-religious group. In 1911, their numbers were slightly larger, but because of a significant increase in those claiming no religion, they had shrunk to less than 15 percent of irreligious British Columbians. There were a few significant socio-economic differences between atheists/agnostics and those of no religion that will be discussed elsewhere.[12] However, in terms of the most significant variables, both groups differed in similar ways from the Christian majority.[13]

At the same time, though calling oneself an atheist is pretty clear-cut, the category of "no religion" is a slippery one. Scholars suggest that, in the late twentieth and early twenty-first centuries, this group could encompass a broad spectrum – ranging from a refusal to identify with a particular denomination, to the rejection of all religious institutions but a sense of oneself as "spiritual but not religious," to a complete dismissal of God and all spirituality.[14] This wide array of possibilities may also have been true of those of "no religion" in early-twentieth-century Canada, but we need to recognize the very real differences between that time and the present. Today, it is very easy to tell an enumerator that one has no religion, and indeed in many circles it is more socially acceptable to proclaim religious indifference than to identify as a Christian. This was certainly not the case in early-twentieth-century Canada, even in British Columbia, despite the greater openness to irreligion in the province.

To avoid misrepresenting those of no religion as rejecting more of spirituality than they may have done, while recognizing their distance from norms of the time, I employ "irreligious" as an umbrella category that encompasses all British Columbians who defined themselves as atheists, agnostics, or of no religion. As mentioned above, this refers to "beliefs and activities that are expressive of attitudes of hostility or indifference towards prevailing religion [both organized religion and religion more generally]."[15] The category of irreligious would also have included some of those who might have identified with a Christian denomination for the census-taker but did not attend any church. However, as we will see throughout the book, the latter group is particularly hard to pin down, for while many who did not attend church rejected organized religion, many others retained some shreds of Christian belief or identity.

As noted, the hegemonic power of the churches in late-nineteenth- and early-twentieth-century Canada made it very difficult for people to define themselves as other than Christian. The question remains, then, why did more people openly identify as irreligious in British Columbia than anywhere else in Canada? Was it somewhat easier to do so in the BC context, and if so why? Or if it were not easier, what prompted a significant number of British Columbians to challenge Christian norms? This chapter begins to answer these questions. In doing so, it explores regional differences in the province and the intersection of region with gender, marital status, geographical mobility, family (or absence of family), birthplace, immigration, racialization, and class and class consciousness.

The findings presented here are based on the 1901 and 1911 censuses. I worked with databases of 5 percent samples of the BC and Canadian manuscript censuses for both years; a database of all British Columbians who, in 1901, defined themselves as atheists, agnostics, or as having no religion; and the church membership data provided in the published census of 1901.

Both published and unpublished census data are analyzed using descriptive statistics. I applied logistic regression analysis to the databases that were compiled from the manuscript censuses, as this enabled me to assess the odds of a particular outcome and whether they are statistically significant, further illuminating the particular demographic forces that shaped irreligion in British Columbia.[16]

Comparative Levels of Church Involvement across Canada

Those who told a BC census-taker that they were atheists, agnostics, or of "no religion" were not a minor though extreme aberration in an otherwise Christian province, but on one end of a continuum that included many others who were also largely or completely irreligious. The latter group identified as Christian for the enumerators but remained indifferent to organized religion. Others may have retained some ethnic, spiritual, or moral links to Christianity but did not attend or join a church. High levels of religious indifference are evident in the low levels of church involvement in British Columbia, as compared to the rest of Canada.

At the other end of the continuum were significant numbers of Christians. By the turn of the century, most communities had churches of various denominations. The majority of these churches had developed beyond the "missionary church" stage, during which they had survived on subsidies from parent churches in Eastern Canada, although in smaller towns many still relied on this support.[17] BC Christians were active in the various moral and social reform campaigns that were gaining momentum across Canada in the early twentieth century, particularly temperance and Sunday closing legislation. Yet, the 1901 census makes it clear that British Columbians were less likely than Canadians in any other province to be involved in a church. As always, the census asked about individual religious adherence, but in 1901 it also took the unusual step of adopting an American practice, which was to enumerate the churches themselves, asking them about the number of their communicants. Although "communicant" had somewhat varied meanings among denominations and is relatively meaningless with regard to some religions (such as Judaism), a comparative listing of communicants by denomination is very useful for understanding levels of church involvement. Communicants, or church members as they were more commonly known in certain denominations, would generally have been the most active churchgoers.[18] The published census for 1901 provides information on numbers of communicants by denomination and numbers of those who simply associated themselves with a denomination (whom the census termed "adherents"). Thus, it is possible to determine relative levels of church involvement both between denominations and between regions.[19]

This analysis reveals that British Columbia had the lowest levels of church involvement in the country. In the Maritime provinces and southern Ontario and Quebec, most districts were average or above average in the percentage of Protestant communicants to total adherents (see Figure 4). Most of Northern and Western Canada was below average, with certain BC districts having some of the lowest levels of church involvement among Canadian Protestants.[20] Catholic patterns were generally similar, although a few other western and northern districts competed with British Columbia for the distinction of having the lowest ratios of communicants to adherents.[21]

Low levels of church participation in British Columbia cannot be explained by the province's denominational makeup. Anglicans, who had a low ratio of communicants to adherents, made up a higher proportion of BC Protestants than was the case elsewhere in English Canada, and Catholics, who had a high ratio of communicants to adherents, were under-represented.[22] However, in British Columbia all major denominations had extremely low involvement rates, with the percentage of communicants among adherents being consistently less than 60 percent of the national average. Only 13.4 percent of BC Presbyterians were communicants, less than half of the national average. Among BC Anglicans, only 12.8 percent

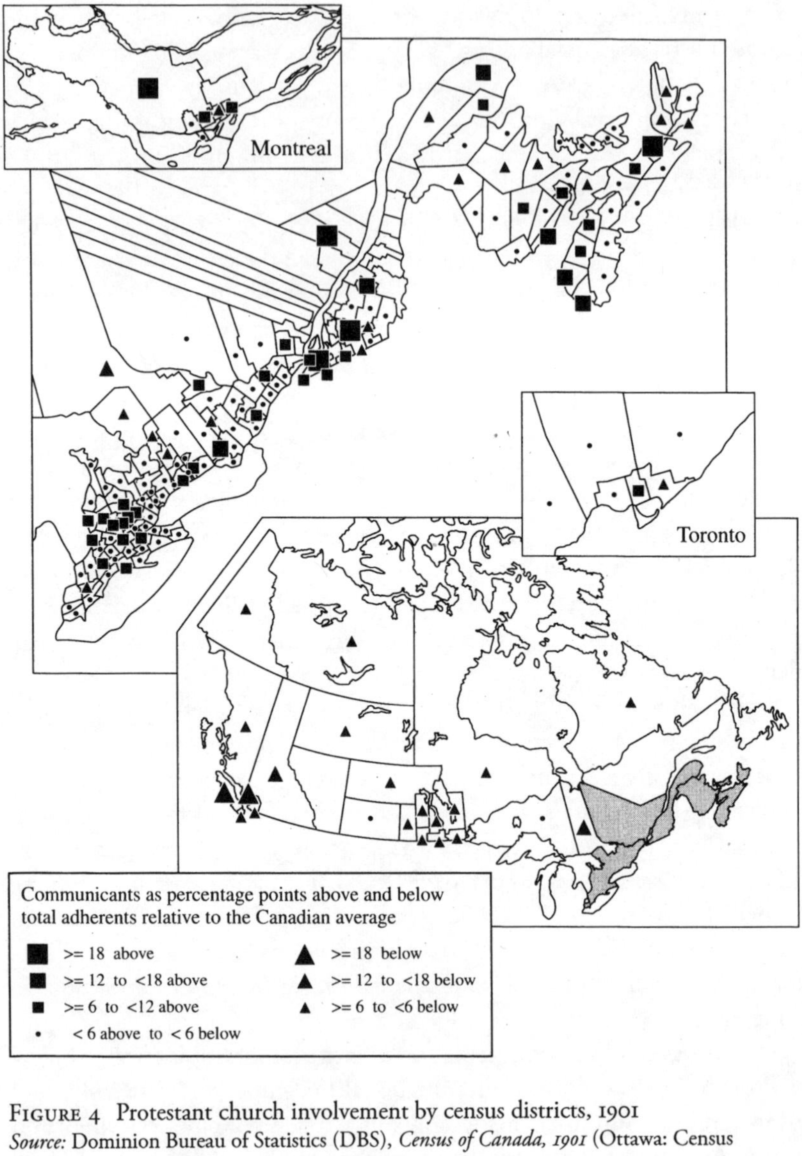

FIGURE 4 Protestant church involvement by census districts, 1901
Source: Dominion Bureau of Statistics (DBS), *Census of Canada, 1901* (Ottawa: Census Office, 1902), vol. 1, Table 8, and vol. 4, Table 19.

were communicants, as compared to 22.1 in Ontario and 30.7 in Quebec, and similar patterns existed for Methodists and Catholics (see Appendix: Table 1). The percentage of communicants in British Columbia was closer to that of the North-West Territories (soon to become the provinces of

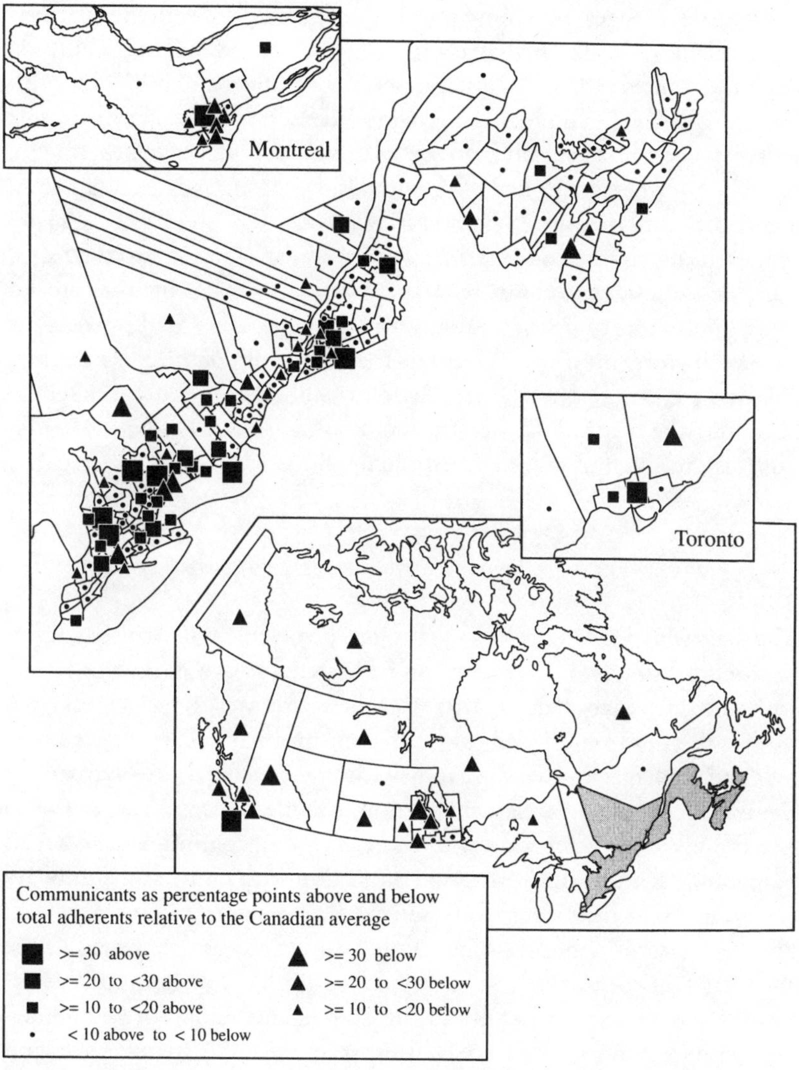

FIGURE 5 Catholic church involvement by census districts, 1901
Source: DBS, *Census of Canada, 1901* (Ottawa: Census Office, 1902), vol. 1, Table 8, and vol. 4, Table 19.

Alberta and Saskatchewan) than to that of the longer-settled provinces in the east. Nonetheless, among all major denominations, the percentages in the sparsely settled Territories were higher than in the relatively more established province of British Columbia (see Table 1 and Figures 4 and 5).

These data suggest that more research needs to be done on the relatively low levels of religious participation in the North and West generally. At the same time, the data highlight especially high levels of religious indifference in British Columbia. The province's demographic character actually serves to underline the gulf between its levels of church involvement and those of elsewhere in Canada. Individuals did not usually become communicants until they were at least thirteen, and many joined a church later in their teens. In 1901, only 32.2 percent of British Columbians were aged fourteen and under, as compared to the Canadian average of 46.2 percent. Thus, the proportion of communicants to adherents should ostensibly have been *higher* in British Columbia than in the rest of the country, since children are included in the calculation of adherents but are unlikely to be among the communicants. The fact that the reverse is true further reinforces the religious gulf between the province and the rest of Canada.

Who Were the Irreligious? Gender and Family Issues

Ministers who decried the lack of religious involvement in British Columbia found various reasons to explain it. Material gain was a major factor, with one missionary arguing that "the chase after wealth has driven from the minds of the majority all care as to their spiritual welfare."[23] American religious leaders who were unhappy with the low church involvement in the Far West voiced similar disapproval.[24] Some BC commentators also noted the loss of connection with Eastern church communities, whereas many more focused on the loss of connection with home and family, relationships that they assumed fostered religious belief and involvement. Similar concerns about transient populations were also expressed in the Western United States.[25] Anxieties about the lack of home influence were closely tied to worries about the over-representation of young men in British Columbia, who were far away from their Christian families and very unlikely to be involved in a church. As one commentator who urged the adoption of new methods to entice young men into church stated, "there are parts of the West into which one may go and find practically none but young men ... And if they are not religious there will be no religion there, for there are no others to lay the foundations."[26]

This over-representation of non-Indigenous men in British Columbia is well documented. Jobs in the primary resource industries such as lumbering and mining attracted many men to the province. Some brought their wives, but many others did not, and large numbers of single men headed west in hopes of making their fortune. As Adele Perry shows for the colonial period, this over-representation of men, particularly unmarried white men (or more specifically, men without white wives) was viewed by authorities as a major barrier to creating a stable, settled, moral society in the province.[27]

Decades later, a variety of elite commentators continued to worry about the range of social problems that were supposedly generated by an excess of young single white men. Church leaders focused on young men's lack of religiosity and attendant moral ruin. The problem extended beyond the province. As one BC minister remarked, "That [the young man] is not with us is only too evident in every city and town the world over. Other circles gain his presence and the influence of his energy, but the Church is looked upon as only the abridgement of his liberties."[28] The churches were well aware that all across Canada few young men stayed in Sunday School once they reached their late teens and that most were neither church members nor active churchgoers. As one Presbyterian missionary noted, many young men "do not think it is good form to be communicants."[29] Young men appear to have rejected the churches because they were associated with feminine characteristics such as piety and emotionalism, preferring instead the alternative of a rougher, more masculine leisure culture.[30] That they courted moral ruin in doing so was a common theme in church periodicals.[31] This problem was seen as exacerbated in British Columbia, in part because many young men were far from the influence of their Christian families, congregating in largely male logging camps, railway construction camps, and mining towns, where drinking, gambling, and the sex trade were predominant.[32]

Religious leaders and women who were active in the churches made various efforts to win the hearts of these young men. They established missions and clubs that targeted them. For example, the Woman's Christian Temperance Union founded a Mission Hall in Victoria in 1900 because,

> In the hearts of some mothers there was a strong, earnest desire to reach the hitherto un-reached portion of the population of the city, the non-church goers ... [and to create] a place ... where men would come in touch, and be to a certain extent under the influence of a kind Christian woman who would take a real personal interest in them, such an interest that none could go away from the Mission ... and say in moments of loneliness "nobody cares how I go or what I do." Words that have been echoed in many a poor fellow's heart when far away from home and those he loves.[33]

There were indeed many "poor fellows" in British Columbia who had abandoned not only the churches but also God. As in other parts of the country and the world, men were much more likely than women to actively define themselves as irreligious – as being agnostic or as having no religion. The 1901 census reveals that over 84 percent of the BC irreligious were male, a higher proportion than one would expect, even with gender ratios skewed toward men. Logistic regression analysis for both 1901 and 1911 confirms that in both Canada and British Columbia, men were dramatically more likely than women to identify as irreligious.[34]

Single men were also somewhat more likely than married men to define themselves as irreligious, although the patterns here are not as strong or consistent. In 1901, the majority (58 percent) of BC non-believers were unmarried men. Given their large numbers in the province, this is not surprising. At the same time, the relatively high proportion of non-believers was not just about the over-representation of single men. In both 1901 and 1911, single men were only slightly more likely than married men to be irreligious.[35] Although, in British Columbia and elsewhere, clerical anxieties focused on the particular "problem" of unmarried young men, age does not seem to have been significant in differentiating between irreligious men and those who claimed a religious affiliation.[36]

Contemporary Christian rhetoric suggested that Christian faith and practice were nurtured in the home, but the fact that single men were only slightly more likely than married men to claim an irreligious identity suggests that the situation in British Columbia was somewhat more complex.[37] Many married men had left their wives behind, whether in Ontario, England, or Italy, to seek their fortune in British Columbia.

Were men, either married or single, who were far from the influence of wives and families most likely to define themselves as irreligious? Not entirely. Irreligious men were as likely to live with their wives as other married British Columbian men.[38] At the same time, there was some reality to this image. Given the over-representation of men in British Columbia, the significant number of all-male households is not surprising. In 1901, among the BC population as a whole, approximately 18 percent of dwellings that housed two or more people included only men. Among dwellings with two or more people that included at least one irreligious person, 34 percent were exclusively male.[39] In 1911, households that were predominantly or exclusively male were also more likely to include irreligious members.[40] As well, in both 1901 and 1911 men who were boarders or lodgers were much more likely than men who lived with their family to be non-believers.[41]

Among the irreligious, the over-representation of lodgers and those who lived in all-male households suggests that for many BC men, moving away from family bonds may have enabled them to shake off religious belief or to be open about doing so. In earlier research, I found that some men who lived in small-town Ontario were willing to define themselves as non-believers in certain contexts but were nonetheless identified as Christians on the census, alongside their churchgoing wives.[42] When such men moved to British Columbia, away from religious wives or mothers, they may have found the freedom to be honest about their lack of faith.

The fact that many boarders and lodgers had not only left family behind but also continued to be quite transient, often moving from place to place in search of work, may also help explain their willingness to challenge religious norms. Transiency made it easier to avoid church and community ties – and church and community oversight. Many transient men had moved "across the Rocky Mountains" from elsewhere in Canada, and census data suggest that this internal migration made a difference. Analysis of the 1911 census demonstrates that Canadians born in other provinces were significantly more likely than the BC-born to define themselves as irreligious.[43] Migration from outside of Canada was even more significant. Immigrants were consistently more likely than the Canadian-born to define themselves as irreligious, both in 1901 and 1911.[44] This issue is discussed further below and in Chapter 4.

Thus far, we have focused on white settler men who defined themselves as irreligious. But what about their wives? And were there irreligious women in British Columbia, single and transient, who left God behind when they crossed the Rocky Mountains? In answering these questions, we must treat the census data with caution. On first glance, the data do suggest that BC women were much more likely than their counterparts elsewhere in Canada to be irreligious. They were much less likely than BC men to be irreligious, but the 1901 census data suggest that they were six times more likely than Ontario women to be irreligious.[45] In British Columbia, married women were slightly more likely than single women to be irreligious, reversing the pattern for men, and they were eight times more likely than their Ontario equivalents to define themselves as irreligious (see Appendix: Table 2). Some BC women were no doubt making their own decisions about religion. Like male lodgers, female lodgers were more likely than women who were part of nuclear family households to be irreligious. In 1901, 4 percent of BC women were boarders or lodgers, and 12 percent of irreligious women were lodgers. Like their male equivalents, some would have been single transient workers who felt able to abandon religious ties and conventions.

One of these was a Miss Moffat, a teacher who lodged with churchgoing Presbyterian Jessie McQueen in Rossland. In an 1897 letter, Jessie described Moffat as "one of no belief."[46] Other irreligious female lodgers were sex trade workers, who felt rejected by the churches because of their "immoral" lifestyle.[47] In either case, most female lodgers were single, and some were willing to draw their own conclusions about Christianity. For irreligious married women, the situation was more murky, linked both to familial assumptions and census conventions. When we look at married couples where at least one spouse was irreligious, we do appear to find many irreligious women. In 41 percent of these families, both husband and wife are listed as agnostics or of no religion (see Appendix: Table 3). These data can be read in various ways. In some instances, they may simply reflect the behaviour of census-takers who listed all family members under the religion of the household head. This was often done, but less so with religion than with certain other variables, as mixed marriages between Christians of differing denominations were often reported. The presence of many irreligious couples may undermine assumptions about wifely piety, but it may also speak to male power and influence within the family. The presence of 4 percent of families (sixteen in total) in which, unlike her Christian husband, the wife defined herself as a non-believer or as having no religion, suggests that at least a few women made independent and unconventional choices in this regard. Hermina Lyons of Victoria, who described herself (and her five children) as atheists, whereas her lawyer husband was given as a Baptist, may be one such instance, although her husband's religious affiliation may have had as much to do with not alienating potential clients as with belief. In any case, although Hermina was not unique, the most common pattern in the census records (at 54 percent of couples) was of a non-believing husband and a Christian wife. This suggests that male non-believer convictions did not always overcome the "naturally" more religious inclinations of women, and that family life with a Christian wife did not always bring skeptical husbands to God (see Table 3). In families where the wife was a Christian, the children generally followed her religion, as was commonly the case with mixed religious marriages.[48] In families where both spouses were listed as irreligious, the children were almost always identified in the same way.[49] Such families lived throughout the province: in Kaslo, for example, a silver miner, his wife, two sons, and three daughters were all recorded as having no religion; in Vancouver, a plasterer, his wife, son, and daughter were enumerated as "secularists"; and also in Vancouver, an accountant, his wife, two sons, and three daughters were listed as "no church." These families would have challenged dominant ideas about family life in which Christianity, and particularly the Christian mother, "glorifies and beautifies the home life" and makes the home "a fragment of heaven on earth."[50]

A study in which I analyzed the irreligious in Victoria and on Vancouver Island between 1881 and 1911 provides a longer view and suggests that the irreligious commitment of at least some white settler wives and mothers was less than solid. This study, based on the ViHistory database, tracked individuals who, in at least one of the 1881, 1891, 1901, and 1911 censuses, stated that they were agnostics or had no religion.[51] Only 28.6 percent (251 of the 751 people who identified as irreligious) could be linked from one census to another, pointing to the transiency of Vancouver Island's population during this period.[52] These results reinforce the findings in Hannah Lane's study of denominational fluidity among Protestants in mid- to late-nineteenth-century New Brunswick, which demonstrate that a significant number of Protestants changed denominational affiliation from one census year to another.[53] In fact, fluidity between Christians and the irreligious on Vancouver Island was significantly greater than among New Brunswick Christians. Just over 16 percent of Vancouver Islanders who identified as irreligious in one census year gave the same self-definition over two census years.[54] Almost 35 percent of islanders who changed affiliation moved from identifying with a Christian denomination to an irreligious category over two census years, whereas over 48 percent shifted from an irreligious category to identifying with a Christian denomination (Appendix: Table 4). This suggests the need for caution in identifying a stable long-term irreligious segment of BC society, although it also indicates that being irreligious was sufficiently acceptable that many could transition fairly easily from Christianity to irreligion, or vice versa. This study found no evidence that British Columbians conformed to the stereotype of embracing atheism in their youth but turning to God in later life. It does, however, suggest that the influence of husbands or fathers was a major factor in reported levels of non-belief among BC women. And it also demonstrates that in some cases, religious wives had some effect on non-believing men.

Women made up just over a quarter (27 percent) of the irreligious who appear at least twice in the ViHistory database. In both the database and the 1901 BC census, almost half of all women who were married to a non-religious man shared his affiliation. Change over time, particularly with the ending of a marriage, offers important clues regarding the true religious or irreligious feelings of certain husbands and wives. The numbers here are very small, but the patterns are suggestive. In two cases that can be traced, wives who were identified as irreligious returned to defining themselves and their children as Christian once they were widowed. In 1881, Ann McLean was listed as having no religion, and in 1891, like her blacksmith husband, John, and her several children, she was classed as a "Freethinker." By 1901, however, John had died, and Ann was enumerated as a widow and a grocer who lived with several of her adult working children. All were now listed as Episcopal, including the two grown sons, a ship's carpenter and a ship fireman. Given the strong likelihood that single young men would be irreligious, one might assume that the sons would maintain their father's approach to religion, but in this case, what appears to be Ann's return to an earlier religious affiliation served as at least the official religion of the entire family. Similarly, Lucy Ross was recorded as a Methodist in 1881 and as a freethinker in 1891, along with her grocer husband and children. As a widow in 1901, she defined herself, and all her grown children then living with her, as Presbyterian. Whereas husbandly influence could sometimes affect the unbeliever status of wives, the reverse was also true. Although it was not uncommon for married couples to consist of an unbeliever husband and a Christian wife, some men, who were listed as Christians when married, came out as unbelievers once they became widowers. For example, James McLay was recorded as a married Presbyterian in 1881 but as both a widower and a freethinker in 1891. In no case did a man shift from being irreligious to a Christian denomination after his wife died. Similarly, three single men who described themselves as unbelievers were enumerated as Christians and married men in a subsequent census. One of these, John Halverson, a Nanaimo miner who defined himself as a freethinker in 1891 when he was single, was identified as an Anglican once he married Susie, an Anglican. There is one counter-example, however, in which Charles Chislett, an unmarried Methodist in 1881, identified both himself and his wife, Elizabeth, as Deists in 1901. However, it is not possible to determine whether Elizabeth was a Deist before her marriage, as she cannot be identified in the database before the time of her wedding. So, who influenced whom remains unknown. It was also very possible for husbands and wives to go separate religious ways, although the gendered patterns were quite clear. For example, John Perry of Nanaimo and his wife, Hannah, were both listed as Methodists in 1891, but each had taken separate spiritual paths by 1901, with Hannah remaining a Methodist and John defining himself as an atheist. Whereas men, both married and single, seemed to be quite comfortable in identifying themselves as irreligious, few women who were not the wives or children of irreligious men followed suit. Of the fifty-seven women linked through the database, only three can be identified as unbelievers without the presence of irreligious husbands or fathers. Two of them, Annie Cox and Ann Scott, were widows: Cox said she was a freethinker in 1881, and Scott called herself an agnostic in 1891. However, ten years later, now in their seventies, both identified as Anglicans, suggesting either that the irreligious impact of former husbands had lost its force or that the power of family, faith, fear of impending death, and issues of respectability had reasserted itself for these elderly women.[55] One other younger widow, Margaret Hirst of Nanaimo, also called herself a freethinker. She worked in a hotel, where her mother, the proprietor, and a few other employees were freethinkers as well.[56]

In assessing shifts between Christian and irreligious affiliations, we need to remember the low levels of church membership in British Columbia, even among those who linked themselves with a Christian denomination on the census. Identifying with a denomination did not necessarily say much about belief. Transferring from freethinker to Methodist, as Frederick Jeune of Victoria did between 1901 and 1911, did not appear to have anything to do with marriage, as his wife was also listed as a freethinker in 1901 and a Methodist in 1911. It may have pointed to a conversion experience for at least one spouse, but it may also have involved a range of more secular calculations, such as Frederick's desire, as a local businessman, for greater acceptance among the Christian Victorians who remained the majority of the city's population. Nanaimo miner Joshua Martell, who defined himself as a Deist in 1881, an atheist in 1891, and a Baptist in 1901, may have returned to a familiar religion or identity as he aged, or he may have been influenced by his Presbyterian wife and mother, both of whom lived with him. They had not prevented him from claiming an atheist identity in 1891 but may have prevailed in at least getting him to identify as a Christian, though not a Presbyterian, by 1901. Age certainly did not always lead to increased piety. Some men, such as Cowichan farmer John Barry, became more religiously radical as they aged. Middle-aged and Catholic in 1881 and 1891, Barry was an agnostic in 1901. His wife, Eliza, never wavered from Anglicanism during this period. Nanaimo miner Joseph Maloney and his wife, Mary, were at least nominal Presbyterians in 1891 but had become freethinkers by 1901, which may suggest a joint decision or that Joseph influenced Mary's affiliation. The willingness to move between categories of belief and unbelief reinforces the sense that identifying with unbelief was more acceptable than in Eastern Canada and also suggests that, in some instances, claiming a religious identity could have been socially advantageous. Hannah Lane argues that identifying with a denomination on the census may sometimes have had more to do with one's ethnic affiliation, a link to family history and religious traditions, than with current faith and church affiliation (or lack thereof). This may have been the case for some irreligious British Columbians. Identification with a denomination may have served more as an assertion of ethnicity and family traditions than as a faith commitment, particularly, but not exclusively, for the men who linked themselves with a denomination after marriage or until widowerhood.

Whereas an analysis of gender and family reveals much about the social contours of irreligion, other variables, such as geography, class, birthplace, and ethnicity, can further illuminate the more secular culture of British Columbia. Regional differences in levels of irreligion are quite striking.

Region and Class

The census district of Yale and Cariboo in the BC Interior had the highest proportion of inhabitants who stated that they were atheists, agnostics, or of no religion, at 2.4 percent of the total population of the district. In 1901, this region also had the most skewed gender ratio in the province. The relationship between a predominance of men and of the irreligious did not always hold, however, as other areas with almost equally skewed gender ratios had relatively low proportions of irreligious residents. Furthermore, in the region that included the City of Vancouver, with the least skewed gender ratio in the province, 1.7 percent of residents identified as agnostics, atheists, or as having no religion.[57]

Gender ratios could be significant, but other factors also came into play. In Yale and Cariboo, class and class consciousness exerted a major influence on many people's attitudes to God and to the churches. In nineteenth- and early-twentieth-century North America and Europe, religious doubt and atheism were certainly not confined to the working class. In the United States, Britain, and to a lesser extent Canada, there was a strong tradition of middle-class freethought, as atheism was commonly known, among those who had been influenced by intellectual currents dating from the Enlightenment. For others, the late nineteenth century was an important turning point, as Darwinism, the Higher Criticism (which perceived the Bible as being written by humans rather than being divinely inspired), and other new ideas cast doubts on many previously accepted religious beliefs. Most Christians were able to accommodate the new understandings, but some moved toward religious doubt and ultimately to unbelief.[58] There was also a tradition of working-class atheism, fuelled partly by similar intellectual currents but also emerging from working-class politics and class consciousness. This type of atheism was grounded in class hostility to clerical authority and the association of the church with the ruling classes and with employers.[59] Whereas some workers rejected the churches and the clergy but not God, others, particularly orthodox Marxists, saw religion as an opiate that impeded workers from recognizing and acting on their true class interests. Atheism was not the dominant current in most working-class politics during this period. Many in the labour movement used Christian rhetoric and Christian belief systems to challenge what they saw as the exploitative un-Christian practices of employers.[60] Christian socialism had a significant influence in Britain, Canada, and the United States. At the same time, some workers and unions in British Columbia and the Western United States were very receptive to orthodox Marxism, with its hostility to Christian belief.[61]

Census data reinforce the perception that working-class atheism was more common in British Columbia than elsewhere in Canada. The 1901 and 1911 censuses list employment categories that allow us to identify class differences, with distinct categories for employers, employees, or those who worked "on their own account."[62] Both the 1901 and the 1911 census reveal that in Canada as a whole, employees were the least likely to identify themselves as irreligious.[63] This suggests that in Canada generally, and particularly in Central and Eastern Canada, the majority of the irreligious continued to emerge from the middle-class intellectual currents of skepticism. However, British Columbia departed from this pattern. Although there certainly were irreligious middle-class British Columbians, analysis of the 1911 BC census demonstrates that employers were the least likely to describe themselves as irreligious. Those who worked on their own account were the most likely to do so, followed by employees. When the analysis is limited solely to explicit unbelievers, those who defined themselves as atheists, agnostics, or freethinkers (not as having no religion), employees were the most likely to define themselves as irreligious.[64] It seems reasonable to assume that many of the employees who identified themselves as atheists or agnostics were working-class Marxists.

Among irreligious working-class men, one occupational group – miners – was particularly over-represented, especially the hardrock miners of the Kootenays, who were almost twice as likely to be irreligious as their representation in the population would suggest (Appendix: Table 5). Most worked in Rossland or Slocan, the Yale and Cariboo subdistricts that had the highest proportion of irreligious people in the province and that were

Figure 6 Percentage of those defined as atheists, agnostics, and of no religion, Rossland, Slocan, and BC, 1901

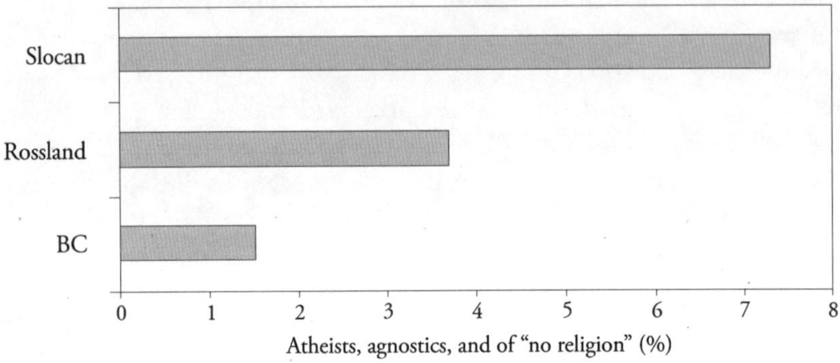

major areas of hardrock mining. In Rossland, 538 people identified themselves as atheists or as having no religion, making up 3.7 percent of its population; in Slocan, the 387 who defined themselves similarly constituted 7.3 percent of the area's residents (Figure 6). The other subdistrict with over 3 percent of irreligious people was the South East Kootenays, which lay nearby and which included some hardrock mining, as well as considerable coal mining in the Crowsnest Pass area. These subdistricts had markedly uneven gender ratios, especially Slocan and the South East Kootenays, where the population was less than 30 percent female (see Appendix: Table 6).[65]

A predominance of men among the white settler population is part of the story, but more importantly, the majority of these men belonged to an extremely transient, and often unmarried, workforce of miners.[66] A significant minority among this group was not only willing to reject religion, but to do so publicly to the census-taker, perhaps because of limited social ties in the community. Transiency may have conferred greater freedom to reject or ignore the forces of family, respectability, and Christian hegemony. These forces may not automatically have made men religious in other parts of Canada, but at a minimum they made it very difficult not to claim some religious affiliation.

The predominance of transient and often single men helps to explain the relatively high levels of unbelief in Slocan, the South East Kootenays, and Rossland, but it doesn't account for everything. These men were not the only irreligious inhabitants of these areas. In Slocan and the South East Kootenays, married men were almost as likely as their single counterparts

Silverton miners of the Standard Silver Mine in the Central Kootenays, 190- | *BC Archives, F-02381*

to be non-believers; in Rossland, where only 30 percent of the population was female, married men were more likely than single men to be irreligious. Also, 2.5 percent of Rossland women were non-believers, though many may have defined themselves as irreligious (or been defined as such by their husbands) due to familial bonds rather than spiritual conviction. Nonetheless, the relatively high proportion of irreligious people in Slocan, the South East Kootenays, and Rossland suggests that what we are seeing is a culture or subculture in which non-belief was an acceptable option. In these communities, this culture was grounded in labour radicalism and socialism.

Older labour histories of the province argued that the starkly oppressive working conditions of its resource industries led to polarized class politics and a labour movement more radical than that of Eastern Canada.[67] Labour relations were certainly bitter and turbulent at the turn of the century. The BC mining regions experienced major strikes during this period: in Slocan in 1899, in Rossland in 1901, in the Crowsnest Pass and on Vancouver Island in 1903, and in Nanaimo and Ladysmith from 1912 to 1914. During these years, the mining districts were electing labour and socialist MLAs,

Columbia Avenue, Rossland, 1896 | *BC Archives, D-07726*

and miners in the Kootenays, the Crowsnest Pass, and on Vancouver Island were affiliated with the Western Federation of Miners, an American union that was considered radical and socialist.[68] Arguments about greater BC radicalism, as part of "western exceptionalism" in labour relations, have been tempered by the work of Jeremy Mouat and John Belshaw. Writing about the Kootenay miners, Mouat states that the leaders of the Western Federation of Miners were more moderate than was previously believed, at least until 1903.[69]

The relatively high numbers of atheists, agnostics, and those claiming no religion in the Western Federation of Miners strongholds of the Kootenays and the Crowsnest Pass suggests that at least some rank-and-file union members may not have been all that moderate. "Western exceptionalism," at least in terms of working-class radicalism powerful enough to reject dominant Christian norms, should not be entirely dismissed. Some people who called themselves atheists or agnostics did so as part of their commitment to a Marxist ideology. These individuals (primarily men) were less likely to identify with "no religion" and more likely to declare for explicit unbelief, as atheists or infidels.[70] Other irreligious workers may not have been Marxists per se, but their non-belief may point to a strong class consciousness bred by the brutal conditions of the mines and the overweening power of capitalists in these communities. Thus, they may have rejected religion and the churches as tools of the employing classes. Such a rejection may have been particularly easy for many relatively transient men who were far from ties of family and Christian respectability, but the combination of transiency and strong class consciousness made public declarations of irreligion possible for many people – single and married, male and female – in this region.

Labour radicalism and relatively high levels of irreligion were correlated in the Kootenay and Crowsnest Pass mining towns. This was much less true in the coal-mining areas of Vancouver Island, where agnostics and those of no religion consistently made up less than 1 percent of the population (see Appendix: Table 6).[71] Relatively low overall levels of irreligion do not mean, however, that the coal miners of Vancouver Island were a particularly pious lot. The 1901 census of communicants reveals that, along with Yale and Cariboo, Vancouver Island (outside Victoria) had the lowest ratios of church members to total adherents in the province. The most populous parts of this census district were the coal-mining communities.[72] Among all denominations except the Catholics, church membership was lower on Vancouver Island than in Yale and Cariboo, giving it the distinction of having the lowest levels of Protestant church involvement in the country (see Appendix: Table 7).

White settlers in the Vancouver Island coal-mining districts were very unlikely to become active church members. This does not seem to have been an issue of transiency, as was true in the Kootenays. Like the rest of the province, the coal-mining areas at Nanaimo had a significant overrepresentation of single men, but women constituted a higher proportion of their population than was the BC norm.[73] The Nanaimo area included far more settled nuclear families than the more transient mining regions of the Interior.[74] It also boasted more relatively long-established churches than was true of the Kootenays.

John Belshaw argues that the churches were important for many Vancouver Island miners because they provided a valuable social and cultural resource, whether in organizing picnics, temperance outings, or the many funerals of those who died in mining accidents, and Lynne Bowen suggests that the miners saw the churches as useful sources of moral education for their children.[75] No doubt, the churches did offer education, social activities, and the solace of ritual and belief in times of crisis, but the low

Coal miners at Ladysmith, Vancouver Island, 191– | *BC Archives, E-01850*

numbers of communicants suggest that many miners and other community members felt at least some ambivalence regarding organized religion. Belshaw's evidence of unusually high levels of inter-denominational marriage, including between Catholics and Protestants, also indicates that denominational ties and loyalties were much weaker in the Vancouver Island coal-mining towns than in Britain and Eastern Canada.[76]

Chapter 3 will look more closely at religious involvement on Vancouver Island, but it seems likely that the powerful labour militancy of island miners may have encouraged a hostility to organized religion that kept many working people, particularly men, out of church. For many who did attend services, a sense of ambivalence regarding Christianity or the church may have prevented them from taking the major step of becoming a member. Some local ministers, at least among the Methodists and Baptists, were sympathetic to the situation of the miners, even during the Great Strike of 1912–14. Nevertheless, the lay leadership of both the Presbyterian and Methodist churches in the coal-mining areas was primarily middle and upper class, and the Presbyterian and Anglican churches received considerable financial support and direction from mine owners and managers, facts that no doubt had a dampening effect on church involvement among many miners and their families.[77]

At the same time, very few Vancouver Islanders were willing to go to the extreme of calling themselves atheists or stating that they had no religion.

Finding an explanation for this brings us back to questions of gender and family. Women were less likely than men to be irreligious and were more numerous on the island than in the Kootenays, particularly in Nanaimo. As noted above, Vancouver Island married men were much less likely than their single counterparts to identify as atheists or as having no religion. The study of irreligious Vancouver Islanders from 1881 to 1911 suggests that at least some men who were living with Christian wives faced family pressure that prevented them from defining themselves as irreligious, at least while their wives were alive. More generally, in more settled long-term communities, it may have been more difficult for some men to challenge dominant Christian norms by "coming out" publicly as atheists or those of "no religion."

Although settled family life may have made it harder for men to define themselves as atheists, it didn't bring them into the churches. The very low level of church involvement in these areas challenges the dominant discourse of the time, which promoted family life as creating moral, stable, Christian communities.[78] If family and gender differences don't fully explain the large discrepancy between levels of explicit irreligion in the Vancouver Island coalfields and in the Kootenays, John Belshaw's argument about the fundamental conservatism of the British colliers on Vancouver Island is suggestive here. This conservatism may have led miners to unionization and to strikes in their efforts to protect their income and way of life, but it may have prevented most from totally rejecting the faith of their childhood.[79]

Ethnicity, Immigration, Birthplace, and Race

Did ethnic identity and birthplace have an impact on levels of irreligion, not only in the Vancouver Island coalfields, but across the province? What about race and racialization? In the latter case, the profoundly racist way in which census enumerators dealt with religion makes any meaningful census-based analysis of the relationship between race and irreligion impossible, while simultaneously revealing a great deal about how outsider status was constituted through both religion and race. A brief examination of how census-takers enumerated the religion of non-Euro-Canadians reveals this clearly. Enumerators very rarely identified Indigenous people as atheists, agnostics, or of no religion. By 1901 and 1911, most Indigenous people were enumerated with a Christian denomination, although a significant number, particularly on the west coast of Vancouver Island, were still defined as "pagan," a racialized term that resonated with images of primitive people. Other census takers recorded certain Indigenous people as "heathens," another extremely negative racialized term. Whereas many Indigenous people who were identified with a Christian denomination had become devout Christians, the syncretic beliefs of many others, who integrated Christian and traditional spiritualities, were invisible to enumerators.[80]

In 1901 and 1911, many Asian immigrants were listed as Buddhist or Confucian, demonstrating at least a minimal knowledge of Asian religions but no recognition of the complex mix of traditions followed by the majority of Chinese people.[81] Some enumerators simply made wild guesses, based on racial/religious stereotypes; for example, some defined all or almost all the Chinese individuals in their districts as either Buddhist or Confucian. Others reported only their prejudices. As noted in the Introduction, one Victoria census-taker listed almost all the Chinese people in his district as "agnostic," expressing his own interlocking prejudices about the Chinese, the non-Christian, and the non-believer. Others similarly recorded all Asian people in their district as "pagan," and sometimes the even more negative and racially loaded "heathen" was used.[82] In many cases, then, both Asian and Indigenous people were "othered" as non-Christians, using identical pejorative terms that entwined racial and religious prejudices, and bore little relationship to actual beliefs or traditions.

The enumeration of white settlers was far from perfect, but it was much less flawed than that of racialized people, and it does permit some analysis of the relationship between birthplace and irreligion. As we have seen, immigrants were much more likely than the Canadian-born to define themselves as atheists or as having no religion. Were some immigrants more irreligious than others? One group – the Americans – stands out clearly. They were far more likely than any other foreign-born immigrants to define themselves as agnostics, atheists, or as having no religion.[83] Although Americans made up only 9.6 percent of the BC population in 1901, over a third (35.0 percent) of all BC residents who defined themselves as atheists or as having no religion were born in the United States. Logistic regression analysis of the 1911 5 percent census sample for British Columbia shows that in this census year Americans were again dramatically overrepresented among the irreligious.[84] This was true in all BC districts, but Americans were particularly concentrated in Yale and Cariboo. In 1901, over 42 percent of the district's irreligious people were American, although only 15 percent of its population came from the United States. Many of the Kootenay hardrock miners were American. About a third of the miners in the Rossland subdistrict came from the United States, and 62 percent of its atheists or those of no religion were also American.[85]

Missionaries certainly perceived Americans as a particular danger. One Presbyterian noted that many of them hailed from "districts where the Lord's house and the Lord's day were either altogether unknown or very largely neglected ... Unless that spirit of religious indifference can be overcome we shall have in some parts of Western Canada the churchless, irreligious communities that have been such a source of anxiety and grief to the earnest-minded Christians of the American Republic."[86] Americans were numerous among the transient miners of the Kootenays. In this period, miners often moved regularly between American and Canadian mines, focusing on the location of work rather than the location of the border. Many may have been converted to socialism, and thus atheism, through the Western Federation of Miners, which represented them on both sides of the border. Other American miners may not have defined themselves as socialists, but the powerful class consciousness developed in the mines may have impelled them to reject Christianity. Whereas class helps to explain the over-representation of Americans among non-believers, gender does not. Americans in the Kootenays were less likely than either British or Canadian-born men to be "rootless" and single, and were more likely to live with other family members.[87] Many of these Americans, both male and female, may have imported a shared class consciousness from the "churchless, irreligious communities" so decried by the "the earnest-minded Christians of the American Republic." Certainly, American historians have suggested that institutional religion was much less powerful in the Far West than elsewhere in the United States during this period.[88]

The fact that Americans were a much smaller percentage of the Vancouver Island mining population than in Yale and Cariboo may help to account for the strong over-representation of the irreligious in the Kootenays.[89] At the same time, their presence does not explain everything. The Kootenays clearly possessed a distinct culture that inspired many people to embrace socialism, radical labour politics, and irreligion, a process that may have been facilitated by high levels of transiency in the district. Americans were in the forefront of this group, but a diverse range of migrants came to define themselves as irreligious once they reached the Kootenays. For example, though Ontarians were slightly under-represented among the irreligious in the district, they came from a province where less than 0.2 percent of the population were atheists or had no religion. Once they arrived in the Kootenays, over 2.0 percent of them defined themselves in this way.[90] Perhaps the Ontarians who headed west were already secular-minded, and given that young men were over-represented among Ontarians in British Columbia there is some truth to this. But at the same time, the ministers' refrain that many men lost their religion "when they crossed the Rocky Mountains" is also reflected in these statistics. In the next chapter, we will look in more depth at the religious and irreligious elements of British Columbia's working-class culture, examining qualitative sources that help to explain why so many workers felt able to tell census enumerators of 1901 that they were non-believers or had no religion, in a country that still very much defined itself as Christian.

2

Pie in the Sky When You Die

Political and Cultural Challenges to Religion

Religion, like old whisky, is not so bad when you only get a taste of it occasionally. But when you fill upon it until it slobbers out of your mouth at every step the evil effects of the jag become apparent. Thousands are addicted to it, and some get it so bad that they are incurable ... Religious intoxication in the past has flooded the world with misery. It has torn many a heart string, mangled many a body on the rack, burned many a noble soul at the stake ... Religious intoxication does not harm the human race so much today. Strong men, by the use of reason, have obliterated much of the evil results of the mania and in another hundred years the civilized world will wonder how we rattled the creed chains so long without discovering the ill effects of filling up on delusions ... If we move forward it means that priests and parsons will soon be unable to hold the masses in bondage by mummery, the waving of hands and bawling long and loud about the fall of man and eternal damnation.

– Lowery's Claim, *July 1901, 24*

So wrote "Colonel" Robert Lowery, famous (or infamous, depending on one's perspective) newspaperman of the Kootenays, in a fairly typical rant against religion and the churches. Like many of his diatribes, it borrowed liberally from the freethought currents of his day, while adding his own forthright blend of outrage and ridicule. One newspaperman alone cannot be held responsible for the particularly high levels of atheism and low levels of church involvement in the Kootenays. Nonetheless, Lowery's anti-religious rhetoric struck a chord in that mining region and may have helped to normalize irreligious beliefs and practices for many. This chapter looks closely at Lowery and other anti-religious journalists of early-twentieth-century British Columbia, as well as those who spoke for the organized and equally godless socialist and syndicalist movements. Their influential discourse was gendered, classed, and racialized. Anti-religious journalists attacked churchgoers as effeminate men or deluded women; the churches as instruments of the employing classes; and clergy as more interested in converting Asian immigrants to Christianity than in trying to exclude them from the province and thus protecting the jobs of white workers. This chapter also explores the largely masculine "rough cultures" of drinking, gambling, and prostitution that existed throughout British Columbia and their stormy relationship with the churches and local Christians.

This rough culture, which was antithetical to contemporary Christian strictures of morality, was similar to masculinized frontier cultures in other settler colonies during this period, and in itself, it provides an explanation for the religious indifference of many working-class men in the province. At the same time, the intense anti-Asian sentiment in British Columbia, as well as racist attitudes toward Indigenous peoples, helped to create a sense of racial commonality and superiority among "white men," regardless of their class.[1] Whiteness was a key marker of superiority, inclusion, and exclusion across North America, as scholars have noted, for the white working class and for other classes.[2] Some scholars have recognized that whiteness was also profoundly interwoven with Christianity, and more specifically with Protestantism.[3] The interlinking of whiteness and Protestantism (and for many, Britishness) was certainly integral to a sense of social superiority for most members of British Columbia's dominant class. However, as we will see in this chapter and the following one, among the BC working class, particularly its men, whiteness and Christianity were much less tightly connected. For many of these men, whiteness, in some cases linked to either Britishness or working-class consciousness or often to both, was enough to provide a sense of social inclusion and self-worth. The deep racial divides of the province allowed many of these men to define their identity primarily in racial, ethnic, and class terms, while rejecting Christianity or remaining completely indifferent to it. This was much less possible in the more hegemonically Christian and less racially diverse Eastern Canada.

Godless Journalists

Robert Thornton Lowery was the best known and most popular of the province's irreligious journalists, though he is little remembered today, outside of local histories of the Kootenays. Born in 1858 to a "God-fearing mother" in Ontario, Lowery moved to British Columbia in 1891. He published a number of local newspapers in towns throughout the Kootenays and the Crowsnest Pass, including Sandon, Slocan, Nelson, New Denver, Fernie, Nakusp, and Greenwood.[4] In addition to editing various community newspapers, he also irregularly published the monthly paper *Lowery's Claim* between 1901 and 1906. Lowery's opinions were evident in every paper that he published, but the *Claim* gave free rein and considerable space to his unorthodox beliefs on a range of topics, including support for women's right to sexual knowledge and freedom, fierce opposition to Prohibition and Sabbatarianism, and scathing contempt for priestly "hypocrites and parasites." Although some of Lowery's writings suggest a belief in a Creator, and in the power of Jesus's teachings, he was generally hostile to religion itself, publishing not only his own attacks on Christianity, but also those of prominent freethinkers.[5]

Colonel Robert Thornton Lowery, freethinking Kootenay journalist, 189– | *BC Archives, B-07979*

A well-known alcoholic himself, Lowery enjoyed comparing religion to alcohol, arguing that "under the influence of religion [man] acts the fool and does things just as ridiculous as if he were under the influence of rye whiskey. Under the intoxication of either of these things man becomes silly, often vicious, and frequently through them lands in jail or the madhouse."[6] Lowery saw religion as at best a "mild form of insanity" and happily reported cases in which it had apparently driven people to madness.[7] In one of many examples, he noted, "Recently Mrs. Fleming of Victoria, while laboring under religious mania, killed her daughter with an axe. Both were devoted church-goers. This is a result of emotional religion."[8] Some of the freethought reprints that Lowery published were even more hostile to Christianity than the editor himself. For example, one reprint declared that "the past attitude of the Agnostic is no longer sufficient. We actually know that the history and postulates of Christianity are false." Remarking that the character of God "is simply revolting," the author condemned the Bible's "foolishness, immorality and obscenity."[9]

Lowery's freethought beliefs don't seem to have been based in socialism. He was wary and often critical of what he saw as overly radical union leaders.[10] However, he was very supportive of the miners in their struggles against the exploitative practices of the mine owners. In part, his critique of the clergy and the churches was class-based. He often stated that the churches favoured the rich and the employers, and "kept the collar on the neck of the working man."[11] For example, he attacked the churchmen of Fernie, who apparently "prayed and invoked the blessing of God" upon the new building of the Crow's Nest Pass Coal Company, a particularly exploitative mining company. Lowery suggested that "while such ceremonies look silly to the scientific they also appear blasphemous to the truly religious. Why should God be rung up over the Methodist, Presbyterian or any other line and be asked to bless a company that by its actions is breeding hatred, fear, bribery and corruption."[12]

Lowery's newspapers, with their class-conscious antagonism to Christianity and the churches, were popular and influential among local miners. One of his papers, the *Ledge,* which also espoused his particular brand of freethought, was informally known as "the Miner's Bible," and the *Claim* was also very popular. George Moir, a pious Christian telegrapher who worked in the Kootenays at that time, stated that every issue of the *Claim* "was eagerly bought up by the rabble [miners] to which he catered."[13] Moir was incensed by one issue of the *Claim,* which denounced Baptists "in statements against Christian people and especially preachers, that were absolutely immoral." In his fury, Moir bought up the entire edition and burnt it all. He noted, "I did not have to wait long before the rising storm broke loose. Lowery had to work overtime for some days to put a new edition on the market."[14]

Lowery's papers were not the only anti-religious media available to BC workers. Kootenay miners could also read William McAdams's *Sandon Paystreak,* which he published from 1899 to 1902 and which was known for "roasting Christianity and the churches."[15] Its proprietor had no time for organized religion, proclaiming at one point that the sooner Sunday Schools "are relegated to oblivion the better for the rising generation."[16] McAdams regularly published a column with excerpts from prominent atheists, titled "Thinkers' Thoughts." On August 11, 1900, he featured work by Ludwig Buchner, who stated that

> one can say without exaggeration that the most religious times and the most religious peoples ... have, generally speaking, been the most immoral ... If to-day is to be otherwise, it is not to religion that we owe the change, but to the spread of education and the progress of intelligence. Experience teaches us that at all times the blackest crimes and the most degraded criminals have been associated with the excess of sanctity.[17]

Like Lowery, McAdams derided Christianity for its apparent immorality and irrationalism, and he presented a clear class analysis of Christianity and the churches, which held that the churches were allies of the capitalist oppressors.[18] Since he believed that the churches opposed the interests of workers, he argued that

> labor organizations are truly the poor man's church. They are for the social, moral, intellectual and financial elevation of mankind. They bind men closer together in friendship, assist each other in attaining a higher efficiency in the various pursuits of the trade upon which depends their daily bread, assist a brother when out of employment. When sickness and death visit a member's family the society furnishes to the bereaved both moral and financial support.[19]

Socialists and Syndicalists

McAdams and Lowery were not the only public voices to speak against religion from a class-conscious perspective. In 1902, a Presbyterian minister commented that "a pronounced Socialist Element is in evidence ... in all this western region. In many cases it is strongly opposed to the ministers and churches, charging them with unfaithfulness to the principles of Christianity in matters having a bearing on industrial and social life."[20] Ten years later, the Methodist superintendent of home missions stated that in some work camps, "we are treated kindly, in some camps rabid socialism prevails and no preachers or church workers need apply." Catholic priests stationed in the Kootenays also complained to their bishop about nominal Catholics who were "heart and soul Socialists."[21]

Ian McKay notes that atheism and hostility to the churches existed within the Canadian left between 1890 and 1920, but he suggests that given the continued importance of Christianity for most Canadian workers, atheism was very much a minority position, despite the efforts of capitalists to brand all socialists as "Godless atheists."[22] A number of socialists would have defined themselves as Christian socialists, and there was a close relationship between many socialists and social gospellers, although the distance between them widened during this period, as increasing numbers of socialists embraced "scientific" socialism. McKay is doubtless correct about the relatively minor position of atheists in the socialist movement across most of Canada, and his evidence – for example, that the atheism of certain socialist leaders alienated many strikers and their families in the mining community of Springhill, Nova Scotia – is instructive.[23] However, though there were many Christian workers in British Columbia, it appears that atheism, and serious critiques of both Christianity and the churches, had a stronger place among pre–First World War BC leftists than elsewhere in the country.

Scholars have acknowledged the hardline Marxist socialism of early BC socialists, seen most clearly in the Socialist Party of British Columbia, later the Socialist Party of Canada (SPC), during the early twentieth century.[24] As Peter Campbell demonstrates, BC SPC leaders, some of whom were from Christian backgrounds, became very critical of Christianity and the churches as they turned to Marxism.[25] The voice of radical BC socialists was expressed most clearly in the *Western Clarion,* an organ of the SPC.

From 1903 onward, the *Clarion* provided BC workers with an unambiguous anti-religious Marxist message that made Lowery and McAdams look almost like Christian apologists. According to the *Clarion,* not only were churches and ministers tools of the capitalist classes, but religion itself was, at best, the opium of the people. The occasional *Clarion* article stated that the socialist movement took no position on religious questions, but the paper's more typical posture was attack – against the churches and sometimes Christianity itself. As the *Clarion* pointed out, "it is futile to suppose that the church, the capitalist church, the church of mammon, whose edifices are built and whose preachers are paid by contributions almost exclusively from wealthy donors, will remain neutral in this mighty struggle between the forces of vested interests and those of industrial freedom." Another article was even more blunt: "In spite of pretense of spirituality the church is as grossly material as any other human institution. Its tap root runs deep down into the plunder that is wrung from the toil and sweat of an enslaved working class."[26] As well as rebuking the churches, the *Clarion* often stated that Christianity itself was so tied up with the capitalist system that it was no longer relevant to working people, or worse, that "religious hobbies" such as Christianity "confine themselves to the teaching of working people to meekly submit to robbery here upon earth, and promise them a harp and a golden crown beyond the clouds as payment for their meekness and humility."[27] Although some Christian socialists challenged the *Clarion*'s stance, for many Western workers, coping with dismal pay and miserable and dangerous conditions in the mines and logging camps, such rhetoric made perfect sense, and it could certainly have either sparked or reinforced anti-religious attitudes.[28]

Socialist ideas about religion and other matters were not only disseminated through the press but also strengthened through a vibrant oral culture. H.H. Stevens, later a cabinet minister under R.B. Bennett, was a Kootenay miner in about 1901. He wrote that every Sunday afternoon in Phoenix, a Western Federation of Miners stronghold, a meeting was held at the local miners' hall, which was attended by five hundred miners or more. On the agenda were "lurid red speakers" who were received with considerable approval by the audience. Stevens himself attended one such lecture and challenged the legitimacy of socialism, upon which he was asked to debate future speakers on various aspects of socialism, something he did for the rest of the winter. Since Stevens was a devout Methodist, it is likely that Christianity, and the socialist critique of it, would have been on the debate agenda.[29]

Scholars such as Ross McCormack have noted the radicalism of BC socialist leaders, particularly in the coalfields of Vancouver Island and in the Kootenays. I argued in Chapter 1 that high levels of irreligion in the Kootenays may point to the strength of such radical values, not just among leaders, but also among the rank and file. Recent scholars of the Vancouver Island coalfields, including John Belshaw and John Hinde, have challenged the "western exceptionalism" of McCormack's approach, suggesting that though some of the island's socialist leaders may have followed pure Marxist doctrine, others were more willing to compromise and that many of their followers were far from being "pure" socialists, even though they voted for socialist representatives.[30]

How did this play out in the religious, or irreligious, arena on Vancouver Island? We saw in Chapter 1 that Vancouver Island coal miners were much less willing than their Kootenay counterparts to take the extreme step of defining themselves as atheists, though they were certainly not avid church-goers. How strongly would the *Clarion*'s anti-religious message have resonated with them? A major conflict that erupted in the pages of the *Nanaimo Free Press* in 1903 points to the strength of irreligious feelings among many Nanaimo socialists. In October 1903, a Frank Ogle, who had recently emigrated from England, resigned from the Socialist Party of British Columbia. As he told the *Free Press,* his major reason for doing so was the anti-religious critiques that he heard at Nanaimo socialist meetings, where the churches were attacked and the Bible was called a "dung heap." A Christian socialist, Ogle could not tolerate such statements. He also remarked that the party's attitude toward Christianity was very different from that in "the Old Country," where Christian socialism was much more central to the movement.[31] His letter immediately provoked vitriolic rebuttals from local socialists, one of whom pointed out that "the foundation of Karl Marx Socialism was Atheism" and expressed surprise at Ogle's "ignorance for expecting Christian sentiment amongst Marxist socialists." The author added that "what [Ogle] failed to extract from books ... he very soon found out when he came in contact with the British Columbia Socialists."[32] The people who wrote these letters do not appear to have been alone in their views: the *Victoria Colonist* reported that Ogle's "letter of resignation was read to the assembly [at a socialist meeting in Nanaimo], who in turn denounced Ogle and 'Christianity, religion, and the Bible.'"[33] However, replying to his challengers in a later letter to the *Free Press,* Ogle inferred that at least some socialist leaders recognized that anti-Christian sentiments could alienate potential voters. He claimed that he had been recruited to work for the Nanaimo socialists by James Hawthornthwaite, the local socialist MLA, who told him that he "was needed to tone down the rabid section of the party [in Nanaimo] and appeal to the religious voters."[34]

Even in British Columbia, some socialists understood that anti-Christian rhetoric could estrange certain workers. At the same time, BC workers, whether in Nanaimo or Rossland, were different from Springhill workers. There is evidence across the province that many were hostile to the churches because they perceived them as allies of the employers. Fewer Nanaimoites may have identified themselves as atheists to the census-taker than was the case in the Kootenays, but radical Nanaimo workers were no more keen on the churches than their Kootenay counterparts. Various discussions in local newspapers about "why the workers are not attending church" echo the comment of a Nanaimo correspondent who stated in 1912 that he would go to church "if it was the church of Christ, but it has been transformed into the church of Mammon ... If your church will divorce Mammon and advocate better conditions for the bottom strata of society, I will come to church."[35] Workers in the coal-mining town of Fernie who were asked about their reluctance to attend church cited the hypocrisy and support for the capitalist class that many ministers displayed, but most did not seem to oppose Christianity itself. A report from the Synod of the Diocese of Kootenay on the alienation of workers from the churches noted that "the working man criticizes the church adversely" because he believes that it "takes a one-sided and bourgeois view in the great labor troubles and social problems of the day."[36]

For many workers, such beliefs may have been inspired and normalized by journalists such as Lowery and McAdams, and reinforced by the *Western Clarion* or by involvement with certain unions and with the Socialist Party of British Columbia. Workers may also have participated in other revolutionary bodies, such as the Industrial Workers of the World (IWW), which also took a dim view of Christianity and the churches.

A syndicalist union movement originating in the United States, the IWW sought to organize skilled and (most particularly) unskilled workers to improve conditions and ultimately to dismantle the capitalist system through the weapon of the general strike. It was very active in organizing many miners, loggers, and other BC workers between 1906 and 1914.[37] The *Industrial Worker,* an IWW paper published out of Spokane, Washington, from 1909 to 1913, was a major source of IWW news and rhetoric for BC workers. Religion was not the main focus of the IWW, and some leaders argued that it was irrelevant to the movement, which concentrated on the material concerns of workers. Nonetheless, as Donald E. Winters notes, some IWW leaders had much to say about Christianity and the churches.

Like many labour leaders of that time and earlier, various IWW leaders and the *Industrial Worker* itself were willing to acknowledge Jesus as a positive role model who challenged the oppression of the poor.[38] They were, however, very critical of organized Christianity, seeing churches and ministers as siding with exploitative employers.[39] They were particularly vitriolic regarding the Salvation Army, which they dubbed the "Starvation Army" and saw as competing with the IWW for the allegiance of unskilled workers. An *Industrial Worker* editorial dismissed the Salvation Army as "always the staunch supporter of the capitalist," which, "in the name of Jesus ... strenuously support[ed] the most vicious practices of the most vicious age. They teach contentment with small means or no means at all."[40] IWW songs, which spread their message far more effectively than any newspaper, used the tunes of hymns to preach a very different message and had little good to say about organized religion. One of the IWW's most famous songs, "The Preacher and the Slave," featured the following well-known response from a minister to hungry workers:

> You will eat, bye and bye
> In that glorious land above the sky;
>
> Work and pray, live on hay,
> You'll get pie in the sky when you die.[41]

The BC labour press, representing trade unions that often saw themselves as competing with the IWW, tended to be less consistently hostile to organized religion, perhaps recognizing that at least some of its trade union readers were churchgoers. It reprinted pro-labour sermons from ministers, noted when ministers supported major strikes, and published letters from Christian socialists. Some letter writers, however, were unfriendly to the churches, accusing them of working hand-in-hand with the capitalists.[42]

BC labour papers certainly agreed with the IWW about the evils of the Salvation Army. The *Western Wage Earner,* the paper of the BC labour movement, was fond of decrying the army's employment schemes for the jobless, less than warmly referring to "that precious crew of pious pirates" and their "sanctified swindle."[43] Parm Pettipiece and other editors of the *Western Wage Earner* and its successor the *BC Federationist* were socialists themselves, and Pettipiece was also the editor of the *Western Clarion.* As a result, they reprinted some pieces from the socialist press that were explicitly antagonistic to the churches and even to religion itself.[44] This could upset readers, as is evident in an outraged letter written by a Catholic trade unionist to the *BC Western Catholic.* Evidently unaware of the overlap between socialists and trade unionists among BC labour leaders and journalists, he complained that the "Vancouver Socialist ... declares an open war on Christ and his Church." He expected no better from the socialists but was furious with the trade unionist leaders who "sow the socialistic tares among the trade union wheat" in local labour papers, attacking Christianity and the Catholic Church.[45]

Gender and Race

The anti-Christian rhetoric in the labour, socialist, and IWW papers, as well as in Lowery and McAdams's newspapers, was not only class-based, but also shot through with gendered and racialized language. Even mainstream culture saw the Christian churches as feminized institutions, and their female-dominated congregations and feminine message of morality, piety, and submission to the word of God fuelled the reluctance of many men, particularly younger men, to attend them.[46] The *Western Clarion* put a particularly socialist spin on this broader concern. Those who accepted the dictates of the churches were lacking in manliness, and participation in Christianity was especially the preserve of women, who were unable to free themselves from the shackles of clerical domination. The *Clarion* accused women of being "the most tractable tools of reactionary forces" and stated that "in woman's attitude toward the church she shows an inclination to crouch most submissively at the feet of those who kick her the hardest."[47] Such rhetoric fit closely with the SPC's position on Christianity – and on women as tending to be much more reactionary than men and less likely than the rational manly Marxist workers of the socialist ideal to join the class struggle.[48]

Gendered rhetoric in the battle against Christianity was not confined to the pages of the *Clarion*. McAdams of the *Sandon Paystreak* did not attack women for supporting the churches but more sympathetically painted them as the main victims of Christianity:

> Many an honest woman has roasted herself over a hot stove to cook a fat chicken for a lazy preacher. Many a spinster and housewife have worn their shoes out tramping the streets to gather in donations for her loafing pastor ... Millions of women have done a cruel penance of this [exhausting themselves in working for the church] or a worse sort in the hope of redeeming her soul of the blight which designing pulpit thumpers have plastered upon it with that legendary cock-and-bull story about the fall of man. Wherever woman has reared her head above mediocrity or manifested a desire to express, or even entertain an opinion of her own, she has been read a stanza about "tempting Adam" and knocked down the bible.[49]

Lowery did not focus on women in his attacks on Christianity and indeed in the *Claim* he often challenged the sexual double standard and supported women's rights to greater equality within marriage and to improved access to divorce.[50] His gendered critiques of Christianity centred on men and masculinity. He characterized freethinkers as manly rationalists – unlike Christians, who were busy "cringing in submission at the risk of fraying [their] pants at the knees." He dismissed ministers as "a lot of sissies and drones who live upon the fear and ignorance of the human race."[51] As other scholars have noted, this kind of anti-Christian gendered rhetoric was part of a larger discourse of manly rationalism among North American freethinkers.[52]

Racist stereotypes were also used to challenge the value of both Christianity and the churches. In one telling editorial, McAdams attacked a government proposal that ministers be exempted from the provincial revenue tax:

> We fail to see why preachers should be bonused. They are of no particular benefit to the community and do a good deal of harm ... If the government is going to exempt preachers it should go the route and exempt salvation army officers, Dowieites [millenarian faith healers], Christian scientists, Siwash [Indigenous] medicine men, Chinese joss agents and the whole push who deal in options on the next world. So far as the B.C. legislature knows, one has as good title as the other.[53]

In associating mainstream Christianity with spiritual practices that were beyond the pale due to their working-class appeal, racialized practitioners, heterodox doctrines and rituals, heathenism, and superstition, McAdams was inferring that religion of any kind was equally suspect. In this way, he undermined the legitimacy of mainstream Christianity by appealing to the racism of his readers and their skepticism about marginalized forms of spirituality.

Like McAdams, Lowery claimed that there was no difference between Christian beliefs and practices and those of non-Christians. He was dismissive of Christian efforts to convert Chinese immigrants, arguing that the Chinese were not interested in conversion and that "they have superstitions of their own and equally as good as ours. All egotistical parsons to the contrary notwithstanding. We have no more right to lead a Mongolian away from his native religion than he has to shove his Joss-house mummery upon us."[54]

Although Lowery might seem to be expressing a "plague on both their houses" attitude here, his hostility to Christian attempts to convert Chinese immigrants was fuelled at least as much by a deep anti-Asian racism as by anti-religious sentiments. Like that of many BC workers and their supporters, his racism focused primarily on "unfair" Asian competition with white labour, and he could not believe that some ministers saw Asian immigration in a positive light, as an opportunity to convert the heathen. In 1903, when the Canadian Presbyterian Church passed a resolution against the restriction of Chinese immigration, Lowery was appalled. He described the Presbyterian ministers as traitors for risking the jobs of white workers in their efforts to "flood this fair land with hordes of yellow boys in order to pump Christ into them." He ranted,

> These fools, mad with a desire to pound their iron-clad creed into anything would sacrifice all this glorious Dominion for the sake of holding up a Presbyterian Christ to the moon-eyed gaze of the Yellow Curse. They would make Canada a place for slaves and masters. They would force poor men in to the ranks of criminals or over the dump of starvation.[55]

This attitude was not unique to Lowery. A letter to the *Victoria Times* attacked a local bishop for referring to those who opposed Chinese immigration as "grumblers." The author argued that "the men who preach for pay; who sit in a temple of ease in Zion, and who probably never knew what a hard day's work means" should not interfere in working men's affairs.[56] Many ministers and church organizations, particularly in British Columbia, did speak out against Asian immigration. However, others did not, both for Christian humanitarian reasons and because of the opportunity to save souls, and many workers and labour leaders saw this stance as further proof that the church did not understand the concerns of the (white) working class. It became one more justification for anti-clericalism and hostility to Christianity.[57] The association of freethought and anti-clericalism with racism in white settler contexts is not unique to British Columbia, although it has not thus far received much scholarly attention.[58]

On rare occasions, BC socialists could work in collaboration with Asian radicals, and they sometimes refused to involve themselves in anti-Asian sentiment. However, as Mark Leier and David Goutor state, they were far more commonly integrated into the broader labour and working-class crusade against Asian workers and Asian immigration.[59] As Goutor points out, whiteness was as essential to the identity of the Euro-Canadian BC working class as it was to the identity of more middle- and upper-class British Columbians. Renisa Mawani argues that for the dominant classes of the province, whiteness was very much imbricated with a sense of Britishness and of Christianity.[60] Whereas Britishness was a proud identity for many members of the BC working class, it was much less relevant to the many Americans who came to the province and to the increasing number of non-British European immigrants. For some of the latter, particularly for Italians and southern Europeans, whiteness was not a given, but remained a contested quality. However, for workers of British and northern and western European origin, whiteness remained a key way of differentiating themselves from the quintessential "others" of BC society – Asians and Indigenous peoples.[61] For many of these BC workers, Christianity was an important component of their belief systems and of their respectable white identity. However, I would argue that for many others, the central role of whiteness in demarcating social acceptance helped to ensure that the public performance of Christianity was less crucial than in other less racially diverse parts of Canada. The valorization of whiteness helped enable many Euro-Canadian workers to remain indifferent to Christianity or to reject it, while still seeing themselves as accepted members of "white British Columbia." Those who could define themselves as both British and white would have been particularly able to maintain a positive self-identity even in the absence of Christian practice, but for many, whiteness and working-class identity alone were sufficient.[62]

"Struggles for Liberty": Rough Culture and the Churches

As Renisa Mawani and Adele Perry demonstrate, the dominant classes in British Columbia did not necessarily agree with this position. For them, whiteness, Britishness, and Christianity were tightly linked. Applying Christian moral terms, they differentiated between good and bad whites, classing the latter primarily as working-class men who participated in the rough culture of drinking, gambling, and the sex trade. Bad whites were seen as setting a terrible example to the Indigenous people whom the dominant classes sought to convert and civilize.[63] For their part, the bad white men remained proud of their whiteness as a badge of superiority to Indigenous people and Asians. Their working-class consciousness distinguished them from employers and from the churches that were identified with the employing classes, and the churches' vocal and frequent attacks on their leisure culture further alienated them from institutional religion and often from Christianity itself.

In many BC communities, there was little or no legislative control over gambling, the sale of alcohol, or the sex trade, and Sabbath legislation, which was common in Central and Eastern Canada, was either non-existent or, when it was passed federally in 1906, largely unenforced in most jurisdictions. The church-based moral reformers, both male and female, who tried to bring in various controls on this rough culture were defied and often portrayed as fussy, feminized killjoys who were undermining the sacred liberty of white Britons by interfering in their manly leisure pursuits.

Alcohol, the sex trade, and gambling were particularly "wide open" in the Kootenay mining towns.[64] For example, the silver-mining town of Sandon, whose population grew rapidly during the late 1890s to about five thousand people, primarily male, saw a dramatic increase in saloons that catered to the miners, as well as to more prosperous businessmen and speculators who were also drawn to the community. Sandon's saloons served copious amounts of alcohol, from cheap beer to "chilled French champagne," often twenty-four hours a day, seven days a week, and they helped Sandon win its reputation as "the Monte Carlo of Canada" "for poker, blackjack, roulette, faro, craps, slot machines – all [the] popular games of chance offered around the clock in the city's many saloons."[65] The red light district of "Lower Sandon" has been termed one of the largest in Western Canada during the late 1890s, with dozens of brothels and 115 sex trade workers.[66] Many miners toiled for weeks or months, living in squalid bunkhouses beside the mines, and then came into town for a few days and spent all their money. As Colonel Lowery noted,

> After a few days of hilarity they usually sober up broke, grow repentant, and then hit the hills for another stake, fully determined that they will never again sip the booze, shuffle the cards or trifle with the painted face of commercial love. As time goes along and their pile grows bigger, the memory of past misery fades, and back they come to camp and history repeats itself.[67]

Sandon may have been particularly famous (or infamous) for its rough culture, but other Kootenay towns embraced it as well.[68] Despite the claims of local boosters that Rossland was far more law-abiding than similar American mining communities, Jeremy Mouat provides considerable evidence to the contrary. Lowery himself wrote that "Boozerino, green cloth [gambling] and the woman in red are too prominent in Rossland."[69] Other towns, such as the regional hub of Nelson, may have been slightly more restrained, but visiting churchmen were nonetheless shocked by their levels of drinking, gambling, and prostitution.

Alcohol was readily accessible throughout most of British Columbia. John Belshaw notes that drinking establishments were very popular in Nanaimo and that its alcohol consumption during the 1890s was twice the provincial average. When a former Nanaimo coal miner was asked by

Hotel saloon interior in Nelson, BC, 1899 | *Photo by G.R. Miller, Touchstones Nelson, Museum of Art and History, TN-59.09.36*

an oral history interviewer whether miners were God-fearing people, he replied, "They didn't go much on religion. They worked hard and they went to the beer parlors, the hotels, and had their beer on the way home, before they even got washed."[70] Clearly, for this man and for many others in the province – and most certainly for the evangelical reformers who were trying to control their activities – rough masculine culture and being "God-fearing" were antithetical. A report from the Presbyterian Church made this clear. Particularly in British Columbia, it lamented, "every Missionary has his experience with the infidel, whose infidelity is the result, not of a change in his convictions, but rather a change in his life ... Missionaries have to tell of positive and aggressive infidelity in their fields, and of disregard for the Sabbath and for the laws of morality."

Like the leaders of other denominations, the Presbyterians who wrote the report blamed Americans for this problem: "In the mining districts the influence of immigrants from the United States is, as a rule disastrous to religion and morals, and this is the preponderant influence in these districts. These men are the pronounced champions and devotees of gambling, drinking and Sabbath desecration." The report added that "many of the finest, most enterprising and best-hearted young men from the Christian homes of Eastern Canada" came to British Columbia, after which "they make a brave stand for their principles for a time, but unless help is given them, they are bound to go under."[71] Such church reports hoped to extract money from the families of the Eastern Canadian "best-hearted young men" for missionary efforts and thus may have exaggerated the American peril. Nonetheless, the over-representation of Americans among the irreligious was quite real, as mentioned in the previous chapter. The largely irreligious homosocial culture of transient miners and other workers, as chronicled by missionaries, was also very much part of life in British Columbia. Writing about the colonial period, Adele Perry discusses the lure of this culture for the hardworking men in the BC resource industries who were often far from family, particularly the (white Christian) wives and mothers who were assumed to exert a civilizing influence.[72] Similar patterns have been observed in other resource frontiers where the gender ratio was skewed toward men.[73]

As noted in Chapter 1, the irreligious were more likely than the BC population as a whole to live in households that were primarily or exclusively male. However, this is one of the few instances in which the pattern for people of "no religion" was markedly different from that for atheists, freethinkers, and others who deviated from the Christian norm. The 1911 census reveals that the latter group was not over-represented in primarily male households, but instead often lived in nuclear families. Many of these people belonged to a socialist atheist subculture that was particularly strong in certain Kootenay towns but also existed elsewhere in the province and often included whole families, who were officially atheist, secular, or freethinkers.[74] Those who identified themselves as having no religion, however, *were* particularly likely to live in households that were largely or exclusively male.[75] Most of them would have participated in the male homosocial culture of mining towns and logging camps. Their alienation from religion may not have reached the level of atheism or freethought, but they were far enough from Christian family influences and felt sufficiently hostile to the churches – perhaps perceiving them as biased in favour of employers and certainly disliking their efforts to control rough leisure – to tell the census-taker that they had no religion. Some men who said they had no religion may have had other reasons for doing so, but the data analysis certainly suggests that this group was especially likely to be associated with homosocial culture.

Some aspects of this culture had a very dark edge. An element of rough culture that may have been particularly common in British Columbia was the abusive treatment of those of Chinese origin. Local newspapers regularly printed short notes about Euro-Canadian boys or men beating up Chinese men, throwing away their belongings, burning down their homes, and committing other violent acts. For example, in September 1894, the *Victoria Colonist* reported that in Nanaimo, "a Chinese man was the victim of a brutal assault and he may die. He was badly ill-used by two white men named John Thompson and George Grey. They brutally kicked him about the body."[76] In November 1899, the *Colonist* noted that in Victoria, "a little Chinese boy, carrying a school bag containing some fruit and a pair of rubbers was assaulted by several large white boys. He was unmercifully beaten and the bag and its contents thrown into the mud and destroyed. The men standing near did not intervene."[77] Eight years later in Victoria, "two Chinese men were attacked at the Post Office by six white men. They were kicked about the face and side and have evidence of numerous bruises."[78] The *Nelson Tribune* of June 22, 1901, reported that "a man is suspected of having kicked in a door in the Chinese quarter. Another is charged with assault in the dipping of a Chinese man in a lake."[79] Just three months earlier, the *Tribune* noted that "two boys assaulted a Chinese man named Wing and threw his basket of vegetables into the creek."[80]

Such behaviour seemed endemic in communities throughout the province. The perpetrators were sometimes charged, with the victims occasionally laying charges, but some victims absented themselves from the trials of their attackers, probably fearing further ill-treatment. Local leaders, particularly churchmen, sometimes criticized such abusive behaviour, but it seemed to be generally tolerated among the white population.

Both Catholic and Protestant clergy were much more concerned about other elements of Euro-Canadian rough culture. By the early twentieth century, many Catholic Italian and central and eastern European workers had immigrated to the Kootenay and Rocky Mountain mining towns. American and Anglo-Canadian workers, who saw them as a threat to their jobs, did not receive them warmly.[81] Their patterns of leisure and religion were nonetheless markedly similar to those of the men who sought to exclude them. Many were very much involved in rough culture and stayed away from local Catholic churches. Catholic clerical and lay leaders sought to solve this problem by providing priests of their own language and culture, a measure that had worked elsewhere.[82] A priest and several Slavic laymen in Fernie were distressed about the situation of local Slavic men and beseeched the bishop to send them a Slavic priest. As a Fernie Slavic layman wrote to Catholic bishop Augustin Dontenwill in 1903,

> I am asking our people why they don't go to church ... Some have excuse always, because they have no [Slavic] priest to go after them. We have two

> Slavonian Hotel[s] in Fernie at present time. Sunday evening you will find more of our people in Bar Room than in church ... People especially the young ones these days need to have bridles on them at all the time. When they get so far they don't go to church for months they don't care to go for year.[83]

Other letters complained of the irreligion and rough and sinful ways of Italian and Hungarian Catholic workers and the need to provide priests who could speak to them in their own language. Father Coccola, an Italian-speaker who was based in Fernie during the early twentieth century, sometimes travelled to other Kootenay towns to provide services to Italian Catholic workers, and the Catholic bishops also brought in American Italian-speaking priests for occasional services.[84]

Protestant church leaders and many laymen also worried about the "sin" they saw around them. For example, George Ferguson, who grew up in a Nelson evangelical congregation, stated that church members "were strict in their sabbatarian observance. Most frowned on card-playing and social drinking," and "regarded with horror the gayer approach to life which was brought to Nelson by the pay days of the mining and lumber camps."[85] Whereas Catholic priests focused on finding ethnic clergy who would bring their countrymen into line, Protestant ministers, particularly more evangelical ones, involved themselves in pitched political battles over issues ranging from banning baseball on Sundays, to closing down brothels, to the issuance of liquor licences to various establishments. The fiercest conflicts turned on Sabbatarian issues. Some labour and socialist leaders, as well as some workers, agreed with church efforts to control gambling, the sex trade, and most particularly the sale of alcohol, seeing such temptations as limiting the options of male workers, especially their ability to organize to improve their lot. However, there was no such agreement concerning Sabbatarianism, which was perceived as attempting to control the limited leisure time of workers.[86]

Battles over "morals issues" and Sunday closing laws occurred throughout the province during these years, including in Victoria and Vancouver, but they were especially bitter in the Kootenays. They were not simply defined by class. Miners might patronize less expensive saloons than local businessmen did, but homosocial culture crossed class in many ways, and middle-class men often participated in it. As Anglican missionary A. Robbins reported of Greenwood, another mining centre, "Drink, I need hardly say, is the curse of the whole place, it seems to affect every class without distinction."[87] This male drinking culture existed elsewhere Canada, in local bars and fraternal halls, but was far stronger, more visible, and unregulated in much of British Columbia, especially the Kootenays.[88] The churches' efforts to close down what were often the only leisure activities available to men far from home certainly did not endear them to many in the Kootenays. The majority of these men may not have defined themselves as atheists, but they did not appreciate religious meddling in their limited leisure options.

One of their strongest champions was John Houston, the outspoken editor of the *Nelson Tribune,* who was later a populist mayor of Nelson for four terms and a two-term MLA for the region.[89] The 1901 census recorded Houston as a freethinker, and he was known as a heavy drinker. He was also well known as a staunch supporter of labour unions.[90] He often used his editorial pulpit to challenge the churches and defend the culture of the Kootenay mining towns. In March 1899, he wrote that "Eastern Canadians do not see us through the same spectacles as we see ourselves. The people of Kootenay, as they see themselves, are orderly and law-abiding, are not obsequious or intolerant, are honest and independent. As seen by Eastern Canadians they are wicked and lawless, are without moral or spiritual backbone, are lacking in common sense and commercial honor."[91] Houston's ideal British Columbian was independent, upstanding, and by implication manly, quite different from that imagined by Eastern Canadians. Houston was not keen on local people who shared these Eastern Canadian views and was always ready to challenge "church people," often in dismissively gendered terms.

When members of the local Baptist and Methodist churches petitioned Nelson's city government to close saloons on Sunday and stop other Sunday recreation, Houston attacked them in print, declaring that, as long as he was mayor,

> every man, woman and child resident in Nelson will be allowed to observe Sunday his or her own way, just as they are allowed to live on weekdays. No church organization or member thereof, will be permitted to dicate [sic] to people who are not members of church organizations as to how they shall spend Sunday or any other day in the week. Nelson ... will not be a church-ridden town.[92]

When an alderman attempted to have stores and saloons closed on Sundays, Houston labelled him "as fussy as an old woman ... and just as useless."[93] As part of a church committee, George Moir met with Mayor Houston to discuss regulating the "gambling and open vice" in nearby Greenwood. Moir recalled that Houston "told me what he thought about

John Houston, mayor of Nelson, MLA, and newspaperman, c. 1900 | *Touchstones Nelson, Museum of Art and History, 84.93.001*

church people or any people who professed Christianity – they were all humbugs and hypocrites, and he threw in a few profane words for good measure."[94]

Like other irreligious guardians of the white working class, Houston also condemned any church effort to defend Chinese immigration. He censured a Reverend Winchester, a Presbyterian missionary to the Chinese in Victoria, for opposing the head tax and other aspects of Chinese exclusion. Houston challenged Winchester's support for Chinese evangelization and "sentimental talk about the brotherhood of man," claiming that the Chinese threatened the livelihoods of white workers and were a "menace to the health and prosperity of the people of British Columbia."[95] Houston's defence of homosocial culture did not extend to the very similar rough culture of Chinese bachelors in towns such as Nelson. He saw their practices as a menace to health and morality.

Thus, he did not agree when Reverend Morgan, a local Baptist minister, characterized British Columbia's treatment of the Chinese as unfair and as counter to the Christian adage "love thy neighbor as thyself." As Morgan pointed out, "Here in Nelson there was a bitter feeling against the Chinese. It was alleged that their immorality was shocking ... Yet the people who raised their voice against the Chinese seemed to overlook the fact that there were in the city houses of prostitution ... and saloons and drunkenness."[96]

As we have seen, Robert Lowery was also unhappy about Christian support for the Chinese. He was equally hostile to churchmen's efforts to control the leisure of white working men, particularly their attempts to impose Sabbath closing laws. In highly gendered terms, he frequently upbraided the "sissy creed promoters" for their attempts to bring in Sabbatarian legislation, stating that "we may want a day of rest in Kootenay, but we do not want it hampered with effete notions from the east." In typically colourful language, Lowery denounced as religious "mania" the endeavours to pass

> stringent and obnoxious laws in regard to the observance of Sunday. If not put in asylums or made to close their valves by public opinion the Sunday fiends will stab liberty and freedom to a sickly finish, and fill any land with gloom, misery, and curses against one of the last efforts of dying theology to keep the rope around the human race with the absurd argument that oppression and persecution is the way to glorify God.[97]

No doubt, Lowery's valiant stance made him popular with miners, and it may have strengthened the anti-church sentiments of many, but it won him no friends among the powerful. Church leaders and other Christians railed against Lowery, particularly against the *Claim,* the paper that most openly and vociferously expressed his anti-Christian and anti-clerical opinions. They succeeded in having the *Claim* banned from the CPR trains early in its publishing history and by 1906 had managed to have it banned from the federal mails, which led to its demise.[98]

Local ministers won this battle against Lowery because the churches retained their hegemony across most of Canada, and thus in federal institutions such as the post office.[99] At the same time, their cultural power was significantly weakened in British Columbia by a range of forces. The left-wing anti-religious arguments disseminated by the *Western Clarion* and IWW organizers struck a chord with many working-class people, normalizing and providing a political justification for both irreligion and outright atheism. Anti-religious and pro-working-class journalists, including Lowery, McAdams, and Houston, also played a significant role, particularly in the Kootenays, where they both reflected and reinforced a culture that embraced irreligion.

These seemingly progressive anti-religious voices were also inflected with less positive messages, such as racist challenges to any clergymen who defended the rights of Asian workers and the dismissal of Christianity as comparable to the religious beliefs of despised "heathen" others. Lowery, Houston, and the *Clarion* all employed gendered language in denigrating Christianity, some of them ridiculing churchgoing women as credulous dupes and others slighting the masculinity of men who were active in the churches, particularly those who challenged the rough culture of many BC men.

As the next chapter reveals, anti-religious attacks on Christian moral reform efforts were popular with male British Columbians who sought to retain their leisure options. Nonetheless, not everyone who participated in rough culture abandoned all forms of Christian practice and belief.

3

Manly White Men, Fuzzy Fidelity, and Practical Christians

Blurred Boundaries of Belief and Chasms of Racialized Difference

The last chapter identified a range of both individual and collective voices that challenged religion and the churches in British Columbia. Committed Christians either ignored or actively resisted such voices, but many other British Columbians responded in a more complex way. A minority identified with the profoundly anti-religious message of the Socialist Party of Canada and lived their lives accordingly, to the horror of ministers and local Christians. Many white settler men enjoyed rough culture and resented clerical efforts to control it, but their attitudes to religion and the churches were nonetheless complex. For many, class consciousness and a shared whiteness provided primary markers of social inclusion, but some vestiges of Christianity remained. Many rejected clerical authority but retained a cultural connection to the broader discourse of Christianity. These "practical Christians," as they called themselves, defined their own religious belief and moral practice, and were not popular with church leaders. They rarely stepped inside a church, but for most, some ethnic, cultural, or spiritual tie to Christianity – even if it were nothing more than enjoying a hymn sing in a local bar, taking pride in being a "good person," or desiring a Christian burial – remained part of what it meant to be human.

This chapter demonstrates the complexity of talking about "the irreligious" in a context where some Christian practices or beliefs – no matter how attenuated – retained a hold on many British Columbians. At the same time, the reduced cultural power of Christianity and the shared sense of whiteness among many British Columbians had social and religious implications that differentiated British Columbia from the rest of Canada. These forces seemed to allow for closer relationships, or at least more peaceful co-existence, between Catholics and Protestants. In Eastern and Central Canada, tensions between these groups were a major social and political fault line, but in British Columbia the more limited power of Christianity and the perceived threat of the non-Christian and non-white Asian immigrant appear to have mitigated such strains.

Manly Miners Sing Hymns

Christian ministers considered themselves embattled in British Columbia, as they struggled valiantly to contest the rough culture that was popular in the Kootenays and many other parts of the province. As Norman Knowles notes in his study of Christianity and the working classes in the Crowsnest Pass region, ministers laboured diligently to present Christianity as a strong, manly option, to counter the view of many workers that Christians, and particularly ministers, were feminized weaklings, "cissy creed promoters," as Robert Lowery called them, who had no place in the manly culture of Western Canada.[1] The novels of Presbyterian minister Charles Gordon (writing under the name of Ralph Connor) are uplifting tales of the struggles of various manly ministers to rescue miners from the sinful allure of rough Western culture. In one of the most popular, *Black Rock,* a heroic minister named Mr. Craig has "good eyes that looked straight out at you, a clean-cut, strong face well set on his shoulders, and altogether an upstanding, manly bearing."[2]

Though real-life ministers may have been less manly than Mr. Craig, they too strove to bring the miners and other resource workers back to church. Their ultimate aim was conversion, to save the men who were "far away from home and those [they] love ... surrounded only with such influences as tend to drag [them] down, deeper and deeper into a life of reckless sinful pleasure from which alas, [they] so surely reap ... in the future the fruit of sin."[3] To inveigle "godless" British Columbians back to church, ministers tried to emulate dominant masculine characteristics and used whatever other techniques they thought might succeed. One of the most effective of these men was "Father Pat," an Anglican minister who served in the Kootenays from the 1880s and into the early twentieth century. He was apparently beloved by many miners and other resource workers, for he lived as they did, sharing his shack with poor or ill miners and giving them clothes. He was not an eloquent or theologically profound

Father Pat (Henry Irwin), Anglican minister of the Kootenays, c. 1909 | *BC Archives, G-04310*

preacher, but he was admired for his kindly ways, for speaking to the men on their own terms, for being very much a "manly man," for moving rapidly in the difficult country of the Kootenays, and for reacting courageously to challenges. He was also a "hard football player" and an excellent boxer who sometimes used his fists against those who "profanely" attacked Christianity.[4]

Canon Alan Greene, who worked as a missionary in isolated parts of the province immediately before and after the First World War, felt strongly that ministers needed to be manly men. In the 1960s, he told an interviewer,

> I think the fortunate thing was that all the men who got into the work on the religious side of it had been men of wide experience in frontier life ... We got a sort of sense of kinship with men, and our approach wasn't stilted, or formal, or clerical. It was as man-to-man, and the result was you got awfully close to men otherwise totally uninterested in religion as such.

He used a boat to reach isolated settlements and logging camps, and as he explained, "the boat gave you an entry among men that nothing else could of. They appreciated the physical adventure and risks involved. They gave you credit for being a man, in spite of your youth."[5]

The churches understood that deep theological knowledge was not the prime qualification for work on the resource frontier. In recommending appropriate men to reach workers in the logging camps, social gospeller Ernest Thomas informed his Methodist superiors that "the church should seek for and train such men of sturdy, invincible Christian spirit, of robust intellect, well trained in economics and philosophy, musical and well-trained for community work. The only preaching which can be effective on this work is that which meets the men on their own ground – a ground utterly unknown to most theological schools."[6]

Being musical was crucial to success. Reports from ministers and missionaries of all denominations record that hymns attracted men to services in mining towns, logging camps, and isolated settlements. For example, Reverend A. Robbins wrote from the mining town of Greenwood in 1900 that "Sundays I have Holy Communion at 8 when six or 8 attend; Evensong is a really hearty Service and our hideous hired concert hall is often full of men, who sing most heartily. I think at this we get some 70 or 80 to a service, especially if they think the hymns will attract them."[7] Ministers transported guitars and other musical instruments for long distances, as they assisted in attracting congregants. For example, an Anglican clergyman, Rowan Ernest Grice-Hutchinson, who served a variety of isolated communities in the Shuswap Lakes immediately before and after the First World War, took a harmonium (a fairly heavy keyboard instrument) with him in his travels. In reporting on various often sparsely attended services, he noted that "once again the harmonium of great assistance."[8] Thomas Green, a Methodist missionary in the Phoenix area during the early twentieth century, walked for miles up a dusty mountain road, carrying his guitar, to sing hymns to the miners at the mine near Phoenix. Initially, they were not interested, but after Green gained permission to sing in their bunkhouse, "they began to ask me to sing certain favorite hymns, as Rock of Ages, Lead Kindly Light, Jesus Lover of my Soul, Nearer my God to Thee ... and Where is My Wandering Boy Tonight." The miners asked him to come again, and he wrote that on subsequent visits "they have been most courteous to me even to the extent of giving up their game of cards while my services were in progress."[9] Ministers often recognized that the hymns were more of a drawing card than the message they were trying to impart. One Presbyterian missionary who visited various mining camps, often preaching in hotels and saloons, stated that

> the discouraging feature is not that there is no response, but that it is so superficial ... Men leave the bar-room at my appeal and come over to the service. They would listen reverently to what I had to say and join heartily in the singing, asking as a special favor that we sing [certain] hymns dear to them because of childhood memories and then when the service was over they would go back again to their drinking and gambling.[10]

For this minister, as for many others, being a Christian entailed accepting the complete package – a conversion experience, welcoming Christ into one's heart, and leading a moral, respectable Christian life. But this was far from the lived religion of many working-class British Columbians. For them, hymns provided fond associations with childhood, with Christian families far away, and perhaps with some form of personal faith. They willingly acknowledged such connections by joining in the singing but did not see this as incompatible with their homosocial leisure culture, anathema though it was to evangelical Christians.

Evangelical Christians employed revivals as major frontal assaults on this leisure culture but with little success. The largest and best-known was the Kootenay Revival Campaign of 1909, which is the subject of an excellent thesis by Stuart Barnard. Organized by the Canadian Presbyterian Board of Moral and Social Reform, and borrowing American revival methods and personnel, it involved two consecutive three-week revivals in a range of Kootenay and Crowsnest Pass towns, including Nelson, Rossland, and Fernie. Hoping to attract irreligious male workers, the revivalists used professional singers and preachers who stocked their sermons with manly, muscular Christian rhetoric. They exhorted their listeners to exchange their sinful leisure ways for evangelical piety and morality, which would transform not just the individual men, but their communities as well. Although the revivalists preached in lumber camps and local public spaces, Barnard notes that they did not address the very real material problems of the workers. Some men may have attended the services, enjoying the excellent singing of well-known gospel hymns, but very few accepted the package of salvation and the abandonment of "sinful" leisure activities. In the years following the revivals, church leaders' lamentations about the sinfulness of the Kootenay towns did not diminish. For the drinking, gambling, hymn-singing miners, nothing had changed.[11]

Fuzzy Fidelity and Practical Christians

In the scholarly literature on secularization and on popular or working-class religion, there has been much debate about people like these miners – the great mass of individuals who occupy a continuum somewhere between unreserved atheism and ardent belief in the religious teachings of a denomination. Historian S.C. Williams has studied the working class of Southwark, in turn-of-the-century London, and suggests that those who professed some type of Christian belief and had a nostalgic fondness for the hymns and prayers of their childhood, but who rarely attended church other than for major life cycle events, nonetheless followed a legitimate form of popular religion. Hugh McLeod, who has studied secularization among the working classes of London and other major cities during the same period, sees such practices as reflecting the "half-secular" approach of many working-class individuals. For McLeod, these practices were a phase in a gradual progression toward complete secularization. Discussing the way in which Americans take up and transform various elements of official religion, making them their own, Robert Orsi argues that this equates to "lived religion" and is not necessarily an indication of secularization.[12] Sociologists of religion have also explored this complex phenomenon. They label individuals who lack strong religious belief and practice but who also lack a clearly secular identity as having "fuzzy fidelity." This may entail belonging to a church without accepting its teachings, believing in God without joining a church, and a host of other options. Most of these scholars see fuzzy fidelity as a way station on the path toward greater secularity.[13]

Turn-of-the-century British Columbia certainly exhibited a range of practices and beliefs that can be identified with fuzzy fidelity, if we see it as occupying the middle ground on the continuum between steadfast atheism and wholehearted espousal of Christianity. Of course, the key question here, one that is much debated, is where to draw the line – where does fuzziness shade into secularity, and where does it become pious religious practice? Orsi would see variations of lived religion as encompassing all but the most avowed atheist, whereas the sociological scholars of fuzzy fidelity are more interested in variations on the continuum, allowing for shades of grey among the more secular.

The term "practical Christian," which had considerable resonance in British Columbia during this period, and also considerable elasticity, illustrates the complexities of this continuum. Practical Christians could be socialist atheists who believed that their concern for their fellow workers made them better, more moral people than churchgoers, whom they saw as hypocrites. Practical Christians could also reject Christianity and the churches but respect Christ for his moral teachings and example. Or they may have had some level of Christian faith but may also have believed that leading a moral life did not necessitate church attendance.

Robert Lowery identified practical Christians simply as those who cared for their fellows, regardless of any religious belief. In response to an easterner's comments on the supposed immorality of the Slocan, Lowery stated that many Slocan men were "practical Christians. They do not spend much time in church howling their complaints to Jesus, but if you are hungry, sick or broke touch some of the boys and see how quick they will respond to your appeal."[14] Lowery attacked a minister for speaking negatively at the death of a "practical Christian" named Allan, who had been very much part of local rough culture. Lowery admiringly declared that "Allan's heart was white with the memory of many a kind deed ... Allan practiced the religion of self-forgetfulness. His toil, his money his grub and cabin were ever ready to assist the needy."[15] The use of "white" here is very much a race-based compliment, reminding us that in this world, a true white man did not need to be a churchgoer. For Lowery and other Euro-Canadian participants in rough culture, whiteness was not necessarily linked to Christianity, as it was for members of the dominant classes who condemned the morals of "bad whites."

The use of "practical Christian" merits further unpacking. What Lowery meant was unselfishness and concern for one's fellow men. Today, we might speak approvingly of following the Golden Rule, though most would not link it to Christianity. Lowery respected the moral teachings of Jesus, and though he had little time for the churches, or even Christianity as a religion, he nonetheless used "Christian" as a term of approbation in describing care for one's fellows. Clearly, "Christian" retained some positive connotations, which demonstrates at least a residual power of Christian culture even among BC unbelievers. "God-fearing" seems to have been used similarly as a positive term, regardless of whether it had anything to do with belief. During an interview, Nanaimo miner Herschel Biggs stated that "as to the hereafter, I'm doubtful whether there is any." Even so, in describing his fellow miners, he said, "They didn't go much on religion, but I think most of the miners were God-fearing. They worked hard and they drank beer and they swore and they did things any miner would do, but they were basically a good, hardworking, clean-minded people."[16]

Wellington Hotel, Wellington, Vancouver Island, c. 189- | *BC Archives, B-02456*

Dave McDonald of Nanaimo was explicit about his lack of belief, but he seems to have fit Lowery's definition of a practical Christian. As he recalled, "I was supposed to go to church when I was young, but when I got old enough I said, 'To Hell with it.' I got fed up with it. I believed in enjoying myself. Mind you, nobody will say anything against me because if I could help someone I always helped 'em. That's my religion."[17] Again, caring for others is defined positively as a religion, even though the practice of Christianity is rejected. The Synod of the Diocese of Kootenay seemed to recognize this stance, suggesting that though many workers rejected the churches as being allied with employers, most remained "Christian in sentiment and ethics."[18] Similar patterns occurred among Catholic working-class men. Priests in Kootenay mining towns frequently complained to their bishop about the lack of church involvement among men. In one instance, a woman came to the local priest because she had been married by a Protestant minister and wanted to make things right with the Catholic Church. But her Catholic husband considered it all nonsense and stated that his only religion was to be an honest man.[19]

Others who called themselves practical Christians felt that caring for one's fellows was important, but they also retained a faith in God and possibly other basic Christian tenets, such as a belief in the afterlife. Even so, they felt no need to attend church. For example, Thomas Greene, an Anglican minister in the mining town of Fairview, wrote that though many of its miners had "no particular religious leanings," their creed was that "if I live a pretty straight, honest life and don't cheat my mates, I shall have a pretty good show at the last."[20] This seems to indicate that the miners believed they would go to heaven if they lived a moral life, defined to include honesty and straight dealing, but definitely not entailing avoidance of strong drink, gambling, and other activities that an orthodox evangelical Christian would see as paving the path to hell.

Similar patterns existed in Nanaimo, which had extremely low levels of church involvement. As noted in Chapter 2, the socialist MLA James Hawthornthwaite may have been concerned about alienating at least some working-class Nanaimo voters with hardline anti-religious rhetoric, but oral history sources suggest that the majority of male Nanaimo workers were not regular churchgoers, although many may have believed in the basic doctrines of Christianity. Albert Tickle of Nanaimo remembered that many of his fellow miners were believers though not churchgoers: "It usually is most common in most miners, most of them were you know Christian believers, but they weren't what you would call someone that went to church every Sunday. I mean they believed and that was good enough for them." Tom Johnston, who was raised in a devout Nanaimo household, said that though "a fair percentage" of Nanaimo residents went to church, "the great majority of the population ... were not regular attendants, but they at least supported what the church taught and stood for."[21] This pattern was very similar to that which S.C. Williams identified in working-class Southwark during the same period. As she argues, people generally felt that if they believed in God, went to church for certain key events, and followed basic Christian precepts, particularly kindness and care for their neighbours, they could define themselves as good Christians. Hugh McLeod also notes that good neighbourliness was identified with practical Christianity in working-class London during this period, regardless of whether those who exhibited it were churchgoers.[22]

Williams suggests that these neighbourly working-class Londoners saw themselves as better Christians than churchgoers who oppressed their employees, displayed unneighbourliness, or were guilty of other faults, and who were branded as hypocrites because they failed to live up to Christian teachings. Similar sentiments were frequently expressed in British Columbia.[23] Alice Barrett Parke of Vernon, a committed churchgoer, noted in her diary that

> I have learned since I came west, that religion and church going are sometimes two widely different things. I think many men do not enter the

> churches, not because they disbelieve in God, or despise His worship, but because they find so little of him in the churches and His professed followers. The Christlike lives are not always lived by those who know most of modern theology. I often think of those words "to do justice, & to love mercy, and to walk humbly with thy God" and they seem a deep reproach to many of us Christians, where the spirit of intolerance, of harshness and spiritual pride reigns.[24]

This theme of churchgoer hypocrisy was very common. Lowery enjoyed skewering the pretense of wealthy churchgoers who oppressed their employees. Thomas Green wrote about debating religion with a miner who held Christian people "up to ridicule for unfaithfulness and inconsistency."[25] Workers who told the *Fernie Free Press* why they did not attend church voiced similar comments. One man stayed away "not because I am not in sympathy with the work that the church purports to do, but because I cannot attend a service without feeling that I have been witness of or participated in a lot of sham and hypocrisy." Another stated that he would attend services "when the parsons and church members can show me that they are living any better than many of us who do not go to church. When I satisfy myself that I would be a better man for attending church services I'll be there." Another declined to attend simply because "I won't associate myself with a bunch of hypocrites."[26]

Baptism and Sunday School

The working-class Londoners whom Williams studied may rarely have attended church, but they seemed to believe that being a Christian parent entailed having their children baptized. Williams suggests that this stress on baptism may have arisen from the orthodox belief that baptism was necessary if the child were to go to heaven and from a more superstitious notion that it would be lucky and provide some supernatural protection for the baby.[27] Norman Knowles notes that many working-class residents of Fernie who rarely attended church wanted to have their children baptized.[28] Canon Alan Greene, an Anglican clergyman who ministered to isolated families on the frontier, recalled that "pioneers that had been there for years and out of touch with the church said 'well, it's about time we had our children christened.' And that might be the first entry in that family. That ... you would baptize the whole family."[29] Rowan Ernest Grice-Hutchinson, an Anglican cleric who hiked many miles and relied on a frequently malfunctioning motor boat in all weathers to serve the often poor and struggling inhabitants of the Shuswap, also reported that a number of non-churchgoing parents of various Protestant denominations wanted to have their children baptized. A German family, which he had never seen at services, "was anxious to have their youngest child baptized." In another family, the first he saw of the mother and aunt was at the christening of the baby.[30] Sometimes, however, he was much more concerned than the parents that the children be baptized, as was the case with a family whose children he referred to as "four little heathens." And in one instance, which he recorded with horror, a mother "asked me what it meant!" when he inquired whether her little boy was baptized.[31]

Williams noted that most of the working-class Londoners in her study also made a point of sending their children to Sunday School. Some of this pattern, which Williams termed "religion by deputy," was echoed among BC workers. One Presbyterian report stated that "even in the all too frequent cases where the parents themselves are non-churchgoers, they are still anxious that their children should come under the influence of Christian teaching in the SS."[32] Interviewees recalled that parents in Nanaimo often sent their children to Sunday School, although they may not have gone to church themselves. Lynne Bowen's study of the town corroborates their memory: "However reluctantly, more children attended church than parents."[33] In Fernie, however, churchmen complained that though parents wanted to have their children baptized, they neither came to church themselves nor sent their children to Sunday School. In 1908, Vancouver Presbyterians complained that "hundreds of Presbyterian children do not attend SS." despite efforts to entice them through school prizes, picnics, and Christmas trees.[34] Even when children did go to Sunday School, the end result was sometimes not what church leaders had hoped for. James Kipp, who grew up in Chilliwack during the late nineteenth century, told Imbert Orchard that he had attended both the Methodist and the Presbyterian Sunday School, one in the morning and one in the afternoon, in hopes of winning two prizes for reciting Bible verses. He described this use of prizes as "commercialized" Sunday School. He worked hard to memorize the verses and was very disappointed when the Methodists decided not to award prizes. Instead, the children were told to "bring something for some poor people that had nothing at all ... 'It's more blessing to give than it is to receive' they said. Well I couldn't see it that way at all." He fared better with the Presbyterians, winning "a nice big red ball ... oh, a good sized one ... Oh, it was something worthwhile." But another child

Sunday School picnic, Nelson, n.d. | *BC Archives, C-07814*

stole it off the Christmas tree, so he was left with nothing to show for his efforts. As he told Orchard, "that just settled me ... And I never went to any church for over twenty years."[35]

Fraternalism and the "Other"

Williams states that many adults in Southwark did occasionally attend church, particularly on important holidays, such as Christmas, Easter, and the annual Harvest Festival. This was also true of many British Columbians who were sometimes drawn to church on important holidays, attracted by the solemn occasion, the elaborately decorated churches, and the special music. For example, regular Sunday services at St. George's Anglican Church in Rossland were generally attended by just twenty to thirty-five people in 1908, with the rector often complaining about "bad attendance" and "very bad attendance" in his service book. St. George's was the only Anglican church in a community of close to six thousand. The rector managed to attract sixty-five people to a "Carol Service" at Christmastime and eighty-four people to a September Harvest Festival, where everyone

Interior of St. George's Church, Rossland, decorated for Harvest Festival, 1905 | *BC Archives, NA-41795*

enjoyed the "very bright and hearty" singing. However, the turnout was greatest during the June "Free Mason's Sunday," when eighty-five people came to church, including "51 Freemasons in regalia." The other Freemason Sunday, in December, drew seventy-three people, more than the carol service that evening.[36]

As various scholars have pointed out, fraternal orders, such as the Masons, the Oddfellows, the Knights of Pythias, and the Orange Order, competed with the churches for the time and energy of men in nineteenth- and early-twentieth-century Canada and the United States. Often, the only form of insurance for death or sickness that was then available to men and their families came from the fraternal orders. They also offered a sense of community and fellowship, the excitement of secret ritual and regalia at all-male meetings, and the relaxation and sociability of convivial lodge socials, where plenty of alcohol was always on tap for the fraternal brothers. In most orders, members were required to assert their belief in a "Supreme Being," but there were no more specific religious requirements, and in fact religious discussions were discouraged, or in many lodges forbidden, as a potential source of discord. For many men, even in Central and Eastern Canada, the lodges provided an appealing, masculine social alternative to

Nelson Oddfellows in full regalia, c. 1900 | *BC Archives, B-04890*

the feminized churches.[37] In the BC resource towns, working-class men also found brotherhood in the local union halls, but joining a union did not preclude involvement in the fraternal orders, and large numbers of men valued their membership in both. Although most literature has focused on the appeal of fraternal orders for men, they commonly had female auxiliaries as well, which attracted many women.

One way of asserting the respectability and social importance of the lodges was the annual or twice annual march of the brothers, in full regalia, into a local Protestant church, where the minister delivered a sermon on an appropriate topic, such as brotherhood. Such sermons were common in Central and Eastern Canada, and the practice appears to have been imported to British Columbia, with similar church parades being held in various towns, including Vernon, Nelson, Rossland, and Nanaimo.[38] However, these parades seem to have been somewhat less common in British Columbia than in Ontario. Even when they did occur, many BC lodge brothers were probably less familiar with the interior of the church than was the case elsewhere in Canada. Certainly, not all lodge members in Central and Eastern Canada belonged to a church, but the dramatic increase in attendance at Rossland's Anglican church when the Masons appeared, and what we already know about the irreligious ways of many BC men, suggests that the overlap between the lodges and the churches was even less than in Central and Eastern Canada. The requirement to believe in a supreme being may have kept the most committed atheists away from the lodges, but it left much space for those of fuzzy fidelity. Some lodges had particularly irreligious reputations. Even in Ontario, members of the Orange Lodges were not likely to be active church members. However, the stern admonitions from two ministers who spoke at the Orange Lodge's July 12 celebrations in Nanaimo, urging the assembled Orangemen not to forget their religious responsibilities, may have been particularly pointed in that town, where most men seemed to prefer local bars over local churches.[39]

Whereas fewer BC Protestants may have combined church involvement with lodge membership than was the case in Eastern Canada, a significant number of BC Catholics tried to do so, though membership in "secret societies" was forbidden by their faith, and those who joined were to be barred from confession and taking communion. Nonetheless, many Catholics joined the orders, a decision that appears to have been much less common in Central and Eastern North America.[40] They would not have considered membership in the anti-Catholic Orange Order and would not have been welcome there, but they did join various other orders, which points to the social and cultural importance of these lodges for both men and women. Fascinating correspondence between Kootenay priests and their bishop indicates that at least some of the Catholics who became lodge brothers or sisters did not wish to lose their church affiliation, although many put commitment to the lodges first.

Priests did not focus on the Catholics who had abandoned the church for the fraternal orders, although they were seen as a problem. Instead, they sought advice regarding the many Catholics who wished to reconcile lodge membership with their Christian faith. Father J.A. Bedard wrote to Bishop Dontenwill for guidance about a Mr. McIsaac in the mining town of Phoenix "who is an active member of the Knights of Pythias and wants permission to take communion on Sunday." Bedard told Dontenwill that McIsaac

> sees no evil in it, that he has spent money for the order but he has taken no insurance; that he would suffer damage socially and financially if he were to abandon the order just now, but would have no objection to abandoning it later on, when he goes away from Phoenix for instance ... There is no peril he claims either for his faith nor his morals.

Bedard supported McIsaac's request because he was a "good boy and means to do what is right." He "promised to make his [McIsaac's] case a test case for there are other boys in Phoenix who await your answer to present themselves to the confessional next Sunday."[41] This letter demonstrates the crucial social role that fraternal orders played in the resource towns. Catholicism was important to McIsaac, but he clearly saw his membership as integral to his position and social ties in Phoenix.

Other Catholics in nearby towns also tried to maintain their links to church and lodge, but if given no choice were willing to abandon their faith. Father Brucker of Grand Forks told Dontenwill in January 1903 that he had refused sacraments at Christmas to many members of secret societies, with the result that many never came back to church, including family men whom Brucker was unhappy about losing.[42] Scholars have shown that men often preferred the lodge to the church, although the focus has been on Protestant men whose choice was less stark than that of their Catholic counterparts. What is particularly fascinating is that many Catholic women in the resource communities seem to have made similar choices. Bishop Dontenwill seems to have failed to instruct Father Bedard in the case of Mr. McIsaac, as eighteen months later Bedard wrote to him again, complaining that "not only the greater number of the Catholic men [of Phoenix and Greenwood] have entered the Eagles and similar secret societies, but now even the women are flocking in the Maccabees, a secret society for women." Bedard pleaded for clear directions on how to deal with these wayward parishioners. Dontenwill was already familiar with this heresy among women, as more than a year earlier Georgionne Madore had written to him from Rossland, saying that she and many other women were both communicants in the Catholic Church and members of the Maccabees. She asked that Dontenwill accept this.[43]

The presence of a significant number of Catholics in BC fraternal orders suggests that the religious strictures of their faith had less power in the province than elsewhere in North America. The fact that Catholics were welcomed into the orders may also indicate that anti-Catholicism was less powerful in British Columbia than in Central and Eastern Canada, and points to the more limited significance of religion and religious differences in the province. Race may also have played a role here. Andrew Reid argues that the presence of Catholics and Jews in the male fraternal orders of late-nineteenth-century Victoria demonstrates that whiteness trumped religious difference.[44] Similar patterns may have applied in the Kootenays. Anti-Asian and anti-Indigenous sentiments distanced those "others" who were clearly racialized as non-white and reduced the power of religious differences among those who were accepted as whites at a time when friction between Catholics and Protestants remained high throughout the rest of Canada.[45] The limited number of active Christians of any denomination in smaller BC communities, particularly in the mining towns, may also have brought Catholics and Protestants together.[46] W.J. Fraser, who was born in 1889 and raised as a Catholic in Revelstoke, argued in 1965 that

> in those days, there was no such thing as [Protestant-Catholic] bigotry at all. All our friends, in most cases, were Protestants. In the earlier days we had the Methodist church, the English church, and the Catholic church. Two of the nearest saints that I could recollect in my memory would be Father Thayer of the Catholic church and Reverend Forbes of the English church ... If there was a celebration during the wintertime the priest and the two ministers appeared on the platform together. It was absolute unity. As I said, no bigotry whatsoever.[47]

Although Fraser may have been reporting relations between denominations with some accuracy, the passage of time may also have softened memories of negative interactions. Catholic-Protestant tensions had not entirely disappeared in British Columbia during this period, even in Revelstoke. As discussed in Chapter 1, even when religious commitment was very attenuated, some ethnic links to denominational identity often remained. The popularity of the Orange Order in a range of BC communities confirms the persistence of a particularly bigoted form of Protestant ethnoreligious identity. The Revelstoke Orange Parade had a large contingent of marchers, although it lacked the enthusiastic audience it would have had in Ontario.[48] The complexity of local situations is revealed by Fraser, who notes that the old man who played King Billy in the Orange Parade was washed and dressed each year by Fraser's Catholic family, to prepare him for his role in the parade.[49]

A letter from Revelstoke's Father Thayer himself to Bishop Dontenwill further illuminates both the existence and the limits of anti-Catholicism in the Kootenays. In December 1903, Thayer wrote from Revelstoke to report that most of his choir had left town and that members of the local Methodist choir had volunteered to fill in. Though Fraser identified Thayer as a saintly model of inter-denominational tolerance, the priest was not comfortable with having Methodists provide the music for his Christmas services. However, he saw no way of refusing their kind offer. Like Fraser, he felt that relations between Revelstoke Catholics and Protestants were harmonious, but he feared that if he refused, a small "contemptible

Orange Parade in Revelstoke, 1900 | *BC Archives, A-09447*

faction" that had stirred up anti-Catholic feeling the year before but was "frowned down by the majority" would have ammunition to incite further sectarian tensions.[50] Although British Columbia was not without religious tensions, the idea of Methodists volunteering to participate in Catholic services would have been unthinkable in Central or Eastern Canada.

White Catholics sought community and brotherhood and sisterhood in the local lodges, and white Protestants were willing to welcome them. The intersection of whiteness and a less religious culture played a role here, and the power of working-class identity and consciousness, most markedly in the Kootenays, may also have limited religious tensions and drawn more workers into fraternal orders, particularly those with a majority of working-class members.

In this context, whiteness was defined quite narrowly. White fraternal brothers and sisters would certainly not have accepted Asian and Indigenous members, but other groups were excluded as well.[51] Newspaperman John Houston wrote tellingly about a railroad work crew that consisted of "160 whites, 65 Italians, and 175 Chinese."[52] At the turn of the century, many Anglo-Canadian workers strongly resented the southern Europeans who immigrated to the Kootenays and the Crowsnest Pass. It is very likely that the fraternal orders would not have accepted the Catholics among them. All the Catholic fraternal brothers and sisters who sought absolution from their bishop had Anglo-Celtic names, and no Italian or Slavic names appear in either this correspondence or among the officers of fraternal orders who are listed in Kootenay newspapers. For some privileged Catholics, race trumped religion in permitting entry to the charmed circle of whiteness, but others who would be deemed white today remained negatively racialized and excluded. Southern and eastern European immigrants formed their own ethno-religious associations, as did both Chinese and Japanese immigrants. These organizations provided crucial mutual support, but this did not diminish the racism that members of these groups faced in BC communities.

Death and Funerals

Although many Catholics were willing to leave the church for the sake of fraternal bonds, their efforts to combine the two pointed to the importance of their faith and a very real fear of dying without priestly absolution. In the mines and other workplaces, sudden death was an ever-present danger. Even nominally Protestant men who absented themselves from church except for an occasional fraternal parade sought its rituals when they died. Most wanted a minister to officiate at their funerals. Bishop Hills of Victoria grumbled in his diary about the frequency with which he was asked to officiate at the burials of people of "doubtful morals" who had never attended church. In February 1890, he recorded that

> today was the funeral at the Cathedral of a Mr. Roller, a German keeper of a Theatre of not good reputation. It is difficult to refuse these applications for Burial Rites over those who not only have never belonged to us but are of a disreputable character. There was a large attendance of a class of persons who are never seen in a place of worship.[53]

Reverend Grice-Hutchinson was also asked to bury men who had never attended his services.[54] The Slavic Catholic layman who asked Bishop Dontenwill to send a Slavic priest to Fernie remarked that less than a third of his compatriots normally attended church but that at funerals you may "see church crowded with Slavonians up to door."[55] In 1895, the Anglican bishop of New Westminster was asked to bury a miner near New Denver and recorded that his workmates "seemed grateful out of all proportion

Funeral at Atlin, 1899, probably held near a mining or logging camp. Note the absence of women | *BC Archives, D-01507*

to the service I had done, but I understood it. However reckless their lives, they hate the idea of being buried 'like a dog.'"[56]

A small minority, generally the most committed atheists, left directions that no "sky pilots," a slang term for ministers, were to officiate at their funerals. Other non-Christians were equally clear, such as the ex-mayor of Victoria, a spiritualist, who instructed that "no other Service should be said over his body but the form used by the Odd Fellows."[57] Most people who barred ministers from their funerals had no desire to be buried "like a dog." Some were interred with due ceremony by the local fraternal order to which they belonged, and some received the "obsequies" delivered by a miners' union, which was involved in many Kootenay funerals.[58] However, even these funerals often had one or more local clergymen officiating. An examination of three Kootenay newspapers reveals that a minister presided at most funerals in these communities.[59] In some cases, this may have reflected the wishes of the more pious spouses, mothers, or other relatives of the deceased, but given the large number of BC men whose families lived elsewhere, it seems likely that, except for committed atheists, they tacitly accepted the value and legitimacy of having a minister preside at their funeral.

Particularly in the Kootenays, most of these men would not have been church members, and many probably never went to church. John Houston is a quintessential example: though he spent his career criticizing Christianity and meddling moralistic churchmen, he was buried by a Presbyterian minister.[60] Clearly, churchgoing was not part of their sense of manhood. Churchgoers could be everything that manly men were not: feminine; craven hypocrites who supported oppressive employers; effete easterners who attacked working men's right to their few enjoyments and who worried more about saving the souls of Asian immigrants than about preventing them from stealing the jobs of white workers. However, it seems that for most, some basic elements of Christianity itself were not antithetical to their sense of masculinity. Christian hymns could provide an emotional link to faraway families, and practical Christianity could serve as the moral basis for relationships in homosocial culture. And for the majority, receiving a proper Christian burial was integral to a sense of decent manhood, or indeed of their very humanity. The fact that the funeral could end with a "drunken orgy," as more than one appalled minister testified, made perfect sense among working-class men in British Columbia.[61]

Increasing Godlessness?

Fuzzy fidelity appears to have had a hold on the majority of British Columbians during the late nineteenth and early twentieth centuries, but this started to change immediately before the First World War, as some BC workers embraced a more fully secular outlook. Increasing numbers of missionaries and ministers found that workers would have nothing to do with them and were now unwilling to listen to services or sing hymns. They blamed several sources for this change, including the Industrial Workers of the World, with its hostility to "religionists," and "socialist Finns" as well as other Scandinavian immigrants who spurned religion and were working in the lumber camps in growing numbers.[62] They also suggested that this attitude revealed the emergence of a new generation, which was being raised with no religious training at all. In 1912, the Methodist superintendent of missions in British Columbia, Reverend J.H. White, wrote,

> The most alarming feature of the situation is the growing indifference and often hostility toward the churches and even towards the Bible and religion

> generally. A few years ago though men might be very rough and even dissipated they had a background of Christian training and tradition to which appeal could be made. A new generation is grown up who have been trained in a different school. There is little use appealing to a man to remember his mother's prayers and his father's God if his mother never prayed and his father scouted [dismissed] religion.[63]

White may have been pointing to a pattern identified by the sociologists of religion who argue that fuzzy fidelity ultimately leads to secularization.[64] As mentioned in Chapter 1, the proportion of atheists or those who had no religion did increase in British Columbia between 1901 and 1911, from 1.5 to 2.0 percent, remaining fairly low but nonetheless strikingly higher than elsewhere in Canada. That this increase occurred even as the BC population mushroomed is also notable. A variety of factors can account for this pattern, including growing numbers of transient male workers from Eastern Canada and internationally, the emergence of a new generation of unbelievers, the message of irreligious journalists, and the popular class-conscious politics of the day. Anti-Asian sentiment also strengthened hostility to churchmen who opposed Asian exclusion, while reinforcing the power of whiteness as a "stand-alone" identity and source of inclusion for working-class men. Whereas anti-Asian racism was certainly strong in late-nineteenth-century British Columbia, it reached more intense levels during the early twentieth century, seen most starkly in the Vancouver anti-Asian riots of 1907 and the racist hysteria that greeted the efforts of the *Komagata Maru*'s South Asian passengers to disembark in Vancouver in 1914.[65]

A range of reasons, then, made it possible, and perhaps increasingly easy, to define oneself as irreligious in British Columbia. However, even among the rough manly miners, some form of fuzzy fidelity seems to have remained much more common than outright atheism, whereas dominant Christian beliefs and practices still had a hold on a significant proportion of the province's white settler population. The next chapter will look more closely at the latter group, which the missionary literature painted as the "faithful and embattled minority" in godless British Columbia.

4
Sundays Are So Different Here
Communities in British Columbia, Ontario, and Nova Scotia

The religious landscape of turn-of-the-century British Columbia differed from the Canadian norm. But what of those British Columbians who mirrored broader Canadian patterns, who regularly attended church and accepted the dictates of Christianity? We know that they were less numerous in British Columbia than in Eastern Canada. Jessie McQueen, recently emigrated from Nova Scotia, lamented in 1888 the "handful of people" who attended church services in her Interior community, as compared to the many who did so in her old home.[1] Eleven years later, E.D. McLaren, pastor of St. Andrew's Church in Vancouver, put things more positively: "There are all through the province earnest, God-fearing men and women, in probably every community." However, he did acknowledge that "the proportion of the people who are actively on the side of the Church of Christ and prepared to subordinate largely other interests to the interests of the Church is a great deal smaller than the proportion, at least, of the Province of Ontario."[2]

This chapter focuses on this "handful of people," the "earnest, God-fearing men and women" who valiantly challenged the godlessness and sin they saw around them. Who were they? Did they live in every community, or did they tend to cluster in certain towns and cities? And were they similar to their counterparts in Ontario and elsewhere in Canada, or did Christianity's diminished hegemony alter the appeal, and thus the social dimensions, of church involvement in British Columbia?

Elsewhere in Canada, the majority of church members were women. Did the dramatic under-representation of non-Indigenous women in British

Columbia affect this pattern? We know that working-class radicalism, the power of whiteness, and the lure of rough culture kept many white men away from BC churches. Nonetheless, some BC men did join a church, even though doing so was less crucial for social inclusion. Who were they? And how different was the situation for white settler women? We know that most women either were not able to, or chose not to, identify themselves as atheists or as those of no religion, except in the company of husbands and fathers. But what did this mean in terms of their commitment to active church membership? This chapter looks closely at a range of variables among church members, including gender, class, race, immigration status, transiency, and marital status to explore the social dimensions of membership, both in British Columbia and, for comparative purposes, in two more religiously observant provinces, Ontario and Nova Scotia.

Taking a closer look at which British Columbians were church members also sheds further light on those who were not. The census can tell us much about the backgrounds of those who defined themselves explicitly as atheists or as having no religion, but church membership patterns provide insights into the many British Columbians who might have defined themselves as belonging to a Christian denomination for the census taker but who never joined a church.

This chapter addresses these issues through comparative local community studies. Thanks to the resources of the Canadian Families Project and many hard-working research assistants, I was able to study eight towns across Canada, linking their church membership records with the 1901 manuscript census. I examined four BC communities, comparing them to two in Ontario and two in Nova Scotia.[3] All were relatively small, with populations ranging from approximately one to six thousand. Selecting small towns improved my ability to generate a clear picture of who was involved in local churches and who was not. In small towns, each denomination is typically represented by just one church. Thus, if the census lists someone as an Anglican but that person does not appear in the membership records of the town's Anglican church, it can be assumed that he or she is not likely to be a church member at all.[4]

This methodological approach has prompted some criticism.[5] It has been suggested that concentrating on small towns can lead one to ignore the greater class consciousness that sometimes exists in larger, more industrialized centres and that may have resulted in lower levels of church involvement there.[6] On the other hand, it has also been suggested that a focus on small towns, with only one church per denomination, necessarily entails the study of cross-class congregations and may in fact underestimate working-class church involvement because it does not permit one to identify the primarily working-class churches to be found in larger centres.[7] The former point seems less relevant to British Columbia, where some of the most class-polarized communities were small resource-based towns. The latter point is more reasonable, and important work has been done on the nature and internal dynamics of working-class congregations in large Central Canadian cities. However, studies of working-class congregations in larger cities still leave open the question of what proportion of workers in these cities were involved in these and other churches, and what proportion stayed away from all religious institutions. The next chapter examines the social dimensions of involvement in a range of Protestant churches in Victoria, allowing me to identify both primarily working-class and mixed-class congregations in that city. However, even for Victoria, a relatively small city for this period, it was not possible to find records for all the churches of any one denomination. Therefore, this chapter scrutinizes small communities to identify both those who were actively involved in the churches and those who were not. Its findings reinforce Chapter 1's census analysis of BC agnostics and those of no religion. A comparative analysis of church membership in BC communities with communities in Central and Eastern Canada also provides crucial information about continuities and discontinuities across Canada.

The Communities and the Communicants

The first Nova Scotia town studied here was Amherst, a highly industrialized community near the New Brunswick border, which had a population of close to 5,000 in 1901. Its two largest jobsites were machine engineering and foundry works, but others included a shoe factory and a woollen mill, which employed a significant number of women. Spatially divided between the industrial workers and their families, and the factory owners, Amherst had already experienced some industrial unrest by 1901, although labour conflict was to escalate during the next two decades.[8] The second Nova Scotia community, Kentville, headquarters of the Dominion Atlantic Railway Company, had slightly more than 1,700 residents in 1901. It had some industry, but it served primarily as an agricultural service and distribution centre in the Annapolis Valley. In both Amherst and Kentville, Baptists were the largest religious group. Both towns boasted a Baptist, Anglican, Catholic, Methodist, and Presbyterian church, and each one had a separate African Nova Scotian church. In Amherst, this was an American Methodist Episcopal church, whereas in Kentville it was a Baptist church.[9]

The two Ontario towns were Campbellford and Dunnville. An agricultural service centre with an industrial base, Campbellford lies north of Lake Ontario in Northumberland County, and Dunnville, a more highly industrialized community, is near the eastern end of Lake Erie, on the Welland Canal.[10] Their population numbers were fairly similar in 1901: Campbellford had 2,485 residents, and Dunnville had just over 2,100. Campbellford had a tradition of fairly paternalistic labour relations in its mills, whereas Dunnville, as part of the industrialized Welland Canal area, already had a history of more polarized class relations. Like many Ontario communities, both towns had a significant plurality of Methodist adherents. Except for the small African Canadian churches in Amherst and Kentville, these four towns were not ethnically or racially diverse; the vast majority of their residents were of British origin.

The BC communities are Nelson, Rossland, Revelstoke, and Vernon, all in the Yale and Cariboo census district. We are already familiar with the Kootenay mining towns of Nelson and Rossland. In 1901, they were at their peak, Nelson with a population of over 5,270 and Rossland at 6,000. Hardrock mining was flourishing in both towns, and Nelson also increasingly served as a supply and distribution centre, as well as an administrative centre for the Kootenays. Both saw their share of labour unrest, though strikes were particularly bitter and contested in Rossland.[11] The largest Christian denomination in both Nelson and Rossland was Presbyterian. Revelstoke was a major CPR centre for the Kootenays and a distribution point for the West Kootenays, and Vernon was a small service centre for the surrounding ranching and agricultural land in the Okanagan Valley.[12] In 1901, Revelstoke had a population of 1,600, and Vernon, the largest community in the Okanagan Valley, had 802 residents, though both would grow significantly over the next decade. In both towns, Anglicans outnumbered other Christians.

Nelson, Rossland, Revelstoke, and Vernon were all newly settled in 1901, having been established within the previous ten to fifteen years. During the late 1880s and early 1890s, all denominations still faced pioneering conditions in these towns, sharing buildings (a former barracks in Revelstoke and a school house in Vernon and Nelson) and taking turns holding services. By 1901, however, all four towns had separate active churches, at least among the mainstream denominations: the Catholics, Anglicans, Methodists, and Presbyterians. The Baptists were a minority, but they did

Nelson, c. 1900 | *BC Archives, G-00658*

have a church in Nelson by 1900, as did the Congregationalists. Each community also had a Salvation Army detachment that included a few adherents, with Nelson having the largest number, at seventy-nine. Despite this small presence, the Salvation Army could sometimes attract large working-class audiences to its intentionally flamboyant "blood and fire" services.[13]

All four towns had significant Chinese populations, ranging from over 100 to almost 240, but they were socially marginalized, as elsewhere in the province, and were not welcome in local mainstream churches. Most communities had some form of Chinese temple, or "joss house" as they were known to the non-Chinese community, and at some point over this period both Euro-Canadian and Chinese missionaries attempted to convert the local Chinese to Christianity, with minimal success.[14] The Vernon area included a number of Indigenous reserves, but very few Indigenous people lived in the town itself, and even fewer lived in or near the Kootenay towns. People of British origin made up almost 80 percent of Vernon's population in 1901, whereas the Kootenay towns were more ethnically diverse.[15] By 1901, significant numbers of Scandinavians, as well as Italian and Slavic Catholics, had moved into these towns, with Rossland being the most multi-ethnic community.[16]

First Anglican church built in Rossland, by Father Pat Irwin, c. 1905 | *BC Archives, Bill Barlee fonds, I-60930*

In this study, I focus on the communicants, or church members as they were more commonly known in certain denominations. These people would generally have been the most active churchgoers. It is true that particularly among Methodists, Presbyterians, and Anglicans, a significant number of churchgoers did not become full members/communicants, choosing instead to attend church on an occasional or regular basis and often providing financial support.[17] We also know that many people of fuzzy fidelity came to church, at least at Christmas and Easter or for life cycle events. Others may have attended on the occasional Sunday, been attracted by popular visiting revivalists, or turned out for evening services to enjoy the hymns. They may have also taken in an occasional local Salvation Army service. As a result, we cannot assume that the numbers listed as communicants represented everyone who went to church. Nonetheless, becoming a member of the evangelical churches, the Presbyterian, Methodist, and Baptist churches, presupposed having some form of conversion experience, entailing repentance for sin and a willingness to give oneself to Christ. Joining a church also involved a formal undertaking to adhere to its religious and moral teachings, and to attend services regularly, particularly communion. Among Anglicans, a conversion experience was not a prerequisite for taking communion; communicants would have been confirmed in the church as children, and the decision to join it as an adult also involved a serious religious commitment. As a result, it seems reasonable to assume that church members/communicants made up the majority of committed churchgoers.

Some scholars have suggested that membership or communicant status is not a good measure of church involvement for the working class.[18] As we have seen, workers in some BC towns commonly retained an attachment to a church, through having their children baptized or sending them to Sunday School, without becoming members themselves. However, many of them were clear that their commitment to the church was less than that of members. In British Columbia, comments from workers express a distinct ambivalence regarding the churches, and perhaps this rather than a sense that membership was irrelevant prevented them from joining (as discussed in Chapter 3). At the same time, as we will see, working-class individuals in some of the communities studied here were as likely as their middle-class counterparts to join a church, especially if they were female. This suggests not that membership was less significant to working-class people, but that certain contexts influenced their attitudes toward the churches, diminishing the likelihood that they would become members. It thus seems reasonable to assume that though many non-members may sometimes have attended services, membership is nonetheless a marker of greater religious commitment, regardless of class.

Belief was certainly a major component of the decision to join a church, but studies suggest that in Eastern Canada, other more social reasons could play a role as well. Faith was very important to many women in this period as an integral part of their personal, family, and feminine cultural worlds, and as a solace in an era of economic uncertainty and high levels of maternal and child mortality.[19] The congruence of the Christian values of morality, submission, and piety with ideal feminine values, and the lack of many alternative social options also helped draw women, both single and married, into membership. Churches offered social interaction, the comfort of communal prayer and preaching, and the shared enjoyment of familiar hymns at regular services and meetings. They also enabled involvement in a variety of women's groups, ranging from local Ladies Aids to female missionary societies that were affiliated with national organizations. These provided welcome sociability with other women, a sense of active Christian purpose, and the capacity, in some small way, to have an impact in the larger world. In Central and Eastern Canada, where churchgoing was a marker of respectability, the need to keep up appearances through regular attendance was a factor that cannot be ignored. Women who stayed away from church risked damaging their feminine respectability, always a fragile construct, and that of their family. For poorer women, church membership provided solace, respectability, and sometimes a small measure of material security – in difficult times, "deserving" women would be especially likely to receive some financial support from the church. Women had a range of reasons for attendance, but among married women the concern for family respectability was a motivation for bringing their husbands into church. Other reasons, particularly a desire to ensure the eternal salvation of their life partners, were also no doubt central.

Scholars suggest that in Ontario and the Maritimes, many men joined a church because of pressure from their wives. Single men often preferred masculine leisure activities to church involvement, but many became members when they married, goaded by wifely pressure, religious belief, and the need to play the part of respectable family breadwinner.[20]

We have seen that both family pressures and the hegemony of the Christian churches were weaker in British Columbia than elsewhere in Canada. Many people were far from family, and anti-Christian and anti-church voices were much stronger, more audible, and more normalized than was true in the East. The power of racial divides also made it easier, at least for white working-class men, to define their respectability and social inclusion with little reference to religion.

In this context, did the reasons for church membership change? Did people join a church to assert the respectability that was essential to church-going in Central and Eastern Canada, or was this considered much less necessary in British Columbia? Was church-based respectability less important for women, for men, or for everyone in the province? If it were, how significant were other factors, such as faith and sociability? How much "common sense" cultural power and authority did the churches retain over British Columbians?[21]

The provincial and regional data on church membership presented in Chapter 1 demonstrate that British Columbians of all denominations were less likely than other Canadians to be church members or communicants, with Nova Scotians and Ontarians having particularly high levels of membership or communicant status. Unfortunately, though these census-based data furnish information on both Protestants and Catholics, data for the eight BC, Nova Scotia, and Ontario towns that are the focus of this chapter deal primarily with Protestants. In some towns, the records for all the Protestant churches were available, whereas in others, the records for only certain denominations had survived.[22] Catholic records were often difficult to access, and they rarely provided lists of individual communicants comparable to those records available in the Protestant churches. No comparable Catholic church records were found for these towns, although letters from BC priests to their bishop provide valuable qualitative information about the nature of church involvement (and non-involvement).

Levels of Church Involvement

A first glance at the basic question of church involvement in the eight towns reveals that local realities can mirror regional ones or can be very different.[23] The four Nova Scotia and Ontario communities had relatively high levels of participation, replicating provincial patterns. Amherst has surviving records for the Baptist and Presbyterian churches. Among its Baptists, 23 percent were members, and 25 percent of its Presbyterians were communicants.[24] In the much smaller agricultural centre of Kentville, rates were slightly lower: 25 percent of Anglicans, 18 percent of Baptists, 35 percent of Methodists, and 20 percent of Presbyterians had joined their local congregations. The membership rates in Campbellford and Dunnville were higher than those of Amherst or Kentville (see Appendix: Table 8).[25]

Some of the BC communities had exceptionally low levels of involvement, reflecting regional patterns. Rossland has surviving records for only the Methodist and Presbyterian churches. Only 14 percent of Rossland's Methodists and 8 percent of its Presbyterians could be linked to church membership lists. Similarly, Nelson had only slightly higher levels of involvement: 8 percent of its Anglicans were communicants, as were 21 percent of its Methodists and 11 percent of its Presbyterians.[26] These low levels do not arise from difficulty in linking church members to the manuscript census. In fact, the success rates in making such linkages for Rossland and Nelson were average or above average.[27] In these BC towns, people were just very unlikely to belong to a church, reproducing both provincial patterns and the particularly low membership levels in the Yale and Cariboo district, as discussed in Chapter 1. In these communities, low participation went hand-in-hand with relatively high levels of irreligion, as reflected in the census categories of "no religion" and agnostic.

Whereas Rossland and Nelson followed the regional norm, Revelstoke and Vernon did not. A railroad community and service centre in the Kootenays, Revelstoke had levels of involvement that were in some cases higher than Eastern communities. Among its Anglicans, 28 percent were communicants, as were 39 percent of its Methodists and 19 percent of its Presbyterians. The local Catholic priest was not positive about church involvement, however, and he complained about the many men who did not take communion.[28] Vernon, in the Okanagan Valley, had higher levels

Trinity Methodist Church, Nelson, 1911| *BC Archives, F-04951*

of participation than Revelstoke: 44 percent of its Methodists and 29 percent of its Presbyterians were church members. Its Catholic priest suggested that most of his parishioners were fairly responsible in fulfilling their religious duties, although he was not pleased about the levels of piety in the local Indigenous community.[29] Vernon membership figures are higher than those for the same denominations in most of the Ontario and Nova Scotia towns studied.

These data show that though regional and district analyses can tell us a great deal, they can also blur local differences. To further explore these differences, we need to take a closer look at each community.

Transiency and Immigration

Bob Stewart, one of the few scholars to have studied the secular nature of British Columbia, argues that its relatively high levels of transiency help to explain the greater reluctance among British Columbians to associate themselves with a church.[30]

Various scholars have confirmed that nineteenth-century Canadian society was generally quite transient.[31] The records of the Ontario and Nova

Scotia churches studied in this chapter regularly noted those who were "dismissed" to move to another community. Many Nova Scotians went to the "Boston States" for work, and Amherst's booming economy attracted many new inhabitants.[32] We must therefore be careful not to idealize a settled Eastern Canada as compared to a transient West. Nonetheless, it is also true that all the BC towns studied became established and settled communities only in the decade prior to 1901.[33] Unlike its Eastern counterparts, British Columbia was a province of immigrants. In 1901, only 48 percent of non-Indigenous British Columbians were Canadian-born, as opposed to over 85 percent of Ontarians and well over 90 percent of Maritimers.[34] In the four BC towns studied here, the proportion of immigrants was much higher than for the province as a whole. Many of these migrants were recent arrivals. In Rossland, over 56 percent of residents had entered Canada after 1890, as had 34 percent of Nelson's population. The proportion of recent immigrants was lower in Vernon and Revelstoke, but they nonetheless composed a sizable part of the community.[35] As we saw in Chapter 1, immigrants throughout Canada were much more likely than the rest of the population to define themselves as irreligious. In the four BC towns, recent immigrants were also very unlikely to join a church (see Appendix: Table 9).[36] George Emery discerns a similar pattern on the Prairies, where recent immigrants, including Europeans, Americans, and Britons, were reluctant to become church members. Even those who relocated to a town that had a church of their denomination often found its rituals and hymns new and unfamiliar, thus discouraging participation.[37]

Transiency was not associated solely with recent immigrants. Lodgers and boarders also tended to be more transient than those who lived in a nuclear family. In Chapter 1, we saw that lodgers and boarders were particularly likely to define themselves as irreligious. In the eight towns studied here, both East and West, lodgers were significantly less likely than those who resided with close kin to be church members.[38] In Rossland, only 4 percent of Methodist boarders were members, whereas 18 percent of Methodists who lived with relatives had joined the church; patterns were similar among Presbyterians.[39] The percentages were higher in Vernon: for example, 56 percent of Methodists who lived with family were church members, as compared to 25 percent of boarders. Nonetheless, the basic pattern was the same as in Rossland, the other BC towns, and the four Ontario and Nova Scotia communities. What differs is the proportion of people who were likely to be lodgers in each region. In British Columbia, 25 percent of men were boarders or lodgers, a significantly higher proportion than in Central and Eastern Canada.[40] The proportion of boarders was consistently higher in the four BC towns than in the Ontario and Nova Scotia ones.[41]

Transiency both increases the willingness to identify as irreligious and reduces the interest in joining a church. Relatively high levels of transiency in British Columbia thus help to explain its higher levels of irreligion and lower levels of church involvement. This is especially true because most transients were men, often far from relatives who could link faith, church belonging, and family or who could coerce participation in a church.

Gender

However, transiency and distance from family are not the whole story. Vernon, with fewer lodgers per capita than Rossland, Nelson, and Revelstoke but still well above Eastern norms, had higher levels of church involvement than most of the Ontario and Nova Scotia communities studied. In at least some BC towns, transiency was also associated with a certain occupation. In the boom-and-bust economy of the Kootenays, miners were especially transient.[42] They were over-represented among the irreligious on the census, and in both Rossland and Nelson were among the least likely to join a church. No Methodist or Anglican miner in Nelson was a communicant, and only two of its Presbyterian miners appeared in the church records, making up 4 percent of Nelson's Presbyterian miners. Rossland miners were slightly more likely to be involved in a church: fourteen Methodist miners were members, at 7 percent of all Methodist miners, whereas only five Presbyterian miners were, at 2 percent of all Presbyterian miners.[43] With so few miners joining a church, those who did were greeted with much enthusiasm. In reminiscing about his time as a Rossland Methodist minister between 1909 and 1911, Reverend J.A. Dow wrote about a popular Bible class: "Part of the exceeding joy was caused by the number of men from the mines who were regular attenders and even boosters for the class."[44]

We know that everywhere in Canada, the irreligious tended to be male, but what role did gender play in church involvement? Like earlier studies, this one shows that Canadian women were more likely than men to associate themselves with a church. In Campbellford, which had generally high levels of participation, Anglican, Baptist, and Presbyterian women were at least twice as likely as their male equivalents to be communicants. Even among Campbellford Methodists, 44 percent of women were members, as compared to 33 percent of men (see Table 10). Although gender differences were not as striking in every community, female church members typically outnumbered their male counterparts.

In "godless" British Columbia, where non-Indigenous men dramatically outnumbered non-Indigenous women in 1901, the bulk of members in most denominations of the four towns were *still* female. This is most striking in Nelson and Rossland. In both towns, the census shows that though male Presbyterian adherents outnumbered female ones by about two to one, female Presbyterian communicants were more plentiful than male ones. For example, in Nelson, only 50 of the more than 729 male Presbyterians were communicants, whereas 68 of the 356 female Presbyterians were. Among Methodists in Rossland and Nelson, men again strikingly outnumbered women, but female church members outnumbered male ones. Even in Vernon and Revelstoke, women outnumbered men in the Presbyterian churches, as they did in the Revelstoke Methodist church, although men consistently outnumbered women in these communities.

This evidence reinforces the popular adage that men left God behind when they crossed the Rocky Mountains. As Reverend J. Robinson noted of Rossland in 1901, many men "who came from fine Christian homes ... forgot their past and became so Westernized that they were of little or no help to the Church numerically, financially or spiritually."[45] Jimmy White, a former gold miner in the Kootenay town of Fort Steele, explained the process more bluntly. Interviewed by Imbert Orchard about Fort Steele religious life during the years before the First World War, he declared, "I quit altogether. I never went inside none of the damn churches after I get away from the East." Asked if many churchgoing people lived in Fort Steele, he replied, "Some women, that's all. Hardly ever a man going to them."[46]

Despite White's dismissal of them, BC women did indeed attend church. For many white women who moved west, the churches served as a symbol of familiarity and community in a strange environment. And when services were not available, they were much missed. While teaching in the Nicola Valley and waiting for a minister to be posted there, Jessie McQueen complained, "It's awful to be so long without preaching." When she moved to Nicola Lake a few years later, she greatly enjoyed its Wednesday night Methodist Bible classes, though there were only six regular students. When the classes were temporarily cancelled in the spring of 1892 due to the minister's overseas trip, Jessie was "left rather forlorn and homeless, so to speak."[47] Her sister Annie, who in 1898 settled with her young family in Tobacco Plains, a remote BC outpost near the Montana border, had even less in the way of religious options, leaving her miserable. In December 1898, she wrote to her mother in Nova Scotia, lamenting that "there is

Jimmy White, panning on the Wild Horse River, Fort Steele | *BC Archives, C-05510*

nothing out here to make life pleasant, not a service, or a lecture, nor a Sunday School ... oh dear! Life is monotonous." This remained a major concern: a few months later, she wrote to her sister, again complaining that there was "no church, no Sunday school ... Nothing of any interest ever going on."

Although social activities that would appeal to Christian women were in short supply, options existed for rougher male sociability. Soon after Annie's arrival in Tobacco Plains, a hotel was built nearby. To her horror, it sold alcohol. As she told her mother, "I do not like the idea of liquor being sold so near to us," but she could not prevent it.[48]

Annie could not get the hotel closed down, but she did what she could about the lack of spiritual options, spending some of her limited "chicken money" on subscriptions to the popular religious journals *Missionary Outlook* and *Youth's Companion,* to give her some spiritual news and inspiration, and to help her provide some Christian education and entertainment for

Annie McQueen Gordon wedding photo 1889 | *Family collection*

her children. In August 1899, a Methodist minister from Montana informed her that he would be holding monthly services nearby. The fact that he was an American made her wary, but at least she could now attend services. To the Presbyterian McQueen, his Methodism seemed less an issue than his Americanness.[49]

Women in British Columbia seemed quite willing to attend the services of other denominations. In Central and Eastern Canada, Presbyterians and Methodists often attended each other's services and co-operated in joint revival campaigns. Interdenominational boundaries appear to have been drawn more broadly in British Columbia, although most evangelicals would not have set foot in a Catholic service. A teacher in Langley, British Columbia, Phoebe McInnes regularly attended her own evangelical Protestant church, usually twice every Sunday. Her diary also occasionally reports that she went to Salvation Army services during visits to nearby Vancouver. In the various small communities where she taught, Jessie

McQueen often went to Methodist services and sometimes Anglican ones as well, although her letters home contain critical assessments of the latter.[50]

The Anglican Sarah Crease was a regular churchgoer in her home city of Victoria. In 1880, she accompanied her husband, Henry, a BC judge, on a trip to Kamloops and Barkerville. Every Sunday during their journey, she made a note of whether the community in which they were stopping had a church. Notations of "no church" appeared often, and with regret. On churchless Sundays, Sarah and Henry read together from the Bible.[51] On one October Sunday, they were in such a rush that they had to travel, and Sarah recorded that they "left at 10 A.M. *very sorry* we could not stop for Mr. Sheldon's morning service." Although she went to services whenever she could, she was not always impressed. In Kamloops, as her journal reported, "we all attended the Methodist Meeting in the Court house ... Mr. Turner (a Ranting radical) addressed the Meeting – painfully unedifying. Hope never to be ... obliged to listen to anything so illogical and irreverential [again]."[52] Women brought both their religious faith and their religious prejudices with them when they came to British Columbia.

Adele Perry points out that though the BC gender imbalance may have given white women an advantage in heterosexual relations, it certainly disadvantaged them in homosocial ones. Perry quotes Jessie McQueen as being "just sick of the faces of men," who hugely outnumbered women in the community where she was teaching.[53] For women like Jessie and her sister, church services offered not only a familiar space, spiritual comfort, and welcome social opportunities in a strange environment but perhaps the only place where the faces of women might outnumber those of men. The provision of social and spiritual comfort helps to explain why the proportion of women who involved themselves in the Revelstoke and Nelson churches was similar to that of the Ontario and Nova Scotia towns, and why female participation in Vernon actually exceeded that of the Eastern ones (see Appendix: Table 10). Rossland is the sole exception here: though its female residents were much more likely than its men to be involved in a church, they were still less likely than women in the East or in the other BC communities studied. Perhaps this sprang in part from class-conscious hostility to the churches among many men and women in what was a polarized mining community, reflected, as we have seen, in relatively high numbers of Rosslanders who had no religion.

Rossland's lower female participation rate may also have been associated with female involvement in rough culture. The town's sex trade workers would not have been welcome in its churches.[54] Rossland may have been a particularly wide open town, but Nelson and Revelstoke had a significant number of brothels. Although "respectable" female residents would see sex trade workers as outcasts, evidence reveals that some were religious and did support the churches financially. Doug Abrahamson, who grew up in turn-of-the-century Revelstoke, mentioned a black madam named Black Mary, who was "a very religious woman despite her occupation." Mrs. Lydia Graham, also of Revelstoke, recalled that its sex trade workers "never mixed with *anybody* but were awfully, awfully good-hearted. If a church wanted say, anything, if they needed money or anything else they could ask the girls and the girls would help them out."[55]

Although more women may have stayed away from Rossland churches than in other BC communities, they were nonetheless more likely than their men to be there. And though membership rates were particularly low in Rossland, its population of over six thousand was served by six churches, with an apparently more-than-respectable turnout each Sunday. Jessie McQueen attended the Presbyterian and Methodist churches in Rossland

Jessie McQueen 1885 | *Family collection*

between 1896 and 1899. As Jean Barman notes, she felt a connection to both ministers because of their Nova Scotia roots, and she found time for regular church services, prayer meetings, and various church-sponsored social activities. She owned a small house in Rossland, where she boarded a number of single working women, many of whom had Nova Scotia connections and most of whom were also active in the churches. Jessie, who was not unaffected by the town's secular outlook, also enjoyed considerably more secular leisure activities than she had in the past, and one of her boarders was a woman "of no belief."[56] At the same time, Jessie's connections with ministers and housemates from Nova Scotia remind us that many women, and some men, brought their religious beliefs and practices with them when they came to British Columbia.

Women's Church Groups

A brief survey of Kootenay newspapers reveals the range of church activities open to white settler women. They were similar to the activities "at home," which were very common in the Ontario and Nova Scotia communities included in this study. Most Protestant churches in Revelstoke, Rossland, Nelson, and Vernon offered weekly prayer meetings in addition to Sunday services and Sunday School (where many women taught). Young people could join the Epworth League, affiliated with the Methodist Church, and young Presbyterians could join the Christian Endeavour society.[57] Both accepted male and female members, but even in Ontario young women predominated in these social and educational organizations. Christian women of all ages could also join Ladies Aid Societies affiliated with their churches. The societies organized a range of activities that were intended as fundraisers for the church, but they also provided social opportunities for members and the larger community. For example, the Revelstoke Anglican Ladies Aid held both a Violet Tea and an "At Home" for local women in February 1901, and that same month the Methodist Ladies Aid and the Presbyterian Ladies Aid each held a musical social. In February 1899, the Nelson Methodist Ladies Aid organized a social tea to raise funds for a new parsonage, in May the Baptist Ladies Aid offered a social that included music, readings, and recitations, and in June the Catholic Ladies Aid held a fundraising dance to furnish the new church.[58] Newspaper reports sometimes mentioned "large attendance" at these events, but some groups seem to have struggled. Even the Catholic dance, which might be expected to arouse much interest, had "not quite so many of the sterner

Kaslo Methodist Ladies Aid Society, 1898. Note the two racialized women, Arvell Perkins and daughter, exceptions to the uniform whiteness of regional churches. | *BC Archives, C-07789*

sex as should have been there."[59] Notations about meetings to "reorganize" some of these bodies, which appear to have lapsed, such as the Nelson Presbyterian women's missionary society and the Revelstoke Presbyterian Christian Endeavour society, hint at ongoing challenges. Father Thayer's letter to his bishop, complaining that his choir had been decimated because a few key families had left Revelstoke, points to the difficulties that such organizations faced in transient communities where church involvement was low.[60] Rossland seemed to have experienced the most problems in this regard. Despite Jessie McQueen's reports, the Rossland newspaper recorded fewer church activities than in Nelson and Revelstoke.[61]

Some women's church groups may have struggled in the BC resource communities, but the women who joined them valued their participation, as is evident in many oral history interviews conducted during the 1960s and 1970s. Except for ministers and a few churchgoing men, most male interviewees said nothing about the churches or, when asked directly, expressed either hostility, indifference, or some limited version of fuzzy fidelity. On the other hand, many women spoke at great length and with enjoyment about church-related social activities. For example, unlike her coal-miner husband, who remarked, "No, no, no, we didn't go to church," Mrs. Edwards of East Wellington, near Nanaimo, had a great deal to say about her church involvement. She "used to walk to Sunday school, up at

Wellington and went to church. I used to go to Sunday school, and church in the English church, and walk home. That would be about 4 miles. I sang in the choir in church too."[62] In another interview collection, Mrs. Esther Gardom of Greenwood, a Kootenay mining community, recalled that "every church had bazaars, and almost everybody, whether they belonged to the congregation or not, provided home baking for every church." Mrs. Muriel Lang of Revelstoke also remembered baking for church teas and stated that "the church was a very important part of people's life at that, in my early days, because ... you went there not only for your church service, and the children went to Sunday School ... They'd have the big Christmas concert."[63] Mrs. Muriel Campbell, also of Revelstoke, mentioned her involvement in the local Presbyterian church, of attending Bible class, and of being active in the Young People's Society. Other women spoke with evident enjoyment of singing in a choir, of attending three services on Sundays, and of participating in women's church organizations.[64] Scholars of North American women's history have long noted the importance of these bodies in providing women with a respectable social space beyond their homes and also conveying some limited power in contexts where the public sphere was primarily male. In the world of British Columbia, which was far more male than the rest of Canada, they furnished women with an accepted space for female sociability.[65]

In *Sojourning Sisters,* Jean Barman discusses Nova Scotians Jessie and Annie McQueen, who taught school in BC locations of varying remoteness. She argues that through their teaching and their religious and moral examples, such women helped "domesticate" British Columbia to fit the more moral and pious mould of Eastern Canada.[66] The McQueens and other white Christian settler women certainly hoped to attain this goal, very much in line with nineteenth-century tropes of white women as a civilizing influence among the wild and rough bachelors of the frontier.[67] However, at least in terms of religious practice, they seem to have achieved little success in British Columbia during this period. Nonetheless, unlike most white men who migrated to the province, these women typically held fast to their religious faith and practices, seeking as much as possible to re-create their religious, social, and cultural worlds in their new home.

Religion, Sexuality, and Race

Re-creating religious, social, and cultural worlds also meant reproducing prejudices and exclusionary practices. In British Columbia, some prejudices were weakened by circumstances, whereas others were sharpened and reinforced. As we saw in Chapter 3, Protestant biases against Catholics were sometimes attenuated in the province. This may have been particularly true among irreligious men, for whom the significance of religious divisions may have faded in tandem with religious belief. Certainly, many pious evangelical women were unwilling to attend Catholic services. Nonetheless, residing in isolated areas where the numbers of white Christians were small meant that some compromises could be accepted. Living in a farming area with very few white neighbours, Annie McQueen excitedly reported to her mother in 1898 that "we have a real live Presbyterian preacher in the house tonight, and had service in the schoolhouse at which nearly all the Landing were present. Our Catholic woman lent her organ, and even played the hymns for us, and brought all her family out to service."[68] The reference to "our Catholic woman" suggests appreciation but perhaps not sisterhood. As we saw in Chapter 3, musical assistance could go both ways, with Methodists volunteering to fill the gaps in a Catholic choir.[69]

In the Kootenay mining towns, female churchgoers often lived within a few blocks or less of the red light district, which would have featured a dozen or more brothels, each with a number of sex trade workers. Many churchgoing women came from regions where prostitution was less visible, so this experience would have been new for them. In some cases, it merely deepened their prejudice, and they aided male church leaders in moral reform efforts to have the brothels closed down and the women forced out of town. Other female church members were less judgmental. Lydia Graham recalled that her mother, who had several children and was a member of the Revelstoke Catholic church, was pleased to accept the assistance of a sex trade worker in helping with her baby, even though the woman had told her, "I guess you won't let me in your house, I'm not a decent girl."[70] Doug Abrahamson, whose parents ran one of Revelstoke's premier hotels, and whose mother was a "great church worker," told the following story:

> One time they were gonna have a clean up in town and one of the ladies of the church called at Mother's place ... and ... told Mother ... "Now, we gotta circulate the petition, we're trying to get those houses downtown ... get the town cleaned up a bit." My mother looked at her and said, "Mrs. So-in-so ... I've been living alongside 'a those women," she said, "for the last 20 to 30 years." She said, "I have yet to see one of them come out on the street and bring any husband or son into them." So, she said "I won't sign your petition."[71]

In this instance, proximity could generate more tolerance than might be expected. However, when racial differences were involved, proximity could occasionally engender a recognition of shared humanity but could not overcome deep-seated racism. White Christian women strongly distinguished themselves from racialized women. In the Kootenays, most of their church groups focused on raising money for the pressing needs of the small churches, but the women's missionary societies that did exist raised money to convert and uplift Chinese and Japanese women overseas or Indigenous women closer to home. The latter may have been an abstraction for some Euro-Canadian women before they came to British Columbia, but they were very present in the province.[72]

Jean Barman points out that, in connection with at least some of the mixed-race children whom she taught, Jessie McQueen was more sympathetic and supportive than most white Christian British Columbians. Nonetheless, she saw these children, and more particularly their Indigenous mothers, as inferior "others" who were not the equals of Euro-Canadian Christian women.[73] A rich literature on the Christian missionary women who worked closely with Indigenous women and girls in British Columbia and the Northwest more generally reveals that though the latter were seen as worthy of salvation and assimilation to "civilized" norms, their perceived racialized characteristics meant that they would never be accepted as full equals.[74]

Other Christian women were more explicit in their racism and sense of distance from Indigenous people. Mrs. Louise Iverson of Port Essington was perhaps most typical in her attitudes about the acceptance of separate worship spaces according to race. Asked about church involvement in her community, she said that any European settlers who "attended church went to the *Anglican* Church, which was at the other end of the town." When the interviewer asked why the European settlers were separated from the Indigenous community, who worshipped in the Methodist church, she replied, "Um, well the um, Native people, the Methodist church would be on the reservation because it ... was definitely the Native church."[75]

White Christian women were also unlikely to cross the racialized boundaries that separated them from Chinese immigrants, sharing the violent anti-Asian racism of their male counterparts. At the same time, many middle- and upper-class Euro-Canadian women employed Chinese men as domestic servants in their homes. Such relationships may have forced some of them to recognize a level of common humanity between themselves and their Chinese employees, but as Lorraine Brown notes, they generally retained racist stereotypes in dealing with their servants, commonly treating them in condescending and even cruel ways. Even a woman whom Brown suggests challenged such behaviour, Alice Barrett Parke of Vernon, was unable to see her servant Loo-Yee as an equal, though she tried to treat him with respect. When she attempted to teach him about Christianity, he rejected her overtures because he felt that most Christians were hypocrites who did not live up to the precepts of their faith. For the frustrated Parke, the refusal of Loo-Yee and other Chinese individuals to accept Christianity created a major gulf between them. As she lamented, "it seems dreadful to think of these poor creatures right at our door, right in our households, having no real knowledge of the true God."[76] Even the Chinese who did convert to Christianity were not seen as equals by their white co-religionists. Male and female missionaries to the Chinese in British Columbia may have challenged Chinese exclusion campaigns and called for more humanitarian treatment, but as in the case of missionaries to Indigenous people, their belief in the equality of souls did not erase racialized social hierarchies.[77] For many working-class white men in British Columbia, whiteness alone defined their sense of respectability, but for white Christian women, and many men, whiteness and Christianity were so tightly interlinked as to leave little possibility for equality with those who did not share both characteristics.

When Euro-Canadians went to church, they brought these attitudes with them. None of the BC towns studied appear to have had any non-white church members, despite significant Asian and First Nations populations in or near them, as well as an African Canadian group in Nelson. The African Canadian women, who were members of nearby Kaslo's Methodist Ladies' Aid, are the only exceptions I found. British Columbians of European origin were not oblivious to the religious practices of the racialized groups who shared their province, but they did not want to worship with them. Asian and Indigenous people were particularly "beyond the pale." Christian missionaries of Chinese origin may sometimes have spoken in mainstream churches, but they seem to have ministered to Chinese converts and those whom they sought to convert elsewhere.[78] Euro-Canadian interviewees referred to the Chinese mission church in Nanaimo, with the very clear sense that all Christian Chinese Canadians would worship there. Revelstoke interviewees knew that the local "joss house," or temple, was a place of worship for Chinese people, and they also mentioned observing the "strange" rituals of Chinese funerals.[79] When missionaries travelled along the coast by boat, trying to convert both "godless" men in logging and mining camps and Indigenous inhabitants in coastal villages, their visits were done separately, as much as possible.[80]

Earlier Methodist camp meetings in British Columbia included both Indigenous and white participants, there is some evidence that a few African Canadians attended certain Victoria churches, and some of the "white" people who worshipped in local churches would have been of mixed European and Indigenous heritage. Nonetheless, I found no evidence of inclusive congregations in Nelson, Revelstoke, Rossland, or Vernon.[81]

The Ontario and Nova Scotia towns were not as completely exclusionary. In Dunnville and Campbellford, both with tiny African Canadian populations, one church member was defined as "Black" in each community. In Kentville, which had a separate African Canadian church, two African Canadians attended the mainstream churches. Racism was integral to Canadian discourse and to institutions across Canada, but race was a particularly charged issue in British Columbia.

In British Columbia, most white Christian women clung to their faith – and to their racism. Most were neither able nor willing to question it, although it limited their social and religious options and intensified their isolation, particularly in small resource communities.[82]

Class and Gender

And what of class? Did Euro-Canadian women of all classes worship together in British Columbia? Oral history interviews suggest that the churches were important for many working-class women, a perception that my eight-community study reinforced. Previous studies of Central and Eastern Canadian towns suggest that class could make a difference in church involvement, but that middle- and working-class women were particularly likely to worship together in smaller communities, a pattern that was also true of at least some men.[83] In British Columbia, class consciousness kept many miners out of church. Did this consciousness extend to women in the four BC towns, or did the churches offer women of differing classes a shared solace? What of working-class men who were not miners? Were they likely to attend church with their middle-class counterparts? More generally, are class divisions in involvement clearer in the West than in the East?

Whereas some generalizations can be made about differences between the BC, Ontario, and Nova Scotia towns, a close study again discloses the importance of local conditions in explaining patterns of church participation.[84] In Campbellford, which had a history of paternalistic industrial relations and no record of class conflict, middle-class people were more involved than their working-class counterparts in the churches. This was true for both men and women. However, gender appeared to be more significant than class, as working-class women were more likely than middle-class men to join a church (see Appendix: Table 11). In Dunnville, an industrial community with links to the nearby industrialized and unionized Niagara region, class was significant for both men and women. Fifty-five percent of middle-class women belonged to a Dunnville church, as compared to only 32 percent of working-class women. The differences among men are not as stark, but there was still a significant gap between the involvement rates of middle- and working-class men. And though women were more likely than men of their class to be church members, middle-class male Dunnville residents were more likely than working-class women to join a church (see Table 11). Dunnville was the only community of the eight where this was the case.

Whereas the class and gender patterns of Campbellford and Dunnville differed to some extent, those of Amherst and Kentville were markedly similar. In both towns, class appeared to be largely irrelevant to church involvement. Women were more likely than men to participate, though this difference was not very large. Most striking is that, in both communities, membership rates were almost identical for women of all classes and men of all classes (see Table 11). Such marked commonalities suggest that membership was not a barrier to working-class people who sought full involvement in a church, but they do raise interesting questions. The absence of class differences may be fairly readily explained in Kentville, a largely agricultural service centre with limited industry, but it is more difficult to explain in Amherst, a heavily industrialized town that was to experience considerable class tension over the coming two decades. Perhaps long-standing family ties to the churches overcame more recently emerging class divisions in Amherst. Cross-class ethnic ties may also have been significant, especially among Presbyterians, most of whom would have been of Scottish or Irish descent. Deeply held religious beliefs may also have overcome class divisions, at least on Sundays.[85] Finally, the fact that Amherst had voted overwhelmingly to be a "dry" community suggests that this town may have had more cross-class moral consensus regarding rough leisure than was the case in many BC communities.[86] Whereas these are all possible explanations, more study is needed to help us understand the complete lack of class differences in church membership patterns in these Maritime towns.

The nature of class differences varied between the Nova Scotia and Ontario towns, but what was consistent was that the presence or the absence of class differences affected men and women similarly. If there were no class differences in church involvement, as in Nova Scotia, this was true for both women and men; in Ontario, any class differences appeared to affect both sexes. But in British Columbia, these patterns were less clear-cut. In Revelstoke, Rossland, and Nelson, working-class men were less likely than middle-class men to join a church, and working-class women were more likely than middle-class men to do so. Particularly striking is that despite class differences in involvement rates among men, the rates for middle- and working-class women are about the same in both Revelstoke and Rossland. Even in Nelson, where the rates of middle- and working-class women differed to some extent, this occurred only among Methodists. Middle- and working-class Presbyterian women were almost equally likely to be communicants, replicating the patterns of Revelstoke and Rossland.

During this period, Revelstoke and Nelson saw their share of class conflict, and Rossland was very polarized by class. Workplace tensions may have kept some men out of church, and conflicts over leisure may have been equally relevant for others. Transiency may also have made church unappealing to many working-class men, both miners and others. These issues appear to have been much less relevant for working-class women. Among both working- and middle-class women in Revelstoke and Nelson, participation rates were similar to those of Eastern Canada. What made the participation rates of Nelson so low was the poor showing of men, especially working-class men. Whereas Rossland women were less likely than their Eastern counterparts to attend services, 17 percent of both middle- and working-class female Rosslanders were active in a church. What does this suggest about working-class BC women? Were they a pious and conservative force, lacking the class consciousness of their men, as the *Western Clarion* and other contemporary socialist rhetoric suggested? Perhaps, but men who rejected the churches had the rich associational life of fraternal orders and unions as well as the enjoyments of homosocial culture. As we saw in Chapter 3, some fraternal orders did have auxiliaries that accepted female members, but the orders were much more available to men. Certainly, any aspect of rough culture was closed to women who wished to define themselves as respectable. Indeed, living in small communities where brothels were very visible, some women may have felt a need to reinforce their own respectability through churchgoing. More importantly, for white working-class women, as for their middle-class counterparts, the church provided much-needed female sociability and the comfort of faith in a new environment.

This is not to say that class was irrelevant for working-class women in mining communities, a point that is particularly germane in the case of Rossland. The data on church membership are based on records linked to the 1901 census, which was taken during the spring. Later that year, Rossland was split by a major strike in the local mines. As a minister who was in Rossland just afterward noted, "When we arrived in Rossland in 1903 we found the city suffering from the after slump of the great strike. The churches suffered very severely and several of them were closed. A spirit of ill will was abroad and the community was divided into hostile camps. It was hard to keep that evil spirit out of the church."[87] In the context of major labour conflict, it would be very surprising if many working-class women who were related to the miners did not choose to leave the church. If they did remain, they probably discovered that Rossland's "hostile camps" extended past the church door and that they and their middle-class sisters were on opposite sides.

Gender and class patterns of church involvement in the three Kootenay towns were relatively similar, but the Okanagan community of Vernon, an agricultural centre of ranching and fruit farming, looks very different. It consisted of fewer than a thousand people, so the numbers in the church records are small, making conclusions tentative. Nonetheless, its working-class men and women appear to have had higher church participation rates than its middle-class men and women. This may reflect the limitations of the data, but it certainly suggests that class concerns did not keep working people away from church. This point is bolstered by Jenny Clayton's study of Vernon, which contends that class was largely irrelevant to the social and community life of the town.[88]

In any event, church participation rates were high for all classes and both genders in Vernon. The centrality of the churches in this and other Okanagan Valley towns even appears to have drawn in many young men, who were often the most reluctant to enter a church. In both oral histories and written reminiscences, men point out that this had little to do with piety. Instead, they saw church as a crucial site of heterosexual interaction. In his written memoirs, C.W. Halliday noted that "all we young Englishmen were quite regular church-goers, certainly not from any religious motives; but there were girls to be seen, and it was a very pleasant way for the married women to gather in a bachelor or two after church and ask them to dinner."[89] When interviewed during the 1960s about early life in the Okanagan, Charlie Shaw acknowledged, "I wasn't very religious, but we all belonged to the church, because you had to ... That was the only amusement. If you wanted to meet a girl at all, or any young people, why

Church of England, All Saints, Vernon, c. 191–. Note that although Vernon was much smaller than Nelson or Rossland, its church was larger and more elaborate than theirs. | *BC Archives, F-09753*

you had to be a member of the church, because the church socials was about all that was going on in those days." Paddy Acland recalled a recommendation on how to secure the company of a girl. The first step was to join the Baptist choir. When he expressed unwillingness to do so, his advisor told him that "if you take the girl around to sing in the choir, you have the pleasure of taking her back in the dark afterwards, and nobody at home knows exactly what time the choir stops singing."[90]

Church involvement in Vernon seemed to parallel that of other BC agricultural areas. Margaret Stewart, who lived in the farming district of Surrey from the mid-1880s on, told Imbert Orchard about the popularity of visiting preachers. Protestant ministers of various denominations, from Anglicans "to real fiery, hot Free Methodists," took turns preaching in the schoolhouse, and all the local Protestants attended these services: "They would all turn out. Even the old bachelors use to come out to a service very good." Everyone came, regardless of denomination, because "see, there wasn't very much going on ... It didn't make very much difference who was doing the preaching, there'd be a crowd anyhow, and they would come out to it." However, a preacher who "said there was no salvation outside of his church" was not popular with this Surrey audience. This pattern parallels Paul Voisey's findings for the Prairies, where people often attended churches regardless of denomination, at least partly for social reasons. Like

Margaret Stewart, they were much happier with ministers who recognized the interdenominational nature of their audience than with those who preached narrowly denominational sermons.[91]

The British and the Americans

With a quarter of its population born in "Britain or the Empire," Vernon prided itself on being "more British than the British."[92] This also helps to explain the high levels of church involvement among all classes in Vernon, since the British-born residents in all four BC towns had much higher levels than the other large immigrant group, the Americans.[93] At the same time, the small size of Vernon, its agricultural base, and its apparent lack of serious class divisions may have been more significant than ethnicity in explaining the importance of the churches to community social life, even for young men. As we have seen, in Nanaimo, which was populated largely by British miners, the majority of men felt some combination of indifference and at best fuzzy fidelity toward the churches. In Vernon, young men went to church to meet young women, but, when asked if he attended church, Nanaimo miner George Edwards responded, "No, no, no, we didn't go to church. No we used to wait till the girls come out o' church!"[94]

The fact that in the Kootenay towns, the British were more likely than the Americans to be church members reflects the pattern discussed in Chapter 1, with Americans making up a disproportionately large share of the irreligious in this region.[95] In Nelson and Rossland, those who participated in a church were likely to be either British- or Canadian-born families. George Ferguson describes Nelson's evangelical community, which was located in "Upper Town," as far as possible from the brothels of "Lower Town." Its members strictly observed the Sabbath, and their leisure activities centred on the church, with strawberry socials and Sunday School picnics. This community was composed of "families from Ontario and some from England."[96] The importance of family ties, and of British or Eastern Canadian roots, in re-creating the church communities of "home" is clear here.

Single Men, Class, and the Churches

Ethnicity was important, but so was the fact that most of these British and Canadian church members lived with their families. What of men on their own? How likely were they to join a church? Certainly, clergy across Canada identified young single men as a problem, and as we have seen, this was exacerbated in British Columbia, where many young men were far from the influence of their Christian families.

But many married male British Columbians also lived and worked far from their wives and families. Did they too kick over the traces once they reached the Wild West, transforming the "young man problem" of the Eastern churches into the "man problem" of the West?

An examination of sex, class, marital status, and church involvement in the Ontario and Nova Scotia towns generally supports previous assumptions about single men's poor participation. In Campbellford, Amherst, and Kentville, single men of all classes had by far the lowest levels of church membership. In Amherst, the membership rate of middle-class single men (less than 4 percent) was actually lower than that of their working-class equivalents (6 percent), but class was largely irrelevant in this town – its single men simply did not join a church (see Appendix: Table 12). Their absence is also confirmed in the Amherst Baptist Church newsletter, which regrets their poor attendance at meetings of the Baptist Young People's Union.[97] Dunnville is somewhat different from Campbellford, Amherst, and Kentville in that its working-class single men – but not their middle-class counterparts – had the lowest levels of church participation. The involvement rate of middle-class single men was close to that of married middle-class men. For single men, as for other social groups in Dunnville, class was the key dividing line when it came to participation in a church.

When one looks at the impact of marital status on church involvement in Nelson, Rossland, Revelstoke, and Vernon, some patterns remain consistent. Among women, marital status and class were largely irrelevant, but the situation was quite different for BC men.

As discussed earlier, the overall figures for male involvement seem to suggest that working-class men in Nelson, Rossland, and Revelstoke were less likely than middle-class men to associate themselves with a church. However, for married men, class did not appear to make much difference. Married working-class male Rosslanders had some tendency to be less involved than their middle-class equivalents, but the pattern is not particularly strong. In Nelson and Revelstoke, middle- and working-class married men were equally likely to join a church. In Revelstoke, 36 percent of married middle-class men and 35 percent of married working-class men did so. This was higher than the proportion of working-class married men who were church members in any of the four Ontario and Nova Scotia towns. The large numbers of less transient and more skilled railway workers in the CPR town of Revelstoke may help to explain its relatively high levels of involvement among working-class married men. Indeed, other studies have shown the importance of respectability for this section of the working class. Even in Rossland, a minister noted the "group of Railroad men who used to occupy very regularly the seats well to the front [of the church] on the right side of the platform."[98]

In Nelson, Rossland, and Revelstoke, very few single men of any class went to church, so no definitive conclusions can be drawn. Nonetheless, some interesting class differences may have existed. In Nelson, both middle- and working-class single men were less involved in the churches than other groups, but even there working-class single men were the least likely to participate (see Table 12). In Rossland and Revelstoke, middle-class married and single men were equally likely to attend a church, whereas single working-class men were again very unlikely to do so.[99] In Rossland's case at least, this may say as much about the generally low levels of church involvement as it does about single men. Nonetheless, these figures suggest that class was more relevant to single men's participation in British Columbia than in most of Central and Eastern Canada, other than in towns like Dunnville, where class was also a central factor. Perhaps in small mining and railroad towns, where class was a major dividing line among men, some bachelors sought to assert their respectability and to identify themselves with the middle class by attending church services.[100] In Nelson and Rossland, up-and-coming middle-class single men could join the Nelson or Rossland Clubs, which were created for successful professionals and business people. The fact that the clubs were equipped with bars and card-playing rooms implies that many of their members may not have belonged to a church, at least not to an evangelical church. But other members would have been communicants and may have drawn aspiring young men with them into the churches. Of course, some middle-class young men who were far from home may also have sought the solace of faith through church involvement.

One must not exaggerate these differences, as the numbers are small, and at least in Nelson, both middle- and working-class single men were very unlikely to go to church, and low levels of involvement among all Rossland men indicate the appealing pull of rough culture.

Other than in Rossland, however, church participation was higher for married men than for single ones. Although they were less likely than married women to attend church, the differences in their membership rates were not that large in most of the four BC towns, suggesting that most married couples went to church together, as was the pattern in the East.

Whereas in Amherst and Kentville, married men and married women of all classes were almost equally likely to attend church, suggesting a solid connection between family and faith, the patterns in Campbellford and Dunnville are much like those of British Columbia. The overall involvement rates of Campbellford and Dunnville tended to be higher, but the gap between the rates of married men and married women of all classes was similar in the BC and Ontario towns (Table 12).

The married couples who did attend a BC church brought with them patterns that also existed in Central and Eastern Canada – either before marriage or soon afterward, the women generally (but definitely not always) managed to bring their husbands into church.[101] The McQueen family provides some telling examples of this. In a letter to Jessie McQueen, her cousin Jessie Olding stated, "how glad I was when Hugh told me that there was nothing to hinder him from being a Christian and that he meant to try to live as a Christian." Soon after this reassuring declaration, the couple were engaged. Jessie's sister Annie, who started her married life in Ontario and then moved back to British Columbia, soon persuaded her husband to join the local Methodist church, where they "commenced family worship."[102] As in Ontario and Nova Scotia, the combination of faith, the need to assert the respectability of the family breadwinner, and wifely nagging prompted many married men to join a church. Once that step was taken, couples attended services with their children, setting a "good example" of moral, Christian family togetherness, values brought with them from Ontario, Nova Scotia, and elsewhere in Canada. In British Columbia, middle-class families were much more likely than working-class ones to be found in church. This pattern is reflected in the diaries and letters of many middle- and upper-middle class BC children, which testify to regular church attendance, as noted in Kathryn Bridge's study.[103]

We must take care not to over-generalize here. Although wives did inveigle their husbands into church, some husbands grew up with firm faith. For example, the daughter of Price Ellison, an early Okanagan rancher, recalled that he "had a great sense of sin and a great sense of righteousness. He was a very, very Christian man and we were brought up that way – the Sabbath day, to keep it holy – and I never knew him to deviate all his life."[104] Lillian Dixon of Nanaimo spoke of the religiosity of her Finnish Lutheran parents, noting that they regularly went to church and that her father, who had "read the bible twice from one end to the other," was "quite religious."[105] Tom Johnston of Nanaimo, who eventually became a minister, mentioned that his parents were converted "as young people before their marriage" and said that both were "involved in the church their whole life

... Sunday was always regarded as a special day. That was Day of Days when father wouldn't be working. He would be home, the whole family would be together."[106]

Such patterns of family church involvement, imported from Central and Eastern Canada, and often from Britain and other parts of Europe, did not automatically disappear in British Columbia. At the same time in some BC communities, particularly more polarized ones like Rossland, one could also find whole families, including children, who told the census-taker that they were agnostics or that they had no religion.

The more irreligious outlook of many British Columbians was very real. Men in particular had more freedom to define themselves as having no religion, or if they identified with a Christian denomination, they could still stay far away from the churches. This was especially true of the many white, single, transient working-class men in the province's resource economy. They faced few family pressures to attend a church and, in a racially divided province, could define their identity solely through class and whiteness.

Families made up the majority of members in the often small congregations of BC towns. Although some men retained the faith of their childhood, the main impetus for family church involvement in British Columbia, as elsewhere, came from women. Even in turn-of-the-century British Columbia, with its skewed gender ratio, almost all churches maintained a majority of female members. Given their minority position, their unwillingness to connect meaningfully with the racialized women around them, their isolation, and their lack of social pursuits, it is not surprising that white women had powerful reasons for seeking the familiarity, cordiality, and comfort of a church.

Community-based studies can tell us only so much, and we must generalize with caution. Nonetheless, they reinforce our understanding of significant differences between the religious cultures of British Columbia and the rest of Canada. Religious involvement in Ontario and Nova Scotia did display some diversity, but certain things are clear: church membership rates were generally higher than in British Columbia. Women were more likely than men to participate in a church, with married men usually being more involved than single ones. In Amherst and Kentville, class differences were largely irrelevant to involvement, whereas in Dunnville, they were so central that they cut across the common pattern of religious indifference among single men.

British Columbia deviated from the configurations of Nova Scotia and Ontario, but it was not a monolithic bastion of secularity. British-based agricultural Vernon, whose levels of church participation were higher than those of the Nova Scotia and Ontario towns, points to the danger of overgeneralizing, and to the fact that some young men, even in British Columbia, could be drawn to a church in the absence of both class tensions and other social options. At the same time, in small communities across the province, it was families, led by women who brought their social and religious norms intact to the new society, that remained the backbone of the congregation.

5
Could Sodom Be Worse?
Christianity, Moral Reform, and the Godless of Vancouver and Victoria

European and American scholars of secularization have long debated whether nineteenth-century cities were in the forefront of secularization or were in fact strongholds of vibrant and diverse forms of religious faith.[1] Although scholars have examined secularization in the urban centres of Ontario, they have not explicitly addressed the rural-urban divide.[2] What about British Columbia's largest cities, Vancouver and Victoria? Were they in the vanguard of unbelief, or were they civilized bastions of Christianity on a godless frontier?[3]

Churches and church communities certainly played major roles in both cities. Anyone who wandered into a BC church during this period might have had difficulty in differentiating the congregation, services, organizations, and campaigns from those of Central and Eastern Canada. However, paying close attention to certain sermons and, more particularly, venturing beyond the church door would reveal that, as in the rest of the province, congregations faced a much broader and more powerful range of challenges to their practical, numerical, and ideological dominance than was the case farther east. This chapter looks at the urban congregations of Vancouver and Victoria, and at the Euro-Canadians of Christian background who remained largely or entirely outside of them, examining conflicts and tensions between Christians and the irreligious. The following chapter outlines major challenges posed to the churches by non-Christian, generally racialized, residents of these cities and the province more generally.

Vancouverites and Victorians were less likely than urbanites in Eastern Canada to be church members, and the irreligious were more common in both cities, particularly among the numerous working-class single men who were more attracted to socialist organizations, rationalist lectures, and rough leisure options than to mission services. These leisure activities were readily available in both Vancouver and Victoria, often seven days a week, and moral reform efforts to control them and to convert the white unchurched had limited success. Some of these struggles ended up on the streets, revealing very public clashes between mainstream Christian faith and alternative religious and irreligious voices.

Churches and Revivals

Churches were prominent features of the urban landscape in Victoria and Vancouver. Even today, large, handsome late-nineteenth- and early-twentieth-century brick-and-stone churches are major landmarks in their downtowns and along main thoroughfares. In recent years, some have been repurposed for a more secular age, such as Victoria's Metropolitan United (formerly Methodist) Church, which was sold to the local music conservatory because an aging and dwindling congregation could no longer maintain it. When the Metropolitan Methodist Church was built in 1891, at a time when Victoria was much smaller than it is now, its substantial membership had both the numbers and the financial capacity to erect and sustain an imposing building. And during the pre–First World War years, when Vancouver's population expanded rapidly from 27,010 in 1901 to 100,401 in 1911, the churches kept pace. In 1910, the Methodists reported that "thirteen new charges have been formed" in the Lower Mainland during the previous four years.[4] Furthermore, eight new church sites had been purchased, and "on six of them churches have either been erected or are under contract while for the coming year several more are projected." In addition, four congregations had "either built new churches or greatly enlarged the old."[5] Other denominations also enjoyed major church growth during this period.

Vancouver and Victoria may not have been "cities of churches," as Toronto has been characterized, but church attendance was clearly important to many residents. As Kathryn Bridge notes, the diaries of Vancouver and Victoria children report faithful attendance at Anglican, Catholic, Presbyterian, or Methodist churches. For example, in March 1880 the Anglican Kathleen O'Reilly wrote in her diary that she "went to church with Papa, Mama and [her brother] Jack." Only illness or bad weather seem to have deterred these middle- and upper-middle-class Anglo children from Sunday services. Most attended with their parents, sometimes turning out for both morning and evening services, as well as Sunday School.[6] Oral history interviews reveal the importance of church attendance for some working-class families. As a child, Duke Ackerman, born c. 1900, went to Victoria's James Bay Methodist Church with his large family. "Sure," he said, "I had to go to church, Sunday school and church about three times a day. I was all dressed up. That's the only time we had a special suit." He also recalled, with evident enjoyment, the church Christmas tree and the "big Sunday school picnic" every summer. Lorraine Bolton attended Vancouver's Dundas Methodist Church in the years before the First World War: "We all attended church three times each Sunday, a morning service; an afternoon Sunday School and an evening service. Church was the centre of social activity ... The summer highlight was the garden party ... It was a family affair and we all had a good time."

Bolton also mentioned the various organizations that were associated with Dundas Methodist Church, including "a strong Ladies Aid, a WCTU [Woman's Christian Temperance Union], Boy Scouts ... [and] a very good choir."[7] Other churches had similar organizations, often including a young people's society and a men's brotherhood. All would have been familiar to Central and Eastern Canadian congregations. An organization of evangelical Protestant women, the WCTU pursued social reform, including the female franchise and Prohibition, and was not associated with a particular denomination. It had strong chapters in Vancouver and Victoria.

The evangelical churches of Vancouver and Victoria sometimes hosted revival teams, such as the cross-Canada team of Hugh Crossley and John Hunter, which came to Victoria in 1891 and 1907. Crossley and Hunter patterned their visits after their regular campaigns in Central and Eastern Canada.[8] They stayed in Victoria for more than two weeks and held nightly meetings in an evangelical church, where they preached the traditional message of sin and salvation in popular, folksy tones, condemned specific sins such as drinking, dancing, and gambling, and sought to convert as many people as possible. The 1891 campaign was popular from the start – newspapers reported that large churches were "crowded to the doors" and that a meeting in the Victoria Theatre, "for men only," was well attended.[9] The second visit, in the late fall of 1907, got off to a much slower start, though the *Victoria Colonist* was able to state on October 30 that "interest in the services is greatly on the increase. The attendance is growing and the speakers are gaining a greater hold upon their audience."[10] A week later, the paper observed that "large crowds are attending the meetings and the enthusiasm is marked."[11] This enthusiasm no doubt gratified Victoria's

Ministerial Association, which had extended the invitation to Crossley and Hunter a few months earlier. Inviting travelling revivalists in hopes of increasing Christian commitment was a common tactic among Canadian churches.[12]

However, Victoria's ministers may have had more to worry about than many of their Eastern counterparts, a factor that is reflected in the Crossley and Hunter revivals themselves. In many ways, the Victoria sessions were quite similar to those in Central and Eastern Canada, but some aspects seem to have been tailored specifically for the West. In all their campaigns, Crossley and Hunter held separate meetings for men, in which they spoke about (sexual) "purity" and various male sins, and their message that men needed to be as willing as women to become Christians was a common one. At the same time, their attacks on male drinking and gambling took on a harder edge in Victoria, a town whose government regulation of such "sins" was much less stringent than in Eastern communities. Challenges to male "skeptics," "scoffers," and the "ungodly" also appeared more frequently in the Victoria campaigns than in those of Eastern Canada.[13] Perhaps Crossley and Hunter did succeed in swaying a few of these scoffers, but despite the large crowds they attracted, their impact on conversion rates seems to have been negligible. Twenty converts was the largest number reported at any one Crossley and Hunter meeting in Victoria, and even the enthusiastic journalist could not identify more than a handful of possible converts at most of their meetings. At the end of their visits, there was no triumphant reference to hundreds or thousands of converts, unlike in many of their other campaigns.[14]

Boosters, Sin, and Moral Reform

Despite the best efforts of the revivalists, the godliness of Victoria was very much contested. Like all cities in this period, both Vancouver and Victoria had their urban "boosters," who proclaimed their economic, social, and moral virtues and their rosy prospects for future growth and prosperity. As part of their larger sales effort, boosters highlighted the presence of active churches and the dynamic moral reform movements associated with them. Karen Dubinsky notes how the moral standing of a town, identified by its levels of churchgoing, standards of sexual conduct, and relative absence of "sinful" behaviour, helped to define a larger sense of urban or regional character and reputation.[15] Like the northern Ontario communities that Dubinsky studied, British Columbia tended to be seen by southern Ontarians as a wild, immoral frontier, an image that was hotly contested by BC urban boosters.

At times, church leaders and reformers were among the most boosterish of moral boosters, as was the case at the November 1901 Metropolitan Methodist Church annual Thanksgiving entertainment. Minister Hayward lauded the many virtues of Victoria, including its "absence of the 'tough' element common to most seaport towns." Although he did acknowledge that "the moral conduct of the city is not all we would wish," he asserted "we may safely say that Victoria, morally is far ahead of most cities of its size." He praised plans to relocate the First Nations reserve outside of town, claiming that this step would improve the city's moral standing.[16] Many reformers blamed racial others, particularly Indigenous people or the Chinese, for the city's moral failings, but others thought the sins of "rough" single white men were as big a problem in BC cities as in the Interior. In 1900, Ontarian J.C. Speer, a Methodist minister who had been in Victoria for a year or two, gave a talk to his "ministerial brethren in Toronto," in which he expressed common Eastern views about British Columbia, stating that BC miners were "detached from the bodies politic and ecclesiastical," and that the sailors in BC cities "get the largest kind of license to do as they like and are a constant menace to morality." He also decried the lack of Sabbath observance and the amount of liquor sold. As he told his listeners, "in Victoria, with its 25,000 inhabitants, there are 98 places in which liquor is sold and there are 100 houses of ill-repute." Six months earlier, Speer had given a similar talk in Victoria, in which he asked "could Sodom be worse?" He claimed that "he had known gentlemen who would not bring their families to reside in Victoria because of the moral condition of the city."[17]

This was exactly the portrayal that BC urban boosters were at pains to challenge, and not surprisingly, they were very unhappy with Speer, as they were with the many other Christian reformers who exposed the supposed moral impurities of BC cities.[18] In a letter to the *Victoria Times*, "Truth First" complained that Speer's attack was "one of the worst, if not the worst, advertisement that could be given to any town." The *Times* editor opined that only "harm is done to the cause which Mr. Speer has at heart by the enunciation and publication of such statements." Like many local boosters, he made a few pointed comments about the moral failings of Toronto: "We have read somewhere that in Toronto the Sabbath is not observed in the manner that it once was ... Torontonians boast of their city of churches and if attendance at Divine service is falling off there, whom does it reflect on?"[19]

Reverend J.C. Speer, n.d. | *BC Archives, B-04194*

Vancouver papers were equally ready to defend their city against charges of lax morals and happy to point out the shortcomings of supposedly more religious centres to the east. In 1899, the editor of the *Vancouver Province* wrote,

> it was once said that there was no Sunday west of the Rocky Mountains ... but it comes as something of a shock to learn that the Christian religion in the old stronghold of Puritanism, New England, is losing its grip ... As to there being no Sabbath on this side of the Rocky Mountains the province of British Columbia stands in open protest. Perhaps in the early days of the gold excitement this applied and it may still apply further north, but at present the Sabbath is remarkably well observed here. The suggestion, however, that there is little religious worship in the land of the Pilgrim Fathers may, perhaps, shatter the Plymouth Rock to its very foundation.[20]

Most clergymen in Vancouver and Victoria, who continually struggled to have laws or bylaws passed (or enforced) to restrict Sunday work and

Sunday recreation, would have dismissed the claim that the Sabbath was remarkably well observed in British Columbia.[21] Their campaign continued even after the federal Lord's Day Act was passed in 1906, which made Sunday excursions on any transportation system illegal and forbade newspaper work and sales, unnecessary railway and steamship work, paid sports, and most other types of work.[22] After an initial refusal to comply, the BC government began to enforce the law, but Victoria persisted in declining to prosecute offenders, claiming that if it did so everyone in town would end up in court.[23]

Conflicts over Sunday work, Sunday sports, and the sale of Sunday newspapers were paralleled to some extent by struggles in other provinces. However, the lack of BC government support for Sabbatarian efforts was quite distinctive. A few BC politicians were earnest Christian reformers, including John Robson, who served as premier from 1889 to 1892. However, Robson could not even get a majority of his own party to support his proposed Sabbatarian legislation in 1891.[24]

Some of the anti-Sabbatarianism in BC newspapers was echoed in Central and Eastern Canadian papers, but some reflected an irreligious outlook that appeared as often in Vancouver and Victoria as it did in the Kootenays, and that clearly had at least some impact on BC government (dis)interest in this issue.

Like Robert Lowery in the Kootenays, some anti-Sabbatarian letters to the editor focused on defending liberty and freedom, and their authors presented themselves as staunch challengers to clerical "tyrants" who sought to limit the people's Sunday options for work and play. One letter in the *Vancouver Province,* its author distressed by successful efforts of religious reformers to close down fruit stores, cigar stands, and refreshment booths on Sundays, railed against "superstitious and narrow-minded religious cranks who strive to acquire the divine favor by curtailing the liberties of their fellow citizens, knowing not that the most genuine method of serving the Divinity is by promoting the happiness and welfare of their fellow creatures."[25] This rhetoric of liberty echoes that of Toronto's great Sunday streetcar battles of the late 1880s and early 1890s, ably documented by Christopher Armstrong and H.V. Nelles.[26] However, some anti-Sabbatarians who wrote to the Vancouver and Victoria papers defined themselves not simply as defenders of liberty, but as opposing all churches, religion, and even God.

For example, "Freethinker" wrote to the *Vancouver Province,* complaining about the attempts to impose Sunday closing and other "blue laws" on Vancouver. As he advised Sabbatarians, instead of

> being ever ready to jump on your agnostic and free-thinking neighbours, you should pause and consider that it is they who give you what liberty you enjoy, for as a body you are too narrow-minded and bigoted to even give yourselves liberty ... So thank your lucky stars that there are enough heretics about to protect your liberty for you.[27]

Paul Laverdure suggests that the predominance of Anglicans in British Columbia accounts for its lax enforcement of Sabbatarian legislation. He also notes the impact of anti-Sabbatarian pressure from BC Catholics as well as the significant number of those adhering to non-Christian religions.[28] The number of "heretics about," in both the largest cities and the rest of the province, would also have played a role.

The heretics, and the less religious outlook of many others in Victoria and Vancouver, were also very exasperating to Christian reformers who sought to address sin in BC cities. Their frustration is evident in the Vancouver Social Survey of 1913. Modelled on larger American urban social surveys, it resembled other surveys undertaken in Canadian cities by leaders of the fledgling social gospel movement.[29] Produced by the Board of Temperance and Moral Reform of the Methodist Church and the Board of Social Service and Evangelism of the Presbyterian Church, the Vancouver Social Survey reflects the Christian moralism of most social gospellers of this period. It reported on a number of labour, health, and social service questions in the city, but it also dealt with specifically moral issues.[30] The authors denounced government toleration of a "segregated district" for prostitution, disapprovingly noted the number of establishments licensed to sell alcohol, and bemoaned that "the vice of gambling is very prevalent in Vancouver." They also decried the immorality of "moving picture shows," and though they acknowledged that some theatres did run educational films, others "should be closed up. In one theatre the audience is 99 per cent men, and it has the atmosphere of an antechamber to darker evils."[31]

The survey's authors were familiar with the Christian forces that were arrayed against these sources of immorality. Significant numbers of evangelical women were involved. The highest-profile female reform group was the WCTU. Its unions organized endless petitions in favour of temperance and Prohibition, pressed for "local option" laws (that enabled local communities to forbid the sale of alcohol), fought to reduce the number of liquor licences issued, and lobbied municipal and provincial governments on a number of morals issues. By the 1880s, the BC WCTU had recognized that the political power of women and their influence over legislation was limited by their inability to vote. As a result, the demand for women's suffrage (on the same basis as men) became a major plank of its reform platform.[32]

The fact that women still could not vote in 1913 may explain why the authors of the social survey focused solely on men in discussing the political influence that church people could bring to bear on problematic issues. In a section titled "Political Activity of Church Brotherhoods," the authors cited the efforts of men to work through the Good Government League and the Adult Bible Class Federation to enforce Sabbatarian legislation, challenge the toleration of the red light district, and prevent any increase in the number of liquor licences issued. Nonetheless, the authors were not optimistic that these efforts would achieve their goals. As they explained, "while the Good Government League has succeeded in having a large percentage of its candidates elected, their success has been more apparent than real" because most candidates did nothing to further the cause of moral reform once they were in office. The authors were particularly scathing in connection with the provincial government, complaining that "the present attitude of the Provincial Government in the matter of a segregated district amounts to an open defiance of the forces organized to promote a clean Vancouver." They acknowledged that "the attitude of the Provincial Government proves that they consider the protests from the Good Government Leagues are the voice of a small minority." The premier at the time, Conservative Richard McBride, may very well have felt that way. As Patricia Roy demonstrates, he did very little to appease Christian moral reformers during most of his time in office. McBride himself was not a frequent church attender.[33]

As in the case of Sabbatarianism, scholars have suggested that the relatively high proportion of Anglicans in the province, who believed in moderate drinking rather than Prohibition, may also have had an impact on government attitudes, at least in regard to liquor legislation.[34] This was probably true, but government recognition that committed male churchgoers were very much a minority in both Vancouver and British Columbia would also have been a significant factor in its reluctance to address morals legislation more generally.

Church Involvement

There was serious concern in Victoria and Vancouver that churchgoers, both male and female, were indeed in the minority. In December 1909, the *Victoria Colonist* published a major article titled "Is Victoria a Church-Going City?" The reporter interviewed clergymen of the twenty largest churches in town, asking about their seating capacity, as compared to average attendance and membership. Interviewees were also asked for their opinion on whether Victoria was a churchgoing city, and if not, why not. The resulting figures were not impressive: in most churches, the seating capacity significantly outstripped either average attendance or membership. On the basis of these statistics, the *Colonist* argued that in a city of 40,000 people, only 5,690 regularly turned out for services.[35] The figures were contested as both over- and underestimating church involvement, but though a few clergy, primarily Catholic priests, defended the devoutness of the community, most interviewees conceded that, regardless of exact numbers, Victoria was not generally a churchgoing city.[36] Some blamed the climate (a frequent argument that persists to the present day), and others asserted that Victoria was no worse in terms of churchgoing than other West Coast cities in Canada and the United States. But there was a general sense that in both attendance and commitment to "church work" (volunteer involvement), it was much worse than most Eastern communities, with many people preferring to spend their Sundays undertaking home repairs, working in their gardens, playing sports, or going on excursions.

One minister postulated that "the early settlement of a place has much to do with its later attitude toward religion and the church. Those who came here with the gold rush years ago were not, I fear, especially inclined to church-attendance."[37] In her study of 1850s California gold-rush society, Laurie Maffly-Kipp made much the same argument, chronicling the long-term impact of this culture and the ways in which the irreligious and heterodox patterns of California were exported to gold rushes around the world (including British Columbia).[38] Two ministers stated that members of the working class were unlikely to attend church in Victoria. This concern was also being expressed across Canada, but it had extra legitimacy in British Columbia. The attitudes of at least some working-class Victorians toward the churches were highlighted by the *Colonist*'s perhaps quixotic decision to include the town's main socialist group with the churches surveyed in its piece "Is Victoria a Church-Going City?" Average attendance at weekly socialist meetings (four hundred) was higher than that for fourteen of the twenty churches listed. The Socialist Party representative was happy to claim a religious dimension for his movement, telling the reporter, "While the chief tenets of the creed are purely economic and material, these, after all, are but a means to an end and the ideals aimed at by Socialism are such as to diffuse intense religious feeling among its adherents."

He added that "the perplexity of the preachers of Victoria over the apparent lack of interest in church doctrines is a source of pleasure to me, personally, and to a majority of the members of the party."[39]

"Is Victoria a Church-Going City?" assumed that Victorians were either churchgoers or not, leaving little or no room for those who did not regularly attend services, but who may have done so at New Year's or Easter, or sent their children to Sunday School. The January 1906 issue of the *Western Methodist Recorder* reported on a late 1905 survey of Sunday School attendance in Victoria. This report, which was acknowledged to have been "carefully though perhaps not completely, done," argued that approximately 60 percent of Victorians under the age of eighteen went to Sunday School, with some denominations, such as the Baptists and the Methodists, achieving much higher numbers.[40] As in the Kootenays, many people who sent their children to Sunday School were not churchgoers themselves, a failing that was decried at a meeting of Vancouver Island Presbyterians in 1908. At this meeting, the distance of many working-class Victorians from the churches was a major concern. It was reported, somewhat bitterly, that "if the pulpit is turned into a forum for the advocacy of revolutionary socialism, speeches to the unemployed and discussion of the Oriental immigration question, the masses would come for a brief time."[41] These Presbyterian leaders understood that they were competing with an anti-religious form of socialism for the souls of BC workers, and as discussed in Chapter 2, they also recognized that the more nuanced and humanitarian position of at least some clergymen regarding Asian immigration was not popular with much of the BC working class.

Socialism was a major rival, but the fraternal orders may have posed a bigger threat. Scholars have identified tension between these societies and the churches in other parts of Canada and in the United States, particularly over the allegiance of men, but this seems to have been a major issue in British Columbia. One of the Victoria ministers whom the *Colonist* interviewed in 1909 stated that his city was "honeycombed with societies the members of which look upon the churches as antagonistic to their interests."[42] This attack on the lodges was more explicit than any produced by a Kootenay clergyman, but the general male preference for lodge over church seems to have held true in both places. In his study of fraternalism in late-nineteenth-century Victoria, Andrew Reid finds that some lodge brothers were also active church members, but he identifies a white, masculine, cross-denominational, and diffuse form of spirituality in the lodges that appealed to men and could provide an alternative to institutional Christianity.[43]

Church leaders in Vancouver were at least as concerned as those of Victoria over the low levels of church involvement in their city.[44] The census of 1901 provides concrete evidence that the remarks of clergy and journalists about low church participation in Vancouver and Victoria were quite justified. As discussed in Chapter 1, this census was unique in Canada: it asked individuals about their religious adherence, but it also asked all churches to provide the number of their communicants, allowing us to differentiate between nominal adherents and church members.

Not every denomination in Victoria and Vancouver reported low levels of involvement. In Victoria's Catholic churches, participation levels were over 100 percent, suggesting that the optimism of their priests was not misplaced. Among Vancouver Catholics, involvement was lower than in Central Canada but nonetheless respectable at almost 50 percent (see Appendix: Table 13). This may in part reflect differences between Catholics and Protestants regarding the definition of "communicant." In theory, Catholic communicants were required to take communion at least once a year, at Easter, but in practice anyone who identified as Catholic would be seen as a member of the parish. In addition, Victoria's large Catholic churches attracted out-of-town worshippers, which also helps to account for the incredibly high level of involvement in that town.

Although all churches provide a sense of community, scholars have highlighted the construction of community in Catholic churches that combines a shared religious and ethnic identity.[45] In the Kootenays, the church hierarchy succeeded in providing only occasional access to Italian priests, and as we saw in Chapter 3, Slavic workers pleaded in vain for a Slavic priest. In the larger cities, accommodating ethnic groups remained a struggle that was exacerbated by ongoing tensions between the predominantly French-speaking Oblates who controlled much of the BC church and the increasing number of secular priests who were coming to the province. Victoria did have some Irish priests who ministered to its largely Irish parishioners into the 1870s, but their less-than-stellar performance led the bishops to prefer Belgian-trained priests after that period, despite their lack of ethnic ties to the community.[46] Vancouver achieved more success in addressing the needs of ethnic congregations. In 1907, the Catholic hierarchy created a French Canadian parish, Our Lady of Lourdes, in Maillardville, a largely French Canadian area near Coquitlam. Sacred Heart Church, founded in 1905 in Vancouver's immigrant Strathcona neighbourhood, ministered to many Italians and had Italian-speaking priests from very early in the history of the parish. To counter the appeal of the fraternal orders, the Sacred Heart parish priests organized a branch of the Catholic Order of Foresters, which provided both social activities and insurance to its members, and appealed primarily to Italian immigrants.[47] The intersection of ethnicity and religion in some urban parishes helped to keep some Catholics at least nominally within the fold, but the limited willingness of the hierarchy to accommodate ethnic concerns in other locales may have reduced involvement in less populated areas.[48]

A few Protestant churches were also organized around ethnic affiliation. For example, a Swedish Lutheran church and a German and English Evangelical Lutheran church had been founded in Vancouver by 1913, and Victoria had a German Lutheran church.[49] Links between Presbyterianism and Scottish and Irish ethnicity also persisted, though they may have become attenuated for the many Presbyterian families that had been in North America for two or more generations. In general, ethnicity appears to have been less of a force in most Protestant churches than was the case for Catholics, and faith alone does not appear to have drawn many nominal Protestants to the Protestant churches of Victoria and Vancouver. Certainly, the overall picture of Protestant church involvement in these cities is much less rosy than for Catholics.

The levels of Protestant church membership were higher in Vancouver and Victoria than on the rest of Vancouver Island and in the Yale and Cariboo district, which had the lowest levels of Protestant involvement in the province. However, participation rates in Vancouver and Victoria were not impressive. In Ontario, church membership tended to be higher in the cities than in the surrounding countryside, as was also true of Winnipeg as compared to the rest of Manitoba. Both Winnipeg and Ontario cities also had higher levels of involvement than either Victoria or Vancouver. For instance, less than 17 percent of Anglicans appear to have been communicants in Vancouver and Victoria, as compared to almost 39 percent in Hamilton, almost 45 percent in London, and over 32 percent in Winnipeg.[50] Figures for Presbyterians were also much lower in Victoria and Vancouver than in London, Hamilton, and Winnipeg. Victoria's Methodist figures were similar to those of these three cities, though its Catholic figures were higher. Vancouver's figures were more consistently lower than those of Hamilton, London, and Winnipeg, regardless of denomination (see Table 13).

If, in general, fewer people chose to participate in a Victoria or Vancouver church than was the case elsewhere in Canada, who did become members? It is not possible to address this question for all denominations, but the surviving Methodist and Presbyterian records for many Victoria churches for 1900 to 1902 provide some answers. These records were linked to a complete census database of Victoria residents in 1901, which gives a sense of who participated in a range of Presbyterian and Methodist churches, including some large downtown congregations and smaller local ones. A similar project was not attempted for Vancouver, but the records for one Vancouver Presbyterian church in a primarily working-class area were linked to a database of the 1901 manuscript census for that city. In both Victoria and Vancouver, the absence of records for many churches means that we cannot get a sense of church involvement and non-involvement for the whole city, as was possible for the small towns studied in Chapter 4. Nonetheless, we can determine who joined certain churches.

There was a significant working-class presence in Victoria churches. Only in the downtown St. Andrew's Presbyterian were middle-class communicants in the majority. In other downtown churches, middle-class members made up over 40 percent of communicants who could be linked to the census database.[51] Certain smaller churches outside the downtown core were largely working class, including the Victoria West Methodist and St. Aidan's Presbyterian Churches.[52] Vancouver's Mount Pleasant Presbyterian Church was located in Mount Pleasant, southeast of downtown. As Ian Buck shows, Mount Pleasant was a mixed residential area, with a majority of skilled, semi-skilled, and unskilled working-class families, but it also included low-level clerks, petty proprietors, and some more middle-class families. The majority (65 percent) of Mount Pleasant members were from working-class families, both skilled and semi- and unskilled, with an additional 27 percent coming from families where the household head worked in a lower-level clerical position.[53]

In the *Colonist*'s 1909 survey of Victoria churches, the majority of clergymen stated that women were more likely than men to attend church – a pattern that held true everywhere in Canada. In Victoria and Vancouver, as in the small towns discussed in Chapter 4, women made up the majority of members in the churches studied, even though men outnumbered them in both cities, at just over 60 percent in Victoria and just under 60 percent in Vancouver. Over 60 percent of members in most of the Victoria churches were female, with the proportion ranging from just over 50 percent in St. Andrew's Presbyterian to over 70 percent in the small working-class Victoria West Methodist Church.[54]

As in the Kootenays, women in Victoria no doubt attended church from some combination of piety, familiarity, respectability, and sociability, but it is also true that gender ratios were less skewed in Victoria and Vancouver than in the Interior. The larger population of these cities would also have provided more opportunities to meet other women than was the case in towns like Rossland. We know from the broader statistics on membership that many women did stay away from the churches in Victoria and Vancouver, as they did in the Kootenays. Nonetheless, they were still more drawn to a church than were men. Some came on their own or with their daughters, but the majority of married women were accompanied by their husbands.[55] As in other BC communities, working-class husbands were somewhat less likely than their middle-class equivalents to be there, particularly those who were semi-skilled and unskilled. They may simply have been less interested than their wives in Christianity, perhaps evincing enough fuzzy fidelity to attend occasional service at Easter and New Year's. Sometimes there were clear religious differences between spouses, as in the case of Mrs. Foreshaw of Mount Pleasant, whose husband was a "tallyman" in a local factory – and an agnostic. Other husbands may have held skeptical opinions, even if they did not define themselves as unbelievers. An entry in the diary of Victoria's Anglican bishop George Hills suggests what this situation might have looked like for some Christian wives. Hills taught a Bible class that was attended by various women "of mature minds." One day, while discussing Noah and the Flood, he mentioned modernist critiques of the story. He asked his students, "Do you hear much of the sceptical opinion upon these points? Several together replied eagerly 'yes, every day.'"[56] Some husbands who absented themselves from church may have joined the four hundred Victorians, primarily male, who regularly attended Sunday socialist meetings. Whereas religious togetherness may have been less common in working-class families than in middle-class ones, it is nonetheless true that in most churches surveyed, in more than half of working-class couples both partners were members.

Christian faith was no doubt important to many married men, but others would have been persuaded into church by the piety of their wives and by the respectability that involvement conferred, as was also the case in Ontario and elsewhere in British Columbia.[57] The respectability of the "middling sort" of family men among Vancouver's working and lower middle classes, identified by Bob McDonald, is evident in the communion roll of Mount Pleasant Presbyterian Church. McDonald identified the Mount Pleasant neighbourhood as being home to respectable family men, such as Thomas Graham, carpenter, and H. Gow, electrician, both of whom joined the church with their wives when it was founded in 1892. In Vancouver and Victoria, church involvement was a signifier of respectability for men of certain classes, but given that so many stayed away, it was clearly not the only one. McDonald argues that being family men of

British background was in itself a basis for respectability in early-twentieth-century Vancouver, as were homeownership and association with fraternal orders, unions, and socialist groups.[58] As noted in Chapter 2, whiteness also equated with social inclusion in a racially divided province. None of these routes to respectability precluded church membership, but they could confer it in their own right, in a manner much less possible in Eastern and Central Canada, where the churches were far more hegemonic.

Godless Single Men in the City

Whereas some white married men found faith, community, and respectability in a church, this was much less true of single men, who were a source of concern to Vancouver and Victoria churchgoers, as they were throughout British Columbia and Canada. The proportion of single men in city churches was lower than that of single women (less than a quarter of all men in most churches), in a context of wider city populations where single men greatly outnumbered single women. As was true throughout Canada, single men preferred the masculine culture of lodges and taverns, sports and gambling halls, which was much more prevalent and available (even on Sundays) in British Columbia than in the East.[59]

Canadian church members were generally well settled. The 1901 census indicates that the vast majority of members of Victoria's larger Presbyterian and Methodist churches had immigrated to Canada over ten years before; many had come well over ten years earlier.[60] Many single men in Victoria and Vancouver had arrived only recently and would soon leave. This floating population of working men, who typically lived in boarding houses, cabins, and hotels, did not seek out community in a church and were much more likely than those living with other family members to define themselves as atheists or of no religion.[61]

Except for Yale and Cariboo, Vancouver had the highest percentage of irreligious people of any district in 1901, at 1.4 percent of the population.[62] Victoria's level of non-belief was lower, at 0.6 percent.[63]

Who identified themselves as atheists or of "no religion" in turn-of-the-century Victoria and Vancouver? As elsewhere in British Columbia, the vast majority were male, but not all were single working-class boarders.[64] In both cities, a significant minority came from the upper or middle class. Over 11 percent of Vancouver's atheists or those of no religion were upper/middle-class managers and professionals, as were over 25 percent of

Vancouver, looking west to Gastown, 1911 | *BC Archives, G-06818*

those in Victoria. Most middle-class irreligious people were married.[65] Members of this group may have subscribed to nineteenth-century middle-class intellectual freethought, and a few may have been middle-class socialists.[66]

The majority of the irreligious in both cities, however, were working class, and most were single. Far fewer irreligious working-class men were married than was true in the Kootenays.[67] McDonald's argument that married working-class Vancouverites were very likely to be respectable and settled resonates here. Even if many never went to church, public declarations of irreligion may have been less acceptable among them than in the more radical working-class culture of the Kootenays.

Respectability was much less important to many single men who defined themselves as irreligious in Victoria and Vancouver. They tended to be significantly over-represented in various "unrespectable" parts of Vancouver, areas of increasing concern to middle-class Christian reformers. Gastown, at the east end of downtown Vancouver, was known for its working-class drifters, unmarried loggers, and other seasonal workers who came into town for the winter, or for a good time. It had the highest proportion of irreligious people in the city. In Poll 16, whose borders in

1901 most closely overlap with Gastown, 42.0 percent of residents were boarders or lodgers, and 8.8 percent of the population defined themselves as atheists or as having no religion, the highest proportion in Vancouver, and indeed, in the province.[68] The proportion of irreligious people in Gastown was in fact over 50 times greater than the proportion of those defining themselves as irreligious in Canada as a whole.[69] Nearby Vancouver polls also had relatively high proportions of boarders and lodgers, and the irreligious were significantly over-represented there as well.[70]

Although the vast majority of rootless working-class irreligious people in both Vancouver and Victoria were men, one group of urban women was also over-represented among the irreligious. Sex trade workers are generally invisible in the census, since they told enumerators that they pursued other female occupations, such as dressmaker and actress. However, Patrick Dunae has developed a complex and convincing method, combining address, income, and other variables, to identify many sex trade workers on the manuscript census for Victoria.[71] Dunae generously permitted me to access his database, and I found that though most Victoria sex trade workers listed a religion to the census-taker, 6.6 percent defined themselves as freethinkers, a much higher proportion than among most Victorians, particularly women. The sample size is very small, so we are talking about only four freethinkers here, but an additional woman listed her faith simply as "Protestant," and the religion of another was "not given." Most of the irreligious sex trade workers lived in Victoria's low-status red light district near the harbour, and they were housed in single-person cabins, or "cribs," rather than the more elaborate and higher-status brothels. Among them was freethinker Nellie Early, an African American who said she was married but who lived alone in a crib on Herald Street. Freethinker Mabel Lockwood, another American, lived in the crib next to Nellie.[72] Most of the irreligious sex trade workers were American.[73] It is not surprising that some of them rejected Christianity, which saw their occupation as sinful and themselves as outcasts, but the fact that most retained a religious affiliation is of interest. Perhaps it signified no more than the false occupations they named for the census-taker. However, as we saw in the Kootenays, such affiliation may also have pointed to a personal faith, as well as a sense of family denominational connection.

Evidence from Vancouver suggests that some sex trade workers retained a commitment to their childhood faith, though they knew that no church would accept them. In Vancouver, Christian social workers who visited sex trade workers reported that "whatever kind of lives they live now, they all told us of early days in Sunday school and church ... It is vain to ask them to *church* – yet some of them go occasionally to the Salvation Army meeting Sunday evening. The brightness and hearty singing, etc., attract them."[74] Again, the hymns of their youth could entice people who otherwise felt alienated from or unwelcome in the churches, or who had actively rejected them.

The sex trade workers and the rootless single men of Vancouver and Victoria were an increasing concern to both male and female Christian moral reformers. The WCTU and male church leaders tried to "rescue" the women and to provide alternative options to the men, such as reading rooms, to dissuade them from frequenting bars and hotels. Some men did avail themselves of the reading rooms, but they seem to have drawn the line at attending a church.[75]

The anxieties of moral reformers about the floating, un-Christian cohort of men intensified after the turn of the century, particularly in Vancouver, where the population expanded by more than three-hundred-fold between 1901 and 1911, leading to dramatically worsened and more visible poverty. Gastown, other low-income parts of downtown, and neighbourhoods just to the east and south of it were populated by growing numbers of poor new immigrants and working-class single men who did not go to church. In 1908, the Vancouver General Ministerial Association, which included ministers from a range of Protestant denominations, decided that something must be done. On November 20, the association concluded that "a service is necessary in the downtown section of the city to meet the requirements of those who do not and will not attend regular Church service."[76]

Social gospel concerns about the material well-being of poor Vancouverites prompted an interdenominational evangelical Protestant group to establish the Central City Mission in 1909. Located on Abbott Street in the heart of Gastown, the mission offered services to the many single men and low-income families in the area. Meals and accommodation were provided to low-income men, as was a free employment bureau. The city missionary visited men in cabins and rooming houses "to search out and reach, as far as possible, those who are without friends in the city and those who have no church connections, and extend to them a hearty invitation to attend the meetings in our Hall." He deplored the fact that "so many people remained untouched" by any church connection. Some of the men whom he visited expressed a class-based critique of Christianity, as they were "embittered against the rich or any who seemed more favoured than they," but he reported that he had brought at least some men to Christ through "a patient and sympathetic hearing of their difficulties."

Whereas he focused on single men, female mission workers visited low-income and immigrant families at home, providing material relief to those who were deemed deserving, as well as the Christian evangelical message to all. As the mission superintendent noted, "while the object of the Central City Mission is the betterment of the entire man – body, mind and soul – yet the crowning work is, after all, the saving of men's souls: for the very moment a man's life is touched by the life of Jesus Christ he becomes a new creature."[77]

In its efforts to convert the unchurched, particularly the unmarried men of downtown Vancouver, the Central City Mission held a range of evangelical services. As it proudly stated in its annual reports, it had nightly services in its new building, through which it claimed to have reached ten thousand individuals over the 1910–11 year. Of course, the report made no mention of the extent to which access to free meals and accommodation may have been linked to attendance at services.

The evangelists at the mission also recognized the need to move into the streets. Preachers held street meetings near the mission almost every evening of the year and tried as much as possible to include among their speakers formerly "sinful" men who had been converted through the mission. The leadership claimed that

> thousands have stood and listened to the fact of Christian experiences as told by those who speak from personal knowledge. The fruits of street meetings are not easily discovered, but we are sure that in the last summing up of affairs many will be found who were arrested and awakened through the messages which were delivered at the corner of Abbott and Cordova streets.[78]

Representatives of the Central City Mission were not alone in taking the evangelical message to the street. The mission was trying to copy the success of the Salvation Army, which had been preaching on the streets of Vancouver, Victoria, and many smaller BC communities for over twenty years.[79] Founded in London, England, in 1878, the Salvation Army was originally an evangelical revivalist movement that sought to bring working-class Londoners to Christ. It used a range of unconventional devices to appeal to the poor, including street meetings, parades, brass bands, female preachers, and various trappings of popular culture. When it first "invaded" Canada in 1882, it was not very popular with the middle classes, who saw it as disruptive and disreputable, and as promoting an overly emotional brand of Christianity.[80] However, its ability to convert the "rough" poor and to transform them into respectable Christians won over the middle class to its methods and even led to their emulation. Certainly, by the time the middle-class leaders of the Central City Mission took up street preaching, the army had become eminently respectable. Its shift to social service work in the 1890s gained it further middle-class support across Canada.[81] This social service focus was evident in Vancouver and Victoria during the years leading up to the First World War. The Vancouver Social Survey of 1913 noted that the Salvation Army ran lodgings for homeless men and a rescue home for sex trade workers, as well as deploying some of its officers in visiting and providing material aid to poor families.[82] In both Vancouver and Victoria, it was also involved in "prison gate" refuges for those released from prison and had operated a rescue home in Victoria during the 1890s.[83]

The literature on the Salvation Army suggests that social service became its main emphasis after the 1890s, but in British Columbia at least, this did not preclude continued revivalist efforts to convert the working-class unchurched.[84] In the early twentieth century, the Salvation Army held regular street services in Gastown, at the corner of Carrall and Hastings, and in downtown Victoria, at the corner of Government and Yates. Most people who attended these street meetings would probably not have defined themselves as adherents but would have lacked a regular church affiliation.[85] For some unemployed workers in Vancouver or Victoria, the army parades and brass bands were free entertainment, and the hecklers who often disrupted the outdoor services merely added to the fun. For others who were not interested in the churches, or comfortable in them, including the sex trade workers mentioned above, the army's street preaching may have provided nostalgic access to childhood prayers and hymns, as well as spiritual sustenance, without requiring the firm Christian commitment (and rejection of rough culture) that both evangelical church leaders and the Salvation Army itself were hoping for.

Whereas some people were attracted to army meetings and parades, more workers who lived in Gastown cabins and lodging houses identified explicitly with unbelief rather than with the Salvation Army.[86] Some local atheists may have been attracted to the secularist-rationalist lectures offered in Vancouver in 1914. From April until well into the fall, a Sam Atkinson, former clergyman and member of the executive of the Pacific Coast Rationalist Association, apparently addressed "the largest Rationalist audience in Canada" every Sunday evening in Vancouver's Globe Theatre."[87] In August of 1914, more infidel heresy was brought to Vancouver from the "unchurched" West Coast of the United States. The *Vancouver Province* reported that an audience "largely composed of men" listened to a lecture titled "The Conflict between Science and Religion," which was offered by C.T. Spalding of the National Rationalist Association at the Labor Temple. In October, he returned to give a series of lectures "from the standpoint of modern scientific rationalism." Active in the American National Rationalist Association, of which the Pacific Coast Rationalist Association was an affiliate, Spalding was apparently "well known all down the Pacific Coast to be a keen and effective speaker."[88]

In addition to providing regular rationalist lectures, Sam Atkinson briefly published the *Vancouver Rationalist* out of a Hastings Street address, a periodical that espoused a secularist-rationalist message. Some of Atkinson's opinions would have been familiar to Robert Lowery and many other irreligious journalists, although couched in less inflammatory language. Atkinson argued against the legitimacy of religion on the basis of rational, scientific principles, and the Rationalist Association with which he and Spalding were affiliated called for the complete separation of church and state, the elimination of Sabbatarian and other laws based in Christian morality, and the abolition of government chaplains and any Christian symbols in government.[89] The main focus of the *Rationalist* was to challenge Christianity and the churches on the basis of rational thought, but Atkinson also espoused an anarchist/co-operative vision of social justice against the evils of an inequitable capitalist society, and he supported equal rights for women. Anti-Asian sentiment was more subtle than in Lowery's work, but it was not absent. The theme of the only extant issue of the *Rationalist* was "The Waste of Human Energy" expended through religion. Whereas the issue concentrated largely on Christianity, it was illustrated with photographs of Hindu men in various religious poses that the author defined as a complete waste of energy, arguing that the 5 million ascetics in India "who spend their lives in meditation ... are all idlers ... How much richer the world would be if these idlers were paying more attention to things of time and sense."[90]

Atkinson presided over the Vancouver branch of the Pacific Coast Rationalist Association and was on the executive of the Rationalist Association of North America, with which it was affiliated. In 1915, the Rationalist Association had branches in eighteen or more major American cities, but the Vancouver branch appears to have been the only Canadian affiliate.[91] However, another active member of the Rationalist Association of North America, Marshall Gauvin, was to become a well-known rationalist speaker in inter-war Winnipeg.[92]

The Rationalists, with their primary focus on the irrationality, wastefulness, and evil of religion, with a secondary focus on the evils of capitalist inequality, seem to have made only a brief impression on Vancouver during this period, and on the city's irreligious white working-class men. The latter were more interested in the messages of the socialists, the IWW, and other more radical elements of the labour movement that concentrated primarily on challenging the oppression of the working class, with a secondary focus on the evils and irrationality of Christianity. Although socialist and IWW rhetoric against most of the churches was largely confined to print, competition between these groups and one particular Christian organization, the Salvation Army, was of a more public nature.

Religion and Irreligion on the Streets

Competition between the Salvation Army and the labour movement and the left for working-class allegiance was very visible on the streets of Vancouver and Victoria during the years prior to the First World War. This rivalry, and the markedly different attitudes of the authorities to the two groups, came into clearest focus in the 1909 and 1911 free speech fights in Vancouver and Victoria.[93] Mark Leier very ably demonstrates what these conflicts can tell us about the limitations of unity between socialists, the labour movement, and the Industrial Workers of the World (IWW).[94] The following brief discussion examines the religious (and irreligious) dimensions of this struggle.

On April 4, 1909, the IWW and the Socialist Party of Canada (SPC) spoke to a working-class crowd on the corner of Carrall and Hastings, while Salvation Army preachers held forth on the opposite corner. The Vancouver city police ordered the IWW and socialist speakers to disperse, declaring they were disrupting traffic, but they ignored the Salvation Army preachers, who were doing the same thing. Six IWW members and socialists were arrested for refusing to comply. In court, they "held that it was clearly discriminatory for a constable to arrest leftists and ignore equally disruptive religionists because they preached a creed more acceptable to the police." The polarized religious perspectives of the two sides were highlighted by one of the IWW defendants, who objected to swearing on the Bible, "complaining that it could harbour germs."[95] The *Vancouver Province* may not have agreed with the messages of the IWW and the socialists, but it did stand up for fair play: "The contention of the Socialists that the bylaw in regard to the holding of street meetings should be enforced against all bodies, if it is to be enforced against them, is perfectly reasonable. The authorities have no right whatsoever to discriminate." For the *Province,* what this meant was that neither Salvationists nor socialists should have the right to hold street meetings. "We have as much respect for the aims and work of the army as any other," it stated, "but in a matter of this kind they are not entitled to special privileges." As the paper pointed out, the army was "not allowed such liberty in the cities of eastern Canada," so there was no reason to countenance it in Vancouver.[96]

A similar attitude prevailed in the free speech fights in Victoria two years later. In July 1911, Victoria City Council told unionists, IWW organizers, and socialists that they could no longer speak downtown but would have to deliver their speeches far from the city core. The Salvationists, however, were permitted to continue preaching downtown, at the corner of Yates and Government. On July 22, after they had preached at the corner with no police objection, IWW and socialist speakers replaced them, whereupon fifteen were arrested. The IWW, SPC, and the Victoria Trades and Labour Council voiced a considerable protest about this attempt to muzzle them and demanded that they be treated in the same way as religious groups such as the Salvation Army.[97] Ultimately, the mayor had a bylaw passed that prevented "any preaching, public speaking or public meeting" in public squares, parks, or streets unless a permit were obtained in advance. As the *Victoria Times* noted, this would "render the street corner congregation, whether for socialistic or salvationistic expression illegal."[98]

When the Salvation Army first arrived in Canada almost thirty years earlier, its preachers had risked arrest for being loud, disruptive, and a threat to public order. By the early twentieth century, however, their efforts to convert the "lower orders," minister to their material needs, and reform their immoral behaviour were seen as a positive force, and one that might help counter the danger posed by socialist and often atheist leftists. The army had become respectable, and in BC towns, where authorities were particularly uneasy about godless leftists, may even have been granted more rights to public space than it enjoyed in Eastern Canada. However, not all street corner preachers received the same consideration as the Salvation Army. In May 1909, as the free speech fights were playing out in Vancouver, the *Province* reported that "for preaching the gospel on the public streets and thereby collecting a crowd which blocked traffic, W.S. Veale, an itinerant preacher, today began a 30-day sentence in the city jail." Veale, who told the judge that "the word of God forbids me to swear," was clearly of a less respectable working-class revivalist tradition than the Salvation Army, and he received no special consideration from Vancouver police.[99]

A few years earlier, the streets of Vancouver and Victoria had witnessed the preaching of another less-than-respectable and very alternative Christian sect – the Zionites. This small faith-healing group was based largely in the United States, and most Canadian Zionites lived in BC cities, primarily Victoria. The response to the Zionites provides some important insights into levels of public support for the mainstream churches. The sect received major press attention after two children in the congregation died, and its leader, Eugene Brooks, was charged with causing their deaths because he had failed to summon a doctor. He served time in jail. This incident is discussed and well analyzed by James Opp in *The Lord for the Body.*[100] The Brooks court cases received a great deal of media attention, but Victorians and Vancouverites were also appalled by certain aspects of Zionite theology, including their bitter attacks on the churches. As an outraged letter to the *Vancouver Province* recounted, a Zionite preacher named Fair claimed that "the churches are run by the devil. There are a lot of devils in them. Oh they don't repent of their sins and get straight with God, they'll go to hell and be damned, every one of them."[101] Eighteen months later, another letter-writer named "Lex" was equally horrified by the preaching of a new Zionite leader, Elder Simmons, who delivered his message on the streets of Vancouver. Lex commented, "If some of us do not attend church every Sunday, still we cannot stand by and hear the religious beliefs of our fathers and mothers denounced or ridiculed by any person, more particularly upon the public street."[102] Lex was challenged by a non-believer who called himself "Impartial Observer." Although he "was not a member of any church or believer in any of their creeds," he felt that in the interests of "justice and fair play," the Zionites should receive an unbiased hearing.[103]

Impartial Observer was also disgusted by the public attacks on the Zionites for their criticism of the secret societies, the fraternal orders, which had large memberships in Vancouver and Victoria.[104] In both cities, it was the Zionite condemnation of the orders – not the churches – that sparked a major public outcry. In Vancouver, Simmons's preaching against the orders appears to have provoked near riots. In October 1900, the first time he denounced the orders on a Vancouver street, a crowd of more than five hundred people pelted him with rotten fruit. At his next attempt, "over a thousand men and boys" drowned him out with shouting. According to the *Vancouver Province,* "strong men who never work left their beer untouched in the saloons in the vicinity and rushed to see the cause of the uproar and they too joined in the big shout." Speaking in his own church, Simmons managed to make himself heard, despite much verbal abuse and heckling. He decried the "filthy rites" of the secret societies and asserted that "there was not a secret society in Vancouver which did not admit to membership men who were not Christian."[105] In Victoria, Eugene Brooks also raised his voice against the fraternal orders, preaching one summer evening on the street, where he encountered a less-than-friendly response. As the *Victoria Times* reported,

> Mr. Brooks and several of the other speakers directed their attention principally to adverse remarks on the secret societies, which were denounced in unmeasured terms. In fact, the evangelist contended that the lodge practice was a reversion to sun worship, and all those who joined a lodge turned their backs on God. This was resented by a number of the audience, who replied with equal vigor.[106]

Though in much more vocal and extreme tones, the Zionite attacks on the orders echo some mainstream church anxieties – that the requirement for members to believe in a supreme being was very far from an acceptance of all Christian dogma. The fraternal orders certainly provided major competition to the churches, particularly among men, and the public reactions to the Zionites suggest who was winning, at least in Vancouver and Victoria. The sect's denunciation of the churches did prompt some angry letters to the editor (as well as some defence by atheist believers in fair play), but the reaction to its attacks on the fraternal orders was much more violent. The relative power and appeal of the two institutions in Vancouver and Victoria seems clear, reinforcing the comment made by the Victoria minister in 1909 that many local men preferred to attend lodge meetings rather than church services.

Soon after these conflicts on the streets of Vancouver and Victoria, most BC Zionites relocated to Illinois, the centre of their ideology. Although the Zionites and the irreligious challenged the mainstream churches, Victoria and Vancouver were much more Christian in the years before the First World War than they are today. There were many committed churchgoers in the major cities of British Columbia. As elsewhere in the country, they tended to be women, both middle and working class. Many middle-class married men and some of their working-class counterparts were also very active in the churches, propelled there by some combination of faith, wifely suasion, and a desire for respectability. However, participation in a church was less crucial to respectability and community involvement than in Eastern cities.

Christianity was not irrelevant in British Columbia's largest cities. Far from it. It was diverse, often vibrant, and much more contested – on the streets and in churches, halls, and homes – than in Central and Eastern

Canadian cities. Protestants and Catholics could try to apply the programs of moral reform, revivals, and simple faith that they had brought with them from Central Canada, but they soon discovered that they were operating in a context where Christian hegemony was often challenged, and from a range of directions. Their efforts to transform the secular culture of drinking, gambling, and Sunday recreation in Vancouver and Victoria met with stiff opposition from large portions of the population and indifference from the government, which recognized that they constituted a small minority of the voting public. The irreligious were more common – and more vocal – than in Eastern Canada. Many Victorians preferred to water their gardens or attend fraternal order or socialist meetings rather than go to church on Sundays, and in working-class Gastown almost 10 percent of the mostly male working-class inhabitants felt the freedom to define themselves as atheists or as having no religion. Church members had to contend with socialist unbelievers and rationalist lecturers, who attacked Christianity and the churches in print as well as on the streets and in packed halls. Attacks on the churches, even from "fanatical sectarians" such as the Zionites, were met with limited protest, unlike the near riots that resulted from Zionite challenges to those bastions of masculine culture, the fraternal orders.

The Zionites represented one small piece of the religious diversity of BC cities. A significant number of religious and racialized groups further undermined the hegemony of mainstream Christianity in Vancouver, Victoria, and other urban centres in the province. These communities and the challenge they posed are the focus of the following two chapters.

6
Under Siege
Non-Christians, Racialized Groups, and White Women's Rights

Churchgoers in Vancouver, Victoria, and across the province struggled with the many Euro-Canadians, primarily working-class men, whose leisure culture was anathema to their values. At best, these irreligious men had no interest in the churches and often spoke against them and Christianity. They were, however, not the only group that either actively or by its very presence challenged the hegemony of the churches. Christian Vancouverites and Victorians shared their cities with a far greater variety and number of non-Christians, including Jews, Buddhists, Sikhs, Hindus, Confucians, and others, than did Christians in other Canadian cities. Most adherents to non-Christian religions belonged to the province's racialized Chinese, Japanese, and South Asian communities. As we have seen, some small towns were also home to significant groups of racialized and largely non-Christian residents, particularly those of Chinese origin. The church leaders perceived most of these groups as a challenge to Christian power and to their efforts to impose Christian moral values on the province. We have seen, for example, how the presence of non-Christian groups was used to help justify the existence of BC's "godless" public schools and how adherents to non-Christian religions were among those who opposed Sabbatarian legislation.[1]

For church leaders, one solution to the "problem" of the racialized non-Christians in their midst was conversion to Christianity. However, attempts at proselytism among these communities achieved little success before the First World War. The Asian population was not the only racialized group that undermined Christian hegemony. Primarily located (or relocated) outside the cities, but not outside the imagination of mainstream Christian settlers, were the Indigenous peoples, most of whom had converted to Christianity by this period, though Euro-Canadian Christians often worried about the depth of their faith.

This chapter looks at non-Christian communities, primarily from the perspective of dominant Euro-Canadian Christians, concentrating on Vancouver and Victoria but also making some generalizations about the broader BC context. Not all non-Christians were seen as equally threatening – Jews were far more accepted than Asians – pointing to the complex intersection of religion and race in constructing the "other" in British Columbia.

This chapter also compares Euro-Canadian irreligious men with the non-Christian and often racialized communities, also largely male, tentatively identifying both similarities and differences between them. Both had their own rough masculine culture, although racial differences and "heathenism" made the leisure activities of the latter appear particularly threatening to many white British Columbians. A brief look at some of the racialized communities demonstrates the complexity of unbelief among them and the diverse ethno-cultural roles played by minority religious institutions in hostile environments.

In seeking to convert the many racialized "heathen" and Euro-Canadian infidels, and to control the leisure culture of both, churchmen needed all the allies they could get. They found supporters among Euro-Canadian women, who were so instrumental in church work. But these allies expected support in return – which they received, particularly in the struggle for the franchise. White BC women were among the first in Canada to gain church acceptance for suffrage rights – both in church and beyond. This may have reflected the progressive nature of the pioneer West, but I argue here that it probably had much more to do with the insecurities of churchmen and the fact that the support – and the votes – of white Christian women were essential in their efforts to Christianize a racially diverse and rather godless province.

Jews: Religion, Ethnicity, and Whiteness

Some non-Christian groups were under-represented in British Columbia, compared to the rest of Canada, whereas others were over-represented. The province's Jewish community was proportionally smaller than in many Eastern provinces, but it was a long-established one: many Jews came to

Temple Emmanu-El, Victoria Synagogue, 190– | *BC Archives, C-09022*

Victoria with the 1858 gold rush, and others arrived during the late nineteenth and early twentieth centuries, as part of the large Jewish immigration from eastern Europe to North America. In Vancouver, Jews made up just under 1.0 percent of the population in 1901 and 1911, whereas in Victoria they made up approximately 0.5 percent in both census years.[2] Victoria's prosperous Jewish immigrants built a beautiful brick synagogue in 1863, which is still in use today, but the Vancouver Jewish community was not large enough to sustain a synagogue until 1907.[3]

When local synagogues were mentioned in the press, it was generally with respect. For example, in October 1900, the *Victoria Times* reported that "the services in connection with the observance of the Day of Atonement by the Jewish residents of Victoria were conducted last evening. Rabbi Klinkenstein delivered two eloquent sermons, one dealing with the historical origin of the Kol Nidre, a portion of the ritual, and the other treating of the doctrine of repentance."[4]

The Jews of Vancouver and Victoria appear to have been relatively well accepted in the Euro-Canadian Christian community, and unlike in Eastern cities, they seem not to have been targeted by proselytizing missionaries. As Andrew Reid notes, both Catholics and Jews could join Victoria's fraternal orders, and the local Freemasons participated in laying the cornerstone of the Victoria synagogue in 1863.[5] Some Victoria and Vancouver Jews, interviewed during the 1960s, 1970s, and 1980s, claimed to have experienced no anti-Semitism, especially those who grew up in the late nineteenth and early twentieth centuries.[6] A number of others recalled incidents of anti-Semitism, particularly from one or two students at school, but most downplayed their significance.[7] Mid-nineteenth-century Jewish immigrants of German and British backgrounds would have been more anglicized, more middle class, and thus more acceptable than the poor Yiddish-speaking Jews who emigrated from eastern Europe in the late nineteenth and early twentieth centuries.[8] However, even the latter do not appear to have encountered much anti-Semitism in British Columbia, at least prior to the 1920s.[9] As was true for BC Catholics, the presence of more strongly racialized others may have made the Jews seem "white" by comparison and thus more accepted than in Central and Eastern Canada and the United States.[10] When asked about anti-Semitism, one interviewee, Josephine Lancaster of Victoria, stated that there was none and added that Jews were fully accepted in the schools. She explained that "people were accepted as people if they were decent clean nice people." Not coincidentally, her next comment was that the Chinese, particularly "the coolie class," did experience prejudice.[11] Jews were more easily incorporated into the white community, despite being non-Christian, than Asian immigrants, who were seen as an economic threat. A comment from another interviewee, Gertrude Weinrobe, daughter of a Jewish businessman in Ladysmith and Wellington, is telling. A Christian with whom her father did business praised him as "a white Jew," meaning that he was fully satisfactory in racial terms, even though he was from eastern Europe and was not part of the earlier and more assimilated wave of Jewish immigration.[12] The small size of the BC Jewish community no doubt helped to mute anti-Semitic feelings, but the presence of more racialized others would also have played a role.

This relative lack of anti-Semitism may have made it easier for young Jewish men to be as irreligious as their Christian counterparts. However, secular Jewish options could draw them together, suggesting that as a minority, even one that did not face significant discrimination, they sometimes sought comfort in ethnic connections. Although most Jews emigrated to Canada as families, a significant number of single Jewish men sought their fortunes on the BC resource frontier.[13] Many stayed away from local synagogues. This was apparent at the 1909 founding of Vancouver's first secular Jewish organization, the Young Men's Hebrew Association (YMHA), which was intended to provide educational, social, athletic, and recreational services to young Jewish men. It had fifty-eight paid-up members, most of whom had no connection with more religious Jewish organizations. Reporting on the YMHA's first meeting, the *Canadian Jewish Times* observed, "it seemed almost incredible to the young men themselves, that there are so many of them in Vancouver, and they regarded each other with astonishment, most of them having met for the first time."[14] The popularity of secular options was also obvious at the YMHA's first social function, the Channukah Ball of December 1909, which "was attended by the largest number of Jews congregated in the city at any prior event."[15] The taste for non-religious activities was not confined to Vancouver. In 1910, twenty Jews, both men and women, participated in Rosh Hashanah services (the Jewish New Year) at Prince Rupert, a northern port town and the terminus of a new railroad, which was then at the height of its early-twentieth-century prosperity. Tellingly, just two months afterward, almost forty Jewish men joined its YMHA, which aimed to "cater to the physical, social, and intellectual welfare of the young men of Prince Rupert."[16] In other words, the number of Jewish men who opted for the secular YMHA was almost double that of the men and women who had attended Rosh Hashanah services at the holiest time of the Jewish year.

Other irreligious Jews did seek ethnic connections in local synagogues. One active member of the Victoria synagogue defined himself as an atheist on the 1901 census, reminding us that then, as now, religious organizations for minority ethno-religious groups could be as much about a sense of cultural belonging as about belief. This was also evident in an interview with Dora Roseman, a Jewish woman who arrived in Vancouver in 1913. By the 1920s, she had become active in an irreligious Jewish socialist women's group and was very dismissive of religious Jews. However, when the interviewer asked her if she and her husband were Orthodox (religiously observant) when they first came to Vancouver, she replied, with a hint of embarrassment, "We had just come, there was no place to go, nothing to do so we just went occasionally, you know, High Holidays – [we] met [Jewish] people there, the people even if they [preferred] somewhere else – still had to go there [because] there wasn't anything else."

She seemed to suggest that she was not alone in this approach, and that other irreligious Jews had to go to synagogue at least occasionally to be with other Jews.[17] In Victoria, this seems to have been particularly true of families, some of whom attended synagogue for similar reasons. Rena Phillips's mother was hostile to Judaism as a religion, and the family had absolutely no Jewish spiritual practices at home when they lived in small BC towns. However, when they lived in Victoria, where "the community was very small but very close knit," they belonged to the synagogue. Everyone attended Friday night services, including her highly irreligious family.[18]

Racialized Communities, Racism, and Religion

Jews were not the only minority group for whom religious institutions provided important ethno-cultural spaces. As we have seen, Catholic churches did the same for Catholic immigrants. Hugh Johnston argues that religious institutions served a similar function for the South Asian community, another relatively small BC minority during this period. Euro-Canadians referred to all South Asian immigrants as "Hindus," othering them through negative perceptions of both race and religion, and demonstrating their bigotry and ignorance. In fact, Sikhs composed over 85 percent of South Asian immigrants to British Columbia, although they were a minority in India. In the years prior to the First World War, they founded temples, or gurdwaras, in Vancouver, Victoria, and nearby towns.[19] Johnston notes that the BC Sikh temples served all South Asians, including Muslims and Hindus, providing meeting places and cultural and social resources in a foreign and racist society.[20] At least some Euro-Canadians may have known of the social and political roles of the gurdwaras, as one Indo-Canadian interviewee stated that the whites "did not want to let people build gurdwaras" because they feared that South Asians would congregate there and "make plans and improve their condition."[21] Indeed, the gurdwaras did provide meeting places for South Asians who struggled against both racist exclusion in Canada and British imperialism in India.

During the pre-war years, South Asians were involved in considerable political organizing to protest rigid immigration restrictions, particularly the infamous "continuous voyage" rule. This required overseas immigrants to make their trip to Canada without stopping along the way, which was impossible from India. Thus, most Indians were barred from legally entering Canada, despite the fact that they were British subjects, many of whom had fought as soldiers for the empire. Political organizers also focused on allowing the wives of South Asian men to enter Canada, and in 1914, to permit the immigrants aboard the *Komagata Maru* to disembark and remain in the country. The federal government's intransigence regarding these issues, and the intense racism faced by South Asian immigrants in everyday interactions, radicalized many. A major political organization that emerged from this radicalization, the Ghadar Party, led primarily by Sikhs, was influential all along the West Coast of North America. As historian Seema Sohi reveals, it emphasized secularism and unity, urging Sikhs, Muslims, and Hindus to set aside their religious differences and work together as Indians.[22]

Canadian scholars have debated whether, like many white workers in the province, at least some of the more radical BC Sikhs became secularized. Peter Campbell argues that even their close association with the Socialist Party of Canada did not have this effect on Sikh radicals, whose challenge to British imperialism in India was grounded in their religious values of social justice.[23] Many may have retained their personal religious values, but they clearly did not want religious differences to undermine organizing in the larger South Asian community.

The largest non-Christian group in Victoria, Vancouver, and British Columbia generally was the Chinese. In 1901 and 1911, they comprised 13.2 percent and 10.9 percent of Victoria residents, and 7.6 percent and 3.2 percent of Vancouverites in the same years. Significant numbers also lived in smaller BC towns.[24] The majority inhabited separate and very much othered Chinatowns, and most were not Christians.[25] Adherence to a single exclusive religion was much less common in China than in the West. The majority of Chinese accepted elements from a range of religious traditions, particularly Taoism and various folk Chinese spiritual practices, including ancestor worship and prayer to various traditional deities. Most also adhered to Confucian values. Buddhist beliefs and practices were important to many.[26]

The Japanese composed the second-largest racialized non-Christian community in British Columbia. They were less than a quarter the size of the Chinese population in 1901, and though their immigration increased over the decade, their numbers were still less than half those of the Chinese in 1911. Very few settled in Victoria, with the majority living in either Vancouver's Japantown or elsewhere in the Lower Mainland. Most were Buddhists. Like the South Asians and the Chinese, they were subject to extreme racism and Euro-Canadian efforts to limit or prevent their immigration to Canada. The following discussion focuses primarily on the Chinese community, as the largest racialized non-Christian group in British Columbia, but the Japanese experience is also addressed where relevant.

Like most South Asians in British Columbia, the vast majority of Chinese and Japanese immigrants were male. Many Euro-Canadians, including many Christian ministers, opposed the immigration of Asian women into Canada, fearing that the Asian population would expand and settle permanently if this were permitted. As Enakshi Dua notes, a minority, primarily of Christian groups, did support the immigration of Asian wives to join their husbands on the grounds that it would prevent miscegenation and other "immoral" behaviour among Asian men.[27] One Presbyterian minister, Reverend L.W. Hall, who served as a missionary to the Chinese in Victoria, went to Ottawa with a party of South Asian men to lobby the government to permit the entry of the wives of several South Asian men who were already in Canada. The Methodist minister J.C. Speer, focusing specifically on the Chinese, argued,

> It is always a disaster for men to congregate together ... without the blessed influences of a home in which there are women and children. This is true of thousands [of Euro-Canadian men] who spend their years in the lumber-camps, and in the mines ... It is a poor home indeed that is totally void of some uplifting influence, and as for the most part these Chinamen leave their wives and children in China they are in a most dangerous and degrading environment.[28]

Whereas Speer and a few other Euro-Canadian Christians saw marriage (to women of the same race) as a moral, domestic solution for Asian men, as they did for white men, this was never the majority view, which continued to concentrate on exclusion.[29]

BC newspapers often printed stories about "exotic" Chinese religious and cultural rites in local Chinatowns. Some were more respectful than others, though none seemed very knowledgeable about actual practice. For example, a *Vancouver Province* article titled "A Strange Chinese Ceremony" informed its readers,

> Twice a year the Chinese offer up food and papers at the graves of their dead. They have a large stone platform erected in each of their cemeteries, with two large stone chimneys at the end of each. Two men place a roast pig, drink, fruit, and several other kinds of food on the platform, while two others are engaged in lighting fires in the chimneys. After this they kneel and offer a prayer, then rising, they chant a long dreary kind of song. By this time the fires are out in the chimneys. They then leave the wood on the platform while they drive home. It is the Chinese belief that Satan comes down in the night to steal away the bodies of their dead friends; but if, on arriving at the graves, he finds a meal laid out for him, he is so pleased that he sits down and eats, and then flies away afterwards so satisfied that he either forgets to take the bodies, or else repents of having intended doing so, their relatives being so obliging.[30]

Palace of the Saints, headquarters of popular Chinese religions in Victoria's Chinatown c. 1899. In the late nineteenth and early twentieth centuries, it would have been one of many similar locations in North American Chinatowns called "joss houses" by white settlers because of the joss sticks, or incense sticks, burned as gestures of respect and worship to the statues of respected historical figures and popular gods located there. | *City of Victoria Archives, M05580*

Other stories of Chinese religious practices were more critical. Of course, missionaries took a particularly negative stance. Reverend Speer's detailed description of a Chinese temple, or "joss house," was fairly representative.[31] He remarked on the dreariness and "gloomy precincts of this idolatrous temple" and mentioned "the malignant expression of the idol [god]" and the "charnel house" smell of incense and roasted meat offerings. He commented condescendingly that "the sincerity of the heathen none can doubt, but the childishness of the matter is saddening to those who have learned the better way."[32] Mainstream newspapers did not always focus on "heathenism," but they sometimes noted social disturbances ostensibly caused by Chinese religious practices. In 1899, the *Province* reported that the Chinese had "made the night hideous" with the sound of firecrackers on Chinese New Year.[33]

Chinese New Year could also provide an opportunity for social contact, as many Euro-Canadians visited Chinatowns to observe and be entertained by the exotic celebrations and to receive food, drink, and other gifts from their Chinese hosts. Some scholars and Euro-Canadian commentators have suggested that these interactions were more positive and friendly than might be expected. However, Patricia Roy points out that they sometimes furnished an excuse for vandalism and theft by Euro-Canadian visitors.[34]

Euro-Canadian descriptions of and involvement with Chinese religious celebrations could range from positive and interested to dismissive and exploitative, but there was much less ambivalence in the profoundly racist articles regarding Chinese sanitary practices, supposed immorality, and competition with white labour that appeared regularly in BC papers during this period.[35] Some Christian ministers supported such attacks and advocated the exclusion of the Chinese from the province. As Peter Ward and Patricia Roy demonstrate, many ministers were hostile to Chinese immigrants, sharing the fear that they threatened the jobs of British Columbians, while also decrying certain leisure activities, particularly gambling, opium smoking, and trafficking in Chinese prostitutes, which they believed would contaminate the morals of BC society and further degrade the leisure practices of white men.[36] Some Christian lay people also participated in anti-Asian efforts. An active member of Mount Pleasant Methodist Church, H.H. Stevens was very much part of Methodist social reform initiatives in Vancouver. A vocal supporter of Asian exclusion, he worked to expose what he saw as the bad influence of Chinese gambling dens on Euro-Canadian clerks, and he pressured authorities to shut down the opium trade, which he argued had a negative impact on Chinese people and Euro-Canadians alike.[37]

Moral issues were somewhat less of a focus with regard to Japanese immigrants, though they too faced virulent racism and suspicion. All the clergymen who testified before the Royal Commission on Chinese and Japanese Immigration in 1902 opposed Asian immigration. Some were in the forefront of anti-Asian sentiment: As Patricia Roy documents, when the Asiatic Exclusion League organized an infamous 1907 rally in Vancouver, several were on hand to address the crowd. Incensed by inflammatory speeches, the rally ended in a major riot, during which a white mob attacked Chinatown and Japantown. Among the ministers who spoke at the rally was Reverend G.H. Wilson of Mount Pleasant, whose working-class Anglican parishioners would have shared his racist views about Asian competition. A few months later, his colleague Reverend St. George Buttrum of Holy Trinity parish in the neighbouring working-class suburb of Fairview spoke at a meeting of the Asiatic Exclusion League, arguing that "instead of trying to Christianize the heathen in foreign lands ... money should be spent upon the white men that we have at home."[38] Other ministers agreed, feeling that their primary focus and responsibility was to bring white men into the Christian fold. Accepting Chinese immigration would run counter to the interests of the Euro-Canadian working class, which would simply increase its hostility toward the church. The Methodist minister Edwin Scott of Vancouver testified before the Royal Commission on Chinese and Japanese Immigration in 1902 that the clergy "have to draw our support from the [Euro-Canadian] labouring people and they are affected because labour can be obtained so cheaply [from Asian workers]."[39] As Presbyterian churchmen in British Columbia pointed out to their Eastern Canadian colleagues who opposed Asian exclusion, such a stance reduced Presbyterian support in the province.[40]

Whereas hysteria about growing numbers of Asian immigrants led some churchmen to support their exclusion from British Columbia, others believed that conversion was the only way to nullify the threat. In 1917, the Methodist minister S.S. Osterhout foretold that if British Columbians failed to Christianize the Asians, "they will in a measure Orientalize us."[41] Others feared a wholesale takeover. Reverend Neville Ward, an Anglican, envisioned a bleak future should this occur. Referring to Shaughnessy and Rockland, fashionable residential districts in Vancouver and Victoria, and to Vancouver's Catholic cathedral, he warned that "unless we Christianize the Chinese and Japanese in our midst, the day may come when there will be Buddhist and Shinto temples on Shaughnessy Heights and Rockland Avenue, and a temple erected to Confucius where now stands the cathedral of the Holy Rosary!"[42]

Not all of those who supported conversion were as hostile or as frightened. Roy and Ward argue that Anglican, Methodist, and Presbyterian missionaries to Asian immigrants tended to be more sympathetic than their racist counterparts who did not work closely with these communities. The missionaries did not see Asians as their racial equals, but they took a different approach, either from a sense of humanitarian Christian brotherhood or in the belief that BC Asians presented a divine opportunity for conversion. They opposed exclusionary legislation as un-Christian and urged their colleagues to funnel more resources into conversion and assimilation programs.[43]

We have seen that many BC workers did not appreciate ministers who criticized Asian exclusion campaigns. Such attitudes extended beyond the working class, with at least some newspaper editors also chastising the churches on this issue. For example, in the summer of 1900 the editor of the *Victoria Times* bitterly attacked a former Victoria minister for

> enumerating all the virtues of the Chinaman, such as his industry and his frugality ... saying that his one bad fault is that he is a worshiper [sic] of Buddha or Confucius. We are sure that if the rev. gentleman had been perfectly candid he could have enumerated a few more very objectionable traits ... but the great point is that [Chinese immigrants are] economically objectionable. We suppose if the ministers and the missionaries are to remain true to the principles which guide their way of life it is their duty to ignore this important point to men of the world and to advocate nothing which will retard the great day which they are doing their utmost to hasten.[44]

Conversion Efforts and Asian Response

Many missionaries were certainly doing their best to hasten "the great day" by trying to convert Chinese immigrants. They hoped that conversion would reform the immorality of the largely male Chinese community, whose rough leisure practices did not differ markedly from those of the Euro-Canadian workers whom the churches also sought to convert and reform. Alison Marshall's description of the pre-conversion life of the Chinese Canadian Christian missionary Ma Seung, which included at least a few bouts of opium smoking, being tempted to visit sex workers, and more long-term interests in Chinese opera and the various forms of gambling popular in his community, provides some insights into the rough culture of Chinese immigrant men.[45]

Between the 1880s and 1914, the Methodist, Presbyterian, and Anglican Churches established various missions that targeted Chinese and Japanese immigrants, seeking to draw them in by offering English classes, which employed Bible readings and hymns as teaching tools.[46] Most missions were in Victoria and Vancouver, though some were founded in other urban centres, such as Cumberland, Nelson, and Nanaimo. A major concern about Chinese immorality focused on the apparent trafficking in Chinese sex workers, so the Methodist Church also set up a Chinese Rescue Home in Victoria during the 1880s to save these women. The church asked the Methodist Women's Missionary Society (WMS) to run the home, and a committee of local Methodist WMS members played an active role in its administration.[47] With other women's church groups, they also supported missions to Asian men in both Victoria and Vancouver.

Despite various missionary efforts, as church leaders bemoaned and scholars have demonstrated, proselytism had little success among either

Chinese Rescue Home, Victoria, May 1906. By this period the home was accepting more younger children, as their efforts to "rescue" Chinese women were not very successful, as many rejected the Christian domestic training provided by the home. | *BC Archives, C-07913*

the Chinese or the Japanese. As Marilyn Whiteley notes, many of the sex trade workers who took refuge at the Chinese Rescue Home soon returned to Chinatown, finding the strict domestic routine and missionizing atmosphere not to their liking. Some women did use the home for their own purposes, particularly to escape abusive husbands or first wives, to receive care during illness, and to obtain an education in English for themselves and their children. A minority, especially those who came to the home as young girls, did remain for many years and were converted to Christianity and Euro-Canadian domesticity.[48]

The majority of Asian men were also indifferent to missionary efforts. Some were actively hostile, as the 1900 attempt to blow up the Victoria

Chinese mission church most clearly attests.[49] Chinese resistance to missionary efforts was well known to both the public and the missionaries themselves. One letter to the *Victoria Times* avowed that "the Chinese don't want Christianity," and an Anglican missionary wrote that "only by secular teaching we could get hold of them. Chinamen will come anywhere to learn English ... Some have gone away because they did not wish to belong to a 'Christian school.'"[50]

Other missionaries complained about the strength of "heathenism" among Asian immigrants. One Presbyterian missionary contended that the Chinese had to be converted from "the centuries of darling superstition, demonaltry, ancestral worship and faith in false gods," and a Methodist bemoaned that missionaries were "face to face with a more powerful heathenism, strong, subtle, deep."[51] Certainly, the fact that Chinese immigrants had their own religious and cultural beliefs can in itself explain their lack of interest in the missionary message. Political changes in China could also affect their attitudes to conversion. Historian Jiwu Wang suggests that they became more willing to listen to the missionaries after 1911 because the new republican government was more friendly than its predecessor to Christianity.[52] No doubt, there is some truth to this, but the number of Chinese converts in British Columbia remained very low.

Scholars have offered various explanations for this lack of interest. Norman Knowles proposes that the predominance of young male "sojourners" in the Chinese community was a major factor. In their search for the best jobs, sojourners moved around a great deal, and most planned to stay in Canada only until they made money. Thus, they were uninterested in conversion. Knowles presents similar arguments to explain the churches' relative lack of success in converting the smaller sojourning Japanese community.[53]

Perhaps, like other young men, many Chinese sojourners were simply indifferent to religious matters. An intriguing article in the *Province* quotes a "prominent Chinaman," who stated that the local Chinese were not interested in their own religion either. In Vancouver, he explained, Chinese New Year was more a national than a religious holiday:

> There are no religious rites or observances in connection with the new year ... The new year is not regarded as a religious festival by the majority of Chinese in this country as it is in China. The Chinaman away from home tends to forget his religious rites and duties. He leaves them in China ... He belongs, perhaps, to what you call the freethinkers. But in fact he does not think at all about religious matters.[54]

At least some men did visit the temples in local Chinatowns, so this was probably an exaggeration.[55] An article in the *Victoria Colonist* reported that in 1909 working-class Chinese men violently protested middle-class Chinese men's efforts to close down the "Joss Houses" in Chinatown.[56] However, Alison Marshall points out that among Chinese families, it was primarily women who were responsible for certain facets of customary religious observance, such as making offerings to ancestors and to traditional deities. Thus, given the largely bachelor culture of Chinese immigrants in British Columbia, there might be some truth in the *Province*'s portrayal of "the Chinaman away from home."[57] When Hong Low was interviewed in 1980 about his early life in Victoria, he noted that at one point in his life he regularly attended the Chinese Presbyterian Mission and visited a number of Chinese temples, but when asked if he believed in Christianity or in (Chinese) gods, he said no, stating, "I'm not a big believer in gods." When the interviewer asked whether his wife had believed in gods, he responded that "women tend to believe in gods."[58]

Although some male Chinese sojourners might not have been as interested in their own religious practices as their female relatives were, it is very clear that most Chinese people in British Columbia were not attracted to Christianity, a phenomenon that appears to have been particularly BC-based. Even in 1931, the first year in which published statistics analyzed religious affiliation according to race, only 6.5 percent of British Columbians of Chinese origin were defined as Christian, as compared to almost 50.0 percent of their counterparts in Ontario and over 30.0 percent in Manitoba and Saskatchewan.[59] Focusing on Manitoba, Alison Marshall suggests why the Chinese residents of that province, most of whom were also sojourning bachelors, were much more willing than those in British Columbia to identify as Christians. Marshall refers to "efficacy" as an important concept in understanding Chinese religious practices – individuals chose their religion on the basis of its value and use, or efficacy. Marshall suggests that at least ostensible adherence to Christianity was efficacious for many Chinese bachelors in Manitoba. They lived in small towns with few other Chinese people, and they had regular contact with Euro-Canadian Christians. Therefore, presenting themselves as Christian was important because it made them more accepted and facilitated some level of assimilation. At the same time, however, public adherence to Christianity did not necessarily equate with religious transformation. Although significant numbers of Chinese people in Manitoba told the census-taker and other public officials that they were Christians, most did not formally convert, and identification as Christian did not preclude the continued acceptance of traditional Chinese religious practices and beliefs.[60]

Why were British Columbians of Chinese origin so much less likely to define themselves as Christian than those elsewhere in Canada? Most of them lived in Chinatowns, whose social and cultural organizations met their needs, making them less interested in connecting with Christian missions.[61] Jiwu Wang argues that particularly for working-class Chinese people, the extreme racism of white BC Christians made missionary claims regarding the virtues of Christianity, and of Christian brotherhood, ring very hollow indeed. Many missionaries were aware of this. As Presbyterian missionary A.B. Winchester noted in 1894, why should a Chinese person embrace the religion "of the people who ... by the many he comes in contact with he is despised, slandered, wronged and persecuted in every way that malice, cupidity and ignorant race-hatred and prejudice can devise and effect?"[62] As a poster placed on the walls of Vancouver's Chinatown shortly after the First World War by the Union for Opposing Christianity averred, "Christianity is not Equality" and "Christianity is not Love."[63]

Wang states that middle-class Chinese had other reservations regarding Christianity: they feared that conversion would undermine Chinese ethnic identity and lead to assimilation. The opposition to missionary efforts meant that Chinese individuals who showed an interest in Christianity or sought conversion were often harassed or ostracized by their families or ethnic organizations.[64] Perhaps the general lack of interest in Christianity among most Chinese immigrants in B.C. also reveals an understanding that it was not particularly central in British Columbia and was thus a less important mechanism for social acceptance than in Central and Eastern Canada. Regardless, the churches' failure to convert the Chinese population of British Columbia simply highlighted the limitations of their influence, power, and cultural reach in the province.[65]

Intersecting Challenges

BC churchmen struggled valiantly to re-create the Christian hegemony that they could take for granted in Central and Eastern Canada. They faced significant challenges from godless radicals, and the many white settler men who preferred "rough culture" to church involvement, as well as from members of a range of racialized non-Christian communities who had little or no interest in Christianity. Even the Indigenous peoples, whom missionaries claimed to have converted by the turn of the century, were a source of anxiety. Both European observers and many churchmen believed that though some Indigenous people were sincere Christians, many others had combined new and old beliefs in distressing ways. In recent years scholars have done important work to demonstrate the ways in which many B.C. Indigenous people accepted key facets of Christian belief, while at the same time integrating them with existing spiritual beliefs and traditions in ways that worked for them.[66] Missionaries did not, however, see things this way.

Some noted that the more isolated Indigenous groups remained largely "pagan" and that many converts were merely nominal Christians or potential backsliders.[67] In a 1914 address titled "Indian Work," Reverend Freeman cautioned the Vancouver Ministerial Association that "the Christian Indians are in danger of lapsing in large numbers back into Paganism."[68] As Paige Raibmon reveals, some Indigenous people enjoyed flouting missionary assumptions about their Christian status by demonstrating their continued adherence to Indigenous spiritual beliefs and practices. Although few were able to do so as spectacularly as the group of Vancouver Island Kwakwaka'wakw who staged a "cannibal dance" at the Chicago World's

Indigenous people and Catholic missionaries at Fort Fraser, 1900–01. Left to right: Chief George Tsadias, Reverend Emile-Marie Bunoz, Reverend Nicholas Coccola, Leon Ketlo, and Allan Ketlo | *BC Archives, D-00445*

Fair in 1893, missionaries realized that their hold on the Indigenous population was less firm than they desired, despite their growing ability to call on the power of the state to outlaw Indigenous spiritual practices and enforce mandatory Christian indoctrination in residential schools.[69]

"Godless" white men and "heathen" Asians exacerbated the problems that Christian missionaries faced in "civilizing" Indigenous people and in deepening their conversions. Missionaries frequently complained of the bad example that drinking and gambling Euro-Canadian men set for their Indigenous charges, demonstrating very clearly to Indigenous people that many Euro-Canadians did not themselves follow the dictates of Christianity. As Renisa Mawani shows, churchmen and many politicians were very concerned that both "bad" Euro-Canadian men and Chinese men debauched Indigenous people by encouraging them to gamble and by illegally providing them with alcohol. Sexual relations between Euro-Canadian men and Indigenous women were also viewed as a moral danger to both the men and the women involved.[70]

Although the Christian churches did not enjoy complete social acceptance among all Canadians across the country, it was only in British Columbia that Christian belief systems, moral precepts, and power structures were challenged so strongly and from so many directions. The groups that were either indifferent to Christianity or strongly opposed to it did not work together and indeed were sometimes intensely hostile to each other. Nonetheless, their combined efforts and presence undermined the hegemonic power of Christianity, in turn creating more social and cultural spaces in which people could be free to define their own religious or irreligious choices.

Seeking Allies

Given this, it is not surprising that churchmen sought for allies wherever they could find them. They worked closely with Euro-Canadian Christian women on a range of Christianizing and civilizing missions. As we have seen, Euro-Canadian women typically retained their church affiliation after their arrival in British Columbia, and many undertook moral and social reform work. The Woman's Christian Temperance Union (WCTU) organized various campaigns, ranging from battling to end gambling and the sale of liquor to setting up reading rooms and canteens for single men and rescue homes for young women who had been led astray.[71] The women's groups of specific churches were also active, sometimes supporting the WCTU in various endeavours and also contributing to their own denominations' efforts at conversion and moral reform. Many women worked in a variety of female Christian organizations.[72] One of the more active groups was the Methodist Women's Missionary Society, which ran Victoria's Chinese Rescue Home. The minutes of church-based women's missionary societies and other women's church groups reveal a variety of activities, including sending quilts to Indigenous communities that were being missionized, providing financial or volunteer support to the Chinese missions or Chinese rescue homes in their own towns, and raising funds and organizing and signing petitions for other Christian social and moral reform causes.[73] Many Christian women also worked in secular women's reform groups and clubs. As Gillian Weiss finds, whereas the Local Councils of Women and other female associations were ostensibly secular, Presbyterian and Methodist women were very much over-represented in them. The secular groups were less overtly focused on Christianization, but as Chris Clarkson notes, they were nonetheless committed to bringing in reforms that would help to "civilize" and domesticate the province, improve the situation of white women and children, and ensure that British Columbia was grounded in strong white families.[74]

As Canadian women worked toward these ends, they became increasingly frustrated by their lack of power in both the churches and the broader political sphere. Nineteenth-century Canadian women did not have a vote or representation on most church councils. Nor did they have the federal or provincial franchise, and as the BC WCTU recognized quite early on, this lack was both a galling reminder of inequality and a major impediment in compelling governments to implement their demands. Indigenous people and Asian immigrants, whether male or female, could not vote either, which enabled governments to legislate against their interests with impunity. For example, Indigenous reserves were reduced in size, and hunting and fishing rights were severely limited. A range of restrictive legislation was passed against Asians in the areas of employment and immigration.[75] At the same time, as we have seen, the BC government had little interest in enacting moral reform legislation, which would control the leisure of white male voters and Asian and Indigenous people alike.[76] As the men who supported such legislation were a minority of the electorate, and the women had no vote, their wishes were relatively easy to ignore.

This may help to explain why, though many Christian women across Canada were demanding the vote in church councils and the broader political sphere, their voices were most likely to be heard by their Christian brothers in British Columbia. Some scholars have examined Canadian women's struggle for the vote on church councils and the right to be delegates to such councils, but none have focused on the fact that most BC mainstream denominations supported their demands for the provincial franchise and granted them ecclesiastical representation and voting rights earlier than elsewhere in Canada.[77]

Even so, the BC churches certainly voiced opposition to women's rights, as was the case across Canada. Bible verses that advocated female subordination in church were handily quoted, as elsewhere, and concerns were raised that women's proper place was in the home. As Ruth Brouwer suggests, some of the opposition arose from fears that granting women equal rights on church councils could further feminize the churches by reducing the "manly character" of their governance structures.[78] It is also clear that not all Christian women wanted such rights, although many became increasingly supportive during the years before the First World War, particularly as British and American women in their own denominations received them.[79]

Even in British Columbia, change took decades to achieve. And not all BC churches were particularly progressive – the Presbyterians seem not to have taken a leadership role in regard to women's rights. Nonetheless, most BC churches were in the vanguard on this issue. For example, Canadian women had been trying to get the vote on Anglican vestries (local church governing bodies) since 1878. Although BC clergymen proved recalcitrant, and the motion to grant the vote was regularly defeated, the Anglican provincial synod finally conferred it in 1913, becoming the first Canadian synod to do so.[80] In 1890, the BC Conference of the Methodist Church was the first Canadian conference to push for increased women's rights in the church, although without success.[81] Efforts to grant women voting rights in the church were regularly defeated at the national level in the ensuing decades. Such attempts also received support from beyond British Columbia, but the wealthier and most urban Central Canadian delegations were consistently hostile.[82]

In 1910, the East Kootenay District of the Methodist Church simply ignored the rules about excluding women from church councils: it appointed Mrs. Florence Hall, president of a Vancouver suffrage association and wife of a progressive minister, as a delegate to the BC annual conference. The church's national Court of Appeal rejected her claim to sit as a delegate.[83] In 1914, almost all the BC delegates to the national Methodist conference voted in favour of female representation on church councils, but opposition from Central and Eastern Canadian delegates scuttled the motion. In 1918, the BC Methodist conference was the first Canadian conference to grant women full equality with men in church governance rights; later that year, the national conference followed suit.[84] Among Baptists, the BC church was the first in Canada to name female delegates to a conference, doing so in 1897. The Prairie provinces did not follow its lead until 1912.[85]

When it came to the provincial and federal franchise, the churches did not move quickly, even though the BC WCTU began regularly demanding it during the 1880s. Nonetheless, BC Baptists and Methodists were in the forefront of Canadian churches in advocating the broader franchise for white women. In 1913, the BC Methodist conference officially supported it, evidently the first Methodist conference in Canada to do so. From 1914 onward, regular "suffrage sermonettes" appeared in the *Western Methodist Recorder,* the BC Methodist paper, written by feminist Florence Hall, who had tried to sit as a conference delegate four years earlier. BC Baptists endorsed women's suffrage even earlier, in 1912.[86]

The fact that many BC churches were ahead of their Eastern equivalents on this issue could be viewed as part of a wider Western pattern, in both the United States and Canada. White women in the West generally won the franchise earlier than those in Eastern Canada and the Eastern United States. Various theories have been put forward to account for this, and some scholars have pointed to a greater progressivism in the West, rooted in pioneer partnerships between settler men and women on the frontier. American historian Rebecca Mead has developed a much more complex and multi-faceted perspective, suggesting that, at least in part, the racial politics in certain Western states and territories enabled white women to acquire political rights. In demanding the vote, they reminded white men that their presence and efforts helped to maintain white hegemony and "civilization" in the face of Asian immigrants and Indigenous populations. Mead also refers to progressive alliances between suffragists and the white working class, but such links could also reinforce anti-Asian sentiments.[87] Patricia Grimshaw makes similar arguments for frontier Australia, where white women won the vote relatively early. She speculates that male politicians sought to contain the potential power of racialized Asian and Aborigine people by increasing the white vote.[88]

In British Columbia, racial issues, entwined with religious concerns, played a significant role in generating church support for women's rights. As we have seen, clergymen felt very much under siege from a range of directions – from the numerous Asian immigrants, from the perhaps-not-fully Christianized Indigenous people, and from the many Euro-Canadian men, particularly working-class men, who scorned or ignored the message of the gospel.

Across Canada, Christian women who sought equal rights often employed the maternal feminist argument that women, who were naturally more moral, pious, and pure than men, would be very valuable in helping the churches to achieve their social and moral reform aims. Such reasoning was not always effective, but it clearly struck a chord among BC clergymen. Many stated that they supported the female franchise because Euro-Canadian Christian women made such a major contribution to their joint project of transforming British Columbia into a more Christian, civilized, and moral province. In affirming that women should have a vote on vestries, Anglican men praised their crucial role in maintaining and supporting the church. As one Anglican explained, in "the rural districts at least the women are the mainstay and hardest workers of the church."[89] Giving Anglican women the vote was more than a reward for their hard work. A perhaps more honest comment was made two years earlier by another Anglican clergyman. He advocated that women should be allowed to vote for vestry members and even to become members themselves, which would be a good thing for the rural districts.[90] What he left unsaid was that due to low levels of church involvement, many vestries had difficulty functioning. Permitting women to serve might actually produce enough candidates to keep them going. The Methodists, who were particularly active in the social and moral reform movement of the province, were very clear that granting women the provincial suffrage would be a positive development because it "would greatly aid in the moral uplift of social and political affairs for which we are all working."[91] They also contended that the female franchise would help to counter the votes of irreligious white men, a point pursued by feminist Florence Hall in a *Western Methodist Recorder* suffrage sermonette:

> For if, as Ralph Waldo Emerson said, "the wants, passions, vices, are allowed a full vote through the hands of a half-brutal, intemperate population, it is but fair that the virtue, the aspirations, should be allowed a full voice as an offset through the purest of the people", in the interests of ... the great work of the establishment of the kingdom of God upon this earth, the church at large should recognize and welcome the full co-operation or partnership of the greater half of its constituency with the other half ... Especially in this age, when the Church is actively engaged in social problems ... such as the white slave trade, gambling, drink evil, housing questions, commercialized sport, Sabbath observance, population eugenics ... and the care of the young,

Delegates to the Women's Missionary Society conference. Metropolitan Methodist Church, Victoria, 1912 | *BC Archives, E-01216*

> these are problems the solution of which can never be attained without the united efforts of man and woman.[92]

Similarly, in 1912 the Baptists supported women's suffrage because it "promised much for the rapid advance of Social and Moral legislation."[93] Clearly, these churchmen agreed with the maternal feminist arguments of many Euro-Canadian feminists.

The *Champion,* a pro-suffrage paper published by the feminist Political Equality League in Victoria between 1912 and 1914, was very interested in clerical attitudes regarding votes for women. Maria Grant, one of its co-editors, was an ardent Methodist who had long been active in church and WCTU work in the city. In an "Open Letter to Clergymen," the editors of the *Champion* stated that granting municipal suffrage rights to women had led to the decline of vice and the election of more moral officials. They also presented testimonials from various clergymen who applauded the influence of women's municipal suffrage on their parishes.[94] In 1913, the editors of the *Champion* congratulated the Methodist Church for endorsing the female franchise and reported with pleasure that several Anglican clergymen were moving in that direction.[95] Also in that year, they canvassed three hundred BC clergymen for their opinions about granting the franchise to women "on the same terms as it is given to men." Almost a third of the clergy responded, and though a small minority opposed suffrage, the vast majority did not. The *Champion* published some of their responses. A few pro-suffrage clergy advanced what have been called "equal rights" arguments, asserting that women deserved the vote on the basis of simple justice and equality. For example, Reverend Duncan Campbell of Enderby supported suffrage "as a matter of justice and fairness." However, most clergy advocated the franchise because, as Reverend Carson of the Congregational Church of Victoria said, "it will help in the moral upbuilding of the province." In Vancouver, Father Connelly of Holy Rosary Cathedral concurred and added that "it is certainly nauseating to see pure and honest women deprived of a vote which is given to frequenters of saloons and houses of immorality." He also noted the importance of white women's votes to "questions that concern the welfare of the race."[96]

Father Connelly was probably thinking in terms of the Caucasian race, and female suffragists across Canada echoed his comment about the injustice of drunken white men having the vote whereas pure white women did not.[97] In 1912, a *Champion* article stated that the clergy and feminists should be united in the social and moral reform movement so that they could work to build "a grander race."[98] Canadian feminist scholars have engaged in lengthy debate about the degree to which suffragists were racist.[99] There is certainly evidence that some BC suffragists shared the racist, exclusionary attitudes of white men, with at least one BC suffrage petition noting that granting the vote to white women would strengthen the electorate and facilitate the exclusion of Asians from the province. And though not all suffragists were Christian, the majority definitely were: their activism sprang from their work with the churches and the WCTU, and their demand for the vote was justified by the belief that it would help to create a more moral and Christian province.[100]

In the years before the First World War, British Columbia was the most religiously and racially diverse province in Canada. This was particularly visible in the larger cities. The province's Asian population consisted largely of single men whose "immoral" leisure interests bore some resemblance to those of their white male counterparts, and there is some evidence to suggest that at least some of the single Chinese working-class men were not much more interested in religious traditions than were their white counterparts. At the same time, religious institutions in racialized minority communities could provide a sense of belonging in a foreign and hostile land. Christian efforts to convert the Asian population were generally unproductive, and though the churches claimed far more success among Indigenous people, they recognized that many conversions were less complete than they had hoped.

BC churchmen, both religious and lay, saw themselves as beleaguered by godless, immoral white men and racialized heathens in need of religious and moral transformation. As these groups were othered, minorities that might normally have been viewed with suspicion became more acceptable. Jews were generally perceived as white, and their numbers were so small that they were not seen as a threat to Christian hegemony.

The input of white Christian women was crucial for the embattled churches of British Columbia, a factor that motivated more BC clergymen to support their demands for suffrage and ecclesiastical representation than was true elsewhere in Canada. This does not mean that all BC churchmen were ardent suffragists. Some remained opposed to women's rights, believing that women's place was in the home. But most mainstream BC churches increasingly favoured the granting of women's rights, both within and outside the church. If they were to rescue British Columbia from godlessness and moral decay, they needed the active support and the votes of white Christian women.

7
Subtler and More Dangerous Forms of Error
Metaphysical Religions

Unbelievers and non-Christians were not alone in contesting Christian hegemony in British Columbia. Various alternative religions, most with at least tenuous ties to Christianity, were more popular in the province than elsewhere in the country, and they presented challenges to the orthodox churches. On a typical December Sunday in 1907, interested Victorians had their pick of several religious options, as publicized in the *Victoria Colonist.* The paper listed mainstream church services, but it also announced the following:

> *Christian Science:* The Christian Science society hold their Sunday service in the K. of P. Hall ... at 11 am. Subject today: "God the Only Cause and Creator." All are welcome.
>
> *Christadelphians:* Bible lecture. Labor hall, Douglas street at 7 pm. Mr Wilkinson will take for his subject "Salvation: From What?" All welcome.
>
> *Universal Brotherhood:* Universal Brotherhood and Theosophical Society Centre No 87 holds a public meeting at 76 Government street ... when addresses are given on living questions of the day from the Theosophical standpoint and questions answered. Unsectarian and non-political. All are invited.
>
> *Spiritualism:* R.H. Kneeshaw lectures at 175 Chatham street ... at 7:30 pm. Subject "A New Religion." All are welcome to the meeting.
>
> *Psychic Research:* Meeting at AOUW hall, room 7, upstairs 8 pm. All are welcome.[1]

Scholarly debates about secularization have often connected religious diversity with the emergence of more secular cultures. Some scholars have traced secularization to the Reformation, arguing that if people could identify alternatives to one true faith, at least some people could eventually imagine the alternative of no faith at all.[2] What role might religious diversity have played in British Columbia's acceptance of unbelief and high levels of religious indifference? We have already discussed some aspects of BC diversity. This chapter introduces other strands, focusing on spiritualism, Theosophy, and Christian Science, all of which were more appealing to British Columbians than to most Canadians. Catherine Albanese defines them as "metaphysical religions," and with their belief in spirits, in the occult, and in faith healing, they would certainly be considered alternative, both then and now. Robert Fuller views these religions, with their rejection of traditional institutional Christianity, as precursors to the popular "spiritual but not religious" approach of many North Americans today (particularly those on the West Coast).[3]

Whereas the over-representation of these metaphysical groups may help to explain the greater openness of British Columbians to irreligion, scholars of the more recent spiritual history of the Pacific Northwest have suggested that causation may go in the other direction: that the rejection of institutional religion leaves open a space for a range of alternative spiritualities.[4]

Historians of late-nineteenth- and early-twentieth-century metaphysical religions have elaborated on this point. Alex Owen argues that the late-nineteenth-century "crisis of faith," inspired largely by Darwinism and Biblical criticism, led many away from orthodox Christianity. For some, this process led directly to a secular world view and atheism. For others, however, a godless universe had little appeal, and they turned to the metaphysical religions, seeking more rational, scientific, and modern approaches to life's big questions that did not discard the mystical and the spiritual.[5] This shift was a gendered one. Women who questioned mainstream Christianity were more willing than men to opt for the metaphysical religions rather than unbelief, as they were also less willing to abandon all spiritual belief.

The question of whether interest in alternative religions provides space for unbelief or whether more acceptance of unbelief provides more space for alternative religions may remain unresolved, but certainly the popularity of both unbelief and alternative religions reinforces the legitimacy of a broader range of religious and irreligious choices than may be possible in more dominantly Christian regions. Laurie Maffly-Kipp has sketched the colourful realities of religious and irreligious heterogeneity in mid-nineteenth-century California gold-rush society, and the link between the two phenomena appears clear in the Pacific Northwest, both today and in the past.[6]

Although British Columbians were more likely to be irreligious than to follow a metaphysical faith, the relative popularity of these faiths nonetheless posed a challenge to the mainstream churches. Ministers railed against the "errors" of the metaphysical religions, seeing them as not much better, or indeed no better, than unbelief. Their sermons aimed at correcting the faulty theology but also reflected their fears that the new heretical movements would purloin their congregants or, what was more insidious and perhaps more common, that members of their flock would integrate the new beliefs into Christianity, developing a form of lived religion that worked for them but was anathema to orthodox Christian leaders. It was not just the boundaries between metaphysical faiths and orthodox Christianity that could be porous. We might view unbelief as being incompatible with metaphysical spirituality, but this was not necessarily the case for many British Columbians.

Earlier chapters have shown that social activism could be linked to both unbelief and Christianity. This chapter discusses the connections between activism and alternative spiritualities. For example, Theosophy was significantly shaped by certain core beliefs of Eastern religions, particularly Hinduism. Some connections were made between South Asian immigrants and Theosophists, and Theosophists were more likely than most Canadians to challenge racist norms.

At the same time, almost all BC Theosophists were Euro-Canadians, as were spiritualists and Christian Scientists. This chapter does not claim to provide a definitive account of these faiths, seeking instead to examine them as part of, and contributors to, the larger story of the more spiritually open, and less hegemonically Christian, religious landscape of British Columbia. It also seeks to identify any relationship that may have existed between the significant number of British Columbians who publicly defined themselves as irreligious and the smaller but still significant number who identified with alternative forms of spirituality.

Adherents of metaphysical religions were not confined exclusively to British Columbia. Ontario had significant numbers, most of whom were based in Toronto, though some lived in smaller towns. Ontario spiritualists and Theosophists have received serious scholarly treatment.[7] The existence of these groups reminds us not to overemphasize the hegemony of conventional Christianity in Ontario, even during this period. Nonetheless, the evidence presented earlier in this book shows that Ontarians were far more likely than British Columbians to be mainstream Christians, and the dramatic over-representation of metaphysical religions in British Columbia suggests that an important story remains to be told.[8]

Spiritualists

Spiritualists comprised one of the largest metaphysical religious groups in British Columbia during this period. They differed sharply from mainstream Christians in believing that they could commune with the spirits of the dead, generally through mediums both male and female, who served as channels for the spirits. The spirits demonstrated their presence by rapping on tables, playing musical instruments, speaking through the medium, and in some cases, materializing. Mediums operated in both small, home-based seances and larger, more public ones. Originating in the United States during the mid-nineteenth century, spiritualism spread to a number of countries, including Canada and Britain. It continued to draw adherents throughout the twentieth century and into the twenty-first as well, particularly among those who sought to communicate with dead relatives.[9] And though spiritualists lived in small towns and large cities across Canada, especially in Ontario, they were particularly over-represented in British Columbia.[10]

In 1901, British Columbians accounted for only 3.3 percent of Canada's population, 5.4 percent in 1911, and 6.0 percent in 1921. Of the 616 Canadian spiritualists listed in the 1901 census, almost a quarter lived in British Columbia, and more than a quarter did so in 1911. In 1921, over 20 percent of the 1,558 Canadian spiritualists were British Columbians (see Appendix: Table 14). Perhaps the province's greater religious diversity and openness encouraged more people to publicly define themselves as spiritualists than was the case elsewhere in Canada. Nonetheless, the striking numbers of BC spiritualists also suggests that the faith had a certain appeal in the province. Of course, many Canadians dabbled in spiritualism, attending an occasional seance or meeting without ever defining themselves as spiritualists to the census enumerator.[11] Among the better known of these was the artist Emily Carr. She and her family attended the Reformed Episcopal Church of Our Lord in downtown Victoria, but this did not prevent Emily from choosing in February 1905 to attend a private seance with Robert Kneeshaw, a local medium and leader of the Spiritualist Society. However, the spirits apparently chose not to reveal themselves at that time.[12]

Spiritualism was not popular in all BC towns, but when Carr attended her seance, it had won a significant following in Victoria. Spiritualist associations were founded in Victoria and Nanaimo during the late 1880s, and they remained vibrant well into the twentieth century. Victoria gained an ordained spiritualist minister in 1915 and Nanaimo in 1926.[13] In 1901, forty-three Victorians defined themselves as spiritualists, and many more attended their meetings. In the Nanaimo area, with its smaller population, eighty people told the census-taker that they were spiritualists.[14] As we've seen, Nanaimoites typically opted for some level of fuzzy fidelity, with nominal adherence to mainstream Christian denominations. Nonetheless, the eighty spiritualists outnumbered the irreligious in Nanaimo by about two to one, as only forty-four residents defined themselves as atheists or of "no religion" in 1901. This ratio is atypical, as the irreligious in other BC towns significantly outnumbered the adherents of metaphysical religions in both 1901 and 1911.

Many Nanaimo spiritualists were miners or members of a mining family. Of the twenty-six spiritualist Nanaimo men who listed occupations on the census, twenty, or 77 percent, were miners. Perhaps the high number of fatal accidents in the mines led at least some colliers and their wives to spiritualism, which offered the hope of reconnecting with a loved one. An address of appreciation from George Campbell, chair of the Nanaimo Spiritualist Association, to visiting medium George P. Colby stressed the importance of this. Campbell thanked Colby for his work in the community as "Test Medium and Inspirational Lecturer," noting that the association felt "grateful for the privilege we have had of communing with those of our loved ones who have joined the greatest throng of immortals in the summerland beyond – for the words of sympathy that have comforted bruised hearts bringing to them a realization of the presence of their supposed dead and a knowledge of the measureless possibilities of life."[15]

Although spiritualism was popular among many people who sought connection with lost loved ones, it was far from popular with certain segments of BC society. Protestant church leaders attacked it as occultism and rank heresy. Such criticism was not new at the turn of the century. In 1870, Edward Cridge, dean of Victoria's Christ Church Cathedral and soon to become the first bishop of the Carr family's Reformed Episcopal Church, published a sermon titled *"Spiritualism:" or Modern Necromancy,* in which he denounced spiritualism as "divining or soothsaying by means of the dead." He warned readers that it was "a very ancient wickedness. Its various forms are enumerated and condemned in the Book of Deuteronomy ... The Christian who meddles with spiritualism stands on the verge of an abyss." Cridge clearly knew that at least some of his flock had experimented with spiritualism because he acknowledged that curiosity or a desire to commune with departed loved ones could tempt people to try it. However, he proclaimed firmly that "this practice is denounced in Holy Scripture under the severest penalties ... That which is hateful to God, and punishable by his law with death, cannot be a thing for a Christian to touch, but to shun with abhorrence."[16] Other Protestant ministers were also strongly opposed to spiritualism, and the Catholic Church declared that spiritualists were trafficking with demons and evil spirits.

Both church leaders and people of a more secular and scientific bent enjoyed unmasking visiting mediums as frauds.[17] For example, in July 1900, a lengthy *Vancouver Province* article titled "Some Shady Shades" attacked a recent visiting medium as a charlatan and provided a more detailed critique of a "Professor Raymond" – a dubious traveller "in the path of easy money" – who was then in town. It described a Raymond seance, complete with several female "victims" of the deception and typical spiritualist manifestations, such as rapping and the playing of musical instruments by unseen hands in the dark. The reporter clearly believed that Raymond himself was the source of all these phenomena, and he commented snidely that "the guitar banging shade was careless, for not only did it drop the guitar, but it most reprehensibly jabbed an elbow into the eye of the little girl."[18]

For their part, spiritualists recognized that some mediums were frauds, but they strongly defended the authenticity of most mediums and of spiritualism as a legitimate religious alternative. In late-nineteenth-century Ontario, the criminal courts did not always agree. In 1899, some Toronto mediums were charged under the witchcraft section of the Vagrancy Act for telling fortunes or conjuring spirits.[19] The BC courts seemed less concerned with this issue, and at least some BC authorities were willing to grant legitimacy to spiritualist organizations. For example, spiritualists petitioned Nanaimo City Council in 1897, protesting a bylaw that forced local mediums and seers to pay a fifty-dollar licence fee every six months, lumping them in with fortune tellers and other occultists. They insisted that spiritualism be treated like any other church, and council complied with their wishes. The words "medium" and "seer" were removed from the bylaw, though fortune tellers still had to pay the fee.[20] The fact that a year afterward, a leading Nanaimo spiritualist was elected mayor reinforces the acceptability of this alternative movement in the community.

Whereas orthodox Christian ministers condemned spiritualist beliefs, some spiritualists claimed that their movement could bolster Christian faith, as it proved the existence of life after death and therefore negated the arguments of atheists and other "infidels." For example, George Colby, who gave a talk in Nanaimo titled "What Good Has Spiritualism Done," argued that "with the advance of material science, the people became more materialistic in their opinions and boldly denied the immortality of the soul. What theology failed to prove, Spiritualism, with its phenomena practically and in a scientific manner demonstrated the truth that we continue to live after the dissolution of the body."[21] As Timothy Noddings notes, mainstream Christians, unbelievers, and adherents of metaphysical religions all employed the rhetorical weapons of science, rationality, and modernity in their debates with each other, with each side labelling the other as irrational and unscientific.[22]

Although these groups often painted themselves as antithetical to the others, scholars have demonstrated that like Emily Carr, many spiritualists in the United States and Central Canada, particularly many middle-class spiritualists, saw nothing incompatible with practising spiritualism, especially in the privacy of their homes, while remaining members of Protestant churches. Some clergy dabbled in spiritualism themselves, but the Canadian Protestant churches had limited tolerance for such behaviour, as Stan McMullin reveals in chronicling the expulsion of Reverend B.F. Austin from the Methodist ministry for heresy in 1899.[23] Robert Lowery, the infidel newspaperman of the Kootenays, certainly felt that Christianity and spiritualism had much in common, none of it good. As he explained in an article, "You are not expected to examine the Bible; neither are you permitted to investigate the seance. How like as two peas are twin sisters of superstition."[24]

Spiritualism may have attracted many Christians, but others came to it from more secular roots. Alex Owen argues that particularly in England's mining districts, it was popular among British working-class secularists, whose belief in science and rationalism led them to spiritualism, which claimed to provide scientific evidence of a spirit world.[25] The spiritualist community in Nanaimo, made up primarily of British miners and their family members, may have derived in part from this tradition. The manuscript census of 1911 suggests that the smaller spiritualist community in Vancouver was also primarily working class, whereas in turn-of-the-century Victoria, adherents were more evenly distributed between the working and middle classes.[26]

Although scholars argue that most middle-class individuals with an interest in spiritualism remained officially affiliated with a Protestant church, this was not always the case. The president of the British Columbia Society of Spiritualists was Oregon C. Hastings, a prominent Victoria photographer.[27] He played a central role in the society, but he listed his religion in both 1881 and 1891 as "infidel" and in 1901 as "agnostic." The census recorded that his wife shared his irreligious leanings. Other prominent spiritualists also spurned the churches, despite the contrary opinions of family members. The death of a former mayor of Victoria, James Fell, revealed the complex relationship that could exist between secularism, spiritualism, and mainstream Christianity. In 1890, the Anglican bishop Hills noted in his diary that Fell had just passed away and had "left directions no other Service should be said over his body but the form used by the Odd Fellows. Poor man he held spiritualist opinions in which he persevered to the last. He used occasionally to come to the Cathedral where he had a pew. His family are much vexed at the directions left." Fell's son asked Hills for permission to have his father buried in the Church of England section of the cemetery, despite the lack of an Anglican burial service. Hills agreed, apparently because "Fell had many excellent qualities was benevolent and never minded what trouble he took for the poor and the sick. Under these circumstances I consented to the request and indeed felt it to be a relief that the service of the Church was not required."[28]

Whereas Fell seems to have been one of the many BC men who challenged the conventional Christian beliefs of their family, spiritualism often outdid irreligion in bringing families together, because wives were much more likely to join their husbands in professing spiritualism than in declaring for atheism or "no religion." As we have seen, men were much more likely than their wives to be irreligious, and irreligious men greatly outnumbered irreligious women. A study of the Vancouver Island population from 1881 to 1911 (using the ViHistory database) demonstrates that the reverse was true among spiritualists – women often outnumbered men. For example, in Nanaimo, where men predominated, the 1901 census lists twenty-one adult men and twenty-eight adult women as spiritualists. In Victoria, where women made up only 40 percent of the population, 56 percent of spiritualists were female. In Vancouver in 1911, just over 40 percent of residents were female, but 53 percent of spiritualists were women.[29] When the Vancouver spiritualists formed the First Spiritualist Church of Vancouver in 1918, four of its five founding directors were female.[30] In 1921, the first year that the published census provided gender-based divisions of religious affiliations, 52 percent of the 319 BC spiritualists were female, although among the non-Indigenous population men still significantly outnumbered women.

As several scholars have noted, women were much more attracted to spiritualism than to irreligion. Owen speculates that many who turned to the alternative religions in Britain may have been alienated by the cold scientific rationalism of unbelief, as it left no room for a spiritual dimension. Women may have been drawn to spiritualism because their natures were assumed to be more spiritual than those of men. The gender ideology of the time, which defined women as sensitive and passive, made them especially suited as mediums, and many took on this role.[31] As well, infant mortality rates in the nineteenth century were much higher than they are today. Although both fathers and mothers mourned dead children, and both sought reconnection through spiritualism, this option appears to have appealed chiefly to women, who had generally had close ties to their children. The fact that the census lists so few unmarried spiritualists may indicate that a number of wives brought their husband to spiritualism, as many did to the Christian churches. For example, the 1881 census records Mary Ann Hardy of Nanaimo as a spiritualist, whereas her miner husband, Thomas, is enumerated as a Unitarian. In the 1891 census, both Mary Ann and Thomas defined themselves as spiritualists, as they also did in 1901. A few husbands identified themselves as spiritualists, whereas their wives remained orthodox Christians (at least officially), but these cases were the exception, unlike those involving unbelieving husbands and Christian wives. Some married women differed from their husbands in defining themselves as spiritualists, as was true of well-known Victoria photographer Hannah Maynard. She and her husband were both Anglicans in 1881, but after her youngest daughter died of typhoid in 1883, she began to attend seances, incorporating ghostly figures into some of her photographic work. Her desire to reconnect with lost family members was intensified by the deaths of another daughter and a daughter-in-law within the next ten years.[32] In 1891, the census identified her as a spiritualist, whereas her husband's religion was "not given."

Some people remained firmly committed to spiritualism for decades, but many others seem to have oscillated between mainstream Christianity and spiritualism, with occasional forays toward unbelief. Hannah Maynard, for instance, had at least officially returned to Anglicanism by 1911, a few years before her death. This fluidity is evident among the sixty-nine Vancouver Islanders who appeared in at least two censuses between 1881 and 1911, and who were listed as spiritualists during at least one of those years. Twenty-five percent of them remained faithful to spiritualism over at least two decades, 39 percent appear to have exchanged it for orthodox Christianity, and a further 28 percent moved from mainstream Christianity to

Multiple exposure of photographer Hannah Maynard and her grandson, c. 1893) | *BC Archives, F-05031*

spiritualism. For the remaining 7 percent, all of whom were men, spiritualism was a way station on the path to atheism or having no religion. One woman shifted from unbelief to spiritualism after being widowed.[33] These data provide further suggestive evidence of the religious (and irreligious) flexibility of many Vancouver Islanders during this period. At the same time, given the many people who attended spiritualist meetings and seances without defining themselves as spiritualists to the census-taker, these numbers are just the tip of the iceberg.

An 1894 petition to the Legislative Assembly allows us to look more deeply at potential interest in and support for spiritualists on Vancouver Island. The petition, a first effort to eliminate the licence fee for clairvoyants, who were lumped in with astrologers, seers, and fortune tellers under the Municipal Act, was signed by 186 people, 58 from Victoria and the rest from Nanaimo. This is significantly more than the 123 Victorians and Nanaimoites who were listed on the 1901 census as spiritualists (a large minority of whom were children, who do not sign petitions). The petitioners stated that they were "Spiritualists, and profess that form of religious

Spiritualists' picnic at Cordova Bay, near Victoria, 1890. Hannah Maynard is seen in profile, seated at the far right | *BC Archives, F-05059*

belief commonly known as Spiritualism, and others are their friends."[34] Many could not be linked to either the 1891 or the 1901 census, but of the Victoria petitioners who could be traced, five were spiritualists and five were infidels or freethinkers, pointing once again to the connection between the two. Ten belonged to mainstream denominations. The latter pattern was even clearer among the Nanaimo petitioners, most of whom identified with orthodox denominations, primarily as Methodists, Anglicans, or Presbyterians. Seven Nanaimo petitioners were listed as spiritualists in the census, one was an atheist, and over thirty were officially Christian (including a Quaker and a Unitarian).[35] Perhaps the Methodist, Anglican, and Presbyterian signatories were simply friends of spiritualists, but it seems much more likely that most would have had at least some level of interest in the alternative religion, perhaps attending an occasional seance or other spiritualist event, and revealing once again that the census omitted many people who had a significant interest in this form of spirituality.

The Sivertz family, which emigrated from Iceland to British Columbia in 1888, is a case in point. Bent Sivertz wrote a detailed account of his parents' working-class lives in Victoria and Vancouver before the First

World War, and his parents, Elinborg and Christian, can also be found on the Victoria census of 1911, which lists them as Lutherans. Bent, however, tells a different and more complex story. Although his mother was raised a Lutheran, she had left the church well before 1911, disenchanted by its hellfire-and-damnation preaching. She spent some years with a Baptist church but had become much more interested in spiritualism by 1910, perhaps influenced by a female friend who had joined the faith. She "gradually over half a dozen years, left off attendance at the Baptist Church in favour of séances."[36] This did not deter her from praying for her children as they grew up or from attending at least one revival meeting at the Metropolitan Methodist Church. Like many other people, Elinborg created a lived religion that worked for her but did not necessarily correspond to the clear divisions preferred by theologians. Although she had a close relationship with her husband, she did not have his support in her spiritual explorations, as he "preferred not to go to church" and practised what his son termed a "kindly agnosticism."[37] Whereas the majority of Victoria's married spiritualists shared their belief in the supernatural with their spouse, the Sivertzes reflect a not uncommon BC pattern of fluidity between alternative and mainstream religions, and a familiar gendered pattern of an agnostic husband and a believing wife. But this configuration was invisible to the census-taker, as either he or the Sivertzes themselves conflated their ethnic and religious identities – in Iceland, where they grew up, the Lutheran Church was the official denomination. Or perhaps, even in the religiously open climate of British Columbia, these working-class immigrants simply felt safer in naming a relatively mainstream denomination than in telling the enumerator that they were an unbeliever and a spiritualist.

The Sivertzes also reflect links between unbelief, alternative religions, and political activism that were not uncommon in British Columbia and Canada more generally. A labour leader, Christian Sivertz was president of the B.C. Federation of Labour by 1912. He was no socialist, though, and he opposed radicalism in the labour revolt of 1919.[38] Unbelief was typically linked to the more radical BC socialists, but Christian demonstrates that it had a broader reach among at least some less radical BC labour leaders. Elinborg was involved in the major suffrage organization in Victoria, the Political Equality League, and in other social reform endeavours. Although BC suffragists tended to be Christians, as discussed in Chapter 6, some were not. Scholars have noted the link between alternative religions, such as spiritualism, and social activism, including the struggle for women's rights, a connection that certainly applied in Elinborg's case.[39]

Theosophists

For many "seekers," spiritualism was a way station en route to other, newer forms of metaphysical religion.[40]

Mark Leier recounts the story of Robert Gosden, a radical activist in the BC Industrial Workers of the World (IWW) who later turned labour spy and whose life illustrates some of this flexibility. Although Leier does not say so, Gosden very probably disavowed Christianity during his IWW period, as most radical IWW leaders did. Leier is certainly clear that Gosden was a materialist at this time, and in 1911 he dismissed spiritualism as "metaphysical dope [that] especially appeals to some emasculated persons." Like many socialists, Gosden denounced any association with spirituality as effeminate weakness. However, a few years later, after a stint as a labour spy, when Gosden was "nearly forty years old, with no career, stable job, or home life," he turned to spiritualism and "became particularly interested in Theosophy."[41]

Theosophy had emerged from spiritualism during the 1870s but was quite different in many ways. Even so, the two movements did maintain some relationship with each other, and in the United States, Britain, and Canada a number of people, especially social activists, feminists, intellectuals, and artists, appear to have moved from spiritualism to Theosophy during the late nineteenth and early twentieth centuries.[42] Theosophy espoused the Western occult tradition but was also influenced by many ideas from Eastern religions – Buddhism and most particularly Hinduism. As a result, karma and reincarnation were integral to its beliefs, and cremation, a Hindu practice, was common among Theosophists at a time when it was beyond the pale for most Euro-Canadians. As Gillian McCann reveals in her study of the Toronto Theosophical Society, the adoption of many major tenets of Hinduism led Theosophists to respect and appreciate Eastern religions. They were very critical of the Christian missionaries who attempted to convert the followers of these religions. They were not immune to the "Orientalism" that pervaded Euro-Canadian society, however, and they sometimes viewed Eastern religions and cultures as exotic "others," but they were much more positive than other Canadians about these religions and were generally respectful of the South Asians who occasionally provided lectures on links between Hindu teachings and Theosophical beliefs.[43]

The intent of Theosophy was to reach a deeper understanding of the divine. As Michele Lacombe points out, Theosophists believed in "a divinity indistinguishable from a Universe which is living, conscious, and endlessly evolving." This evolution moved toward a positive endpoint, which included the brotherhood of mankind.[44] Not all Theosophists subscribed to the same views, but a belief in the interconnectedness of the world and in universal brotherhood was central for all. During the early twentieth century, Canada had few Theosophists (at least as listed on the census), but between 1901 and 1921 more than 30 percent lived in British Columbia, and the province claimed over 35 percent in 1911 and 1921, although even by 1921 British Columbians composed only 6 percent of the Canadian population (see Table 14).

Theosophy made its first official appearance in British Columbia in 1892, with the establishment of a "headquarters" in downtown Victoria. By 1894, this headquarters was also equipped with a free library of Theosophical books.[45] The Victoria chapter seems to have been one of Canada's first three Theosophical Societies.[46] The Theosophists offered regular public lectures, provided by their own members or visiting speakers, and though their numbers were small, the new religion appears to have aroused considerable public interest. Sometimes the local paper noted that their talks attracted large audiences, as in the case of visiting speakers Dr. Griffith and Sidney Coryn, whose 1896 and 1898 lectures were titled "Theosophy in Ancient Egypt" and "Adepts and the Mysteries of Antiquity."[47] In the spring of 1911, Mr. C. Jinarajadasa, a protégé of international Theosophical leader Annie Besant and a member of the executive of the International Theosophical Society, gave a series of three lectures in Victoria titled "The Growth and Evolution of the Soul," "Theosophy in the Christian Church," and "The Laws of Reincarnation." After his lectures, a letter appeared in the *Victoria Colonist* from a local Sikh leader, protesting the fact that even Hindus "of good social standing" like Jinarajadasa had difficulty entering the country because of its racist immigration laws.[48] Jinarajadasa was not the only Theosophist lecturer to discuss the relationship between Christianity and Theosophy, as this was an occasional topic at the Victoria Theosophical Society's public lectures in the decades preceding the First World War. Titles such as "What Is True Christianity?" and "Some Forgotten Teachings of Jesus" imply that Theosophists hoped to interest Christians in shared Theosophical and Christian beliefs such as universal brotherhood – beliefs that they felt many Christians failed to practise.[49]

Such lectures would merely have deepened the unhappiness of Victoria ministers, who saw Theosophy as no more welcome than spiritualism. As in the case of spiritualism, at least some ministers worried that Theosophy might lead their flocks astray. In the summer of 1894, Reverend P.M. MacLeod of the James Bay Presbyterian Church in Victoria preached a lengthy sermon on the evils of Theosophy. He began by saying (over-optimistically) that "infidelity in its grosser form is dying out." But this was no cause for complacency, since "subtler and hence more dangerous forms of error are taking its place." He explicitly linked the attraction of Theosophy to the secular leanings of many British Columbians: "There are so many people on this Pacific coast who have as yet no definite views with regard to religion and we can readily understand their willingness to listen to any teacher who begins by justifying their attitude of indifference to Christianity, and who promises to show them a more excellent way." MacLeod was appalled by Theosophical critiques of Christianity, especially their focus on the violence caused by conflicts between rival Christian denominations. In case his listeners might be hoping to integrate Theosophy with Christianity (as sometimes occurred with spiritualism), MacLeod ended by pronouncing that the two faiths were totally incompatible: Theosophy offered no personal saviour and no hope of a heavenly afterlife for individual souls.[50]

Perhaps such clerical hostility had an impact in Victoria, particularly among women. In Britain and the United States, Theosophy's belief in an asexual divinity and in equality between the sexes appears to have attracted many women.[51] However, the four Victorians who identified as Theosophists on the 1901 census were all men, almost all middle class, and all Euro-Canadian. Three of them were married, and the census identified their wives with mainstream Christian denominations. Of the other three Theosophists on Vancouver Island, the two married men also had Christian wives. It appears that during this early period, Theosophy was still far too unconventional to appeal to the respectable middle-class women of Victoria and the island, or at least too far beyond the norm for them to admit an interest. In Vancouver, however, both sexes were identified with the movement in 1901 and 1911, and in 1921 almost half of the small band of BC Theosophists were women.[52] Unlike spiritualists, BC Theosophists were more likely to be middle class than working class, as was true elsewhere in Canada. Eighty percent of the Vancouver Theosophists who appear on the 1911 manuscript census can be defined as middle class, and again, all were Euro-Canadian.[53]

Just before the First World War, another Theosophical Lodge was founded in British Columbia, this time in Kelowna, in the Okanagan Valley.[54] Its 1913–15 minutes have survived, and they give us further insights into the concerns and nature of BC Theosophists. The Kelowna group seems to have been quite small, with only twelve names appearing in its minutes. Half of the members were female, with half of the women being married and half single. Meetings of the Kelowna Theosophical Society followed the structure of middle-class Christian organizations of the period, with the business of the association being followed by the reading of a paper – in this case, of course, on a Theosophical topic.

The Kelowna Lodge also allowed for those "desirous of studying Theosophy, but who had not made up their minds on the subject," to become "fellows" of the society, rather than members.[55] Again, in addition to those willing to define themselves as members of alternative religions, others were interested in exploring them. Some may have wished to do so while remaining affiliated with the churches, and there are hints that Kelowna ministers were no happier than the Victoria ones with the local Theosophists. For example, in August 1913 the Kelowna group approved a letter to be sent to "Rev. T. Green in reply to an article in the Parish Magazine."[56] Despite the displeasure of Kelowna ministers, the Theosophists continued with their meetings, where they heard and discussed papers on a range of topics, including the relationship of Theosophy to Christianity, as well as more "orthodox" Theosophical subjects such as karma and reincarnation. The group seemed divided regarding the latter topic, with a number of members arguing that the "evidence of reincarnation was inadequate and faulty."[57] The Kelowna Theosophists knew that Theosophy also provided answers to broader social concerns. In June 1913, they read a pamphlet titled *Social Problems and How Theosophy Solves Them.*[58]

Although there is no evidence that any Kelowna Theosophists became socially active during 1913–15, it appears that this was not uncommon among other BC Theosophists. Robert Gosden was certainly not alone in combining Theosophy with alternative political views. Scholars of Theosophy in Central Canada, the United States, and Britain note that Theosophy appealed to a number of feminist and socialist activists, even more than spiritualism did. Many activists in the BC women's movement were very involved in the mainstream churches and most claimed an orthodox Christian affiliation, but there is evidence to link a few BC feminist activists with Theosophy. One of these was Helena Gutteridge, a radical labour and women's rights activist who had worked with the London Theosophical Society for five years. Although she resigned from the society before emigrating from England to British Columbia in 1911 and seems never to have rejoined it, her biographer suggests that her political beliefs remained influenced by Theosophy.[59] Another activist in the BC suffrage campaign, Mary Graves of Victoria, had been a pious Catholic, but she lost her faith and stopped attending church after her husband and infant child died in 1896. A friend invited her to join the Victoria Theosophical Society in the late 1890s, where she became an active member and met her second husband. Soon afterward, she joined the suffrage movement, often giving speeches on suffrage issues, and she became involved in the Local Council of Women. How long she remained with the Theosophical Society is unknown, but in her later years she apparently also occasionally preached a sermon at the local Unitarian church, suggesting that she had not lost her interest in alternative religious options.[60]

Maria Grant, a major activist in Victoria's first-wave feminist movement, also participated in an alternative religion. For the first part of her life, she was a steadfast Methodist, and like many feminists of her day, she embarked on her social reform work and women's rights activism in part because of her Christian faith. However, the death of her husband left her in financial difficulties during her middle years, and she apparently experienced a crisis of faith. She left the Methodist Church for a metaphysical religion called New Thought, which had some links to Theosophy.[61] Maria was central to the development of Victoria's Unity Church, a branch of New Thought, while remaining active in the struggle for the vote. In later years, she was a preacher at the Unity Church.[62]

There is less definitive evidence that another important Victoria women's rights activist, Agnes Deans Cameron, may have had some links to Theosophy. A pioneering teacher, principal, and journalist who believed strongly in equal rights in the workforce and in politics, Cameron was listed as a Presbyterian on the 1901 Victoria census, which also recorded that she lived with her unmarried sister and her mother, both of whom were active members of St. Andrew's Presbyterian Church.[63] Agnes herself does not seem to have belonged to the church. When she died in 1912 at the young age of forty-eight, a funeral service was held at St. Andrew's, but she was then cremated and her ashes were scattered in the Georgia Strait, as she had wished. In 1912, cremation was extremely rare in Canada and was closely associated with the Theosophists. Two very active Ontario feminist Theosophists, Emily Stowe and Flora Macdonald Denison, were among the first Canadians to be cremated.[64] In opting for cremation, Agnes may simply have wished to follow the example of feminists whom she admired, but it seems more than possible that she also shared some of their Theosophical beliefs, although living with her pious Presbyterian mother and sister may have made it difficult to express them.

We may never know whether the ostensibly Presbyterian Cameron believed in the tenets of Theosophy, but some people did manage to integrate Theosophy and Christianity. Whereas clergymen like Reverend MacLeod may have seen these as incompatible, not all Theosophists agreed.

Gillian McCann argues convincingly that the leader of Theosophy in Ontario, A.S. Smythe, merged some elements of his Christian and Theosophist beliefs. In the 1890s, Smythe taught Christian Scripture classes through the Toronto Theosophical Society and contended that his social gospel approach, which sprang from his Methodist upbringing, was reinforced by Theosophist ideas about universal brotherhood.[65]

Theosophy's focus on the brotherhood of man and the amalgamation of Eastern and Western religious beliefs led at least some Canadian Theosophists to follow the example of their international leaders, such as Annie Besant, in attacking racism and British imperialism. Not surprisingly, this critique tended to concentrate on the behaviour of the British government and Christian missionaries in India, although in the Canadian context considerable focus was also placed on Canada's racist immigration and citizenship laws. Hugh Johnston points out that both this critique and the adoption of Hindu beliefs forged links between BC Theosophists and at least a few South Asian immigrants, who were themselves highly critical of both Canada's immigration laws and British rule in India. Johnston discusses Teja Singh, a well-educated and pious Sikh immigrant who was planning to undertake graduate work at Harvard and who spent some time in Vancouver during the pre-war years. Local Theosophists lionized him, "treating him as a guru and inviting him to their homes for intimate philosophical talks."[66] Canadian security officials considered Singh a subversive at least in part for his efforts to assist his compatriots in dealing with Canada's racist immigration laws.[67] Gillian McCann identifies another South Asian man, Kartar Singh, who immigrated to Vancouver during the pre-war years, moved to Toronto during the war, and became involved with the Toronto Theosophists. He returned to Vancouver in the late 1920s to assist the BC Sikhs in their struggle to become Canadian citizens.[68]

Johnston also mentions another Sikh immigrant, Kapoor Singh, who was associated with the Theosophists. Singh came to British Columbia in 1912 as a labourer and became a businessman and community leader, developing increasingly close links with Theosophists in both Toronto and Vancouver. He was initially attracted to them because of their respect for Indian religious traditions and beliefs.[69] Some Euro-Canadian Theosophists assisted South Asians in dealing with a racist society wherever they could, and by the interwar period were actively involved with them in challenging Canada's immigration laws.[70] Some Theosophists studied and practised their religion with the despised "Hindus" while also working to address their oppression in Canada, but the new religion was not socially transformative for everyone. Some Toronto Theosophists, who could not escape the values of Euro-Canadian society, treated visiting South Asian speakers in a highly racist manner.[71]

Whereas some Theosophists challenged racial oppression or fought for women's rights, others were strong socialists.[72] Robert Gosden, although a complex figure by the time he embraced spiritualism and then Theosophy in the mid- to late 1910s, retained at least some of his socialist ideals.[73] Perhaps the most famous BC activist to incorporate both socialist and Theosophist ideals in the years before the First World War was Matti Kurikka, the leader of Sointula, a Finnish socialist utopian community on Malcolm Island, just off the northeast coast of Vancouver Island. The extent to which the Sointula community accepted Kurikka's Theosophical beliefs is not clear. Certainly, his embrace of the free-love currents of Theosophical thought helped to break up the community fairly soon after its founding.[74] Those who remained, however, stayed true to socialist, co-operative beliefs but seemed more irreligious than Theosophist. As a long-time resident told Imbert Orchard in the 1960s, long-time inhabitants of Sointula "were all pretty against" the church and Christianity.[75]

Most scholars have focused on the relationship between socialism and Theosophy in Ontario, whereas Samuel Wagar provides an in-depth exploration of the subject in the BC context. He concentrates largely on the 1920s, when active socialist and Theosophist Jack Logie ran a number of summer camps in the Okanagan that promoted both Theosophist and socialist beliefs.[76] However, Wagar also identifies earlier links between socialism and Theosophy, arguing that materialism was not the only model available to BC socialists, since a number of prominent socialists espoused Theosophy. Wagar discusses a major front-page article titled "Socialism and Theosophy," which appeared in the April 1903 issue of the *Western Socialist,* an organ of the Socialist Party of British Columbia. It was written by Phillips Thompson, an Ontario Theosophist and well-known leftist, whose career reflects an ongoing spiritual journey. In the 1880s, Thompson had promoted a radical Christian social gospel critique of capitalism, and later in the century he became involved in spiritualism. He was also an active member of Toronto's freethought community for a time but had embraced Theosophy by the early 1890s, which he saw as the best way of integrating spirituality with socialism.[77] As he told *Western Socialist* readers, "I am a class-conscious Socialist from the ground up, and I claim that my Socialism is reinforced by [Theosophy]; in fact, I might go further and say based upon the truths of Theosophy."[78] Thompson was clear that he did not accept Christianity, but at the same time, his article was rather different from the general hostility to religion that characterized Marxist journals in British Columbia. Wagar notes that in 1907, Jack Logie ran as a candidate for office in the Socialist Party of Canada, although he does not provide evidence that Logie was a Theosophist at the time. He has clear evidence that by 1920 some individuals combined Theosophy and socialism: for example, socialist James Taylor was also president of the Vancouver Theosophical Society in 1920, and A.M. Stephen, president of the Julian Theosophical Society in Vancouver during the early 1920s, was also a committed Marxist and a well-known author and poet.[79] Those who integrated Theosophy and socialism were able to abandon a capitalist-tainted Christianity but retain a spiritual belief system that focused on human betterment and the brotherhood of man.

Christian Scientists

The third significant metaphysical movement of this period offered not just ultimate universal betterment, but also improved individual health in the here and now. It is therefore perhaps not surprising that Christian Science soon transcended its very modest beginnings in British Columbia to become the most popular and significant metaphysical religion in the province. It claimed a close affinity to Christianity, but as scholars have revealed, it also owes considerable intellectual debts to spiritualism and has links to Theosophy.[80] Like its spiritual cousins, it may have claimed ties to Christianity, but orthodox Christian leaders saw it as quite distinct and heretical.

Christian Science was developed by American Mary Baker Eddy during the 1870s. With the publication of *Science and Health* in 1875, she began the popularization of the movement, which contended that ill-health emerged from a mistaken belief in the separation of spirit and matter. Eddy maintained that there was no such thing as matter, that people were all part of the great Life Soul, and that those who accepted this belief, and thus achieved harmony with God, could be healed of their ailments. Claiming to have cured herself of various serious afflictions in this way, she began to train practitioners, both male and female, who used her spiritual methods to work with and heal those who accepted Christian Science teachings.[81]

Christian Science appears to have come late to British Columbia, given its increasing popularity in the United States during the 1880s and 1890s. In 1901, most Canadian Christian Scientists lived in Ontario, with only a small band of 94 in British Columbia. In 1911, however, they were over-represented in the province, which was now home to almost 15 percent of all Christian Scientists in Canada. With 757 adherents, they also outnumbered BC spiritualists and Theosophists. Their ranks continued to grow after 1911, so that in 1921 over 3,700 Christian Scientists lived in British Columbia, making up almost 27 percent of Christian Scientists in Canada (see Table 14).

Christian Scientists were apparently met with significant hostility from American mainstream clergymen.[82] Although Christian Scientists comprised a minuscule portion of the BC population in 1900, a prominent Victoria Methodist minister had clearly heard of their reputation from American colleagues. He vigorously denounced the movement in March of that year, even though it does not seem to have had any organized presence in the city. Reverend J.C. Speer preached a sermon titled "The Fads of Faith," in which he cautioned his flock that "out of the heart of the devil has never been given to the world, under the name of religion, anything which, were it universally practiced, would tend to such hellish results." With an anxiety that verged on paranoia, he claimed to have proof that Christian Science agents "were to be found in all our cities working quietly to undermine the faith of the church members." Speer's concerns resembled those of ministers who feared the detrimental effects of combining Christianity with spiritualism or Theosophy, but he may have had more to worry about because, as he himself stated, Christian Science was becoming increasingly popular in the United States and Eastern Canada. In establishing that it was incompatible with Christianity, Speer had a more difficult time than those who condemned spiritualism and Theosophy, because Mary Baker Eddy claimed closer links to Christianity than the other two metaphysical religions did. Speer dismissed this reasoning out of hand: "We know of no other sect which has so systematically trampled upon everything which has been dear to the heart of the Christian church." He enumerated the many ways in which Christian Science diverged from Christianity, including apparently abandoning a belief in sin and the core Christian faith that Jesus had died for the sins of man.[83]

Speer's attack on Christian Science not only took an orthodox Christian approach, but also a highly gendered one. Given that Christian Science was the only significant religious movement of the time to be led by a woman, this is perhaps unsurprising. Speer sneeringly denounced Eddy as "the 'female messiah' of the nineteenth century," disparaged her theology as an "effeminate nightmare," and derided Christian Science practitioners as "religious birds of prey" who were "leading captive silly women and effeminate men." Rational socialist unbelievers may have characterized

Christianity as effeminate, but Christian leaders wrapped themselves in the mantle of rational masculinity as they censured the irrationality of a female-dominated sect, one that had the temerity to steal and delude good Christians.[84]

Although there were no publicly identifiable Christian Scientists in Victoria when Speer preached his sermon, he may have known that they had taken up residence across the water in Vancouver. In 1897, Carrie and Charles Varey, who were full-time Christian Science practitioners, moved to that city and began holding services in their living room, as well as Sunday School classes and Wednesday evening testimony meetings, in which members of the congregation "bear witness to experiences of healing, guidance and spiritual regeneration." The movement aroused so much interest that the services soon relocated to a rented hall, and by 1899 the congregation was organized as First Church of Christ, Scientist, Vancouver. By 1907, the congregation was large enough to purchase its own building on West Georgia Street, and by 1918 it had grown and prospered to the point it built its own large and handsome church across the street from the original building. By 1912, there were also Christian Science societies in New Westminster and North Vancouver.[85] In 1901, two members of the Vancouver Christian Science Church, Nancy and Samuel Greenwood, moved to Victoria and started offering services in their living room. Over the next ten years as the congregation grew, they held services in various halls and built their first church on Pandora Avenue in 1910. During the early 1900s, the church was twice able to fill the Victoria Theatre (with a capacity of a thousand) for visiting Christian Science speakers, which reveals broader interest in the movement.[86]

Christian Science soon spread well beyond Vancouver and Victoria. In 1908, former members of the Victoria church began services in Duncan, and a few Christian Scientists met together in Nanaimo from 1900. There was also considerable interest in the Interior, where Christian Science societies were founded in Nelson and Kamloops in 1908, in Rossland in 1909, in Kelowna in 1910, and in Greenwood in 1914. In some cases, services were held even before formal societies were established. These societies tended to be fairly small, since those with sixteen or more members could become churches, which none did before the First World War (the Nelson Christian Science Society became a church in 1915).[87]

As the congregations expanded, they continued to face hostility, not only from orthodox Christians, but also from proponents of science. In 1904, "W.L.B." wrote to the *Victoria Colonist,* ridiculing Christian Scientists for believing that prayer could stop the action of microbes. As James Opp states, the discovery that germs caused disease created increasing difficulties for all varieties of faith healers in the early twentieth century, as ignoring the reality of contagious illnesses was now seen as not just deluded, but as dangerous to public health.[88] Even so, Samuel Greenwood, a leader of Victoria's Christian Scientists, was not fazed. He challenged the Christian credentials of W.L.B. by declaring that "if prayer to God is of no avail, a terrible farce is enacted in the churches of the world every Sunday." He enlisted the arguments of rational empiricism:

> The majority of Christian Scientists have had experience with medicine and all other material ways before adopting Christian Science, and their only reason for adopting it is because they have found the most help in it. Facts are the final court of decision for human reason and judgment, and when one has received help and cure in a new method after all the old ones had failed to meet the need, is he wise or foolish for believing in it?[89]

Hostile letters to the editor could be rebutted, and always were, but allegations of Christian Science involvement in preventable deaths were more difficult. In 1907 and 1909, BC coroner's inquests investigated suspicious deaths related to Christian Science. The first case involved Gilbert Mann and his wife, Christian Scientists who lived in Victoria. When Gilbert fell ill, they did not call a physician, though repeatedly urged to do so by their neighbours. However, a doctor testified at the inquest that death was "due to an aneurism of the aorta, which was beyond the aid of medical practice," so the jury returned a verdict of "death from natural causes."[90] The second case, which was more complex, received considerable press attention in both Vancouver and Victoria. It related to a wealthy Vancouverite, John J. Harrison, who took his own life in March 1909. Witnesses at the coroner's inquest stated that the main Christian Science practitioner, Charles Varey, tried to convince Harrison to destroy his will, which left everything to his wife. Varey told Harrison that he needed to "renounce all ... connections with any society or party, either political or religious, also to cancel all insurance policies, wills and other unnecessary encumbrances that would injure [his] spiritual recovery." According to newspaper reports, this advice so depressed Harrison that he committed suicide. The coroner's jury declared that "one Mr. Varey, a Christian Science leader in this city, is largely the cause of Mr. Harrison's despondency and demise."[91]

This kind of negative press may not have impressed the general public, but it did not obstruct the growth of Christian Science in British Columbia. Who was particularly attracted to the new movement? As scholars have noted, and practitioners have claimed, most Christian Scientists came from the middle class. Of the eighty-nine Vancouver Christian Scientists who listed an occupation on the 1911 census, 70 percent can be defined as middle class. All appear to have been Euro-Canadians. The majority of Christian Scientists in the province were also female, as was the case elsewhere in Canada and the United States. In 1911, 57 percent of Victoria's Christian Scientists were female, as were 52 percent of their Vancouver co-religionists.[92] The published census for 1921 shows that 57 percent of BC Christian Scientists in that year were female, again in a province where non-Indigenous men greatly outnumbered non-Indigenous women.

A range of factors attracted women to Christian Science. Some had lost faith in mainstream religion, but more commonly they had lost faith in mainstream medicine. The latter offered limited relief from the illnesses and problems that arose due to repeated pregnancies, often involving humiliating and intrusive treatments that sometimes made things worse.[93] Women could also make a respectable living as Christian Science practitioners. In British Columbia before the First World War, twenty-nine of the thirty-two practitioners were female, and all but one of the women appear to have been either married or widowed.[94]

Despite the disapproval of orthodox clergymen, women who sought assistance with their health problems may have preferred to consult a female practitioner rather than a male doctor, as women could provide a familiar source of comfort. Before 1911, the numbers of BC Christian Scientists were so small that it is impossible to make definitive statements about their family relationships. Nonetheless, a small study of Victoria's Christian Scientists suggests that some couples joined the church together, whereas in other cases wives joined on their own. Most Christian Scientists came from mainstream churches.[95]

Whereas most of Victoria's Christian Scientists came from the conventional denominations, one couple abandoned irreligion for the new movement. And a famous unbeliever also seems to have viewed it positively, although it is not known whether he joined the church. Robert Lowery, the harshest critic and lampooner of churches and Christianity in the Kootenays, appears to have developed a soft spot for Christian Science. Unlike many journalists, who gleefully attacked or ridiculed it, he was uncharacteristically even-handed and then increasingly positive. In 1900, a reprinted article in Lowery's *New Denver Ledge* inferred that medicine and Christian Science were about equally efficacious: "There is a howl that rends the welkin when some one dies under Christian Science treatment, but the drug advocates can keep funeral processions in constant motion year in and year out without a whispered protest."[96] Lowery did reprint a couple of low-key humorous notes against Christian Science, but in 1907 he declared that it was the only altruistic church.[97] In 1908, he stated that "Christian Science, with its optimistic methods of teaching religion is fast becoming the great church of America. In less than 30 years there will be practically only two churches on this continent – the Roman Catholic and Christian Science, with here and there a Presbyterian." In 1912, he concluded that Presbyterians were a doomed species and that only Christian Science and Catholicism would survive. He had great expectations for Christian Science, whose teaching of "love, life and truth will eventually lift us out of the mud and kill fear, greed and selfishness, the three great curses of the world."[98] Lowery also printed a major article in which an American senator testified to the success of Christian Science in curing himself and his wife of their ailments, and his son of alcoholism.[99] In 1913, he reprinted two lengthy articles from the *Victoria Week* that defended Christian Science against the attacks of orthodox Christian ministers, avowing that it brought "comfort and hope to lives which have hitherto known nothing but gloom" and was "exercising successfully the most remarkable curative system of modern times."[100]

It is unclear why Lowery, that scourge of religious hypocrisy and cant, portrayed Christian Science in such a positive light. Perhaps he did join the church, and it helped to cure some of his recurring health problems, most of them apparently caused by overindulgence in alcohol. Certainly by 1913, one of his papers, the *Greenwood Ledge,* was regularly printing notices of local Christian Science services, which Lowery may well have attended. Christian Science may also have appealed to his strong sense of justice and fairness, which had made him such a nemesis to the mainstream churches. We may never know the answer, but Lowery's case indicates that even the most hardened and cynical male unbeliever could sometimes be drawn to the new metaphysical religions, in search of some combination of spiritual meaning, social justice, and physical healing.

The stresses and fears of the First World War may also have prompted British Columbians to explore the metaphysical religions. Some Christian leaders hoped that the war would bring unbelievers back to church, but at least one major clergyman, the Anglican bishop Doull of Kootenay, thought otherwise. In 1917, the *Toronto Globe* reported on a speech given by the bishop, which argued that

> while no Province in Canada was more given over to ungodliness and materialism before the war [than British Columbia], many are now turning

> to spiritual matters, though instead of turning to the Christian Church they are patronizing all sorts of creeds, such as Christian Science, Spiritualism, Russellism, Theosophy and New Thought, which, the Bishop said, would never bring the satisfaction of soul they were seeking. This, therefore, constitutes a great opportunity for the Church, and it is earnestly to be hoped that full advantage will be taken of it. The war will have done something, indeed, a great deal, if only people are enabled to realize that materialism cannot possibly meet the deepest needs of man. And yet it is equally clear that nothing short of the Person and Work of Christ can truly satisfy the soul.[101]

After the war, the proportion of British Columbians who declared that they had no religion did in fact decline slightly, to levels similar to those of 1901. Perhaps Bishop Doull was right about the spiritual impact of the war, or perhaps the fact that the provincial gender ratio was gradually evening out provides more of the answer. Regardless, the war certainly did not lead all British Columbians back to the mainstream denominations. The 1921 census shows a marked increase in the number of adherents of the metaphysical religions. This also occurred across Canada, but spiritualists, Theosophists, and Christian Scientists remained significantly overrepresented in British Columbia (see Table 14). As well, the published census of 1921 listed the 258 Canadian members of New Thought, an offshoot of Theosophy, 90 percent of whom lived in British Columbia.

A DETAILED STUDY OF the impact of the war and the post-war years on irreligion and alternative faiths must be left to future scholars, but it is clear that current intersections between New Age spirituality and high levels of irreligion can be glimpsed in turn-of-the-century British Columbia. The porous boundaries between the irreligious and those who sought spirituality outside of traditional religious forms were already evident. In this period, some secularists decided that, though orthodox Christianity was no longer meaningful or credible, a godless universe did not answer their spiritual yearnings, leading them to embrace a range of metaphysical alternatives, either temporarily or for the longer term. Such decisions were often gendered, or rooted in family choices, as people sought contact with lost loved ones or a spiritual path to improved health. Among those who remained committed to irreligion, men greatly outnumbered women, and many of the women who abandoned the mainstream churches for metaphysical religions never ventured to a fully secular world. Many others, both male and female, are listed on the manuscript census as Christians, but the fulminations of their ministers reveal that they took what they needed from the new metaphysical faiths, fashioning their own lived religion in a province that allowed for considerable openness and diversity.

Some also challenged other orthodoxies. Whereas socialism fuelled the skepticism of many BC men, and Christian beliefs bolstered the social reform efforts of many women and men, a number of British Columbians, particularly among Theosophists and spiritualists, found that alternative religions further inspired and motivated their socialist, feminist, or anti-racist activism.

For the orthodox Christian ministers who sought to reclaim the Christian hegemony that they could take for granted in Central and Eastern Canada, all of this provided not inspiration but frustration and despair. Some ministers, like Doull, recognized the dangerous interconnections between irreligion and alternative religions, but all of them saw both as major challenges to Christian hegemony in British Columbia, challenges that when combined with the lack of interest in Christianity among racialized immigrant communities, significantly weakened Christian authority and legitimacy – opening a range of cultural spaces where British Columbians had a unique freedom to shape their own irreligious, religious, or alternative spiritual destinies.

Conclusion

Godless Past and Present

Today, British Columbia is in the forefront of a secularizing English-speaking world, with over 44 percent of its inhabitants stating that they have no religion. This level of indifference or unbelief exceeds that of any other Canadian province.[1] British Columbia has consistently led the country in levels of "no religion" throughout the twentieth century and into the twenty-first.

Although levels of irreligion were much lower in British Columbia during the late nineteenth and early twentieth centuries, they were significantly higher than in Central and Eastern Canada, where Christianity was still hegemonic, the taken-for-granted basis of how people understood the world. Even during this early period, significant numbers of the white BC settler population declared that they had no religion, when this was almost unheard of elsewhere in Canada. Furthermore, the church involvement rates of those who identified themselves as Christians were much lower than elsewhere in the country. In exploring irreligion in British Columbia, this book examined questions of gender and family, class and class conflict, immigration, transiency, birthplace, racism, and racialization.

The irreligious, the indifferent, and the occasional churchgoers of early British Columbia cannot be understood in isolation from their Christian neighbours and family members. Therefore, this book peered inside the province's Christian churches. They enjoyed higher levels of membership and much more social and cultural clout than they do today, but being a pious churchgoer was much more of a minority experience than elsewhere in Canada. As church leaders surveyed their disappointingly meagre flocks and bemoaned the significant numbers of infidel and indifferent Euro-Canadians, and of racialized "heathens," they recognized that their cultural power and reach was much more limited and contested than in Central and Eastern Canada.

The majority of the irreligious and the indifferent were white settler men. This should not be surprising, since men were significantly over-represented among the non-Indigenous population of British Columbia before the First World War, and white men, particularly single men, were less religious than their female counterparts across Canada. Men were especially over-represented in the transient resource towns, where dominant versions of masculinity normalized challenges to Christianity, enabling many men to abandon religion along with the families they left behind. Some brought irreligion with them, particularly the Americans who came up from the neighbouring Western states, which had a longer tradition of irreligion than British Columbia. Other imports, from both the United States and Britain, included forms of labour radicalism that rejected both God and the churches as tools of the employing classes. The secular radicalism of the socialists and the Industrial Workers of the World was attractive to many workers who endured the brutal conditions of the BC resource frontier. Other men may not have completely discarded God but embraced the rough culture of drinking, gambling, and the sex trade, which often left little room for Christianity beyond the appeal of childhood hymns, an acceptance of basic moral precepts that had some lingering association with Christianity, and the desire for a proper Christian burial.

Certain forms of masculine irreligion were highly visible in the resource towns, but they had a much broader geographical reach. Transient workers in Vancouver's Gastown brought significant currents of both militant socialist atheism and religious indifference to that growing urban centre, and Victoria's ministers lamented the fact that Victorians would rather cultivate their gardens or turn out for a socialist meeting than attend a church service. Again, men (primarily working-class men) were seen as the main problem, although middle-class men were also more likely to be irreligious in British Columbia than elsewhere in Canada.

If we wish truly to understand these irreligious white men, and how they came by their freedom to loudly proclaim their irreligion, we must understand them in their unvarnished, and not always pretty, complexity. Class consciousness was certainly part of many working-class men's hostility to the churches, but this hostility was also fuelled by racism. The willingness of at least some clergymen to critique policies of anti-Asian racism and exclusion exacerbated anti-Christian feelings among many white working-class men. Virulent anti-Asian and anti-Indigenous racism also allowed many white working-class men to define their social respectability and inclusion in racial and class terms alone, without needing to affirm Christian connection and respectability.

This was less true for most white settler women. Some working-class women became part of the secular, class-conscious cultures that were prominent in the Kootenay mining towns, and the many sex trade workers in these and other BC communities were not welcome in church. But for many Euro-Canadian settler women, the Christianity they brought with them served as a bulwark of faith, community, and familiarity in a foreign and largely masculine world. Whereas white women were a minority throughout British Columbia, they remained a majority in most churches, as they were in Eastern Canada. Through both church attendance and involvement with a range of Christian women's organizations, they tried to re-create the social connections they had left behind and to transform their new society into something more moral and Christian. In British Columbia, as in regions farther east, many women, especially middle-class women, managed to bring their husbands to church. Nonetheless, the predominance of men among the irreligious and indifferent points to a starkly gendered divide in the province. White settler women's racism was as deep as that of white settler men, but it had different implications. Their refusal to include racialized women in their church communities increased their own isolation, while in trying to reform their new society they sought to "civilize" and Christianize not only their men, but also the racialized men and women whom they defined as heathen others.

The association of irreligion with masculinity caused difficulties for at least some women who rejected Christianity, unless they did so in the company of a godless, class-conscious husband. Other women who were dissatisfied with Christianity tended not to reject all religion but instead sought an alternative form of belief and turned to metaphysical religions such as spiritualism, Theosophy, and Christian Science. Some people who sought progressive change found both spiritual sustenance and activist inspiration in these faiths. Such religions were more popular in British Columbia than elsewhere in Canada, again pointing to the province's greater openness to heterodox beliefs (or non-beliefs) and to the more limited authority of the churches.

British Columbia was also far more racially and religiously diverse than the rest of Canada. By the late 1880s, Indigenous people were no longer a majority presence, but they remained a significant part of the population, and they faced systemic and daily racism from white settlers and the state.

An irony of this period is that though the churches had at least officially succeeded in converting most Indigenous peoples, they failed to sway a significant proportion of the settler population, which missionaries saw as setting a poor example to their newly converted charges. The influence of "bad" white men amplified missionary anxieties about the maintenance of Christian belief and behaviour among Indigenous people.

Other racialized groups, particularly the relatively large Chinese, Japanese, and South Asian communities, who came to the province with their own religious traditions and proved reluctant to convert to Christianity, further limited the cultural influence of the churches. Unwillingness to convert was grounded in a number of issues. Like many of their white counterparts, Asian immigrants were bachelors, more interested in the excitements of rough culture than in religious practices in traditions of any type. Many were sojourners who hoped to soon return home and were thus uninterested in espousing a foreign religion. Unlike Asian immigrants elsewhere in Canada, they also lived in relatively large racialized communities, which provided the supports they needed, so conversion, even nominal conversion, had less appeal than in parts of the country where it was necessary to fit in. Asian immigrants in British Columbia, particularly those of Chinese origin, risked ostracism from their own communities if they converted. They may also have understood that Christianity was not central to broader social acceptance in the province, and the fierce racism that they encountered certainly undermined Christian promises of love and brotherhood.

The presence of non-Christian racialized communities combined with the acceptance of irreligion among many British Columbians, strengthened certain alliances and reduced some social cleavages among white settlers. BC churchmen were more willing than their colleagues in other provinces to accept the demands of white Christian women for political rights, both in the churches and in broader society. They viewed Christian women as crucial allies in their campaigns to Christianize and "civilize" godless white men and "heathen" Asians, as well as to shore up their power over Indigenous peoples. Many white Christian women were eager to participate in these campaigns for social and moral reform. In a context where religion (and thus religious differences) mattered less, and racialized Asians were seen as the primary enemy, relations between white Catholics and Protestants were more cordial than in Eastern Canada. And despite not being Christian, Jews were generally perceived as white, which meant that they experienced less prejudice than elsewhere in the country.

The dominant Christian institutions of British Columbia would have been very familiar to most Canadians, and their message of social and moral reform was common across the country. Some BC agricultural and ranching communities had high levels of church involvement, with the churches serving as centres of faith and as social hubs. But despite the many devout Christians in the province, and their efforts to strengthen and empower its Christian culture, British Columbia was different. Church members could live good Christian lives in their new home, and the province did remain ostensibly Christian, but a range of voices – racialized and marginalized non-Christians, militant Marxist atheists, followers of various metaphysical spiritualities, irreligious former Christians, and nominal Christians with limited or no interest in Christian traditions – weakened and fractured the possibility of Christian hegemony.[2] The challenges posed by these groups were mutually reinforcing, creating many opportunities and cultural spaces for ignoring Christian power and oversight. These opportunities were especially available to white settler men in the province, many of whom made use of their freedom to ignore the churches or to declare their atheism or indifference loudly and clearly.

This study has focused on the BC situation, but what can it tell us about broader international debates regarding secularization and irreligion? I would argue that it reinforces analyses that move away from overarching interpretations of secularization toward understanding irreligious cultures in specific localized contexts. Only by looking closely at the BC case can we come to understand the intersecting forces that allowed many men to shrug off the Christian norms that were hegemonic elsewhere in Canada. This regional study demonstrates the importance of integrating a range of variables and closely tracing out their intersections to answer questions about the relative power and force of religion and irreligion in particular cultures. Whereas class and gender have become important foci in studying religion, irreligion, and secularization in various national and transnational contexts, issues of race, racialization, and racism have been largely overlooked. This book suggests that historians need to take a closer look at potential relationships between religion, irreligion, racialization and racism.

This study also points to the potential impact of larger regional cultures on local patterns of irreligion. Americans from the western United States had a significant impact on the irreligious culture of British Columbia during the years before the First World War. Elements of this culture can be traced to the frontier gold-rush society of mid-nineteenth-century

California, more directly to the later nineteenth-century mining camps of the American West, and to broader patterns of religious indifference along the Pacific Coast.

While recognizing the complexity of British Columbia's contested religious culture of the late nineteenth and early twentieth centuries, one is left with the question of how we got from there to here. How did irreligious influences become increasingly dominant in the province by the late twentieth century? Although this question must be left largely to other scholars, a few thoughts are in order.

No one has looked closely at religion and irreligion in British Columbia between 1914 and 1945, but the limited information available suggests that irreligious elements did not grow during these decades. After increasing between 1901 and 1911, the percentage of British Columbians who defined themselves as atheists/agnostics or as having no religion declined to 1901 levels in 1921 and fell a bit farther in 1931, although remaining significantly higher than in the rest of Canada. In absolute numbers, the irreligious population remained stable between 1911 and 1931.[3]

The First World War may not have had the dramatic impact that Bishop Doull of Kootenay hoped in turning people from "infidelity," but it did temporarily strengthen popular support for certain Protestant causes, as in the rest of the country. The passage of Prohibition legislation during the war (as a result of a referendum) saw the short-lived success of a major Protestant goal, and the enfranchisement of white women in 1917 increased the proportion of actively Christian voters in the province. Nonetheless, the fact that in 1920 British Columbia became the first anglophone province to repeal Prohibition (as the result of another referendum) points to the continued force of its less pious voices.[4]

The slight decline in the proportion of those of "no religion" during the interwar years may reflect the evening out of gender ratios in the province.[5] The emergence of certain Christian movements may also have had an impact. Robert Burkinshaw chronicles the rise of conservative evangelicalism among BC Baptists and Pentecostals after 1917.[6] This movement expanded significantly and held very popular revivals. The best known, the Charles Price Pentecostal healing revivals of the 1920s in Vancouver and Victoria, drew in thousands. As James Opp shows, Charles Price and other Protestant revivalists worked hard to diminish the feminine image of Christianity and thus to attract men to their events.[7] Their efforts may have helped to reduce the stark gender disparity in BC church involvement. The Price revivals also appealed to people of Asian origin: in 1923, more than eight hundred Chinese British Columbians attended a Price revival in Victoria's New Chinese Theatre.[8] Whereas even by 1931 the vast majority of Chinese British Columbians did not define themselves as Christians, missionaries enjoyed increasing success in converting at least some of them during the interwar years.[9] Members of the Japanese community, which included growing numbers of women and children, were also more likely to convert to Christianity during these decades.[10] This does not appear to have had any impact on levels of racism in the province, which remained virulent, rising to a fever pitch against Japanese Canadians with the coming of the Second World War. The relationship between anti-Asian racism and irreligion among Euro-Canadian British Columbians in this period remains to be explored.

Christianity may have strengthened its power and appeal in the interwar years, but the irreligious did not disappear. As Reverend J.H. White stated in the immediate pre-war period, and as Callum Brown argues for the 1970s and 1980s, the children of the irreligious, "raised in a domestic routine largely free of the intrusion of organized religion," are less likely than those raised in Christian households to turn to religious belief and practice.[11] This may have been less true in the 1920s than in the 1980s, but it seems very probable that at least some children of committed socialist atheists of the pre-war period would have maintained their parents' allegiances, and those raised in "indifferent" households (or at least with irreligious fathers) may also have had little interest in religion. In addition to generational patterns of irreligion, regional cultures of irreligion, particularly in the Kootenays, may also have had longer-term resonance. More research is needed to address this issue in depth.

Whereas the gender imbalance that fuelled BC secularism may have diminished after the First World War, the radical working-class tradition that also fostered it remained very much alive. Particularly in the Depression years, BC communist leaders gained a major following among the many unemployed. Peter Campbell and Elliot Hanowski demonstrate that many socialist and communist leaders in both British Columbia and across Canada were committed to atheism during the interwar years.[12] We know less about their followers, but it seems reasonable to assume that despite the continued appeal of the social gospel among some progressives, many BC leftists of this generation would have shared their predecessors' distaste for religion.[13] Certainly, Hanowski has shown that in Manitoba and Ontario rationalist speakers, with their primary message of rational atheism and a tinge of socialism, became more popular, and more socialist, during the interwar period. We can fairly safely conjecture that something similar would have happened in British Columbia.[14]

The interwar years may have been a period of consolidation for the churches and of relative stagnation for more irreligious British Columbians, but the number of those of "no religion" began to increase after the Second World War. In 1951, the number of British Columbians in this category more than tripled from 1931 totals, growing to 2.2 percent of the provincial population, while remaining at 0.4 in Canada as a whole. The 1960s had a secularizing impact across Canada but especially so in British Columbia, as those of no religion increased to over 13.0 percent of the provincial population by 1971, as compared to 4.3 percent of Canadians generally.[15] The province's more secular nature in these years is also reflected in the fact that Canada's first post-war humanist (secularist) association was founded in Victoria during the early 1950s. Other BC humanist organizations followed in the 1970s and 1980s, and BC secularists played a role in the founding of the Canadian Humanist Association in 1968.[16]

Scholars have ably studied BC secularization during those years: Callum Brown argues that growing levels of irreligion in British Columbia and the English-speaking world were produced largely by women's new willingness to abandon religion. Tina Block's fine-grained comparative study of British Columbia and Washington State notes that in the 1950s, 1960s, and 1970s, the image of the irreligious white male worker as the quintessential secular British Columbian retained much rhetorical power but no longer reflected reality. Many of the secular British Columbians whom Block studied were women, and mothers of families. Although many were torn by the social expectation that they would provide Christian training for their children, they were clear that religion was not important to them or their families.[17]

Social expectations concerning women and religion were more powerful before the First World War, even in British Columbia. During the years studied in this book, most white women were either unwilling or unable to define themselves as irreligious, unless in the company of an irreligious husband or father, a fact that helped to limit the strength of British Columbia's more secular minority. Nonetheless, even as a primarily male phenomenon, this irreligious minority was part of what made the province different from the rest of Canada in the period before the First World War. At this time, Christians still dominated in many ways, but their dominance was not so culturally ingrained as to be normal, natural, and "just the way things were." Bitter critiques of religion and even of God were a standard feature of public discourse. *Lowery's Claim* may eventually have been banned from the federal mails after more than five years of lambasting Christianity and the churches, but no BC politician challenged its editor's right to express his opinions. And no BC court attempted to silence either Lowery or his equally atheistic colleagues. As Elliot Hanowski demonstrates, such was not the case in Eastern Canada. During the interwar period, activists in Ontario and Quebec who made similar claims against religion and Christianity were charged, convicted, and jailed for "blasphemous libel."[18] It seems unthinkable that this could have happened in British Columbia.

As newcomers move to British Columbia and marvel at its beauty, while being surprised and in some cases shocked by its level of secularism and racial and class cleavages, it is important for them to understand the roots of this story – some pieces of which are with us still, for better and worse. Examining the lives of the racist, socialist, atheist white men, the white and Asian workers who enjoyed their leisure time and had little interest in organized Christianity (if for very different reasons), the spiritualists and Theosophists who sought spiritual fulfillment beyond the churches, and the pious white settler women and embattled ministers who allied with them enables us to see the importance of irreligion and religion to British Columbia's past. Religion and irreligion need to be understood in relation both to each other and to other major forces that shaped this province. Knowing about these people and these powerful interrelated forces can also inform our understanding of the province's social relations and culture today, illuminating why British Columbia remains in many ways distinctive from the rest of Canada.

Appendix: Tables

TABLE 1 Percentage of communicants to total adherents, major denominations, by selected provinces and territories, 1901

Province		Communicants		
		#	%	Total adherents
BC	Anglican	5,193	12.8	40,689
	Baptist[a]	1,383	21.3	6,500
	Methodist	4,373	17.5	25,047
	Presbyterian	4,555	13.4	34,081
	Roman Catholic	11,513	34.2	33,639
Nova Scotia	Anglican	13,192	20.0	66,107
	Baptist[a]	29,573	35.5	83,233
	Methodist	16,790	29.2	57,490
	Presbyterian	28,903	27.2	106,381
	Roman Catholic	82,440	63.6	129,578
Ontario	Anglican	81,393	22.1	367,937
	Baptist[a]	40,643	34.9	116,320
	Methodist	201,632	30.3	666,388
	Presbyterian	138,284	29.0	477,386
	Roman Catholic	243,694	62.4	390,304
Quebec	Anglican	25,024	30.7	81,563
	Baptist[a]	3,126	36.9	8,480
	Methodist	14,431	34.3	42,014
	Presbyterian	16,870	29.1	58,013
	Roman Catholic	889,055	62.2	1,429,260
The Territories[b]	Anglican	3,901	15.4	25,366
	Baptist[a]	1,185	21.9	5,416
	Methodist	4,126	18.6	22,151
	Presbyterian	5,093	18.3	27,806
	Roman Catholic	13,172	43.8	30,073
Canada	Anglican	148,469	21.8	680,620
	Baptist[a]	108,217	34.2	316,477
	Methodist	269,610	29.4	916,886
	Presbyterian	226,228	26.9	842,442
	Roman Catholic	1,356,019	60.8	2,229,600

a Baptists also include Free Baptists.

b Includes Alberta, Assiniboia, and Saskatchewan but not the unorganized territories.

Source: Dominion Bureau of Statistics, *Census of Canada, 1901* (Ottawa: Census Office, 1902), vol. 1, Table 8, and vol. 4, Table 19.

TABLE 2 Agnostics and those of no religion, BC and Ontario, 1901

	BC irreligious #	Percentage of total population %	Ontario irreligious #	Percentage of total population #
Single women	182	0.5	62	0.1
Single men	1,502	2.0	197	0.2
Married women	203	0.8	62	0.1
Married men	609	1.7	152	0.2

Note: The Ontarians are a percentage of the total population of the cities and counties included in the Ontario sample.
Sources: Canadian Families Project, 1901 database of atheists/agnostics and those of "no religion" for BC and selected towns and counties of Ontario, 1901 manuscript census; Dominion Bureau of Statistics, *Census of Canada, 1901* (Ottawa: Census Office, 1902), vol. 1, Table 7.

TABLE 3 Atheism and non-atheism among spouses, BC, 1901

	#	%
Both spouses non-believers	156	41
Husband non-believer, wife Christian	205	54
Wife non-believer, husband Christian	16	4
Total couples	377	100

Source: Canadian Families Project, 1901 database of atheists/agnostics and those of "no religion" (using SPLOC variable).

TABLE 4 Religious and irreligious fluidity between at least two of the census years of 1881, 1891, 1901, and 1911, as found in the ViHistory database

	1881–91	1891–1901	1901–11	Total	
	#	#	#	#	%
Remained in an irreligious category[a]	10	25	1	36	16.3
Moved from irreligious to religious category	18	63	23	104	48.4
Moved from religious to irreligious category	19	49	7	75	34.9

Note: As previously mentioned, the ViHistory database includes Vancouver Island's total population between 1881 and 1901 but only the population of Victoria for 1911, which helps explain the smaller numbers in the 1901–11 column.
a Some shifted from one irreligious category to another, such as from infidel to atheist, or from agnostic to secularist.

Table 5 Proportion of the BC irreligious who were miners, by type of miner, 1901

	Irreligious		5% sample of total population	
	#	%	#	%
Gold miner	155	6.0	105	2.6
Silver miner	178	6.9	149	3.7
Coal miner	61	2.4	130	3.3
Total irreligious people	2,588*		3,999	

Note: "Irreligious" refers to those who defined themselves as atheist/agnostic or of no religion.

* The 1901 database of atheists/agnostics and those of no religion gives a total of 2,588 people, as opposed to a total of 2,674 in the published census. The latter may have included 86 individuals whose language in describing themselves as irreligious did not correlate with the definition of irreligious as used for the database. Alternatively, some form of clerical error may have occurred during the compilation of the published census.

Sources: Dominion Bureau of Statistics, *Census of Canada, 1901* (Ottawa: Census Office, 1902), vol. 1, Table 8; Canadian Families Project, 1901 database of atheists/agnostics and those of "no religion"; Canadian Families Project, 5 percent sample of total BC population, from the National 5 percent sample of manuscript census, 1901.

Table 6 Percentage of population atheists or of no religion and percentage of population female, by selected Vancouver Island and Yale and Cariboo subdistricts, 1901

	No religion/atheist			
	#	Percent of population	Total population	Percent of population female
Vancouver Island				
Comox	22	0.6	3,493	29
Cowichan	29	0.8	3,613	32
Nanaimo City	43	0.7	6,130	43
Nanaimo North	4	0.3	1,439	33
Nanaimo South	26	0.5	5,146	35
Yale and Cariboo				
Kootenay East South Riding	208	3.2	6,508	29
Kootenay West Nelson Riding	85	1.2	7,102	31
Kootenay West Revelstoke Riding	66	2.2	3,003	32
Kootenay West – Rossland Riding	538	3.7	14,603	30
Kootenay West Slocan Riding	387	7.3	5,321	26

Sources: Canadian Families Project, 1901 database of atheists/agnostics and those of "no religion"; Dominion Bureau of Statistics, *Census of Canada, 1901* (Ottawa: Census Office, 1902), vol. 1, Table 7.

Table 7 Percentage of communicants to total adherents, major denominations, for BC and the Vancouver Island and Yale and Cariboo districts, 1901

		Communicants		Total adherents
		#	%	
BC	Anglican	5,193	12.8	40,689
	Methodist	4,373	17.5	25,047
	Presbyterian	4,555	13.4	34,081
	Roman Catholic	11,513	34.2	33,639
Vancouver Island (excludes Victoria)	Anglican	427	7.5	5,718
	Methodist	452	11.3	4,001
	Presbyterian	475	9.2	5,170
	Roman Catholic	1,524	34.1	4,463
Yale and Cariboo	Anglican	1,147	9.3	12,355
	Methodist	968	13.8	7,032
	Presbyterian	1,301	10.7	12,170
	Roman Catholic	4,886	27.2	17,955

Source: Dominion Bureau of Statistics, *Census of Canada, 1901* (Ottawa: Census Office, 1902), vol. 1, Table 10, and vol. 4, Table 19.

TABLE 8 Church involvement, by denomination, for selected Ontario, Nova Scotia, and BC communities, 1901

		Anglicans			Baptists			Methodists			Presbyterians		
		Comms.	Adh.	%	Comms.	Adh.	%	Comms.	Adh.	%	Comms.	Adh.	%
Ontario	Campbellford	57	208	27	33	75	44	261	667	39	130	507	26
	Dunnville	163	431	38	70	306	23	205	547	37	62	207	30
Nova Scotia	Amherst	n/a			185	813	23	n/a			171	672	25
	Kentville	81	328	25	66	358	18	59	170	35	39	198	20
BC	Revelstoke	94	330	28	n/a			78	198	39	53	284	19
	Vernon	n/a			n/a			55	125	44	66	228	29
	Nelson	70	905	8	n/a			114	545	21	118	1085	11
	Rossland	n/a			n/a			94	691	14	77	951	8

Note: Includes only those over the age of twelve. Comms. = communicants. Adh. = adherents

Sources: Canadian Families Project, 100 percent databases of the 1901 manuscript census for Revelstoke, Nelson, Vernon, Amherst, Kentville, Campbellford, and Dunnville; 100 percent database of the 1901 manuscript census for Rossland, from Jeremy Mouat; local church records in the following archives: Anglican Diocesan Archives, in Kelowna, Hamilton, and Toronto; Atlantic Baptist Archives, Wolfville; Canadian Baptist Archives, Hamilton; Presbyterian Church in Canada Archives, Toronto; Public Archives of Nova Scotia, Halifax; United Church of Canada Archives, Toronto; United Church of Canada, British Columbia Conference Archives, Vancouver; United Church of Canada, Maritime Conference Archives, Sackville.

TABLE 9 Church membership by year immigrating to Canada, in four BC communities

	Year immigrated	Anglican			Methodist			Presbyterian		
		%	Comm.	Adh.	%	Comm.	Adh.	%	Comm.	Adh.
Nelson	After 1890	3	9	266	6	7	117	8	19	237
	1880–90	10	21	219	36	16	45	13	19	143
	1860–79	12	6	52	36	10	28	13	7	56
Vernon	After 1890		n/a		33	3	9	19	6	31
	1880–90		n/a		62	8	13	39	14	36
	1860–79		n/a			n/a			n/a	
Rossland	After 1890		n/a		12	48	405	5	14	310
	1880–90		n/a		15	7	47	12	11	90
	1860–79		n/a		*			*		
Revelstoke	After 1890	17	10	59	39	11	28	8	3	39
	1880–90	35	29	84	27	10	37	28	14	50
	1860–79	*			*			*		

Note: Comm. = number of church members/communicants. Adh. = total number of that denomination. Only individuals who were over the age of twelve are included. Pre-1860 immigration numbers were too small to include in all four communities.

* Numbers too small to include.

Sources: Canadian Families Project, 100 percent databases of the 1901 manuscript census for Revelstoke, Nelson, and Vernon; 100 percent database of the 1901 manuscript census for Rossland, from Jeremy Mouat; local church records in the following archives: Anglican Diocesan Archives, Kelowna; United Church of Canada, British Columbia Conference Archives, Vancouver.

Table 10 Church involvement, by gender and denomination, for selected Ontario, Nova Scotia, and BC communities, 1901

			Anglicans			Baptists			Methodists			Presbyterians		
			Comms.	Adh.	%	Comms.	Adh.	%	Comms.	Adh.	%	Comms.	Adh.	%
Ontario	Campbellford	Female	43	117	37	24	42	57	163	367	44	95	288	33
		Male	14	91	15	9	33	27	98	300	33	35	219	16
	Dunnville	Female	98	228	43	43	173	25	118	279	42	42	105	40
		Male	65	203	32	27	133	20	87	268	32	20	102	20
Nova Scotia	Amherst	Female	n/a			102	414	25	n/a			93	278	33
		Male				83	399	21				78	349	22
	Kentville	Female	53	189	28	34	173	20	36	86	42	24	103	23
		Male	28	139	20	32	185	17	23	84	27	15	95	16
BC	Revelstoke	Female	46	126	37	n/a			43	83	52	32	101	32
		Male	48	204	24				35	115	30	21	183	11
	Vernon	Female	n/a			n/a			26	42	62	34	88	39
		Male							29	83	35	32	140	23
	Nelson	Female	28	315	9	n/a			64	196	33	68	356	19
		Male	42	592	7				50	349	14	50	729	7
	Rossland	Female	n/a			n/a			48	250	19	40	291	14
		Male							46	441	10	37	660	6

Note: Only those who were over the age of twelve are included. Comms. = communicants. Adh. = adherents.

Sources: Canadian Families Project, 100 percent databases of the 1901 manuscript census for Revelstoke, Nelson, Vernon, Amherst, Kentville, Campbellford, and Dunnville; 100 percent database of the 1901 manuscript census for Rossland, from Jeremy Mouat; local church records in the following archives: Anglican Diocesan Archives, in Kelowna, Hamilton, and Toronto; Atlantic Baptist Archives, Wolfville; Canadian Baptist Archives, Hamilton; Presbyterian Church in Canada Archives, Toronto; Public Archives of Nova Scotia, Halifax; United Church of Canada Archives, Toronto; United Church of Canada, British Columbia Conference Archives, Vancouver; United Church of Canada, Maritime Conference Archives, Sackville.

TABLE 11 Church involvement, by gender and class, for selected Ontario, Nova Scotia, and BC communities, 1901

		Comms.	Adh.	%	Comms.	Adh.	%
Ontario							
		Campbellford			*Dunnville*		
Female	md. cl.	92	188	49	115	208	55
	w. cl.	138	368	38	96	303	32
Male	md. cl.	49	157	31	79	199	40
	w. cl.	76	327	23	71	322	22
Nova Scotia							
		Amherst			*Kentville*		
Female	md. cl.	55	185	30	55	183	30
	w. cl.	95	312	30	57	204	28
Male	md. cl.	47	189	25	33	155	21
	w. cl.	77	313	25	41	193	21
BC							
		Vernon			*Revelstoke*		
Female	md. cl.	13	30	43	47	106	44
	w. cl.	23	45	51	58	139	42
Male	md. cl.	13	42	31	41	121	34
	w. cl.	17	39	44	48	195	25
		Nelson			*Rossland*		
Female	md. cl.	57	168	34	27	157	17
	w. cl.	55	223	25	51	297	17
Male	md. cl.	44	226	19	30	182	16
	w. cl.	37	300	12	41	394	10

Note: Only those over the age of twelve are included. Comms. = communicants. Adh. = adherents. Communicants and adherents for Campbellford, Dunnville, and Kentville include Methodists, Presbyterians, Baptists, and Anglicans. Communicants and adherents for Amherst include Baptists and Presbyterians. Communicants and adherents for Revelstoke include Anglicans, Methodists, and Presbyterians. Communicants and adherents for Nelson, Rossland, and Vernon include Methodists and Presbyterians.

Sources: Canadian Families Project, 100 percent databases of the 1901 manuscript census for Revelstoke, Nelson, Vernon, Amherst, Kentville, Campbellford, and Dunnville; 100 percent database of the 1901 manuscript census for Rossland, from Jeremy Mouat; local church records in the following archives: Anglican Diocesan Archives, in Kelowna, Hamilton, and Toronto; Atlantic Baptist Archives, Wolfville; Canadian Baptist Archives, Hamilton; Presbyterian Church in Canada Archives, Toronto; Public Archives of Nova Scotia, Halifax; United Church of Canada Archives, Toronto; United Church of Canada, British Columbia Conference Archives, Vancouver; United Church of Canada, Maritime Conference Archives, Sackville.

TABLE 12 Church involvement, by gender, class, and marital status, for selected Ontario, Nova Scotia, and BC communities, 1901

		Comms.	Adh.	%	Comms.	Adh.	%
Ontario							
		Campbellford			*Dunnville*		
F (married)	md. cl.	53	103	51	68	119	57
	w. cl.	83	209	40	60	191	31
F (single)	md. cl.	36	76	47	43	77	56
	w. cl.	50	143	35	32	95	34
M (married)	md. cl.	41	144	28	50	118	42
	w. cl.	56	208	27	49	197	25
M (single)	md. cl.	8	52	15	28	76	37
	w. cl.	16	108	15	20	104	19
Nova Scotia							
		Amherst			*Kentville*		
F (married)	md. cl.	40	103	39	38	101	38
	w. cl.	72	195	37	35	121	29
F (single)	md. cl.	13	69	19	13	67	19
	w. cl.	23	111	21	20	74	27
M (married)	md. cl.	42	99	42	24	100	24
	w. cl.	67	197	34	34	115	30
M (single)	md. cl.	3	84	4	8	53	15
	w. cl.	6	100	6	7	73	10
BC							
		Vernon			*Revelstoke*		
F (married)	md. cl.	11	22	50	38	77	49
	w. cl.	20	30	67	45	105	43
F (single)	md. cl.	2	7	29	7	22	32
	w. cl.	3	14	21	12	33	36
M (married)	md. cl.	9	25	36	29	80	36
	w. cl.	15	24	63	39	111	35
M (single)	md. cl.	3	14	21	12	36	33
	w. cl.	2	15	13	9	81	11
		Nelson			*Rossland*		
F (married)	md. cl.	26	66	39	27	115	23
	w. cl.	24	60	40	44	238	18
F (single)	md. cl.	4	25	16	6	36	17
	w. cl.	2	13	15	9	48	19
M (married)	md. cl.	18	70	26	20	116	17
	w. cl.	18	68	26	34	243	14
M (single)	md. cl.	5	42	12	11	62	18
	w. cl.	2	42	5	8	145	6

Note: Only those over the age of twelve are included. Comms. = communicants. Adh. = adherents.
Communicants and adherents for Campbellford, Dunnville, and Kentville include Methodists, Presbyterians, Baptists, and Anglicans. Communicants and adherents for Amherst include Baptists and Presbyterians. Communicants and adherents for Revelstoke include Anglicans, Methodists, and Presbyterians. Communicants and adherents for Nelson, Rossland, and Vernon include Methodists and Presbyterians.
Sources: Canadian Families Project, 100 percent databases of the 1901 manuscript census for Revelstoke, Nelson, Vernon, Amherst, Kentville, Campbellford, and Dunnville; 100 percent database of the 1901 manuscript census for Rossland, from Jeremy Mouat; local church records in the following archives: Anglican Diocesan Archives, in Kelowna, Hamilton, and Toronto; Atlantic Baptist Archives, Wolfville; Canadian Baptist Archives, Hamilton; Presbyterian Church in Canada Archives, Toronto; Public Archives of Nova Scotia, Halifax; United Church of Canada Archives, Toronto; United Church of Canada, British Columbia Conference Archives, Vancouver; United Church of Canada, Maritime Conference Archives, Sackville.

Table 13 Percentage of communicants to total adherents in major denominations, for BC, Ontario, Vancouver, Victoria, and selected Ontario and Manitoba districts, 1901

Province/district/city		Communicants #	Communicants %	Total adherents
BC	Anglican	5,193	12.8	40,689
	Baptist	1,383	21.3	6,500
	Methodist	4,373	17.5	25,047
	Presbyterian	4,555	13.4	34,081
	Roman Catholic	11,513	34.2	33,639
Ontario	Anglican	81,393	22.1	367,937
	Baptist	40,643	34.9	116,320
	Methodist	201,632	30.3	666,388
	Presbyterian	138,284	29.0	477,386
	Roman Catholic	243,694	62.4	390,304
Vancouver City	Anglican	1,066	15.1	7,063
	Baptist	437	28.1	1,554
	Methodist	759	20.1	3,785
	Presbyterian	1,244	19.1	6,506
	Roman Catholic	1,500	49.0	3,064
Victoria City	Anglican	1,079	16.4	6,588
	Baptist	434	46.1	941
	Methodist	828	27.2	3,043
	Presbyterian	744	20.6	3,604
	Roman Catholic	2,035	101.7	2,001
Hamilton City	Anglican	4,819	38.7	12,443
	Baptist	1,182	42.0	2,814
	Methodist	3,935	28.6	13,737
	Presbyterian	4,509	39.1	11,542
	Roman Catholic	7,320	82.5	8,872
London City	Anglican	2,825	44.5	6,347
	Baptist	547	37.8	1,449
	Methodist	2,010	27.8	7,219
	Presbyterian	1,804	39.8	4,537
	Roman Catholic	3,677	104.9	3,506
Winnipeg City	Anglican	3,312	32.6	10,175
	Baptist	773	37.6	2,055
	Methodist	2,105	31.2	6,741
	Presbyterian	2,783	27.4	10,172
	Roman Catholic	2,925	56.9	5,143

Note: Vancouver City and Victoria City are sub-districts, whereas the other cities are census districts, because they are larger.
Source: Dominion Bureau of Statistics, *Census of Canada, 1901* (Ottawa: Census Office, 1902), vol. 1, Table 7, and vol. 4, Table 19.

TABLE 14 Alternative religious groups in BC and Canada, 1901–21

		Total in BC	%	Total in Canada	BC population as % of total Canadian population
1901	Spiritualists	143	23.2	616	3.3
	Christian Scientists	94	3.6	2,619	
	Theosophists	34	31.8	107	
1911	Spiritualists	184	27.3	674	5.4
	Christian Scientists	757	14.9	5,073	
	Theosophists	68	38.4	177	
1921	Spiritualists	319	20.5	1,558	6.0
	Christian Scientists	3,711	26.8	13,826	
	Theosophists	135	36.9	366	

Source: Dominion Bureau of Statistics, *Census of Canada, 1901* (Ottawa: Census Office, 1902), vol. 1, Table 8; DBS, Census of Canada, 1911 (Ottawa: C.H. Parmelee, 1913), vol. 1, Table 1; DBS, Census of Canada, 1921 (Ottawa: F.A. Acland, 1924), vol. 1, Table 35.

Notes

Introduction

1 I was born in England after my parents had emigrated from South Africa, but I was raised on their stories of the evils of apartheid, and made several family visits to apartheid South Africa in my teens and early twenties.

2 *Westminster,* April 1, 1899, 349.

3 Data for Figure 1 taken from Dominion Bureau of Statistics (DBS), *Census of Canada, 1901* (Ottawa: Census Office, 1902), vol. 1, Table 8; DBS, *Census of Canada, 1911* (Ottawa: C.H. Parmelee, 1913), vol. 1, Table 1; DBS, *Census of Canada, 1921* (Ottawa: F.A. Acland, 1924), vol. 1, Table 35; DBS, *Census of Canada, 1931* (Ottawa: J.O. Patenaude, 1935), vol. 3, Table 20; DBS, *Census of Canada, 1951* (Ottawa: E. Cloutier, 1956), vol. 10, Table 36; Statistics Canada, *Census of Canada, 1971* (Ottawa: Information Canada, 1972), Catalogue no. 92-724, Table 10-2; Statistics Canada, *Census of Canada, 1981* (Ottawa: Statistics Canada, 1982), Catalogue no. 92-912, Table 1; Statistics Canada, *Census of Canada, 1991* (Ottawa: Statistics Canada, 1992), Catalogue no. 96-304E, 106; Statistics Canada, "Population by Religion, by Province and Territory (2001 Census)," in *Census of Canada, 2001,* Statistics Canada (online); Statistics Canada, "Religion (108), Immigrant Status and Period of Immigration (11), Age Groups (10) and Sex (3) for the Population in Private Households of Canada, Provinces, Territories, Census Metropolitan Areas and Census Agglomerations," Catalogue no. 99-010-X2011032, in *2011 National Household Survey,* Statistics Canada (online).

In 2001, almost 36.0 percent of the BC population claimed to have no religion, as compared to 16.5 percent of all Canadians. The 2011 data, which are taken from Canada, National Household Survey, 2011, are not fully comparable to the 2001 census data. Since the Household Survey was voluntary, a significant number of people did not complete it, making it less representative of the entire population. Scholars have noted that in recent years a significant proportion (approximately a third in the United States) of those who define themselves as having no religious affiliation see themselves as "spiritual but not religious." See Robert C. Fuller, *Spiritual, but Not Religious: Understanding Unchurched*

America (New York: Oxford University Press, 2001); and Mark Oppenheimer, "Examining the Growth of the 'Spiritual but Not Religious,'" *New York Times,* July 18, 2014, http://www.nytimes.com/2014/07/19/us/examining-the-growth-of-the-spiritual-but-not-religious.html?_r=2. For Canada, see Siobhan Chandler, "The Social Ethic of Religiously Unaffiliated Spirituality" (PhD diss., Wilfrid Laurier University, 2011). Sarah Wilkins-Laflamme argues, however, that only a minority of British Columbians who define themselves as being of "no religion" are spiritual but not religious. See Sarah Wilkins-Laflamme, "Religious-Secular Polarization Compared: The Cases of Quebec and British Columbia," *Studies in Religion/Sciences religieuses* (forthcoming).

4 *Vancouver Sun,* October 30, 1996. My thanks to Patricia Roy for this reference. For the 2015 data, see Angus Reid Institute, *Religion and Faith in Canada Today,* March 26, 2015, http://angusreid.org/wp-content/uploads/2016/01/2015.03.25_Faith.pdf. The 2015 data referred only to Canada, but levels of those rejecting religion would be much lower in the United States. Since 1986, British Columbians have almost always reported the lowest levels of church attendance in the country, with only 23 percent of them attending services at least once a month in 2012. Pew Research Centre, "Canada's Changing Religious Landscape," http://www.pewforum.org/2013/06/27/canadas-changing-religious-landscape/. For further discussion of current irreligion in British Columbia, see Wilkins-Laflamme, "Religious-Secular Polarization Compared."

5 Pew Research Center, "Canada's Changing Religious Landscape." Also see Lee-Anne Goodman, "Religion Marks a Divergent Path in Canadian-US History," *Global News,* May 8, 2013, http://globalnews.ca/news/544455/religion-marks-a-divergent-path-in-canadian-us-history/.

6 Samuel Reimer, "A Look at Cultural Effects on Religiosity: A Comparison between the United States and Canada," *Journal for the Scientific Study of Religion* 34, 4 (1995): 445–57.

7 Report of the Columbia Mission (1882–1883), 18–20, quoted in Vincent J. McNally, "Church-State Relations and American Influence in British Columbia before Confederation," *Journal of Church and State* 34, 1 (Winter 1992): 108–9.

8 J.W. Winslow, Nicola Lake, 29 January 1890, *Missionary Outlook* 10, 3 (March 1890): 47, quoted in Jean Barman, *Sojourning Sisters: The Lives and Letters of Jessie and Annie McQueen* (Toronto: University of Toronto Press, 2003), 103.

9 *Westminster,* April 1, 1899, 349–50; "Report of the Home Mission Committee of the Presbyterian Church in Canada (Western Section) for 1895-96," in *Acts and Proceedings of the Twenty-Second General Assembly of the Presbyterian Church in Canada* (June 1896), xxxiv, United Church of Canada Archives, Toronto. For similar concerns, also see *Presbyterian,* September 20, 1902, 362; "The Voice of the West," in A.M. Sanford Scrapbooks, vol. 1, United Church of Canada, British Columbia Conference Archives, Vancouver; "Methodism in B.C.," *Wesleyan,* 1903.

10 For a discussion of hegemonic discourses, see Gail Bederman, *Manliness and Civilization: A Cultural History of Gender and Race in the United States, 1880-1917* (Chicago: University of Chicago Press, 1995), Introduction. Also see Robert Bobcock, *Hegemony* (London: Tavistock, 1986). Hugh McLeod uses the concept of "Christendom" in referring to the hegemonic power of Christianity in Europe over several centuries. See Hugh McLeod and Werner Ustorf, eds., *The Decline of Christendom in Western Europe, 1750-2000* (Cambridge: Cambridge University Press, 2003), particularly Introduction.

11 Nancy Christie and Michael Gauvreau, "Modalities of Social Authority: Suggesting an Interface for Religious and Social History," *Histoire sociale* 36, 71 (2003): 1-30. Lynne Marks,

Revivals and Roller Rinks: Religion, Leisure, and Identity in Late-Nineteenth-Century Small-Town Ontario (Toronto: University of Toronto Press, 1996), also demonstrates the hegemony of Christianity in late-nineteenth-century Ontario, while noting that differing social groups often "read" Christianity somewhat differently. Peter Beyer, "Modern Forms of the Religious Life: Denomination, Church, and Invisible Religion in Canada, the United States, and Europe," in *Rethinking Church, State, and Modernity: Canada between Europe and America*, ed. David Lyon and Marguerite Van Die (Toronto: University of Toronto Press, 2000), 189–200. Beyer briefly acknowledges more recent religious/irreligious differences between British Columbia and the rest of English Canada but then ignores them, whereas Christie and Gauvreau do not discuss the province.

12 That this issue remains very much contested was revealed during the founding conference of the International Society for Historians of Atheism, Secularism and Humanism, Conway Hall, London, United Kingdom, June 2016, which was characterized by spirited debates as to whether those who rejected Christianity and the churches should be defined as unbelievers, atheists, or the irreligious.

13 Colin Campbell, "Irreligion," in *Encyclopedia of Religion and Society*, ed. William H. Swatos, Jr. (Hartford Institute for Religion Research, Hartford Seminary), 998, http://hirr.hartsem.edu/ency/irreligion.htm.

14 Jean Barman, *The West beyond the West: A History of British Columbia*, 3rd ed. (Toronto: University of Toronto Press, 2007), 120–22. Toward the end of the nineteenth century, fruit growing began to replace ranching in the Okanagan.

15 Rossland's population declined from 6,159 in 1901 to 2,826 in 1911, and that of Nelson diminished from 5,273 in 1901 to 4,476 in 1911. John Belshaw, *Becoming British Columbia: A Population History* (Vancouver: UBC Press, 2009), 196.

16 Jeremy Mouat, *Roaring Days: Rossland's Mines and the History of British Columbia* (Vancouver: UBC Press, 1995); A. Ross McCormack, *Reformers, Rebels, and Revolutionaries: The Western Canadian Radical Movement, 1899-1919* (Toronto: University of Toronto Press, 1991).

17 Adults were defined as being fifteen and older. Barman, *The West beyond the West*, 429, 435.

18 The Indigenous population declined slightly between 1891 and 1911, from 27,305 to 20,174. Ibid., 429.

19 Americans made up 11.5 percent of the non-Indigenous population in 1901 and 10.1 percent in 1911, whereas Continental Europeans increased from 6.3 percent of the non-Indigenous population in 1901 to 10.8 percent in 1911. The British-born increased significantly over this decade, from 21.4 percent to 31.3 in 1911, outnumbering those who came to British Columbia from elsewhere in Canada, who made up 23.2 percent of its non-Indigenous population in 1911. Ibid., 429, 430.

20 For further discussion of race and racialization, see Timothy Stanley, *Contesting White Supremacy: School Segregation, Anti-racism, and the Making of Chinese Canadians* (Vancouver: UBC Press, 2011), 47–70.

21 In 1901, approximately 90 percent of Asians in Canada lived in British Columbia, whereas in 1911 over three-quarters of them lived in the province.

22 The Chinese lost the franchise in 1874, the Japanese in 1895, and the South Asians in 1907. For further discussion of anti-Asian racism, see Patricia Roy, *A White Man's Province: British Columbia Politicians and Chinese and Japanese Immigrants, 1858-1914* (Vancouver: UBC Press, 1989); Renisa Mawani, *Colonial Proximities: Crossracial Encounters and Juridical*

Truths in British Columbia, 1871-1921 (Vancouver: UBC Press, 2009); and Stanley, *Contesting White Supremacy*.

23 *Census of Canada, 1911* (Ottawa: C.H. Parmelee, 1913), 2:370–71. There were some African Canadians in British Columbia at this time, but their numbers were very small.

24 In 1901, Saskatchewan had a more diverse population than British Columbia, but at this point it was still part of the North-West Territories and was only beginning to experience large-scale immigration. In this period, 19.4 percent of its population was Indigenous. However, due to deaths from disease and malnutrition, and because of an immigration-fuelled five-fold increase in Saskatchewan's population, Indigenous people constituted only 2.4 percent of the province's population by 1911. In that year, Saskatchewan had the second-most diverse population in Canada, almost 16 percent of which was racialized as non-white. Of this group, over 13 percent were southern and eastern Europeans. Ibid.

25 More Jews lived in Quebec than in any other province, but even there they composed only 1.5 percent of the population. Ibid. Of course, though Canada was almost uniformly Christian, differences between Catholics and Protestants served as a major source of tension throughout much of the country.

26 See, for example, Laura Schwartz, *Infidel Feminism: Secularism, Religion and Women's Emancipation, England, 1830-1914* (Manchester: Manchester University Press, 2013), 21–26.

27 David Marshall, *Secularizing the Faith: Canadian Protestant Clergy and the Crisis of Belief, 1850-1940* (Toronto: University of Toronto Press, 1992); Callum Brown, *The Death of Christian Britain: Understanding Secularisation, 1800-2000* (London: Routledge, 2001); Hugh McLeod, *Piety and Poverty: Working-Class Religion in Berlin, London and New York, 1870-1914* (New York: Holmes and Meier, 1996); Callum Brown, *Religion and the Demographic Revolution: Women and Secularisation in Canada, Ireland, UK and USA since the 1960s* (Woodbridge, UK: Boydell Press, 2012).

28 McNally, "Church-State Relations"; Adele Perry, *On the Edge of Empire: Gender, Race and the Making of British Columbia, 1849-1871* (Toronto: University of Toronto Press, 2001).

29 Robert Orsi, "Everyday Miracles: The Study of Lived Religion," in *Lived Religion in America: Toward a History of Practice*, ed. David D. Hall (Princeton: Princeton University Press, 1997), 3–21; Robert Orsi, "Who Cares about Religion? The Blind Spot in Contemporary Historiography" (paper presented at Qualicum History Conference, Parksville, BC, January 30, 2003); S.C. Williams, *Religious Belief and Popular Culture in Southwark, c. 1880-1939* (Oxford: Oxford University Press, 1999).

30 See Ingrid Storm, "Halfway to Heaven: Four Types of Fuzzy Fidelity in Europe," *Journal for the Scientific Study of Religion* 48, 4 (2009): 702–18; and Callum Brown, "The People of 'No Religion': The Demographics of Secularisation in the English-Speaking World since c. 1900," *Archiv fur Sozialgeschichte* 51 (2011): 37–61.

31 Jon Butler, "Jack-in-the-Box Faith: The Religion Problem in Modern American History," *Journal of American History* 90, 4 (March 2004): 1357–78. Also see Mark Noll, "What Happened to Christian Canada?" *Church History* 75, 2 (June 2006): 245–73. Charles Taylor, in *A Secular Age* (Cambridge: Harvard University Press, 2007), has also argued for a much more complex understanding of secularization and the secular.

32 See, for example, Peter Beyer, "Questioning the Secular/Religious Divide in a Post-Westphalian World," *International Sociology* 28, 6 (2013): 663–79; and David Zeidan, *The Resurgence of Religion: A Comparative Study of Selected Themes in Christian and Islamic Fundamentalist Discourses* (Leiden: Brill Academic, 2003).

33 Christie and Gauvreau, "Modalities of Social Authority"; David Nash, "Reconnecting Religion with Social and Cultural History: Secularisation's Failure as a Master Narrative," *Cultural and Social History* 1, 3 (2004): 302–25.

34 See McLeod and Ustorf, *The Decline of Christendom in Western Europe, particularly Introduction;* McLeod, *Piety and Poverty; and Brown, Religion and the Demographic Revolution,* 43–47.

35 See, for example, Hannah Lane, "Tribalism, Proselytism, and Pluralism: Protestants, Family, and Denominational Identity in Mid-nineteenth-century St. Stephen, New Brunswick," in *Households of Faith: Family, Gender, and Community in Canada, 1760-1969,* ed. Nancy Christie (Montreal and Kingston: McGill-Queen's University Press, 2002), 103–37; Marks, *Revivals and Roller Rinks;* Melissa Turkstra, "Working-Class Churches in Early Twentieth Century Hamilton: Fostering a Distinctive Working-Class Identity and Culture," *Histoire sociale* 41, 82 (2008): 459–503; Michael Gauvreau, "Factories and Foreigners: Church Life in Working-Class Neighbourhoods in Hamilton and Montreal, 1890-1930," in *The Churches and Social Order in Nineteenth- and Twentieth-Century Canada,* ed. Michael Gauvreau and Ollivier Hubert (Montreal and Kingston: McGill-Queen's University Press, 2006), 225–73; and Bonnie Morgan's fine study "Conceiving Christianity: Anglican Women and Lived Religion in Mid-20th Century Conception Bay, Newfoundland" (PhD diss., University of New Brunswick, 2014). An early exception that does look at irreligion, but in a more intellectual history frame, is Ramsay Cook, *The Regenerators: Social Criticism in Late Victorian English Canada* (Toronto: University of Toronto Press, 1985).

36 For newer work on the relationship between irreligion and the left, see Ian McKay, *Reasoning Otherwise: Leftists and the People's Enlightenment in Canada, 1890-1920* (Toronto: Between the Lines, 2008), Chapter 4, "The Religion Question"; and Elliot Hanowski, "A Godless Dominion: Unbelief and Religious Controversy in Interwar Canada" (PhD diss., Queen's University, 2015).

37 See, for example, Nancy Christie and Michael Gauvreau, *A Full-Orbed Christianity: The Protestant Churches and Social Welfare in Canada, 1900-1940* (Montreal and Kingston: McGill-Queen's University Press, 1996); Marshall, *Secularizing the Faith;* David Marshall, "Canadian Historians, Secularization and the Problem of the Nineteenth Century," *Historical Studies* (Canadian Catholic Historical Association) 60 (1993–94): 57–81; Cook, *The Regenerators;* Marguerite Van Die, *Religion, Family and Community in Victorian Canada: The Colbys of Carrollcroft* (Montreal and Kingston: McGill-Queen's University Press, 2005); and Catherine Gidney, *A Long Eclipse: The Liberal Protestant Establishment and the Canadian University, 1920-1970* (Montreal and Kingston: McGill-Queen's University Press, 2004). Van Die focuses on gender in her challenge to the secularization thesis. For work in which gender is central to the analysis of secularization, see, for example, Brown, *The Death of Christian Britain;* and Brown, *Religion and the Demographic Revolution.*

38 Nancy Christie and Michael Gauvreau, eds., *The Sixties and Beyond: Dechristianization in North America and Western Europe, 1945-2000* (Toronto: University of Toronto Press, 2013).

39 See Tina Block, *The Secular Northwest: Religion and Irreligion in Everyday Postwar Life* (Vancouver: UBC Press, 2016); for American literature, see Rodney Stark and William Sims Bainbridge, *The Future of Religion: Secularization, Revival and Cult Formation* (Berkeley: University of California Press, 1985); Patricia O'Connell Killen and Mark Silk, eds., *Religion and Public Life in the Pacific Northwest: The None Zone* (Walnut Creek, CA: AltaMira Press, 2004). Also see Brown, *Religion and the Demographic Revolution.*

40 Bob Stewart, "That's the B.C. Spirit! Religion and Secularity in Lotus Land," *Canadian Society of Church History Papers* (1983): 22–35; Norman Knowles, "'Christ in the Crowsnest': Religion and the Anglo-Protestant Working Class in the Crowsnest Pass, 1898-1918," in *Nation, Ideas, Identities: Essays in Honour of Ramsay Cook,* ed. Michael D. Behiels and Marcel Martel (Toronto: Oxford University Press, 2000), 57–72; Stuart Barnard "The Kootenay Revival Campaign of 1909" (master's thesis, University of Calgary, 2010). John Belshaw's work on demography is also relevant, revealing particularly high levels of Catholic-Protestant intermarriage in British Columbia, which suggests that religion may have been less important in this province than elsewhere in Canada. Belshaw, *Becoming British Columbia.* Also see Barman, *The West beyond the West,* 223.

41 McNally, "Church-State Relations," 105. In 1977, the Social Credit government began to fund BC Catholic schools as part of a broader compromise in which all "independent schools" received some public funding.

42 "An Act Respecting Public Schools," Appendix A, no. 16, *Journals of the Legislative Assembly of the Province of British Columbia,* Session 1872-73 35 Vic., Volume 1; Vincent J. McNally, "Challenging the Status Quo: An Examination of the History of Catholic Education in British Columbia," *Historical Studies* (Canadian Catholic Historical Association) 65 (1999): 127–28.

43 This was true after 1882. Joan Helen Townsend, "Protestant Christian Morality and the Nineteenth Century Secular and Non-sectarian British Columbia Public School System" (master's thesis, University of British Columbia, 1974).

44 *Vancouver Province,* August 2, 1900, 2. The Catholic priest asserted that Bible readings for Catholic students must come from the (Catholic authorized) Douai Bible, not the King James version. For opposition to the school board plan, see *Vancouver Province,* August 4, 1900, 4; August 7, 1900, 3; and October 17, 1900, 6. For concerns about the lack of Bible reading in the schools from Catholic and Anglican clergymen, also see *Victoria Week,* January 10, 1913, ix and xvii; and for more general church concerns about this issue, see *Victoria Colonist,* November 4, 1918, 4; and *Vancouver Sun,* May 10, 1928, 12.

45 Nancy Christie and Michael Gauvreau, *Christian Churches and Their Peoples, 1840-1965* (Toronto: University of Toronto Press, 2010), 9–13. Christie and Gauvreau make this argument with regard to early settlers in Upper Canada.

46 See Marguerite Van Die, "'A Woman's Awakening': Evangelical Belief and Female Spirituality in Mid-nineteenth-century Canada," in *Canadian Women: A Reader,* ed. Wendy Mitchinson et al. (Toronto: Harcourt Brace, 1996), 49–68. For a discussion of women's predominance in the churches and other analyses of women and Christianity in this period, also see Hannah Lane, "'Wife, Mother, Sister, Friend': Methodist Women in St. Stephen, New Brunswick, 1861–1881," in *Separate Spheres: Women's Worlds in the 19th Century Maritimes,* ed. Janet Guildford and Suzanne Morton (Fredericton: Acadiensis Press, 1994), 93–117; Ann Braude, "Women's History *Is* American History," in *Retelling U.S. Religious History,* ed. Thomas A. Tweed (Berkeley: University of California Press, 1997), 87–107; and Marks, *Revivals and Roller Rinks.* For work that complicates the ideal of women's greater religiosity, see Sue Morgan and Jacqueline de Vries, eds., *Women and Religious Cultures in Britain, 1800-1940* (London: Routledge, 2010); and Schwartz, *Infidel Feminism.*

47 Marks, *Revivals and Roller Rinks.* For Christian domestic masculinity, see Van Die, *Religion, Family and Community*; and John Tosh, *A Man's Place: Masculinity and the Middle-Class Home in Victorian England* (New Haven, CT: Yale University Press, 1999).

48 Schwartz, *Infidel Feminism*; Evelyn Kirkley, *Rational Mothers and Infidel Gentlemen: Gender and American Atheism, 1865-1915* (Syracuse: Syracuse University Press, 1999).

49 For the impact on Indigenous and white women, see, for example, Perry, *On the Edge of Empire;* Sylvia Van Kirk, *Many Tender Ties: Women in Fur-Trade Society, 1670-1870* (Winnipeg: Watson and Dwyer, 1998); and Barman, *Sojourning Sisters.* For labour radicalism, see McCormack, *Reformers, Rebels, and Revolutionaries.*

50 At the same time, one needs to use the concept of frontier with caution, given its problematically Euro-centric history, as defined by Frederick Jackson Turner, particularly in earlier American historiography. See Tiziano Bonazzi, "Frederick Jackson Turner's Frontier Thesis and the Self-Consciousness of America," *Journal of American Studies* 27, 2 (August 1993): 149–71.

51 Laurie Maffly-Kipp, *Religion and Society in Frontier California* (New Haven, CT: Yale University Press, 1994); Sandra Sizer Frankiel, *California's Spiritual Frontiers: Religious Alternatives to Anglo-Protestantism, 1850-1910* (Berkeley: University of California Press, 1988).

52 Marilyn Lake, "Frontier Feminism and the Marauding White Man," *Journal of Australian Studies* 20, 49 (1996): 12–20; Patricia Grimshaw, "Settler Anxieties, Indigenous Peoples and Women's Suffrage in the Colonies of Australia, New Zealand and Hawai'i, 1888-1902," *Pacific Historical Review* 69, 4 (2000): 553–72.

53 Lake, "Frontier Feminism and the Marauding White Man"; Nancy Forestell, "Bachelors, Boarding-Houses, and Blind Pigs: Gender Construction in a Multi-ethnic Mining Camp, 1909-1920," in *A Nation of Immigrants: Women, Workers, and Communities in Canadian History, 1840s-1960s,* ed. Franca Iacovetta, Paula Draper, and Robert Ventresca (Toronto: University of Toronto Press, 1998), 251–90. For the colonial period in British Columbia, see Perry, *On the Edge of Empire;* Robert Hogg, *Men and Manliness on the Frontier: Queensland and British Columbia in the Mid-nineteenth Century* (London: Palgrave Macmillan, 2012); Elizabeth Vibert, *Traders' Tales: Narratives of Cultural Encounters in the Columbia Plateau, 1807-1846* (Norman: Oklahoma University Press, 1997).

54 For important work on religion and masculinity in the British context, see Lucy Delap, "'Be Strong and Play the Man': Anglican Masculinities in the Twentieth Century," in *Men, Masculinities and Religious Change in Twentieth–Century Britain,* ed. Lucy Delap and Sue Morgan (London: Palgrave Macmillan, 2013), 119–45; and Sue Morgan, "'Iron Strength and Infinite Tenderness': Herbert Gray and the Making of Christian Masculinities at War and at Home, 1900–40," in Delap and Morgan, *Men, Masculinities and Religious Change,* 168–96. For an American perspective, see Gail Bederman, "'The Women Have Had Charge of the Church Work Long Enough': The Men and Religion Forward Movement of 1911–12 and the Masculinization of Middle-Class Protestantism," *American Quarterly* 41, 3 (September 1989): 432–65.

55 Van Die, *Religion, Family and Community;* J.L. Little, "The Fireside Kingdom: A Mid-nineteenth-century Anglican Perspective on Marriage and Parenthood," in Christie, *Households of Faith,* 77-100; Tosh, *A Man's Place.*

56 In the American context, see, for example, William Sutton, "Tied to the Whipping Post: New Labor History and Evangelical Artisans in the Early Republic," *Labor History* 36, 2 (1995): 251-81; Kenneth Fones-Wolf, *Trade Union Gospel: Christianity and Labor in Industrial Philadelphia, 1865-1915* (Philadelphia: Temple University Press, 1989); and Jama Lazerow, *Religion and the Working Class in Antebellum America* (Washington, DC: Smithsonian Institution Press, 1995). Also see McLeod, *Piety and Poverty;* and Lynne Marks, "Challenging

Binaries: Working-Class Women and Lived Religion in English Canada and the United States," *Labor: Studies in Working-Class History of the Americas* 6, 1 (Spring 2009): 107–25.

57 Christie and Gauvreau, "Modalities of Social Authority"; Michael Gauvreau and Ollivier Hubert, "Introduction," in Gauvreau and Hubert, *The Churches and Social Order,* 3-45; Greg Kealey and Bryan Palmer, *Dreaming of What Might Be: The Knights of Labor in Ontario* (Cambridge: Cambridge University Press, 1982).

58 My approach did not satisfy scholars of either perspective, and their critiques suggested that *Revivals and Roller Rinks* either overemphasized the religiosity of workers or did not take it seriously enough. See Bryan Palmer, "Historiographic Hassles: Class and Gender, Evidence and Interpretation," *Histoire sociale* 33, 65 (2000): 105–44; Lynne Marks, "Heroes and Hallelujahs: Labour History, Bryan Palmer and the Social History of Religion in English Canada," *Histoire sociale* 34, 67 (2001): 169–86; and Christie and Gauvreau, "Modalities of Social Authority."

59 See McCormack, *Reformers, Rebels, and Revolutionaries*; Carlos A. Schwantes, *Radical Heritage: Labor, Socialism, and Reform in Washington and British Columbia, 1885-1917* (Vancouver: Douglas and McIntyre, 1979); John Belshaw, *Colonization and Community: The Vancouver Island Coalfield and the Making of the British Columbian Working Class* (Montreal and Kingston: McGill-Queen's University Press, 2002); and Jeremy Mouat, "The Genesis of Western Exceptionalism: British Columbia's Hard-Rock Miners, 1895-1903," *Canadian Historical Review* 71, 3 (1990): 317–45. Also see Gregory Kealey, "1919: The Canadian Labour Revolt," *Labour/Le travail* 13 (Spring 1984): 11–44.

60 McKay, *Reasoning Otherwise,* Chapter 4.

61 Peter Ward, "Class and Race in the Social Structure of British Columbia, 1870-1939," *BC Studies* 45 (Spring 1980): 17–35; Rennie Warburton, "Race and Class in British Columbia: A Comment," *BC Studies* 49 (Spring 1981): 79.

62 See, for example, John Stenhouse, "Imperialism, Atheism, and Race: Charles Southwell, Old Corruption, and the Maori," *Journal of British Studies* 44, 4 (2005): 754-74, and Leigh Eric Schmidt, *Village Atheists: How America's Unbelievers Made Their Way in a Godly Nation* (Princeton, NJ: Princeton University Press, 2016), 135-42.

63 Patricia Roy, "Anglicans and Asians in British Columbia: An Ambiguous Relationship" (unpublished paper, n.d.); Peter Ward, "The Oriental Immigrant and Canada's Protestant Clergy, 1858-1925," *BC Studies* 22 (Summer 1974): 40–55; Mawani, *Colonial Proximities.*

64 For a discussion of how many Indigenous peoples continued to challenge the churches' efforts to eradicate their cultural and religious practices, see Paige Raibmon, *Authentic Indians: Episodes of Encounter from the Late-Nineteenth-Century Northwest Coast* (Durham: Duke University Press, 2005).

65 See, for example, Susan Neylan, *The Heavens Are Changing: Nineteenth-Century Protestant Missions and Tsimshian Christianity* (Montreal and Kingston: McGill-Queen's University Press, 2002); Laura Peers, "'The Guardian of All': Jesuit Missionary and Salish Perceptions of the Virgin Mary," in *Reading beyond Words: Contexts for Native History,* 2nd ed., ed. Jennifer Brown and Elizabeth Vibert (Peterborough, ON: Broadview Press, 2003), 284-303; Michael Harkin, "Power and Progress: The Evangelic Dialogue among the Heiltsuk," *Ethnohistory* (Columbus, OH) 40, 1 (Winter 1993): 1-33; and Sergei Kan, "Shamanism and Christianity: Modern Day Tlingit Elders Look at the Past," *Ethnohistory* (Columbus, OH) 38, 4 (Fall 1991): 363–87.

66 The Canadian Families Project (CFP) was funded by the Social Sciences and Humanities Research Council, and the Canadian Century Research Infrastructure Project (CCRI) was

funded by the Canadian Foundation for Innovation (CFI). While I was a co-investigator with the CFP and thus had access to its databases, I gained access to the CCRI databases through the generosity of Eric Sager, a CCRI co-director in Victoria. The ViHistory database is available at http://www.vihistory.ca/.

67 Bruce Curtis, *The Politics of Population: State Formation, Statistics, and the Census of Canada, 1840-1875* (Toronto: University of Toronto Press, 2006). Also see Peter Baskerville and Eric Sager, *Unwilling Idlers: The Urban Unemployed and Their Families in Late Victorian Canada* (Toronto: University of Toronto Press, 1998); and Chad Gaffield, "Language, Ancestry and the Competing Constructions of Identity in Turn-of-the-Century Canada," in *Household Counts: Canadian Households and Families in 1901,* ed. Eric Sager and Peter Baskerville (Toronto: University of Toronto Press, 2006), 423–40.

68 Curtis, The Politics of Population.

69 Dominion Bureau of Statistics (DBS), *Census of Canada, 1901,* volume 1, "Introduction," (Ottawa: Census Office, 1902), xix. Also see Patrick Dunae, "Sex, Charades, and Census Records: Locating Female Sex Trade Workers in a Victorian City," *Histoire sociale* 42, 84 (2009): 267–97.

70 See Gaffield, "Language, Ancestry and the Competing Constructions of Identity."

71 See Marks, *Revivals and Roller Rinks,* Chapter 1.

72 Dunae, "Sex, Charades, and Census Records"; DBS, *Census of Canada, 1901,* Schedule 1.

73 Such records are called circuit registers among Methodists and communion rolls among Presbyterians.

74 When only surnames were provided, links could not be made. Similarly, if names were too common (such as John Smith), it was not possible to make reliable links.

75 Lynn Abrams, *Oral History Theory* (London: Routledge, 2010); Joan Sangster, "Telling Our Stories: Feminist Debates and the Use of Oral History," *Women's History Review* 3, 1 (1994): 5–28; Marlene Epp, "The Memory of Violence: Soviet and East European Mennonite Refugees and Rape in the Second World War," *Journal of Women's History* 9, 1 (Spring 1997): 58–87.

76 Although I read many of these newspapers on microfilm, this project also benefitted from the digitization of BC papers in recent years.

Chapter 1

1 *Westminster,* June 17, 1899.

2 *Westminster,* April 1, 1899, 349–50; "Report of the Home Mission Committee of the Presbyterian Church in Canada (Western Section) for 1895-96," in *Acts and Proceedings of the Twenty-Second General Assembly of the Presbyterian Church in Canada* (June 1896), xxxiv, United Church of Canada Archives, Toronto. For similar concerns, also see *Presbyterian,* September 20, 1902, 362; "The Voice of the West," in A.M. Sanford Scrapbooks, vol. 1, no. 22, United Church Archives, British Columbia Conference, Vancouver (UC Archives, BC); "Methodism in B.C.," *Wesleyan,* 1903; Report of the Committee on Church Life and Work, 1908, Presbyterian Synod of B.C., UC Archives, BC.

3 In 1901, British Columbians were ten times more likely than other Canadians to define themselves as atheists or as having no religion. In 1911, they were over five times more likely to do so. Dominion Bureau of Statistics (DBS), *Census of Canada, 1901* (Ottawa: Census Office, 1902), vol. 1, Table 8; DBS, *Census of Canada, 1911* (Ottawa: C.H. Parmelee, 1913), vol. 1, Table 1.

4 See, for example, Nancy Christie and Michael Gauvreau, "Modalities of Social Authority: Suggesting an Interface for Religious and Social History," *Histoire sociale* 36, 71 (2003): 1–30.

5 Lynne Marks, *Revivals and Roller Rinks: Religion, Leisure, and Identity in Late-Nineteenth-Century Small-Town Ontario* (Toronto: University of Toronto Press, 1996), Chapter 1.

6 See, for example, ibid., 6, 22–51; David Marshall, *Secularizing the Faith: Canadian Protestant Clergy and the Crisis of Belief, 1850–1940* (Toronto: University of Toronto Press, 1992); and Ramsay Cook, *The Regenerators: Social Criticism in Late Victorian English Canada* (Toronto: University of Toronto Press, 1985).

7 As mentioned in the introductory chapter, British Columbia was the only Canadian province that did not provide funding for separate religious schools (until 1977). Its 1872 Public School Act stated that public schools were to teach "no religious dogma," although recitation of the Lord's Prayer and the Ten Commandments was allowed. Vincent J. McNally, "Challenging the Status Quo: An Examination of the History of Catholic Education in British Columbia," *Historical Studies* (Canadian Catholic Historical Association) 65 (1999): 71-91.

8 On religious denominations as ethnicity, see Hannah Lane, "Tribalism, Proselytism, and Pluralism: Protestants, Family, and Denominational Identity in Mid-nineteenth-century St. Stephen, New Brunswick," in *Households of Faith: Family, Gender, and Community in Canada, 1760-1969*, ed. Nancy Christie (Montreal and Kingston: McGill-Queen's University Press, 2002), 103–37. For the importance of denominational affiliation in defining who one might board with, see Peter Baskerville, "Familiar Strangers: Urban Families with Boarders, Canada, 1901," *Social Science History* 25, 3 (Fall 2001): 321–46. On respectability, see Marks, *Revivals and Roller Rinks;* and for being a Christian as part of one's sense of humanity, see Enrico Carlson Cumbo, "Salvation in Indifference: Gendered Expressions of Italian-Canadian Immigrant Catholicity, 1900-1940," in Christie, *Households of Faith,* 203–33.

9 See, for example, James Turner, *Without God, without Creed: The Origins of Unbelief in America* (Baltimore: Johns Hopkins University Press, 1985), xi-xiii.

10 See Marks, *Revivals and Roller Rinks,* especially 44–49; and Cook, *The Regenerators,* 41–64. In the American context see Leigh Eric Schmidt, *Village Atheists: How America's Unbelievers Made Their Way in a Godly Nation,* (Princeton, NJ: Princeton University Press, 2016), 22-24.

11 In 1901, 1,069 British Columbians defined themselves as agnostics, atheists, freethinkers, infidels, secularists, skeptics, or unbelievers, with the largest number being agnostics; 1,605 said they had no religion. Among both groups, they made up about a third of those claiming these designations in Canada at the time. DBS, *Census of Canada, 1901,* vol. 1, Table 8.

12 One difference between the two groups was that in the 1911 census, those who were most explicitly irreligious (atheists, agnostics, and so on) were more likely to be employees rather than employers or self-employed – working "on their own account" – whereas among all of the irreligious in 1911 (both atheists and those of no religion), those who worked on their own account were most numerous. This is discussed more fully below. The other difference is that in 1911 those of no religion were more likely than atheists and agnostics to live in primarily or all-male households. Chapter 2 will return to this topic.

13 The 1911 census showed almost identical patterns of significant difference from the norm in terms of ethnicity, gender, and marital status for those of no religion and atheists/agnostics. The ViHistory database for Vancouver Island shows that the self-identification

of non-religious individuals could shift between census years: some people moved from no religion to atheists/agnostics or vice versa, and some shifted from the irreligious categories to Christian ones. (For further discussion of the latter point, see page 41–44.) ViHistory database, University of Vancouver Island and University of Victoria, http://www.viHistory.ca.

14 Callum Brown, "The People of 'No Religion': The Demographics of Secularisation in the English-Speaking World since c. 1900," *Archiv fur Sozialgeschichte* 51 (2011): 37–61; Ingrid Storm, "Halfway to Heaven: Four Types of Fuzzy Fidelity in Europe," *Journal for the Scientific Study of Religion* 48, 4 (2009): 702–18; Grace Davie, *Religion in Britain since 1945: Believing without Belonging* (Cambridge, MA: Blackwell, 1994); Robert C. Fuller, *Spiritual, but Not Religious: Understanding Unchurched America* (New York: Oxford University Press, 2001); for the Canadian context, see Siobhan Chandler, "The Social Ethic of Religiously Unaffiliated Spirituality" (PhD diss., Wilfrid Laurier University, 2011).

15 Colin Campbell, "Irreligion," in *Encyclopedia of Religion and Society*, ed. William H. Swatos, Jr. (Hartford Institute for Religion Research, Hartford Seminary), 1998, http://hirr.hartsem.edu/ency/irreligion.htm.

16 Logistic regression estimates the change in log odds associated with each value in the independent variable, in relation to the dependent variable (which in this analysis is the dichotomous variable of either "has stated religion" or is "atheist/agnostic or has no religion"). The SPSS software used to calculate the regression converts log odds to an "odds ratio." Thus, if the independent variable is "sex," and if the odds for male are 37/11, the odds ratio is 3.365, which can be interpreted as saying that the odds for men being irreligious are 3.365 higher than for the reference value (female). The program also calculates the significance value of the odds ratio. A significance value of .000 is the strongest indication of significance, but a value up to and including .05 is generally viewed as a finding of significance, in that ninety-five times out of a hundred this result cannot simply be attributed to random chance. I am sincerely grateful to Eric Sager for explaining logistic regression to me and for running a series of logistic regressions, using the 1901 and 1911 5 percent census samples, with religion/irreligion as the dependent variable.

17 Elsie G. Turnbull, *Church in the Kootenays: The Story of the United Church of Canada in Kootenay Presbytery* (Trail, BC: Trail Times, for Kootenay Presbyterial United Church Women, 1965).

18 It is true that particularly among Methodists, Presbyterians, and Anglicans, a significant number of churchgoers did not become full members/communicants but attended services on an occasional or regular basis. Nonetheless, the majority of committed churchgoers were generally members/communicants.

19 Conducting this analysis would not be possible in the United States. Although American censuses do record numbers of communicants by denomination, they do not ask individuals regarding their religious adherence. In certain Protestant denominations, the word "adherent" refers to individuals who often attend church and may contribute to it financially but do not become members or communicants. My use of the word, to refer to anyone who identified with a particular denomination, follows that of the census. Nonetheless, the term is not ideal: telling a census-taker that one was a Methodist or a Presbyterian, and thus an "adherent" for census purposes, reveals nothing about how likely one was to attend church.

20 Vancouver Island took pride of place as the only district in the lowest category of church involvement. British Columbia's Yale and Cariboo district as well as the northern Ontario

district of Nipissing stood alone in the second-lowest category. Yale and Cariboo, at 11.1 percent of Protestant communicants of total adherents, was considerably lower than Nipissing, at 14.8 percent of Protestant communicants of total adherents.

21 The figures for Catholics can be problematic. Some districts that lay in urban areas or adjacent to them may have been listed as having very few communicants because their Catholic residents attended church, and were counted as attending church, in another district. This also explains why in some urban districts, such as Kingston, Ontario, communicants outnumbered adherents.

22 Anglicans accounted for 22.7 percent of British Columbians, as compared to 16.1 percent of all Canadians outside Quebec, and 18.8 percent of British Columbians were Catholic, as compared to 21.5 percent of all Canadians outside Quebec. Quebec, where Catholicism was the majority faith, is excluded here because of its very different religious makeup.

23 *Westminster,* June 17, 1899, 654; also see April 1, 1899, 349.

24 See, for example, Douglas Firth Anderson, "'We Have Here a Different Civilization': Protestant Identity in the San Francisco Bay Area, 1906–1909," *Western Historical Quarterly* 23, 2 (1992): 199–221.

25 Rodney Stark and William Sims Bainbridge, *The Future of Religion: Secularization, Revival and Cult Formation* (Berkeley: University of California Press, 1985), 94–95; Anderson, "'We Have Here a Different Civilization,'" 219–21.

26 *Presbyterian,* June 6, 1903, 737. See also "The Voice of the West," in A.M. Sanford Scrapbooks, vol. 1, no. 22, UC Archives, BC; *Presbyterian,* September 20, 1902, 361, and December 13, 1902, 746.

27 Adele Perry, *On the Edge of Empire: Gender, Race and the Making of British Columbia, 1849-1871* (Toronto: University of Toronto Press, 2001). Also see Jean Barman, *The West beyond the West: A History of British Columbia,* 3rd ed. (Toronto: University of Toronto Press, 2007), 208–10; and John Belshaw, "The West We Have Lost: British Columbia's Demographic Past and an Agenda for Population History," *Western Historical Quarterly* 29, 1 (1998): 42–45.

28 *Presbyterian,* June 6, 1903, 736.

29 "Report of the Home Missions Committee of the Presbyterian Church in Canada," Appendix 1 in *Acts and Proceedings of the 21st General Assembly of the Presbyterian Church in Canada* (June 1895), xvii, United Church of Canada Archives, Toronto.

30 See Marks, *Revivals and Roller Rinks,* 30–37, and 81–139.

31 See, for example, *Catholic Register,* July 23, 1896, 6; *Religious Intelligencer,* May 20, 1896, 3; *Messenger and Visitor,* September 7, 1898, 10; *Parish and Home,* April 1897, 46; and *Canadian Epworth Era,* April 1901, 31.

32 For Christian concerns about this masculine culture and efforts to bring young men back into the fold, see Norman Knowles, "'Christ in the Crowsnest': Religion and the Anglo-Protestant Working Class in the Crowsnest Pass, 1898–1918," in *Nation, Ideas, Identities: Essays in Honour of Ramsay Cook,* ed. Michael D. Behiels and Marcel Martel (Toronto: Oxford University Press, 2000); and the novels of Ralph Connor (Reverend Charles Gordon), particularly Ralph Connor, *Black Rock: A Tale of the Selkirks* (Toronto: Westminster, 1898).

33 *Western Methodist Recorder,* December 1900, 6.

34 CFP, National 5 percent sample 1901, shows an odds ratio of over 3.7 – so the odds are 3.7 higher that men will be irreligious as compared to women (significance .000). The ViHistory database, which includes everyone who lived on Vancouver Island in 1901, also showed a

strong and significant odds ratio for the over-representation of men among the irreligious: the odds ratio is that women are .611 as likely to be irreligious as men (significance .001). The BC portion of the CCRIP National 5 percent sample, 1911 provided similarly strong results for the over-representation of men among the irreligious, since the odds ratio for women was a very low .301, as compared to men (significance .000).

35 In 1901, 2.0 percent of all single men versus 1.7 percent of all married men in British Columbia defined themselves as being atheists/agnostics or as having no religion. The logistic regression odds ratios for marital status were significant for the 1911 5 percent sample for BC, but were not very strong, at .901 odds ratio for married (with the reference category being single). So the odds ratio suggests that married people were slightly less likely than single people to be irreligious across British Columbia (significance of .002). An analysis of the 1901 census (complete census) for Vancouver Island provides an odds ratio of .713 for married (reference category being single), with a significance of .007, suggesting that marital status (being single) was a more important predictor of being irreligious on Vancouver Island than in the province as a whole.

36 Age was not a significant category (controlling for other categories), using logistic regression for either the 1901 or the 1911 census samples.

37 For a discussion of the ideal relationship between Christianity and family life, see, for example, Lynne Marks, "'A Fragment of Heaven on Earth?': Religion, Gender and Family in Turn-of-the-Century Canadian Church Periodicals," *Journal of Family History* 26, 2 (April 2001): 251–71.

38 Sixty-six percent of irreligious married men cohabited with their wives, whereas 67 percent of all married men did so. The figures for all BC married men are derived from CFP, National 5 percent sample, 1901. The figures for both the irreligious and all BC married men are derived using the constructed "SPLOC" variable, which determines whether spouses cohabit and thus also tells us when they do not.

39 The figures for all BC households are derived from CFP, National 5 percent sample, 1901.

40 For the 1911 census data, the logistic regression demonstrating this is statistically significant, at .000 – but only when both atheists/agnostics and those of no religion are included. When only atheists/agnostics are included, there is no statistically significant relationship between the proportion of men in a household and the irreligion of its members, a topic that is explored further in Chapter 2.

41 In 1901, 25 percent of all BC men were lodgers, and 48 percent of male non-believers were lodgers. The percentage of lodgers of all men in the province is based on an analysis of CFP, National 5 percent sample, 1901. A regression analysis of the CCRIP, National 5 percent sample, 1911 for British Columbia also reveals that lodgers were significantly more likely to be irreligious than the head of household and those related to the head. Lodgers were irreligious at an odds ratio of 1.679, as compared to household heads and their relatives (significance .000).

42 Marks, *Revivals and Roller Rinks,* 44–49.

43 BC-born people had a significantly lower odds ratio (likelihood of being irreligious), at .674, as compared to the Canadian-born reference category (.000 significance level), using the CCRIP National 5 percent sample for 1911.

44 The odds ratio is consistently significant and consistently much higher for immigrants than for the Canadian-born in both the 1901 and 1911 censuses: in the 1911 5 percent sample for British Columbia, the odds ratio is .461 for non-immigrants compared to immigrants (with a .000 significance); in the Vancouver Island (ViHistory) census database for 1901,

the odds ratio is .515 for non-immigrants as compared to immigrants (significance of .000); and in the national 5 percent sample for 1901, the odds ratio is 1.986 for immigrants as compared to non-immigrants (significance of .000).

45 In British Columbia, 0.6 percent of women defined themselves as irreligious, as compared to 0.1 percent of Ontario women; 1.9 percent of BC men defined themselves as irreligious, as compared to 0.2 percent of Ontario men. The BC data include all who defined themselves as atheists or as having no religion in the BC 1901 census, whereas the Ontarians who defined themselves as irreligious were a percentage of the total population of four cities and eight counties included in an Ontario sample of all agnostics and those of no religion in the 1901 census. CFP database of atheists/agnostics and those of "no religion," BC and Ontario, 1901; DBS, *Census of Canada, 1901,* vol. 1, Table 7.

46 Jessie McQueen to Catherine McQueen, January 15, 1897, Rossland, Atlantic Canada Virtual Archives, University of New Brunswick, McQueen Family Collection. Despite Jessie's remark, Moffat did attend the Presbyterian church with her, even though she refused to contribute to it financially. Jessie McQueen to Catherine McQueen, December 11, 1898, Rossland, McQueen Family Collection.

47 See Chapter 5 for a further discussion of the over-representation of female sex trade workers among the irreligious.

48 See Bonnie Morgan, "Conceiving Christianity: Anglican Women and Lived Religion in Mid-20th Century Conception Bay, Newfoundland" (PhD diss., University of New Brunswick, 2014).

49 Census enumerators were instructed to assume that children shared the faith of their parents unless the children themselves indicated otherwise, in which case the children's stated religion was to be entered. *Census of Canada, 1901,* Schedule 1, Library and Archives Canada.

50 *Western Methodist Recorder,* October 1901, 7; *Canadian Churchman,* February 2, 1899, 76. Also see *Canadian Churchman,* April 27, 1899, 268; and *Messenger and Visitor,* August 3, 1898, 2. See Marks, "'A Fragment of Heaven?'"

51 The online ViHistory database includes nominal-level information (name, sex, age, birthdate, religion, occupation, and so on) for everyone who was listed in the Vancouver Island census for 1881, 1891, and 1901. It also gives the same information for 1911, but only for residents of Victoria.

52 Nineteen of these linkages involve people who were linked between more than two census years.

53 Lane, "Tribalism, Proselytism, and Pluralism." Also see Morgan, "Conceiving Christianity."

54 By comparison, Lane, "Tribalism, Proselytism, and Pluralism," found that, among New Brunswickers, an average of between 70 and 80 percent remained in a particular Christian denomination between two census years.

55 Cox and Scott first appear in the ViHistory database as widows, so we cannot be sure that their husbands were irreligious, but given the broader patterns described here, it seems likely.

56 Margaret's mother is listed as being married, but her husband was not living in the household. It is possible that these women were involved in some aspect of the sex trade, but there is no definitive evidence of this here (see Chapter 5 for a discussion of the relationship between freethought and prostitution).

57 In Yale and Cariboo, women composed 32.4 percent of the population in 1901. In New Westminster and Vancouver Island, they made up approximately 37.0 percent of the

population. Only 0.6 of the population in both regions were defined as irreligious. In Vancouver, 41.0 percent of the population was female. CFP irreligion databases; DBS, *Census of Canada, 1901,* vol. 1, Table 7.

58 See, for example, Cook, *The Regenerators*; Turner, *Without God, without Creed,* 171–225; Susan Jacoby, *Freethinkers: A History of American Secularism* (New York: Metropolitan Books, 2004); Evelyn Kirkley, *Rational Mothers and Infidel Gentlemen: Gender and American Atheism, 1865-1915* (Syracuse: Syracuse University Press, 1999); and Paul Stob, "Religious Conflict and Intellectual Agency: Robert Ingersoll's Contributions to American Thought and Culture," *Rhetoric and Public Affairs* 16, 4 (Winter 2013): 719–51.

59 See, for example, Edward Royle, *Radicals, Secularists and Republicans: Popular Freethought in Britain, 1886-1915* (Manchester: Manchester University Press, 1980), 218–45; Susan Budd, *Varieties of Unbelief: Atheists and Agnostics in English Society, 1850-1960* (London: Heinemann, 1977), 81–103; Hugh McLeod, *Piety and Poverty: Working-Class Religion in Berlin, London and New York, 1870-1914* (New York: Holmes and Meier, 1996); and E.P. Thompson, *The Making of the English Working Class* (New York: Pantheon Books, 1964).

60 See Herbert Gutman, "Protestantism and the American Labor Movement," in Herbert Gutman, *Work, Culture, and Society in Industrializing America: Essays in American Working-Class and Social History* (New York: Vintage Books, 1977), 79–117; Marks, *Revivals and Roller Rinks,* Chapter 6; and Kenneth Fones-Wolf, *Trade Union Gospel: Christianity and Labor in Industrial Philadelphia, 1865-1915* (Philadelphia: Temple University Press, 1989), 145–98.

61 See, for example, Janice Newton, *The Feminist Challenge to the Canadian Left, 1900-1918* (Montreal and Kingston: McGill-Queen's University Press, 1995), 22–25; Ian McKay, *Reasoning Otherwise: Leftists and the People's Enlightenment in Canada, 1890-1920* (Toronto: Between the Lines, 2008), 242–44; Donald E. Winters, Jr., *The Soul of the Wobblies: The I.W.W., Religion, and American Culture in the Progressive Era, 1905-1917* (Westport, CT: Greenwood Press, 1985); and Chapter 2 in this volume.

62 For further analysis of the class implications of these categories, see Eric Sager, "The National Sample of the 1901 Census of Canada: A New Source for the Study of the Working Class" (paper presented at the Social Science History conference, Amsterdam, March 1998), http://web.uvic.ca/hrd/cfp/publications/Eric%20W.%20Sager.pdf; and Peter Baskerville and Eric Sager, "Finding the Work Force in the 1901 Census of Canada," *Histoire sociale* 28, 56 (1995): 521–38. Baskerville and Sager also note that individuals could identify with more than one employment category, but only a small minority did so.

63 An analysis of the CFP National 5 percent sample, 1901 demonstrates that employers were the most likely to identify as having no religion or as being atheists or agnostics, as compared both to employees and those who worked on their own account. This result is significant to .000, with an odds ratio of 2.064 compared to the reference category of "own account." Analysis of the CCRIP National 5 percent sample, 1911 shows that those who were working on their own account were significantly more likely to be irreligious than either employers or employees, again with a significance level of .000. The comparator reference category was "working on own account," and the odds ratio of both employers and employees was under .7.

64 This is based on an analysis of the BC data from CCRIP, National 5 percent sample, 1911. When people of no religion are excluded, employees have a significantly higher odds ratio of being atheists, agnostics, or freethinkers than do employers or those who worked on

their own account. The comparator reference category is "employee," and both other categories have odds ratios of under .64. When those of no religion are included, employers are the least likely to be identified as irreligious, those who worked on their own account are most likely, and employees are also more likely than employers to identify as irreligious. It is not possible to use the CCRIP 1901 national sample at the BC level, as the numbers are too few. However, an analysis of the database of everyone in British Columbia who identified as irreligious for the 1901 census shows a slight over-representation of the working class, compared to the middle class: 10.7 percent of the total population were middle class, a cohort that accounted for 8.9 percent of the irreligious. Working-class irreligious people were slightly over-represented; 89.3 percent of the population were working class, and 91.0 percent of the irreligious came from this group. Total population figures are from the CFP, National 5 percent sample, 1901, and figures for the irreligious are from the CFP database of atheists, agnostics and those of no religion, 1901, BC.

65 For a discussion of the Slocan area, and its over-representation of men, see R. Cole Harris, "Industry and the Good Life around Idaho Peak," in R. Cole Harris, *The Resettlement of British Columbia: Essays on Colonialism and Geographical Change* (Vancouver: UBC Press 1997), 194–218.

66 See Jeremy Mouat, *Roaring Days: Rossland's Mines and the History of British Columbia* (Vancouver: UBC Press, 1995), 129; and Harris, "Industry and the Good Life," 202–3.

67 See A. Ross McCormack, *Reformers, Rebels, and Revolutionaries: The Western Canadian Radical Movement, 1899-1919* (Toronto: University of Toronto Press, 1991); and Carlos A. Schwantes, *Radical Heritage: Labor, Socialism, and Reform in Washington and British Columbia, 1885-1917* (Vancouver: Douglas and McIntyre, 1979).

68 See McCormack, *Reformers, Rebels, and Revolutionaries;* Mouat, *Roaring Days;* Schwantes, *Radical Heritage;* and Allen Seager, "Socialists and Workers: The Western Canadian Coal Miners, 1900-1921," *Labour/Le travail* 16 (Fall 1985): 23–59.

69 Jeremy Mouat, "The Genesis of Western Exceptionalism: British Columbia's Hard-Rock Miners, 1895-1903," *Canadian Historical Review* 71, 3 (1990): 317–45; John Belshaw, "The British Collier in British Columbia: Another Archetype Reconsidered," *Labour/Le travail* 34 (Fall 1994): 11–36; John Belshaw, *Colonization and Community: The Vancouver Island Coalfield and the Making of the British Columbian Working Class* (Montreal and Kingston: McGill-Queen's University Press, 2002). Also see Gregory Kealey, "1919: The Canadian Labour Revolt," *Labour/Le travail* 13 (Spring 1984): 11–44.

70 This would help to explain why workers (or "employees," in census parlance) very clearly predominated among those who associated themselves with such labels.

71 The high levels of irreligion among coal miners in the Crowsnest Pass were offset by the low levels of explicit irreligion among their Vancouver Island counterparts, which meant that, overall, coal miners accounted for 2.4 percent of BC agnostics and those claiming to have no religion (see Table 5). Coal miners made up 3.3 percent of the BC workforce in 1901.

72 Fishing, farming, and forestry were also important to the district's economy, but coal mining was most significant.

73 In the Nanaimo area, 43 percent of the population was female, as opposed to 36 percent for British Columbia as a whole.

74 Allen Seager and Adele Perry, "Mining the Connections: Class, Ethnicity, and Gender in Nanaimo, B.C., 1891," *Histoire sociale* 30, 59 (1997): 55–76; and Belshaw, *Colonization and Community.*

75 Belshaw, *Colonization and Community*, 182–87; Lynne Bowen, *Boss Whistle: The Coal Miners of Vancouver Island Remember* (Nanaimo, BC: Rocky Point Books, 2002), 186–87.
76 Belshaw, *Colonization and Community*, 184–85.
77 For evidence of church support for the 1912–14 strike, see Bowen, *Boss Whistle*, 122. For information about the Methodist and Presbyterian leadership, and the impact of mine owner James Dunsmuir on the Presbyterian church, see Belshaw, *Colonization and Community*, 183–84. For the impact of the coal company managers and owners on the Anglican churches in and around Nanaimo, see Diary of Bishop Hills, June 27 and October 22, 1891, and April 7, 1892, Bishop George Hills sous-fonds, Anglican Synod of the Diocese of British Columbia and the Yukon fonds, Anglican Provincial Synod of BC Archives, Vancouver. For oral history of religious ambivalence among Nanaimo miners, see Chapter 3.
78 Perry, *On the Edge of Empire*, 3–19, 139–66; Marks, "'A Fragment of Heaven?'"
79 Belshaw, "The British Collier."
80 For a discussion of Indigenous syncretism, see for example, Susan Neylan, *The Heavens Are Changing: Nineteenth-Century Protestant Missions and Tsimshian Christianity* (Montreal and Kingston: McGill-Queen's University Press, 2002) and Michael Harkin, "Engendering Discipline: Discourse and Counterdiscourse in the Methodist-Heiltsuk Dialogue," *Ethnohistory* 43, 4 (Fall 1996): 643-61.
81 Although the census categorized Confucianism as a religion, many commentators have argued that it is a set of ethical and philosophical values. For further discussion of Chinese religion, see Chapter 6.
82 Other enumerators listed the religion of Chinese immigrants simply as "Chinese," or they left the religion category blank. A similar approach occurred in connection with Japanese immigrants.
83 Of course, some of the American-born would have been racialized African Americans or of Asian origin, but a large majority of the American-born in British Columbia were Caucasian. Individuals who were born in Norway, Sweden, or Germany were also overrepresented among the irreligious, but less dramatically, and they also made up a much smaller proportion of the BC population.
84 The British Columbia portion of CCRIP, National 5 percent sample, 1911, reveals that the odds ratio of Americans being irreligious was 4.384 (with Canadians as the comparator reference), with significance of .000.
85 For figures on the percentage of Rossland miners who were American, see Mouat, *Roaring Days*, 124.
86 W.R. McIntosh, ed., *Canadian Problems* (Toronto: R. Douglas Fraser, Presbyterian Publications, 1910), 12.
87 See Lynne Marks, "Irreligion, Immigration, Racialization and Ethnicity in British Columbia at the Turn of the Nineteenth Century" (paper presented at the annual meeting of the Social Science History Association, Vancouver, November 3, 2012).
88 Laurie Maffly-Kipp, *Religion and Society in Frontier California* (New Haven, CT: Yale University Press, 1994); Douglas Todd, ed., *Cascadia, the Elusive Utopia: Exploring the Spirit of the Pacific Northwest* (Vancouver: Ronsdale Press, 2008); Patricia O'Connell Killen and Mark Silk, eds., *Religion and Public Life in the Pacific Northwest: The None Zone* (Walnut Creek, CA: AltaMira Press, 2004); Stark and Bainbridge, *The Future of Religion*.

89 Seven percent of Vancouver Islanders were born in the United States, as compared to 15 percent in Yale and Cariboo.
90 Yale and Cariboo had 10,460 Ontario-born residents, 225 of whom were atheists.

Chapter 2

1 Renisa Mawani, *Colonial Proximities: Crossracial Encounters and Juridical Truths in British Columbia, 1871-1921* (Vancouver: UBC Press, 2009); David Goutor, *Guarding the Gates: The Canadian Labour Movement and Immigration, 1872-1934* (Vancouver: UBC Press, 2007); Timothy Stanley, *Contesting White Supremacy: School Segregation, Anti-racism, and the Making of Chinese Canadians* (Vancouver: UBC Press, 2011); John Lutz, *Makúk: A New History of Aboriginal-White Relations* (Vancouver: UBC Press, 2008).
2 See, for example, David Roediger, *The Wages of Whiteness: Race and the Making of the American Working Class* (London: Verso, 1991).
3 See, for example, Edward J. Blum, *Reforging the White Republic: Race, Religion and American Nationalism, 1865-1898* (Baton Rouge: Louisiana State University Press, 2005); Tracy Fessenden, *Culture and Redemption: Religion, the Secular, and American Literature* (Princeton: Princeton University Press, 2007); and Edward J. Blum et al., "Forum: American Religion and 'Whiteness,'" *Religion and American Culture* 19, 1 (Winter 2009): 1–35.
4 *Kaslo Kootenaian,* March 14, 1968, 2.
5 Lowery's attacks on Christianity (as well as his racism and support for women's sexual freedom) place him in a similar cultural and intellectual cohort as the male atheists profiled in Leigh Eric Schmidt's, *Village Atheists: How America's Unbelievers Made Their Way in a Godly Nation* (Princeton, NJ: Princeton University Press, 2016), although Lowery worked within a more sympathetic irreligious environment than those described by Schmidt.
6 *Lowery's Claim* (Nelson), December 1905, 3.
7 *Lowery's Claim* (Nelson), October 1905, 1. Also see November 1905, 4, and September 1902, 249.
8 *Lowery's Claim* (New Denver), September 1902, 245.
9 *Lowery's Claim* (New Denver), May 1902, 182–83.
10 *Lowery's Claim* (Nelson), October 1905, 1.
11 *Lowery's Claim* (New Denver), September 1902, 253. Also see October 1905, 8.
12 *Lowery's Claim* (Nelson), November 1905, 6.
13 George T. Moir, *Sinners and Saints: A True Story of Early Days in the Farthest West by an Old Timer, Written and Told by Himself* (Victoria: n.p., 1948), 109.
14 Ibid.
15 *Sandon Paystreak,* December 29, 1900, 7. Founded in 1896 by Lowery, the *Paystreak* was later taken over by McAdams. Sandon Museum, http://www.sandonmuseum.ca/characters/73-colonel-robert-thornton-lowery.
16 *Sandon Paystreak,* May 11, 1901, 4.
17 *Sandon Paystreak,* August 11, 1900, 2.
18 *Sandon Paystreak,* September 7, 1901, 4.
19 *Sandon Paystreak,* October 26, 1901, 2.
20 *Presbyterian,* September 20, 1902.
21 Reverend J.H. White (Superintendent of Missions for BC Conference of the Methodist Church of Canada) to Reverend James Allen (General Secretary of Missions in Toronto),

April 22, 1912, United Church Archives, BC Conference, Vancouver, box 2 78.099C. Regarding Catholic complaints, see Father J.A. Bedard to Bishop Dontenwill, Greenwood, September 2, 1902, Catholic Archdiocesan Archives, Vancouver (CAAV), Chancery Office fonds, GR 1, box 4, folder 6.

22 Ian McKay, *Reasoning Otherwise: Leftists and the People's Enlightenment in Canada, 1890-1920* (Toronto: Between the Lines, 2008), 213–78. For a study of Canadian atheists on the left during the 1920s and 1930s in Winnipeg, Toronto, and Montreal, see Elliot Hanowski, "A Godless Dominion: Unbelief and Religious Controversy in Interwar Canada" (PhD diss., Queen's University, 2015).

23 McKay, *Reasoning Otherwise*, 249–50.

24 The Socialist Party of British Columbia became the Socialist Party of Canada (with a BC section) in 1905.

25 Peter Campbell, *Canadian Marxists and the Search for a Third Way* (Montreal and Kingston: McGill-Queen's University Press, 2000), 34–37, 81.

26 *Western Clarion*, July 9, 1904, 4, and June 16, 1906, 2. Also see *Western Clarion*, October 21, 1905, 1, and September 23, 1905, 4; and Socialist Party of Canada *Religion – Thy Name Is Superstition* (Vancouver, 1912), Socialist History Project, http://www.socialisthistory.ca/Docs/PreWWI/Religion.htm.

27 *Western Clarion*, June 10, 1905, 1, and July 1, 1905, 2. Also see *Western Clarion*, November 4, 1905, 2.

28 For letters to the editor from Christian socialists complaining about the *Clarion*'s anti-Christian position, and responses from atheist socialists, see, for example, *Western Clarion*, May 15, 1909, 3, May 22, 1909, 3, and May 29, 1909, 2–3. Also see Eric Crouse, *Revival in the City: The Impact of American Evangelists in Canada, 1884–1914* (Montreal and Kingston: McGill-Queen's University Press, 2005), 150–52.

29 Stevens claimed that by the end of the winter, half of the audience was on his side, whereas the other half remained rabid socialists. "Notes of a Talk with H.H. Stevens," Library and Archives Canada, MG 27, series IIIB9, vol. 209.

30 John Belshaw, *Colonization and Community: The Vancouver Island Coalfield and the Making of the British Columbian Working Class* (Montreal and Kingston: McGill-Queen's University Press, 2002), 144–49; John R. Hinde, *When Coal Was King: Ladysmith and the Coal-Mining Industry on Vancouver Island* (Vancouver: UBC Press, 2003), 142–44.

31 *Nanaimo Free Press*, October 21, 1903, 2, and October 27, 1903, 2. Ogle was also unhappy about the fact that, unlike in Britain, the Socialist Party of British Columbia would not formally ally itself with the labour movement.

32 *Nanaimo Free Press*, October 24, 1903, 2. Also see October 21, 1903, 2.

33 *Victoria Colonist*, October 22, 1903, 2.

34 *Nanaimo Free Press*, November 11, 1903, 3.

35 *Nanaimo Free Press*, November 18, 1912, 2. Of course, in 1912–14 the Nanaimo coal miners were engaged in a bitter strike. A Methodist and a Baptist minister stood with the men, but most clergy did not. See Lynne Bowen, *Boss Whistle: The Coal Miners of Vancouver Island Remember* (Nanaimo, BC: Rocky Point Books, 2002), 122.

36 *Fernie Free Press*, 30 December, 1910; *Journal of the Sixth Session of the Synod of the Diocese of Kootenay, June 7 and 8th*, 1905, 17, quoted in Norman Knowles, "'Christ in the Crowsnest': Religion and the Anglo-Protestant Working Class in the Crowsnest Pass, 1898–1918," in *Nation, Ideas, Identities: Essays in Honour of Ramsay Cook*, ed. Michael D. Behiels and Marcel Martel (Toronto: Oxford University Press, 2000), 63–64.

37 See Mark Leier, *Where the Fraser River Flows: The Industrial Workers of the World in British Columbia* (Vancouver: New Star Books, 1990).

38 See, for example, Lynne Marks, "The Knights of Labor of the 1880s," Chapter 6 in Lynne Marks, *Revivals and Roller Rinks: Religion, Leisure, and Identity in Late-Nineteenth-Century Small-Town Ontario* (Toronto: University of Toronto Press, 1996). Also see Herbert Gutman, "Protestantism and the American Labor Movement: The Christian Spirit in the Gilded Age," *American Historical Review* 72, 1 (1966): 74-101; Herbert Gutman, *Work, Culture, and Society in Industrializing America: Essays in American Working-Class and Social History* (New York: Vintage Books, 1977); and Kenneth Fones-Wolf, *Trade Union Gospel: Christianity and Labor in Industrial Philadelphia, 1865-1915* (Philadelphia: Temple University Press, 1989).

39 Donald E. Winters Jr., *The Soul of the Wobblies: The I.W.W., Religion, and American Culture in the Progressive Era, 1905-1917* (Westport, CT: Greenwood Press, 1985), 20–24.

40 *Industrial Worker,* October 8, 1910, 2, quoted in ibid., 51. The IWW also saw itself as competing with the Salvation Army in the Vancouver "free speech fights" of 1909 and 1912, where the police allowed the Salvation Army to preach on street corners but arrested IWW leaders for speaking in similar venues. See Leier, *Where the Fraser River Flows,* 62–77.

41 Industrial Workers of the World, "The Preacher and the Slave," in *Songs of the Workers: To Fan the Flames of Discontent* (Chicago: Industrial Workers of the World, 1973), quoted in Winters, *The Soul of the Wobblies,* 54.

42 For articles that were positive about the church or Christianity, see, for example, *Western Wage Earner,* November 1909, 21; and *BC Federationist,* January 20, 1912, 2, October 12, 1912, 1, and June 27, 1913, 1. For letters to the editor critiquing the churches, see, for example, *BC Federationist,* July 27, 1912, 1, August 1, 1913, 3, and August 8, 1913, 3.

43 *Western Wage Earner,* March 1909, 2–3, April 1909, 21; *BC Federationist,* September 12, 1913, 5.

44 See, for example, *Western Wage Earner,* July 1909, 16, and August 1909, 22.

45 *BC Western Catholic,* February 7, 1913, 6.

46 See Marks, *Revivals and Roller Rinks,* 14.

47 *Western Clarion,* December 22, 1906, 3.

48 Janice Newton, *The Feminist Challenge to the Canadian Left, 1900-1918* (Montreal and Kingston: McGill-Queen's University Press, 1995).

49 *Sandon Paystreak,* April 28, 1900, 2.

50 See, for example, *Lowery's Claim* (New Denver), December 1901, 112, February 1902, 131, and July 1902, 213. This connection between greater sexual equality and autonomy for women and freethought was a not-uncommon pattern in the nineteenth-century British and American freethought movements.

51 *Lowery's Claim* (Nelson), June 1906, 2.

52 Evelyn Kirkley, *Rational Mothers and Infidel Gentlemen: Gender and American Atheism, 1865-1915* (Syracuse: Syracuse University Press, 1999), and Schmidt, *Village Atheists,* 132.

53 *Sandon Paystreak,* March 30, 1901, 4.

54 *Lowery's Claim* (Vancouver), June 1903, 1.

55 Ibid. For another example of Lowery's anti-Asian racism, see *Lowery's Claim* (Nelson), December 1905, 4. For the labour movement's attack on Asian immigration, see Goutor, *Guarding the Gates.* For further discussion of anti-Asian racism in British Columbia, see Patricia Roy, *A White Man's Province: British Columbia Politicians and Chinese and Japanese Immigrants, 1858-1914* (Vancouver: UBC Press, 1989); and Stanley, *Contesting White Supremacy.*

56 *Victoria Times,* July 9, 1900, 4. Also see *Victoria Times,* June 28, 1900, 4.

57 For differing attitudes among the clergy toward Asian immigration, see Peter Ward, "The Oriental Immigrant and Canada's Protestant Clergy, 1858-1925," *BC Studies* 22 (1974): 40–55; and Patricia Roy, "Anglicans and Asians in British Columbia: An Ambiguous Relationship" (unpublished paper, n.d.). The moderate position of the *BC Federationist* regarding the churches is also reflected in a church report it printed regarding the BC Presbyterians' opposition to further Asian immigration – a position that *Federationist* readers would view positively. The national Presbyterian Church tended to be less hostile to Asian immigration than BC Presbyterians. *BC Federationist,* September 19, 1913, 6.

58 John Stenhouse has written about the irreligious roots of mid-nineteenth-century attacks on New Zealand clergy for their support of Maori rights. John Stenhouse, "Imperialism, Atheism, and Race: Charles Southwell, Old Corruption, and the Maori," *Journal of British Studies* 44, 4 (2005): 754-74.

59 For a rare example of co-operation between South Asian radicals and BC Euro-Canadian socialists, see Peter Campbell, "East Meets Left: South Asian Militants and the Socialist Party of Canada in British Columbia, 1904-1914," *International Journal of Canadian Studies/Revue internationale d'études canadiennes* 20 (Fall 1999): 35–65. For evidence of anti-Asian sentiment among BC socialists and trade unionists, see Goutor, *Guarding the Gates;* and Mark Leier, *Red Flags and Red Tape: The Making of a Labour Bureaucracy* (Toronto: University of Toronto Press, 1995).

60 Goutor, *Guarding the Gates*; Mawani, *Colonial Proximities.*

61 For rural and working-class white identity in British Columbia, see Karla Greer, "Race, Riot and Rail: The Process of Racialisation in Prince Rupert, B.C., 1906-1919" (master's thesis, University of Victoria, 1999); and Elizabeth Furniss, *The Burden of History: Colonialism and the Frontier Myth in a Rural Canadian Community* (Vancouver: UBC Press, 1999). For a discussion of how European workers came to define themselves as part of the white working class in the United States, see Roediger, *The Wages of Whiteness.*

62 For a discussion of the value of Britishness to the Canadian working class, and the way that even non-British immigrant workers sought to adopt this identity in order to improve their status in Canadian society, see Kurt Korneski, "Britishness, Canadianness, Class, and Race: Winnipeg and the British World, 1880s–1910s," *Journal of Canadian Studies* 41, 2 (2007), 161-84.

63 Mawani, *Colonial Proximities;* Adele Perry, *On the Edge of Empire: Gender, Race and the Making of British Columbia, 1849-1871* (Toronto: University of Toronto Press, 2001). Mawani and Perry state that interracial relationships were another source of concern, but they are rarely mentioned in the sources I examined for the 1890–1914 period. By this time, with significantly amplified European immigration to British Columbia, sexual relationships between white men and Indigenous women appear to have diminished in number, particularly in urban areas, and were subject to increased social sanction. See, for example, Sylvia Van Kirk, "Tracing the Fortunes of Five Founding Families of Victoria," *BC Studies* 115–16 (Autumn-Winter 1997–98): 149–80.

64 For a Presbyterian critique of the "open towns" of the Kootenays, see "The Battle for a Clean Town," *Presbyterian,* April 9, 1904, 470.

65 Sandon Historical Society, "'Knights of the Green Cloth': Gamblers, Card Sharks and Sandon's Saloons," Sandon Museum, February 23, 2011, http://www.sandonmuseum.ca/characters/74-knights-of-the-green-cloth.

66 Sandon Historical Society, "The 'Soiled Doves' of 'Lower Sandon': Madames, Brothels and the Infamous Red Light District," Sandon Museum, February 23, 2011, http://www.sandonmuseum.ca/characters/76-the-soiled-doves-of-lower-sandon. Also see R. Cole Harris, *The Resettlement of British Columbia: Essays on Colonialism and Geographical Change* (Vancouver: UBC Press, 1997), 205–7.

67 *Sandon Paystreak* (no date provided), quoted in Sandon Historical Society, "'Knights of the Green Cloth.'"

68 Clare McAllister, "Women of the West Kootenay," *B.C. Historical News* 10, 3 (April 1977): 13.

69 Jeremy Mouat, *Roaring Days: Rossland's Mines and the History of British Columbia* (Vancouver: UBC Press, 1995), 127–28; *Sandon Paystreak,* August 12, 1899.

70 Belshaw, *Colonization and Community,* 178–81. Herschel Biggs interview transcript, interviewed by Myrtle Bergren, June 6, 1979, BC Archives, Victoria, Coal Tyee Society Oral History Collection, T4051:10. For a description of the beer-drinking habits of Nanaimo miners, and the range of hotels and saloons available to them, see Bowen, *Boss Whistle,* 182–84.

71 "Report of the Home Mission Committee of the Presbyterian Church in Canada (Western Section) for 1895–96," in *Acts and Proceedings of the Twenty-Second General Assembly of the Presbyterian Church in Canada* (June 1896), xxxiii, xxxiv, United Church of Canada Archives, Toronto.

72 Perry, *On the Edge of Empire.* Also see Nancy Forestell, "Bachelors, Boarding-Houses, and Blind Pigs: Gender Construction in a Multi-ethnic Mining Camp, 1909-1920," in *A Nation of Immigrants, Women, Workers, and Communities in Canadian History, 1840s-1960s,* ed. Franca Iacovetta, Paula Draper, and Robert Ventresca (Toronto: University Toronto Press, 1998), 251–90.

73 See, for example, Mary Murphy, *Mining Cultures: Men, Women and Leisure in Butte, 1914-41* (Urbana: University of Illinois Press, 1997); Susan Lee Johnson, "Bulls, Bears and Dancing Boys: Race, Gender and Leisure in the California Gold Rush," *Radical History Review* 60 (Fall 1994): 4–37; and Forestell, "Bachelors, Boarding-Houses, and Blind Pigs."

74 As mentioned in Chapter 1, some of the apparently irreligious women in these households may not have had a deep commitment to irreligion, and a significant number did not define themselves as irreligious with their husbands (see Appendix: Table 3).

75 Atheists constituted only 15 percent of the irreligious in 1911, and when only this group is included in the logistic regression analysis there is no statistically significant relationship between the proportion of men in a household and the irreligion of its members. When all the irreligious are included (with those of no religion being 85 percent of the total), logistic regression demonstrates that there is a statistically significant relationship (at .000 significance) between living in a household that is primarily or exclusively male and being irreligious.

76 *Victoria Colonist,* September 18, 1894, 2.

77 *Victoria Colonist,* November 16, 1899, 5. For other acts of racist violence against the Chinese in Victoria, see *Victoria Times,* February 9, 1900, 6; *Victoria Colonist,* February 24, 1893, 5; *Victoria Colonist,* February 19, 1905, 2; and *Victoria Colonist,* March 18, 1908, 6. For a discussion of the economic and other reasons that served to justify such behaviour in the minds of the Euro-Canadian assailants, see Roy, *A White Man's Province;* and Stanley, *Contesting White Supremacy.*

78 *Victoria Colonist,* September 26, 1907, 5.

79 *Nelson Tribune,* June 22, 1901,4. Also see *Nelson Tribune,* March 8, 1901, 4; March 13, 1901, 4; May 2, 1901, 4; July 17, 1901, 4; January 25, 1902, 4; and *Victoria Times,* February 9, 1900, 6.

80 *Nelson Tribune,* March 8, 1901, 4.

81 See, for example, *Nelson Tribune,* November 2, 1899, 2, and November 7, 1899. This hostility was based in part on efforts of mine owners to bring in Italian workers to break strikes. See *Nelson Tribune,* June 8, 1899, 2, and June 16, 1899, 2. By later in the first decade of the twentieth century, these southern and eastern European miners had become much more integrated into the mining workforce, and the mining unions. Allen Seager, "Socialists and Workers: The Western Canadian Coal Miners, 1900-1921," *Labour/Le travail* 16 (Fall 1985): 23–59.

82 For a discussion of how the Catholic Church succeeded elsewhere in Canada in integrating ethnic communities, see Roberto Perrin, *The Immigrants' Church: The Third Force in Canadian Catholicism, 1880-1920,* Canada's Ethnic Group Series Booklet 25 (Ottawa: Canadian Historical Association, 1998); Roberto Perrin, "Churches and Immigrant Integration in Toronto, 1947-65," in *The Churches and Social Order in Nineteenth- and Twentieth-Century Canada,* ed. Michael Gauvreau and Ollivier Hubert (Montreal and Kingston: McGill-Queen's University Press, 2006), 274–91; and Enrico Carlson Cumbo, "Salvation in Indifference: Gendered Expressions of Italian-Canadian Immigrant Catholicity, 1900-1940," in *Households of Faith: Family, Gender, and Community in Canada, 1760-1969,* ed. Nancy Christie (Montreal and Kingston: McGill-Queen's University Press, 2002), 203–33.

83 J. Matubak to Bishop Dontenwill, February 9, 1903, CAAV, Chancery Office fonds, GR 1, box 4, folder 8. Also see J. Matubak and other Slavic men to Dontenwill, March 16, 1902; and Father Coccola to Dontenwill, December 3, 1903, CAAV, Chancery Office fonds, GR 1, box 4, folder 8.

84 Father Thayer to Bishop Dontenwill regarding Italian workers, December 16, 1902, CAAV, Chancery Office fonds, GR 1, box 4, folder 12. For Hungarian workers, see Father Brucker to Bishop Dontenwill, June 3, 1903, CAAV, Chancery Office fonds, GR 1, box 4, folder 7. For a discussion of visiting Italian-speaking priests, see *Revelstoke Herald,* March 27, 1901, 4; and *Nelson Tribune,* April 30, 1899, 4.

85 George V. Ferguson, "Queen of the Kootenays," *Beaver* 19 (March 1960): 21.

86 Knowles, "'Christ in the Crowsnest,'" 62–63. Also see *Ladysmith Ledger,* March 25, 1905, 2; and Belshaw, *Colonization and Community,* 180.

87 A. Robbins, letter to editor, *Work for the Far West,* April 1900.

88 See Marks, *Revivals and Roller Rinks,* 81–139, for a discussion of masculine cross-class rough culture in late-nineteenth-century small-town Ontario. Also see Mouat, *Roaring Days.*

89 Wolfe, "Tramp Printer Extraordinary." Also see Nelson History Theatre Society, "A History of John Houston," http://www.johntruthhouston.com.

90 One supporter noted that Houston "has been the staunchest champion of the rights of Labor during the past two years. Houston was fighting our battles when practically the whole press of the country was against us." James Wilke to W.L. Nayler, May 27, 1900, Rossland Museum and Archives, Rossland, BC. Also see *Nelson Tribune,* April 18, 1899, 2, June 17, 1899, 2, and January 13, 1900, 2.

91 *Nelson Tribune,* March 21, 1899, 2.

92 *Nelson Tribune,* July 10, 1900, 2. Also see *Nelson Tribune,* June 16, 1894, 2.

93 *Nelson Tribune,* August 26, 1899, 2.

94 Moir, *Sinners and Saints,* 104–5. When Moir lived in Slocan City, another Kootenay mining town, he also observed hostility from most miners, and many businessmen, to church efforts to control their leisure activities (and, for hotel, saloon, and brothel owners, their businesses). As he recalled, "On going to church with my wife one Sunday morning we saw a number of men on the street, who showed evidence of a last night's banquet. We approached one, a mining speculator holding his horse by the bridle, and when I said 'Good morning' without answering my salutation, he replied with an oath: 'You church people can all go to hell.'" Ibid., 108.

95 *Nelson Tribune,* July 2, 1900, 2. Houston defined the "people of British Columbia" in very narrow racial terms. He actively supported the exclusion of both Chinese and Italian workers, as he subscribed to labour arguments that they threatened the livelihoods of the white working class. See *Nelson Tribune,* November 2, 1899, 2, and June 20, 1899, 2.

96 *Nelson Tribune,* March 25, 1901, 4.

97 *Lowery's Claim* (Nelson), February 1906, 2–3. Also see *Lowery's Claim,* December 1905, 1 and 3, and January 1906, 7.

98 Welwood, R.J., "Lowery, Robert Thornton," *Dictionary of Canadian Biography Online,* http://www.biographi.ca/en/bio.php?id_nbr=8251.

99 This was certainly the argument of the Toronto journal *Secular Thought,* which claimed that Lowery's paper was banned from the mail because the post office was "bound 'hand and foot' to the Preachers Union." *Secular Thought,* 1906, 480.

Chapter 3

1 Norman Knowles, "'Christ in the Crowsnest': Religion and the Anglo-Protestant Working Class in the Crowsnest Pass, 1898–1918," in *Nation, Ideas, Identities: Essays in Honour of Ramsay Cook,* ed. Michael D. Behiels and Marcel Martel (Toronto: Oxford University Press, 2000), 66.

2 Ralph Connor, *Black Rock: A Tale of the Selkirks* (Toronto: Westminster, 1898). For further discussion of "muscular Christianity" in Canadian fiction of this period, see Daniel Coleman, *White Civility: The Literary Project of English Canada* (Toronto: University of Toronto Press, 2008), Chapter 4.

3 *Western Methodist Recorder,* December 1900, 6.

4 Anne Mercier, *Father Pat: A Hero of the Far West* (Gloucester, MA: Minchin and Gibbs, 1909).

5 Canon Alan Greene interview, interviewed by Imbert Orchard, January 1969, BC Archives, Imbert Orchard Collection, T944–005, side 2.

6 Ernest Thomas to the Crosby Mission Committee, June 1922, United Church of Canada Archives, Toronto, Fonds 14: Methodist Church (Canada) Missionary Society, series 4: Home Mission Records, accession 78.099C.

7 A. Robbins, letter to editor, *Work for the Far West,* April 1900.

8 Diary of Reverend Rowan Ernest Grice-Hutchinson, November 7, 1913, Anglican Diocesan Archives, Diocese of Kootenay, Kelowna, BC, Rowan Ernest Grice-Hutchinson fonds.

9 Thomas Green, "BC Experiences," 31, 34, United Church of Canada Archives, Toronto, Thomas Green fonds (fonds 3110). Also see Canon Alan Greene interview, BC Archives, Imbert Orchard Collection, T944–005, side 2.

10 H.R. Pickup, "Helping Men in the Kootenay," *Presbyterian,* October 22, 1908, 448.

11 Stuart Barnard, "The Kootenay Revival Campaign of 1909" (master's thesis, University of Calgary, 2010). Also see J.H. White to James Allen, annual report of the Home Missions for 1909, United Church of Canada, British Columbia Conference Archives, Vancouver (UC Archives, BC), British Columbia Conference Records.

12 S.C. Williams, *Religious Belief and Popular Culture in Southwark, c. 1880-1939* (Oxford: Oxford University Press, 1999); Hugh McLeod, *Piety and Poverty: Working-Class Religion in Berlin, London and New York, 1870-1914* (New York: Holmes and Meier, 1996); Robert Orsi, "Everyday Miracles: The Study of Lived Religion," in *Lived Religion in America: Toward a History of Practice,* ed. David D. Hall (Princeton: Princeton University Press, 1997), 3–21; Robert Orsi, "Who Cares about Religion? The Blind Spot in Contemporary Historiography" (paper presented at Qualicum History Conference, Parksville, BC, January 30, 2003).

13 See, for example, David Voas, "The Rise and Fall of Fuzzy Fidelity in Europe," *European Sociological Review* 25, 2 (2009): 155–68; Ingrid Storm, "Halfway to Heaven: Four Types of Fuzzy Fidelity in Europe," *Journal for the Scientific Study of Religion* 48, 4 (2009): 702–18; Callum Brown, "The People of 'No Religion': The Demographics of Secularisation in the English-Speaking World since c. 1900," *Archiv fur Sozialgeschichte* 51 (2011): 31–61; and Grace Davie, *Religion in Britain since 1945: Believing without Belonging,* Making Contemporary Britain series (Cambridge, MA: Blackwell, 1994).

14 *Sandon Paystreak,* March 18, 1899, 4.

15 *Lowery's Claim* (Nelson), November 1905, 3.

16 Herschel Biggs interview transcript, interviewed by Myrtle Bergren, June 6, 1979, BC Archives, Coal Tyee Society Oral History Collection, T4051:10.

17 Dave McDonald interview transcript, interviewed by Myrtle Bergren, February 7, 1979, BC Archives, Coal Tyee Society Oral History Collection, T4051:0081.

18 *Fernie Free Press,* December 27, 1910, 8; Journal of the Sixth Session of the Synod of the Diocese of Kootenay, June 7 and 8th, 1905, 17, quoted in Knowles, "'Christ in the Crowsnest,'" 63–64.

19 Father Brucker to Bishop Dontenwill, February 23, 1905, translated from French by the author, Catholic Archdiocesan Archives, Vancouver (CAAV), Chancery Office fonds, GR 1, box 4, folder 7. For more discussion of low levels of church involvement, see Father Bedard to Bishop Dontenwill, November 5, 1903, CAAV, Chancery Office fonds, GR 1, box 4, folder 6.

20 Thomas Greene, "Report from Fairview, Anglican Diocese of New Westminster," *Monthly Record,* January-February 1895, Anglican Provincial Synod of British Columbia Archives, Vancouver, Anglican Provincial Synod of British Columbia and Yukon fonds.

21 Albert Tickle interview transcript, interviewed by Bernard McNichol, June 20, 1979, BC Archives, Coal Tyee Society Oral History Collection, T4051:119; Tom Johnston interview transcript, interviewed by Myrtle Bergren, June 13, 1979, BC Archives, Coal Tyee Society Oral History Collection, T4051:65–66.

22 Williams, *Religious Belief and Popular Culture,* 113–21. McLeod, *Piety and Poverty,* 140. Nancy Ammerman has identified what she calls "Golden Rule Christianity" among many twentieth-century American Christians. Their primary focus was on the need to care for their neighbours and to treat others as they themselves would wish to be treated, with much less emphasis on theological and evangelical concerns. She suggests that this practical approach has existed among various Christians throughout the centuries. See Nancy T.

Ammerman, "Golden Rule Christianity: Lived Religion in the American Mainstream," in Hall, *Lived Religion in America,* 196–216.

23 Williams, *Religious Belief and Popular Culture,* 113–14.

24 Jo Fraser Jones, ed., *Hobnobbing with a Countess and Other Okanagan Adventures: The Diaries of Alice Barrett Parke, 1891-1900* (Vancouver: UBC Press, 2001), 161.

25 Green, "BC Experiences."

26 *Fernie Free Press,* December 27, 1910, 8.

27 Williams, *Religious Belief and Popular Culture,* 104, 89.

28 Knowles, "'Christ in the Crowsnest,'" 63.

29 Canon Alan Greene interview, BC Archives, Imbert Orchard Collection, T944–005, side 2.

30 Grice-Hutchinson diary, March 5, 1914, and March 11, 1915.

31 See ibid., September 10 and November 5, 1913, over his eagerness to baptize the "four little heathens" of various ages. Also see December 7, 1913.

32 Report of the Committee on Church Life and Work, of the Presbyterian Synod of B.C., Vancouver, 1908, UC Archives, BC.

33 Lynne Bowen, *Boss Whistle: The Coal Miners of Vancouver Island Remember* (Nanaimo, BC: Rocky Point Books, 2002), 186. Also see, for example, Wilf Brodrick interview transcript, interviewed by Bernard McNichol, July 5, 1979; George Bodovinick interview transcript; and Tom Johnston interview transcript, both interviewed by Myrtle Bergren, June 13, 1979, BC Archives, Coal Tyee Society Oral History Collection, T4051:16, T4051:0014, and T4051:65–66.

34 Report of the Committee on Church Life and Work, 1908, UC Archives, BC.

35 James Kipp interview, BC Archives, Imbert Orchard Collection, T0308:0002.

36 Service Register, St. George's Anglican Church, 1908, Anglican Diocesan Archives, Diocese of Kootenay, Kelowna, BC, St. George's Parish (Rossland, BC) sous-fonds, St. Andrew's Parish (Trail, BC), fonds, Vital Records, box 43, book 2. This service register covers May to December of 1908, so it unfortunately does not include attendance figures for Easter services, which would probably also have been relatively high.

37 Andrew Reid discusses the belief in a supreme being in "Not So Secret Societies: Fraternities and Masculine Identity in Victorian Victoria, 1860-1890" (major research paper, Department of History, University of Victoria, 2012), 8–9. For fraternal culture and masculinity, see Lynne Marks, *Revivals and Roller Rinks: Religion, Leisure, and Identity in Late-Nineteenth-Century Small-Town Ontario* (Toronto: University of Toronto Press, 1996), Chapter 5; Mary Ann Clawson, *Constructing Brotherhood: Class, Gender and Fraternalism* (Princeton: Princeton University Press, 1989); and Mark Carnes, *Secret Ritual and Manhood in Victorian America* (New Haven, CT: Yale University Press, 1989).

38 Jenny Clayton, "Local Connections: Stories from Early Vernon" (honours essay, Department of History, University of Victoria, 1999), 44–46; *Nelson Tribune,* February 14, 1899, 2, April 28, 1899, 4; *Nanaimo Free Press,* July 8, 1897, 4.

39 *Nanaimo Free Press,* July 13, 1897, 4.

40 See, for example, Clawson, *Constructing Brotherhood;* and Adam G. Kendall, "The Whitewash Committee of 1914: The Knights of Columbus, Freemasonry and Anti-Catholicism in California," *European Journal of American Culture* 33, 1 (2014): 49–60.

41 Father J.A. Bedard to Bishop Dontenwill, September 2, 1902, CAAV, Chancery Office fonds, GR 1, box 4, folder 6.

42 Father Brucker to Bishop Dontenwill, January 14, 1903, CAAV, Chancery Office fonds, GR 1, box 4, folder 7, translated from original French by author.

43 Father Bedard to Bishop Dontenwill, March 4, 1904, CAAV, Chancery Office fonds, GR 1, box 4, folder 6; Georgionne Madore to Bishop Dontenwill, January 12, 1903, CAAV, Chancery Office fonds, GR 1, box 4, folder 10.

44 Reid, "Not So Secret Societies."

45 See, for example, Kevin Anderson, "'This Typical Old Canadian Form of Racial and Religious Hate': Anti-Catholicism and English Canadian Nationalism, 1905–1965" (PhD diss., McMaster University, 2013); and J.R. Miller, "Anti-Catholic Thought in Victorian Canada," *Canadian Historical Review* 65, 4 (December 1985): 474–94.

46 For a discussion of interdenominational co-operation among early BC Christians, also see Ivan E. Antak, "John Robson and His Faith: Church and State in Late Nineteenth-Century British Columbia" (master's thesis, Simon Fraser University, 2012), particularly 96-98.

47 W.J. Fraser interview, interviewed by Imbert Orchard, March 8, 1965, BC Archives, Imbert Orchard Collection, T0935:002.

48 There are certainly other examples of anti-Catholicism beyond the Orange Order. The Protestant Protective Association, a virulently anti-Catholic organization, had at least some presence in Vancouver in 1898, and a New Westminster mayoral candidate blamed his electoral loss on his Catholicism. *Victoria Colonist,* June 8, 1898; *Ledge (New Denver),* July 7, 1898; *New Westminster Columbian,* December 12, 1899. I would like to thank Pat Roy for sharing this research material with me.

49 W.J. Fraser interview, interviewed by Imbert Orchard, March 8, 1965, BC Archives, Imbert Orchard Collection, T0935:002.

50 Father Thayer to Bishop Dontenwill, December 15, 1903, CAAV, Chancery Office fonds, GR 1, box 4, folder 12.

51 Alison Marshall found no evidence of Chinese participation in fraternal orders, other than the Chinese Freemasons (CKT), which was a different kind of organization. Alison Marshall, *Cultivating Connections: The Making of Chinese Prairie Canada* (Vancouver: UBC Press, 2014), 90.

52 Quoted in "John Houston: The Man and His Legacy," http://www.johntruthhouston.com/man.html.

53 Diary of Bishop Hills, February 2, 1890, Anglican Provincial Synod of British Columbia Archives, Vancouver, Bishop George Hills sous-fonds, Anglican Provincial Synod of the Diocese of British Columbia and the Yukon fonds.

54 Grice-Hutchinson diary, July 17, 1913.

55 John Podmillanak to Bishop Dontenwill, February 9, 1903, CAAV, Chancery Office fonds, GR 1, box 4, folder 8.

56 Anglican Diocese of New Westminster, *Monthly Record,* December 1895, 6, Anglican Provincial Synod of British Columbia Archives, Anglican Provincial Synod of British Columbia and Yukon fonds.

57 Diary of Bishop Hills, December 8, 1890, Anglican Provincial Synod of British Columbia Archives, Bishop George Hills sous-fonds, Anglican Provincial Synod of the Diocese of British Columbia and the Yukon fonds.

58 For example, *New Denver Ledge,* May 4, 1899, 1, and February 22, 1900, 1.

59 It is difficult to be exact about the numbers here. In some cases, the newspaper editor may simply have noted that the arrangements were made by a miners, union or a fraternal order and failed to mention whether or not a minister also spoke at the funeral. However, silence regarding the presence of a minister may mean that none were in attendance. In any case, between 1900 and 1905, the *Phoenix Pioneer* reported on thirty-nine local funerals, only 13

percent of which evidently had no minister. A clergyman spoke at twelve of the fifteen funerals organized by the miners' union. The *Ledge,* which published in Greenwood, Nakusp, New Denver, and Fernie between 1894 and 1913, recorded fifty-six funerals, 75 percent of which had a minister in attendance, whereas no clergy were mentioned in connection with the remaining 25 percent. The *Sandon Mining Review* reported on eleven funerals between 1898 and 1902, all of which were arranged by the miners' union. In 36 percent of them, the paper did not mention the presence of a minister. With a total number of only eleven, it is very difficult to make any definitive arguments here. However, the fact that Sandon had the highest proportion of atheists/those of no religion in the province is suggestive.

60 David Scott and Edna H. Hanie, *Nelson: Queen City of the Kootenays* (Vancouver: Mitchell Press, 1972), 77–78.

61 For an example of a funeral conducted by a minister that ended (to his horror) in a "drunken orgy," see Pickup, "Helping Men in the Kootenay," *Presbyterian,* October 22, 1908, 447.

62 See, for example, Carlos A. Schwantes, "The Churches of the Disinherited: The Culture of Radicalism on the North Pacific Industrial Frontier," *Pacific Historian* 25 (Winter 1981): 54–65; and Canon Alan Greene interview, interviewed by Imbert Orchard, January 1969, BC Archives, Imbert Orchard Collection, T:944–005, side 2. Greene suggests that interest in religion diminished in the lumber camps after the coming of the Scandinavians.

63 Reverend J.H. White to Reverend Allen, April 22, 1912, United Church of Canada Archives, Toronto, Methodist Church Missionary Society Fonds, Fonds 14, Series 4: Home Mission Records Methodist Church (Canada) Missionary Society, accession 78.099C.

64 Voas, "The Rise and Fall of Fuzzy Fidelity"; Storm, "Halfway to Heaven."

65 Patricia Roy, *A White Man's Province: British Columbia Politicians and Chinese and Japanese Immigrants, 1858-1914* (Vancouver: UBC Press, 1989).

Chapter 4

1 Jessie McQueen to Catherine McQueen and Dove McQueen Crowell, August 22, 1888, quoted in Jean Barman, *Sojourning Sisters: The Lives and Letters of Jessie and Annie McQueen* (Toronto: University of Toronto Press, 2003), 101–2.

2 *Westminster,* April 1, 1899, 349–50.

3 For a description of the Canadian Families Project, see Peter Baskerville and Eric Sager, eds., *Household Counts: Canadian Households and Families in 1901* (Toronto: University of Toronto Press, 2007). See Appendix: Table 1 for 1901 census data confirming that Ontarians and Nova Scotians were much more likely than British Columbians to become church members.

4 Occasionally, someone might claim one denomination on the census and be a member of another church, but this was fairly rare. For the same phenomenon in New Brunswick, see Hannah Lane, "Tribalism, Proselytism, and Pluralism: Protestants, Family, and Denominational Identity in Mid-nineteenth-century St. Stephen, New Brunswick," in *Households of Faith: Family, Gender, and Community in Canada, 1760-1969,* ed. Nancy Christie (Montreal and Kingston: McGill-Queen's University Press, 2002), 103–37.

5 I employed this methodology in studying religious involvement in small-town Ontario. See Lynne Marks, *Revivals and Roller Rinks: Religion, Leisure, and Identity in Late-Nineteenth-Century Small-Town Ontario* (Toronto: University of Toronto Press, 1996).

6 Bryan Palmer, "Historiographical Hassles: Class and Gender, Evidence and Interpretation," *Histoire sociale* 33, 65 (2000): 105–44.

7 Nancy Christie and Michael Gauvreau, "Modalities of Social Authority: Suggesting an Interface for Religious and Social History," *Histoire sociale* 36, 71 (2003): 1–30. For studies of working-class churches in larger centres, see, for example, Edward Smith, "Working-Class Anglicans: Religion and Identity in Victorian and Edwardian Hamilton, Ontario," *Histoire sociale* 36, 71 (2003): 123–44; Melissa Turkstra, "Working-Class Churches in Early Twentieth Century Hamilton: Fostering a Distinctive Working-Class Identity and Culture," *Histoire sociale* 41, 82 (2008): 459–503; Michael Gauvreau, "Factories and Foreigners: Church Life in Working-Class Neighbourhoods in Hamilton and Montreal, 1890-1930," in *The Churches and Social Order in Nineteenth and Twentieth Century Canada,* ed. Michael Gauvreau and Ollivier Hubert (Montreal and Kingston: McGill-Queen's University Press, 2006), 225–73.

8 Del Muise, "'The Great Transformation': Changing the Urban Face of Nova Scotia, 1871–1921," *Nova Scotia Historical Review* 11, 2 (1991): 1–42.

9 Unfortunately, records for the African Canadian churches have not been found, so the analysis of church involvement in Amherst and Kentville focuses almost exclusively on the white population.

10 I discussed Campbellford in *Revivals and Roller Rinks,* where I linked its church records to the 1891 census.

11 Jeremy Mouat, *Roaring Days: Rossland's Mines and the History of British Columbia* (Vancouver: UBC Press, 1995).

12 Seven of the eight community databases were funded by the Canadian Families Project. I am very grateful to Jeremy Mouat for his generosity in sharing with me the Rossland 1901 census database that he created for his own research.

13 For a discussion of the Salvation Army and the working class in Ontario, see Marks, *Revivals and Roller Rinks,* Chapters 6 and 7. For the Salvation Army in Victoria, see Susan Neylan, "Encountering Spirits: Evangelical and Holiness Revivals in Victoria, B.C., and the 'Colonial Project,'" *Histoire sociale* 36, 71 (2003): 175–204.

14 In 1901, the census defined 162 Vernon residents as "racially" Chinese. Nelson had 178, Revelstoke 104, and Rossland 238 residents defined as Chinese. See Chapter 6 for a discussion of Chinese religious practices and white settler attitudes toward them, and the relationship between Chinese Canadians and the Christian churches. Regarding the Chinese in Rossland, also see Mouat, *Roaring Days,* 121–22; and Ronald A. Shearer, "The Chinese and Chinatown of Rossland: Fragments from Their Early History," http://spiritofred.ca/wp-content/uploads/chinese-in-rossland.pdf. For memories of a Christian missionary of Chinese origin in Nelson, see Reverend Yee Jing Chow interview, interviewed by Theresa Low, June 1980, BC Archives, Chinese Historical Wrongs Legacy Initiative Collection, T3715, translated from Chinese for author by Liang Han.

15 Jenny Clayton, "Local Connections: Stories from Early Vernon" (honours essay, Department of History, University of Victoria, 1999), 8.

16 The 1901 census reported 138 Italians and 403 Scandinavians in the Nelson area. In Revelstoke, there were 119 Italians and 206 Scandinavians. Both towns had only a very few Slavic residents. In Rossland, there were 357 Italians, 238 people who were defined as "Austro-Hungarian" (including "Bohemians, Galicians, Poles and Slavs"), and 793 Scandinavians. More Italians would emigrate to Revelstoke during the next decade, so that by 1911 more than 500 Italians lived there. Dominion Bureau of Statistics (DBS), *Census of Canada, 1901* (Ottawa: Census Office, 1902), vol. 1, Table XI; DBS, *Census of Canada,*

1911 (Ottawa: C.H. Parmelee, 1913), vol. 1, Table 7. For a discussion of Italians in British Columbia, see Lynne Bowen, *Whoever Gives Us Bread: The Story of Italians in British Columbia* (Vancouver: Douglas and McIntyre, 2011).

17 These people were often called "adherents," a term that, sometimes confusingly, was also employed by census enumerators to define anyone who identified with a particular denomination for the census.

18 Christie and Gauvreau, "Modalities of Social Authority," 8–9.

19 See, for example, Marguerite Van Die, *Religion, Family and Community in Victorian Canada: The Colbys of Carrollcroft* (Montreal and Kingston: McGill-Queen's University Press, 2005).

20 For the social reasons that might have brought women into the churches, see Marks, *Revivals and Roller Rinks.* For a discussion of women's pressure on married men to enter the churches, and the relationship between married men's involvement and respectability, see Hannah Lane, "Evangelicals, Church Finance, and Wealth-Holding in Mid-nineteenth century St. Stephen, New Brunswick, and Calais, Maine," in Gauvreau and Hubert, *The Churches and Social Order,* 109–50; Lane, "Tribalism, Proselytism, and Pluralism," 103–37; and Marks, *Revivals and Roller Rinks,* Chapter 1.

21 For the cultural authority of the churches in Central and Eastern Canada during this period, see Christie and Gauvreau, "Modalities of Social Authority."

22 Since all of the communities had only one church of each denomination, if the records of some Protestant churches had not survived this was not a major problem, as members of a particular denomination with existing church records could be compared to non-church members of that denomination in the community.

23 We must remember that the figures discussed below reflect only those individuals who appear on both church membership rolls and the manuscript census. In every community, some individuals who were listed on the rolls could not be linked to the census. Perhaps they were not enumerated because they left town after being listed in the membership roll but before the time of the census. Others may have lived outside the census area, in the neighbouring countryside. And for some, variant spellings of their name made linkages impossible.

24 Only community members over twelve years of age were included in the analysis, as Protestants tended to join the churches in their teens or later.

25 Twenty-seven percent of Campbellford Anglicans and 38 percent of Dunnville Anglicans were church members, and 44 percent of Campbellford Baptists and 23 percent of Dunnville Baptists belonged to their church, as did 39 percent of Methodists in Campbellford and 37 percent in Dunnville, and 26 percent of Campbellford Presbyterians and 30 percent of Dunnville Presbyterians. Included in these numbers are the few people who identified themselves with a certain denomination on the census but were members of another church. I have listed them according to the denomination that they claimed on the census. So, for example, a Campbellford man who told the census-taker that he was a Presbyterian but was found on the Methodist circuit register would be included among Campbellford's Presbyterian communicants. This solution is not ideal, but not ignoring these individuals means that levels of church membership are not under-represented in a community. Their choice of denomination on the census suggests a long-standing religious identity. For a discussion of fluidity in denominational identities, see Lane, "Tribalism, Proselytism, and Pluralism."

26 The Anglican records for Nelson are incomplete, so levels of involvement in the church were probably higher than those reported here.

27 Of Rossland's Methodist church members, 66.9 percent could be linked to the census, as could 42.0 percent of its Presbyterian communicants. Among Nelson's Methodist church members, 68.9 percent could be linked to the census, as could 55.6 percent of its Presbyterian communicants. These figures are as good as or better than Ontario and Nova Scotia rates (34.7 percent of Dunnville Presbyterians, 50.9 percent of Dunnville Anglicans, 51.6 percent of Campbellford Anglicans, 46.5 percent of Campbellford Baptists, and 44.6 percent of Amherst Baptists could be linked between church records and the census).

28 Father Thayer to Bishop Dontenwill, January 9, 1904, Catholic Archdiocesan Archives, Vancouver (CAAV), Chancery Office fonds, GR 1, box 4, folder 12.

29 Father Gilroy to Bishop Dontenwill, January 23, n.d. (probably 1904), CAAV, Chancery Office fonds, GR 1, box 4, folder 9. For concern about "les sauvages" and his refusal to baptize their babies (perhaps because he assumed that they were not good Christians), see Father Gilroy to Bishop Dontenwill, August 19, n.d. (probably 1903), CAAV, Chancery Office fonds, GR 1, box 4, folder 9.

30 Bob Stewart, "'That's the B.C. Spirit!': Religion and Secularity in Lotus Land," *Canadian Society of Church History Papers* (1983): 22–35. For a discussion of how rootlessness could also lead to involvement in evangelical churches, see Robert Burkinshaw, *Pilgrims in Lotus Land: Conservative Protestantism in British Columbia, 1917–1981* (Montreal and Kingston: McGill-Queen's University Press, 1995).

31 See, for example, Michael Katz, *The People of Hamilton, Canada West: Family and Class in a Mid-nineteenth-century City* (Cambridge, MA: Harvard University Press, 1975); and David Gagan, *Hopeful Travellers: Families, Land, and Social Change in Mid-Victorian Peel County, Canada West* (Toronto: University of Toronto Press, 1981).

32 Muise, "'The Great Transformation.'"

33 There was very limited European settlement in Vernon in earlier decades.

34 DBS, *Census of Canada, 1901,* vol. 1, Tables 13 and 11.

35 Twenty-two percent in Vernon and 24 percent in Revelstoke.

36 The four Ontario and Nova Scotia communities did not have enough immigrants for me to make a comparable study.

37 Some Methodist immigrants may have been members of sub-denominations, such as Wesleyan Methodists and Bible Christians, that no longer existed in Canada due to early Methodist union. George Emery, *The Methodist Church on the Prairies, 1896-1914* (Montreal and Kingston: McGill-Queen's University Press, 2001), 120–23.

38 The category of those who lived with relatives encompasses everyone who lived with any related kin, but most lived with either a spouse or at least one parent.

39 Among Rossland Presbyterians, only 3 percent of lodgers were church members, as compared to 12 percent of those who lived with family.

40 This figure is derived from an analysis of Canadian Families Project, National 5 percent sample of manuscript census Canada, 1901. As noted in Chapter 1, boarders and lodgers were primarily male. Only 4 percent of BC women were lodgers in 1901.

41 Proportions ranged from 30 percent of the population being boarders in Rossland and Nelson to just over 15 percent in Vernon. Among the non-BC towns, Amherst had the highest rate: lodgers made up more than 10 percent of its population.

42 See, for example, R. Cole Harris, "Industry and the Good Life around Idaho Peak," in R. Cole Harris, *The Resettlement of British Columbia: Essays on Colonialism and Geographical Change* (Vancouver: UBC Press, 1997), 194–218. As we have seen, American miners were

particularly likely to be atheists and to be associated with "godless" rough culture. However, even in the most American community of Rossland, only a third of miners were Americans, so the reluctance of miners to become church members cannot simply be associated with a particular ethnic group.

43 Among Nelson miners, 21 were Anglicans and none were communicants, 18 were Methodists and none were church members, and 46 were Presbyterians and 2 were church members. In Rossland, 189 miners were Methodists and 14 were church members, whereas 236 were Presbyterian and 5 were communicants.

44 J.A. Dow to Minister of Rossland United Church, September 23, 1929, Rossland Museum and Archives, Rossland, BC, United Church Records of Rossland United Church Anniversary (United Church Anniversary Records). As a part of anniversary celebrations in Rossland, previous ministers were asked to provide their reminiscences.

45 J. Millen Robinson to Minister of Rossland United Church, n.d. (probably 1929), Rossland Museum and Archives, United Church Anniversary Records. Robinson was a Rossland Presbyterian minister from 1901 to 1903.

46 Jimmy White interview, interviewed by Imbert Orchard, November 6, 1964, BC Archives, Victoria, Imbert Orchard Collection, T0302:002. White lived in Golden and Fort Steele from 1889 onward.

47 Jessie McQueen to Catherine McQueen, July 12, 1888, November 26, 1891, and May 9, 1892, quoted in Barman, *Sojourning Sisters,* 102, 119.

48 Annie McQueen Gordon to Catherine McQueen, December 4, 1898, and November 1, 1898, BC Archives, Anne Gordon fonds, MS-0860. Annie McQueen Gordon to Jane McQueen, February 20, 1899, quoted in Barman, *Sojourning Sisters,* 170.

49 Annie McQueen Gordon to Catherine McQueen, August 14, 1899, cited in Barman, *Sojourning Sisters.*

50 Diary of Phoebe McInnes, cited in Kathryn Carter, ed., *The Small Details of Life: Twenty Diaries by Women in Canada, 1830-1996* (Toronto: University of Toronto Press, 2002), 226–35; Barman, *Sojourning Sisters,* 118–19.

51 See, for example, "Sarah's 1880 Journal," September 26, 1880, and September 12, 1880, cited in Kathryn Bridge, ed., *Henry and Self: The Private Life of Sarah Crease, 1826-1922* (Victoria: Sono Nis Press, 1996), 147, 134.

52 Ibid., October 24, 1880 (emphasis in original), and October 17, 1880, quoted in Bridge, *Henry and Self,* 182, 176.

53 Adele Perry, "'Oh, I'm Just Sick of the Faces of Men': Gender Imbalance, Race, Sexuality and Sociability in Nineteenth Century British Columbia," *BC Studies* 105-6 (Spring-Summer 1995): 27-43.

54 Sex trade workers generally lived in the brothels of red light districts. Since the census identified many of them as seamstresses, forming a clear picture of their church participation (or non-participation) is very difficult.

55 Doug Abrahamson interview, interviewed by Imbert Orchard, January 29, 1965, BC Archives, Imbert Orchard Collection, T0343:0001; Mrs. Lydia (née Morgan Graham) interview, interviewed by Christina Meade, March 21, 1977, Revelstoke Museum, Revelstoke and District Historical Association Aural History Collection (Revelstoke Aural History Collection), number 24, tape 1, track 1 (emphasis in original). This image of "good-hearted" sex trade workers is definitely a stereotype, but it may have been based in some reality in this case.

56 Barman, *Sojourning Sisters,* 200–7. Also see Jessie McQueen to Catherine McQueen, January 15, 1897, Atlantic Canada Virtual Archives, University of New Brunswick, McQueen Family Collection.
57 For references to the activities of the Epworth League and Christian Endeavour, see, for example, *Revelstoke Herald,* January 18, 1901, 4, January 25, 1901, 4; and *Nelson Tribune,* January 8, 1900, 3.
58 *Revelstoke Herald,* February 9, 1901, 4; February 16, 1901, 1 and 4; February 23, 1901, 4; March 27, 1901, 4; *Nelson Tribune,* February 28, 1899, 4; April 27, 1899, 1; June 17, 1899, 1; May 20, 1899, 1. Also see *Rossland Evening World,* March 9, 1901, 5.
59 *Nelson Tribune,* June 17, 1899, 1.
60 Father Thayer to Bishop Dontenwill, December 15, 1903, CAAV, Chancery Office fonds, GR 1, box 4, folder 12.
61 *Nelson Tribune,* January 7, 1899, 4; *Revelstoke Herald,* January 25, 1901, 4. For other information about church organizations in Rossland, see A.M. Sanford, "Reminiscences concerning Rossland," Rossland Museum and Archives, United Church Anniversary Collection. Sanford was Rossland's Methodist minister from 1901 to 1903.
62 George Edwards interview transcript, interviewed by Myrtle Bergren, January 30, 1979, BC Archives, Coal Tyee Society Oral History Collection, T4051:39 (also includes material from Mrs. Edwards, although George is the only one listed in archives entry). For other Coal Tyee female interviewees who had positive things to say about church participation, see Elizabeth Inez Freeman interview transcript and Mima Sheppard interview transcript, interviewed by Bernie McNicholl, May 28, 1979, and August 14, 1979, BC Archives, Coal Tyee Society Oral History Collection, T4051:44–45 and T4051:108.
63 Mrs. Esther Gardom interview, interviewed by Lynn Bueckert, 1983, BC Archives, Behind the Kitchen Door Collection, T4058:18; Mrs. Muriel Lang interview, interviewed by Kathy Chopik, August 4, 1983, BC Archives, Behind the Kitchen Door Collection, T4088:35.
64 Mrs. Muriel Campbell interview, interviewed by Reverend L.G. Seiber, June 17, 1975, BC Archives, United Church History Seekers Collection, T:2409:1. In the same BC Archives collection, also see Miss Lorraine Bolton interview, interviewed by Pearl Willows, June 20, 1975, T2410:1; and Mrs. Violet Schroeder interview, interviewed by Alice Philip, May 17, 1976, T:2659:1.
65 For scholarly discussions of women's church organizations, see, for example, Marilyn Fardig Whiteley, *Canadian Methodist Women, 1766-1925: Marys, Marthas and Mothers in Israel* (Waterloo, ON: Wilfrid Laurier University Press, 2005); Nancy Cott, *The Bonds of Womanhood: "Woman's Sphere" in New England, 1780-1835* (New Haven, CT: Yale University Press, 1997); and Mary Ryan, *Cradle of the Middle Class: The Family in Oneida County, New York, 1790-1865* (Cambridge: Cambridge University Press, 1981).
66 Barman, *Sojourning Sisters,* 200, 242–43.
67 White women were also expected to counter white men's "dangerous" mixed-race liaisons with Indigenous women. See Adele Perry, *On the Edge of Empire: Gender, Race and the Making of British Columbia, 1849-1871* (Toronto: University of Toronto Press, 2001).
68 Annie McQueen Gordon to Catherine McQueen, January 4, 1898, BC Archives, Anne Gordon fonds, MS-0860.
69 Father Thayer to Bishop Dontenwill, December 15, 1903, CAAV, Chancery Office fonds, GR 1, box 4, folder 12.
70 Mrs. Lydia Graham interview, interviewed by Christine Meade, March 21, 1977, BC Archives, Revelstoke Aural History Collection, number 24, tape 1, track 1.

71 Doug Abrahamson interview, interviewed by Imbert Orchard, January 29 1965, BC Archives, Imbert Orchard Collection, T0343.

72 See Mariana Valverde, "'When the Mother of the Race Is Free': Race, Reproduction and Sexuality in First-Wave Feminism," in *Gender Conflicts: New Essays in Women's History*, ed. Franca Iacovetta and Mariana Valverde (Toronto: University of Toronto Press, 1992); 3–26; and Adele Perry, "'Fair Ones of a Purer Caste': White Women and Colonialism in Nineteenth-Century British Columbia," *Feminist Studies* 23, 3 (Fall 1997): 501–29.

73 Barman, *Sojourning Sisters*. Also see Perry, "'Oh, I'm Just Sick of the Faces of Men.'"

74 See, for example, Jan Hare and Jean Barman, *Good Intentions Gone Awry: Emma Crosby and the Methodist Mission on the Northwest Coast* (Vancouver: UBC Press, 2006); Mary Ellen Kelm, ed., *The Letters of Margaret Butcher: Missionary-Imperialism on the North Pacific Coast* (University of Calgary Press, 2007); Myra Rutherdale, *Women and the White Man's God: Gender and Race in the Canadian Mission Field* (Vancouver: UBC Press, 2002). For racist attitudes towards Indigenous peoples in BC, also see John Lutz, *Makúk: A New History of Aboriginal-White Relations* (Vancouver: UBC Press, 2008).

75 Mrs. Louise M. Iverson interview, interviewed by Alan William Specht, January 17, 1984, BC Archives, BC Pioneer Series, T4119:1. For a discussion of similar white settler women's attitudes to Indigenous peoples on the Prairies see Sheila McManus, "Their Own Country: Race, Gender, Landscape, and Colonization around the Forty-Ninth Parallel, 1862-1900" in Sterling Evans, ed, *The Borderlands of the American and Canadian Wests: Essays on Regional History of the Forty-ninth Parallel* (University of Nebraska Press, 2006) and Sarah Carter, "Categories and Terrains of Exclusion: Constructing the 'Indian Woman' in the Early Settlement Era in Western Canada," *Great Plains Quarterly* 13 (Summer 1993), 147-161.

76 Lorraine Brown, "Domestic Service in British Columbia, 1850-1914" (master's thesis, Department of History, University of Victoria, 2007), Chapter 4; Clayton, "Local Connections," 69–70; Jo Fraser Jones, ed., *Hobnobbing with a Countess and Other Okanagan Adventures: The Diaries of Alice Barrett Parke, 1891-1900* (Vancouver: UBC Press, 2001), 194 (diary entry February 2, 1897).

77 Peter Ward, "The Oriental Immigrant and Canada's Protestant Clergy, 1858-1925," *BC Studies* 22 (1974): 40–55; Patricia Roy, "Anglicans and Asians in British Columbia: An Ambiguous Relationship" (unpublished paper, n.d.). Also see Marilyn F. Whiteley, "'Allee Samee Melican Lady': Imperialism and Negotiation at the Chinese Rescue Home (Women Missionary Societies Set Up the Chinese Rescue Home to Save Chinese Women from Prostitution)," *Resources for Feminist Research* 22, 3–4 (1992-93): 45-50; Shelly Ikebuchi, "Marriage, Morals and Men: Re/defining Victoria's Chinese Rescue Home," *BC Studies* 177 (Spring 2013): 65–84; and further discussion in Chapter 6.

78 Reverend Yee Jing Chow interview, interviewed by Theresa Low, June 1980, BC Archives, Chinese Historical Wrongs Legacy Initiative Collection, T3715, translated for author by Liang Han.

79 Johnny Robertson interview transcript, interviewed by Dale Lovick, August 13, 1979, BC Archives, Coal Tyee Society Oral History Collection, T4051:106; Mrs. Doris Smith interview transcript, interviewed by Imbert Orchard, November 10, 1964, BC Archives, Revelstoke Oral Histories. For a description of white children watching Chinese funerals, see Mrs. Lydia Graham interview transcript, interviewed by Christina Meade, March 21, 1977, BC Archives, Revelstoke Oral Histories.

80 The white men may have preferred to worship separately from Indigenous peoples, but in such cases it is also true that missionaries feared the moral contagion of white men's rough

culture on Indigenous peoples. "Work of the Methodist Mission Boat 'Udal,'" 1909, in Home Mission Records of the B.C. Conference of the Methodist Church, United Church Archives of BC, Vancouver. Also see Mawani, *Colonial Proximities.*

81 For a discussion of large camp meetings in the Lower Mainland that included both Europeans and Indigenous people in the 1870s and 1880s, see Christine Shaw, "'Sitting at the Feet of Jesus, Clothed and in Their Right Mind': The Convergence of Religion, Culture, and Race in Missionary Discourse in Halkomelem Territory, Southern Coastal British Columbia, 1850–1900" (master's thesis, University of Victoria, 2001), 67–68.

82 For a similar perspective, see Perry, "'Oh, I'm Just Sick of the Faces of Men.'"

83 Marks, *Revivals and Roller Rinks,* Chapter 2.

84 The definition of class is an ever-thorny problem, one that the 1901 census tends to complicate, as it includes not just occupational data but also data that identify people as employers, employees, or working "on their own account." In this chapter, "middle class" refers to white-collar individuals (manufacturers, merchants, professionals, supervisors, clerks) who are either employers, employees, or working on their own account, and blue-collar individuals (both skilled and semi-skilled) who are employers. Blue-collar individuals (including skilled and semi-skilled workers as well as labourers and servants) who are employees or working on their own account are defined as working class.

85 I am grateful to Suzanne Morton and Hannah Lane for these insights.

86 See Michael Boudreau, "'There Is ... No Pernicious Dualism between Sacred and Secular': Nova Scotia Baptists and the Social Gospel, 1880–1914," *Nova Scotia Historical Review* 16, 1 (1996): 109–31.

87 R.F. Stillman to Minister of Rossland United Church, September 17, 1929, Rossland Museum and Archives, United Church Anniversary Collection. For further discussion of the strike, see Mouat, *Roaring Days,* Chapter 5.

88 Clayton, "Local Connections," 58.

89 C.W. Halliday, *The Valley of Youth* (Caldwell, ID: Caxton Printers, 1948), 311. For another comment about how church attendance could secure a good meal, see David Mitchell and Dennis Duffy, eds., *Bright Sunshine and a Brand New Country: Reflections on the Okanagan Valley, 1890–1914,* Sound Heritage Series 7, 3 (Victoria: Province of British Columbia, 1979), 37.

90 Quoted in Mitchell and Duffy, *Bright Sunshine,* 43; Paddy Acland interview, interviewed by Imbert Orchard, December 12, 1964, BC Archives, Imbert Orchard Collection, T1085:0003.

91 Margaret Stewart interview, interviewed by Imbert Orchard, February 7, 1963, BC Archives, Imbert Orchard Collection, T0326:0002. Paul Voisey, *Vulcan: The Making of a Prairie Community* (Toronto: University of Toronto Press, 1988). Some scholars of secularization have suggested that agricultural districts became secularized later than urban areas that included larger numbers of wage earners. Although this might be relevant to British Columbia, other scholars dispute this analysis. For an outline of the debate, see Hugh McLeod, *Piety and Poverty: Working-Class Religion in Berlin, London and New York, 1870-1914* (New York: Holmes and Meier, 1996), xx-xxiii.

92 In Vernon, 24.6 percent of residents were born in "Britain or the Empire," whereas 58.0 percent were native to Canada. Only 6.3 percent were born in the United States. Clayton, "Local Connections," 8.

93 For example, 17.0 percent of British-born Rosslanders over the age of twelve belonged to a church, as compared to 5.0 percent of those born in the United States. In Nelson, 12.0 percent of the British-born and 6.8 percent of Americans were church members, whereas

in Revelstoke 26.8 percent of the British-born and 17.4 percent of Americans were.

94 George Edwards interview transcript, interviewed by Myrtle Bergren, June 30, 1979, BC Archives, Coal Tyee Society Oral History Collection, T4051:39.

95 In Rossland, Americans made up more than a quarter of the population and over 14 percent in Nelson.

96 George V. Ferguson, "Queen of the Kootenays," *Beaver* 19 (March 1960).

97 *Reflector* (Amherst Baptist Church), November 1899, 6–7.

98 W.M. Scott to Minister of Rossland United Church, October 1, 1929, Rossland Museum and Archives, United Church Anniversary Collection. For a discussion of respectability among railway workers in Ontario, see Mark Rosenfeld, "'She Was a Hard Life': Work, Family, Community, Politics and Ideology in the Railway Ward of a Central Ontario Town, 1900–1960" (PhD diss., York University, 1990).

99 This pattern was also true of Vernon, but the numbers there were very small.

100 Stuart Barnard suggests that middle-class men were far more attracted than the working class to the 1909 revivals in the Kootenays because involvement was an important way of defining their faith, their respectability, and their difference from the working class. Stuart Barnard, "The Kootenay Revival Campaign of 1909" (master's thesis, University of Calgary, 2010).

101 For this pattern in the Maritimes, see Lane, "Tribalism, Proselytism, and Pluralism"; for Ontario, see Marks, *Revivals and Roller Rinks.*

102 Jessie Olding to Jessie McQueen, April 28, 1890, quoted in Barman, *Sojourning Sisters,* 107; Annie McQueen Gordon to Catherine McQueen, November 1889, quoted in Barman, *Sojourning Sisters,* 131.

103 Bridge, *Henry and Self.*

104 Quoted in Mitchell and Duffy, *Bright Sunshine,* 8.

105 Lillian Dixon interview transcript, interviewed by Lynne Bowen, November 22, 1984, BC Archives, Coal Tyee Society Oral History Collection, T4343:4.

106 Tom Johnston interview transcript, interviewed by Myrtle Bergren, June 13, 1979, BC Archives, Coal Tyee Society Oral History Collection, T4051:65–66. John Robson, who became BC premier in the late nineteenth century, was another actively Christian British Columbian man. See Ivan E. Antak, "John Robson and His Faith: Church and State in Late Nineteenth-Century British Columbia" (master's thesis, Simon Fraser University, 2012).

Chapter 5

1 Hugh McLeod, *Piety and Poverty: Working-Class Religion in Berlin, London and New York, 1870-1914* (New York: Holmes and Meier 1996), xx-xxiii.

2 See Ramsay Cook, *The Regenerators: Social Criticism in Late Victorian English Canada* (Toronto: University of Toronto Press, 1985); and David Marshall, *Secularizing the Faith: Canadian Protestant Clergy and the Crisis of Belief, 1850-1940* (Toronto: University of Toronto Press, 1992). Nancy Christie and Michael Gauvreau, *A Full-Orbed Christianity: The Protestant Churches and Social Welfare in Canada, 1900-1940* (Montreal and Kingston: McGill-Queen's University Press, 1996), does provide some discussion of secularization in small Prairie communities.

3 Susan Neylan, "Encountering Spirits: Evangelical and Holiness Revivals in Victoria, B.C., and the 'Colonial Project,'" *Histoire sociale* 36, 71 (2003): 175–204, examines some issues regarding religion in Victoria in the 1880s and early 1890s.

4 A charge generally included only one church under Methodist governance but in some contexts could include more than one.

5 Quadrennial Report of Home Missions in the British Columbia Conference of the Methodist Church to June 20, 1910, by J.W. White, to Reverend James Allen, General Secretary, Toronto, United Church of Canada Archives, Toronto.

6 Kathryn Bridge, "Being Young in the Country: Settler Children and Childhood in British Columbia and Alberta, 1860-1925" (PhD diss., University of Victoria, 2012), 94–102; Diary of Kathleen O'Reilly, March 7, 1880, BC Archives, quoted in ibid., 96.

7 Duke Ackerman interview transcript, interviewed by Rich Mole, December 12, 1979, BC Archives, Victoria, Christmas in British Columbia Collection, tape 3582:1; Lorraine Bolton interview transcript, interviewed by Pearl Willows, June 20, 1975, BC Archives, United Church History Seekers Collection, tape 2410:1.

8 See Kevin Kee, *Revivalists: Marketing the Gospel in English Canada, 1884-1957* (Montreal and Kingston: McGill-Queen's University Press, 2006), Chapter 1; and Lynne Marks, *Revivals and Roller Rinks: Religion, Leisure, and Identity in Late-Nineteenth-Century Small-Town Ontario* (Toronto: University of Toronto Press, 1996), Chapter 8.

9 *Victoria Colonist,* November 24, 1891, 1. Also see *Victoria Colonist,* December 1, 1891, 1, and December 16, 1891, 1.

10 *Victoria Colonist,* October 30, 1907, 3.

11 *Victoria Colonist,* November 6, 1907, 7. Also see *Victoria Colonist,* November 9, 1907, 2.

12 Victoria Colonist, August 8, 1907, 7. Also see Marks, *Revivals and Roller Rinks,* 190; and Kee, *Revivalists.*

13 See, for example, *Victoria Colonist,* November 5, 1907, 3; November 9, 1907, 2; and November 22, 1907, 7.

14 Kee, *Revivalists,* 14, 46.

15 Karen Dubinsky, *Improper Advances: Rape and Heterosexual Conflict in Ontario, 1880-1929* (Chicago: University of Chicago Press, 1993), 143–62.

16 *Victoria Times,* November 29, 1901, 2.

17 *Victoria Times,* May 11, 1900, 4.

18 For other Christian critiques of the moral failings of Victoria, in regard to gambling, prostitution, and the liquor trade and how they ruined young white men, see Ivan E. Antak, "John Robson and His Faith: Church and State in Late Nineteenth-Century British Columbia" (master's thesis, Simon Fraser University, 2012), 85-90.

19 *Victoria Times,* May 11, 1900, 4, and December 18, 1900, 4. For attacks on local religious reformers for making Vancouver look bad, see, for example, *Vancouver Province,* December 18, 1900, 2.

20 *Vancouver Province,* May 23, 1899, 4.

21 For comments about the lack of Sabbath observance, see, for example, *Western Methodist Recorder,* August 1900, 8, May 1906, 9; and *Daily World Vancouver,* May 21, 1900, 5, May 22, 1900, 2. For efforts among Protestant Sabbatarians to bring in or enforce laws about Sabbath observance, see, for example, *Victoria Times,* October 4, 1900, 7; and *Vancouver Province,* August 21, 1902, 9.

22 Paul Laverdure, *Sunday in Canada: The Rise and Fall of the Lord's Day* (Yorkton, SK: Gravelbooks, 2004), 45.

23 Ibid., 79. For complaints from certain BC mayors at a meeting of municipalities that the Lord's Day Act was not being enforced as it was in all other provinces, see *Victoria Colonist,* February 28, 1908, 1.

24 Robson had even less success with proposed temperance legislation in the 1880s, although he was able to get limited temperance legislation passed in 1891. Antak, "John Robson and His Faith," 84–85, 71–78.
25 *Vancouver Province,* September 5, 1899, 6. Also see *Vancouver Province,* October 15, 1900, 6.
26 Christopher Armstrong and H.V. Nelles, *The Revenge of the Methodist Bicycle Company: Sunday Streetcars and Municipal Reform in Toronto, 1888-1897* (Toronto: Peter Martin, 1977).
27 *Vancouver Province,* October 17, 1900, 6. Also see *Vancouver Province,* December 20, 1900, 4.
28 Laverdure, *Sunday in Canada,* 60, 66-67. See Chapter 6 for further discussion of the impact of racialized non-Christians on Christian hegemony in British Columbia.
29 See, for example, Alan Hunt, "Measuring Morals: The Beginnings of the Social Survey Movement in Canada, 1913-1917," *Histoire sociale* 35, 69 (2002): 171–94. For a discussion of the Presbyterian and Methodist Churches and moral reform, see Mariana Valverde, *The Age of Light, Soap and Water: Moral Reform in English Canada, 1885-1925* (Toronto: McClelland and Stewart, 1991).
30 The discussion of labour, health, and social service was also deeply imbued with moralism. For example, the authors insisted that the unemployed should not receive relief unless they performed some labour in return.
31 Board of Temperance and Moral Reform of the Methodist Church, and the Board of Social Service and Evangelism of the Presbyterian Church, *Vancouver, British Columbia: The Report of a Brief Investigation of Social Conditions in the City Which Indicate the Need of an Intensive Social Survey, the Lines of Which Are Herein Suggested* (Vancouver, 1913), 31, 12.
32 Lyn Gough, *As Wise as Serpents: Five Women and an Organization That Changed British Columbia, 1883–1939* (Victoria: Swan Lake, 1988).
33 Patricia E. Roy, *Boundless Optimism: Richard McBride's British Columbia* (Vancouver: UBC Press, 2012), 168, 244, 20, and 137. During the First World War, as a result of major public pressure, McBride did bring in the Prohibition plebiscite, but critics argued that his heart was not in it. Ibid., 290–91.
34 Board of Temperance, *Vancouver, British Columbia: The Report of a Brief Investigation,* 25, 26; Jean Barman, *The West beyond the West: A History of British Columbia,* 3rd ed. (Toronto: University of Toronto Press, 2007), 225–26; Laverdure, *Sunday in Canada.*
35 *Victoria Colonist,* December 19, 1909, 2.
36 The minister who argued that attendance numbers were underestimated asserted that the newspaper had ignored some smaller and suburban churches. (It had omitted the local synagogue as well, though this was not mentioned.) The minister also pointed out that Sunday School figures had not been included. The critic who argued that attendance numbers were overestimated stated that "average attendance" ignored the double counting that could occur when people attended both morning and evening Sunday services. Neither noted that 400 of the 5,690 people who were listed as church attenders actually went to a local socialist meeting instead. *Victoria Colonist,* January 2, 1910, 2 and 8.
37 *Victoria Colonist,* December 19, 1909, 3.
38 Laurie Maffly-Kipp, *Religion and Society in Frontier California* (New Haven, CT: Yale University Press, 1994).
39 *Victoria Colonist,* December 19, 1909, 3 and 7.
40 *Western Methodist Recorder,* January 1906, 4.
41 *Victoria Colonist,* February 28, 1908, 7.
42 *Victoria Colonist,* December 19, 1909, 3.

43 Andrew Reid, "Not So Secret Societies: Fraternities and Masculine Identity in Victorian Victoria, 1860-1890" (major research paper, Department of History, University of Victoria, 2012), 32–34. Also see Mark Carnes, *Secret Ritual and Manhood in Victorian America* (New Haven, CT: Yale University Press, 1989); and Marks, *Revivals and Roller Rinks*, 113–14.

44 For example, Anglicans worried about the large numbers of non-practising Anglicans. After the publication of the 1891 census, Anglican leaders noted that it counted "over 10,000 Church people in the diocese of New Westminster, but our returns account for only 5749 ... In the city of Vancouver 3,754 returned themselves as members of the Church of England, while the returns from the 3 Parishes in Vancouver account for only 2,020 altogether ... Our large numerical preponderance in the Province loses much of its virtue if it is found, upon investigation, to dwindle away into a merely nominal one." Diocese of New Westminster, *Monthly Record*, March-April 1893, 5, Anglican Provincial Synod of British Columbia Archives, Vancouver, Anglican Provincial Synod of British Columbia and Yukon fonds.

45 For two excellent studies on this subject, see Robert Orsi, *The Madonna of 115th Street: Faith and Community in Italian Harlem, 1880-1950* (New Haven, CT: Yale University Press, 1985); and Brian Clarke, *Piety and Nationalism: Lay Voluntary Associations and the Creation of an Irish-Catholic Community in Toronto, 1850-1895* (Montreal and Kingston: McGill-Queen's University Press, 1993).

46 Vincent J. McNally, *The Lord's Distant Vineyard: A History of the Oblates and the Catholic Community in British Columbia* (Edmonton: University of Alberta Press, 2000), 191–92.

47 "The Most Sacred of Hearts," *B.C. Catholic*, December 22, 2003, 12; McNally, *The Lord's Distant Vineyard*, 263.

48 In 1901, 25.1 percent of Vancouver Catholics were of English or Scottish descent (or "race"), 28.0 percent were of Irish descent, 17.0 percent were of French descent, and 8.5 were of Italian descent (a proportion that was to increase over the next decade). In 1901, 28.1 percent of Victoria Catholics were of English or Scottish descent, 36.9 percent were of Irish descent, 11.5 percent were of French descent, and 8.5 were of German descent. Canadian Families Project, Vancouver and Victoria 100 percent databases, from 1901 manuscript census, Canada.

49 Board of Temperance, *Vancouver, British Columbia: The Report of a Brief Investigation*, 8; Bruce Shelvey and June Bull, eds., *The Archival Directory of Religious Organizations in the Greater Victoria Region* (Victoria: Centre for Studies in Religion and Society and the Department of History, University of Victoria, 1998). There were also Protestant missions to Chinese and Japanese immigrants, discussed in Chapter 6.

50 I chose to compare Victoria and Vancouver with London and Hamilton not because they had the highest church involvement figures, but because they seemed typical of Ontario urban patterns. Kingston and Ottawa had similarly high figures.

51 The figures for downtown Victoria churches are as follows: of the 127 St. Andrew's Presbyterian communicants who could be linked with the census, 75 were middle class, 51 were working class, and one was unknown. Of the 100 First Presbyterian members, 42 were middle class and 58 were working class. Of the 214 Metropolitan Methodist members, 95 were middle class, 113 were working class, and 6 were other or unknown. First Presbyterian and St. Andrew's Presbyterian Churches, Communion rolls, Metropolitan Methodist Church, circuit register; records of First Presbyterian and Metropolitan Methodist held by First Metropolitan United Church, Victoria, and St. Andrew's records held by St. Andrew's

Presbyterian Church, Victoria; membership records linked to Canadian Families Project, Victoria 100 percent database 1901 manuscript census, Canada.

52 Figures for these churches are as follows: of the sixteen St. Aidan's Presbyterian members who could be linked with the census, two were middle class, six were working class, and eight were other or unknown. Among the twenty-two members of Victoria West Methodist Church, four were middle class and eighteen were working class. Of the thirty-seven James Bay Methodist Church members, thirteen were middle class and twenty-four were working class. Saint Aidan's membership records, James Bay Methodist circuit register, Victoria West Methodist circuit register, all held in United Church of Canada, British Columbia Conference Archives, Vancouver (UC Archives, BC); membership records linked to Canadian Families Project, Victoria 100 percent database 1901 manuscript census, Canada.

53 Forty members of Mount Pleasant Presbyterian were from working-class families, seventeen from families where the father was a clerk, and five where the father was a merchant or professional. Mount Pleasant Presbyterian (later St. Giles United) Church communion roll, UC Archives, BC; church membership records linked with Canadian Families Project, Vancouver 100 percent database 1901 manuscript census, Canada.

54 In Mount Pleasant Church, Vancouver, 61 percent of the congregation that could be linked to the census were female, and 65 percent of working-class members were female. Mount Pleasant Presbyterian Church communion roll, UC Archives, BC; church membership records linked to Canadian Families Project, Vancouver 100 percent database 1901 manuscript census, Canada.

55 The proportion of married men of all men involved in the Victoria churches studied ranged from 77 percent of all male church members in Victoria's First Presbyterian Church to 66 percent in Victoria West Methodist Church.

56 Diary of Bishop Hills, March 4, 1891, Victoria, Anglican Synod of the Diocese of British Columbia and Yukon Archives, Vancouver, Bishop George Hills sous-fonds, Anglican Synod of the Diocese of British Columbia fonds.

57 Marks, *Revivals and Roller Rinks,* Chapter 1. Also see Robert McDonald, *Making Vancouver: Class, Status, and Social Boundaries, 1863-1913* (Vancouver: UBC Press, 1996), for a discussion of the importance of respectability to married middle- and working-class men in Vancouver.

58 McDonald, *Making Vancouver,* Chapter 7.

59 For a discussion of low levels of church involvement among single men, see Marks, *Revivals and Roller Rinks,* Chapter 1.

60 In the larger Presbyterian and Methodist churches, over 80 percent of members had immigrated to Canada before 1890. First Presbyterian and St. Andrew's Presbyterian Churches, Communion rolls, Metropolitan Methodist Church, circuit register; records of First Presbyterian and Metropolitan Methodist held by First Metropolitan United Church, Victoria, and St. Andrew's records held by St. Andrew's Presbyterian Church, Victoria; membership records linked to Canadian Families Project, Victoria 100 percent database 1901 manuscript census, Canada.

61 In Victoria in 1901, over 11 percent of the population were boarders, but fewer than 5 percent of church members were boarders. This analysis includes the records of First Presbyterian and St. Andrew's Presbyterian Churches, Communion rolls, Metropolitan Methodist Church, circuit register; records of First Presbyterian and Metropolitan Methodist held by First Metropolitan United Church, Victoria, and St. Andrew's records held by St. Andrew's Presbyterian Church, Victoria; Saint Aidan's membership records,

James Bay Methodist circuit register, Victoria West Methodist circuit register, all held in UC Archives, BC; membership records linked to Canadian Families Project, Victoria 100 percent database 1901 manuscript census, Canada.

62 In Yale and Cariboo, 2.4 percent of the population defined themselves as atheists/agnostics or as having no religion. Dominion Bureau of Statistics, *Census of Canada, 1901* (Ottawa: Census Office, 1902), vol. 1, Table 8, and vol. 4, Table 19.

63 An initial analysis of the 1901 manuscript census for Victoria suggested that 0.9 percent of the population were atheists/agnostics or of no religion. However, as mentioned in the Introduction, a closer look revealed that one census-taker, a Mr. Phipps, enumerated fifty-four of the fifty-nine Chinese residents in his district as agnostics. This grossly overestimated the proportion of Chinese people who defined themselves as agnostics and was a reflection of the racism and Christian-centric nature of wider BC society, and of Phipps himself. I arrived at the 0.6 percent figure for unbelievers by subtracting fifty of the fifty-four Chinese agnostics whom Phipps enumerated from the total irreligious people in Victoria. This step seems reasonable, as less than 10 percent of Chinese people defined themselves as irreligious in the 1901 BC census. Even Victoria's small minority of irreligious was three times as large as the 0.2 percent of the Toronto population, in the "city of churches," that identified themselves as such.

64 In Vancouver, 76 percent of the 364 irreligious were male, and 78 percent of Victoria's 191 irreligious were male. Canadian Families Project (CFP), Database of atheists/agnostics and those of no religion in BC, 1901 manuscript census.

65 In Vancouver, seventeen middle-class irreligious individuals (agnostics and those of no religion) were married and nine were single. In Victoria, eleven were married and four were single. These figures include only those whose occupations are known. CFP, Database of atheists/agnostics and those of no religion in BC, 1901 manuscript census.

66 For a discussion of middle-class freethought see Cook, *The Regenerators*. For socialism and atheism, see Ian McKay, *Reasoning Otherwise: Leftists and the People's Enlightenment in Canada, 1890-1920* (Toronto: Between the Lines, 2008). At the same time, two of Vancouver's most prominent socialists, J.H. McVety and Parmeter Pettipiece, identified with a mainstream Christian denomination on the 1911 census. This does not mean that they were churchgoers, and they certainly attacked the churches and Christianity in print, but where the census was concerned, they did not go so far as to cite an irreligious identity.

67 Thirty-four working-class irreligious Vancouverites were married and 146 were single. In Victoria, 13 were married and 26 were single. These figures include only those whose occupations are known. CFP, Database of atheists/agnostics and those of no religion in BC, 1901 manuscript census. See Chapter 4 for comparable figures for the Kootenays.

68 Recall from Chapter 1 that in Slocan, which had the highest proportion of the irreligious in the "godless" Kootenays, over 7 percent of the population defined themselves as irreligious.

69 As noted in Chapter 1, 0.16 percent of the total population of Canada defined themselves as atheists or as having no religion in 1901.

70 These data are based on an analysis of the proportion of the irreligious in Vancouver polls that Ian Buck identified as having a particularly high proportion of working-class inhabitants in 1901. Ian Buck, "The Integration Index: Using GIS to Interpret the Residential Structure of Vancouver, British Columbia" (master's thesis, University of Victoria, 2001), 34. In Poll 15, which lay beside Gastown, 30.0 percent of residents were listed as boarders,

roomers, or lodgers, and 3.0 percent defined themselves as irreligious. In nearby Poll 18, 28.0 percent of the population were boarders or lodgers, and 3.5 percent were irreligious; 23.0 percent of Poll 23's population were boarders or lodgers, and 4.5 percent were irreligious.

71 Patrick Dunae, "Sex, Charades, and Census Records: Locating Female Sex Trade Workers in a Victorian City," *Histoire sociale* 42, 84 (2009): 267-97; Patrick Dunae, "Geographies of Sexual Commerce and the Production of Prostitutional Space: Victoria, British Columbia, 1860-1914," *Journal of the Canadian Historical Association* 19, 1 (2008): 115–42.

72 One other freethinking woman should perhaps be included in Dunae's list of sex trade workers. Freethinker Cora Tugwell called herself a teacher and lived alone with her daughter, a seamstress, on Herald Street, just a few doors down from Lockwood and Early.

73 The majority of sex trade workers in Dunae's sample were American.

74 Annual report of the Turner Institute, Central Methodist Church, Vancouver, 1917, 18, UC Archives, BC (emphasis in original).

75 *Vancouver Province*, June 14, 1900, 2; *Western Methodist Recorder*, December 1899, 19.

76 Minutes of a meeting of the Cabinet held in the Dominion Hotel on 20 November, 1908, enclosure in the minutes of the Vancouver General Ministerial Association, November 23, 1908, UC Archives, BC, General Ministerial Association fonds. The impetus for this idea appears to have begun the year before, with the Central City Mission Society, founded in 1907.

77 Second annual report of the Central City Mission, July 1908 to July 1910, Agency of the Evangelical Churches of the City, 1910, Vancouver, BC, 17, 12, 20, UC Archives, BC. Also see Third annual report, Central City Mission, 1911, Vancouver, UC Archives, BC.

78 Third annual report, Central City Mission, 1911, Vancouver, BC, 11–12, UC Archives, BC. The report claimed that three hundred street meetings had been held during the previous year.

79 For a discussion of the early years of the Salvation Army in Victoria, see Neylan, "Encountering Spirits."

80 Marks, *Revivals and Roller Rinks*, Chapters 6 and 7.

81 See, for example, R.G. Moyles, *The Blood and Fire in Canada: A History of the Salvation Army in the Dominion, 1882-1976* (Toronto: Peter Martin, 1977).

82 Board of Temperance, *Vancouver, British Columbia: The Report of a Brief Investigation*, 28.

83 Moyles, *The Blood and Fire*, 66. Also see Bonnie Sawyer, "A Critical History of Social Work, the Canadian Salvation Army, and Female Sexual 'Deviance' in Canada, 1886-1940" (master's thesis, University of Victoria, 2014).

84 This also seems to have been the case on the Prairies. See Ashley Forseille, "Reading Love between the Lines: Religion, Courtship and Correspondence in the Salvation Army, 1906-1910" (master's thesis, University of Victoria, 2012). The Salvation Army also had considerable success in winning Indigenous converts in certain parts of British Columbia. Neylan, "Encountering Spirits."

85 Most people who joined the Salvation Army during this period were the more stable and respectable members of the working class, and most were married. In Vancouver in 1901, 93 percent of Salvationists who listed occupations were working class, as were 89 percent in 1911. They included many labourers but also a significant number of skilled workers. In 1911, in both Vancouver and Victoria less than 15 percent of Salvationists were lodgers or boarders. Most lived with a spouse or other family members. Although the army targeted "down and out" single men and women, in both its social service work and conversion

efforts, there was a gulf between its members and those whom they tried to reform and convert.

86 On the census, Vancouverites who described themselves as having no religion or as being agnostics greatly outnumbered Salvationists. In 1901, 0.41 percent of Vancouverites said they were Salvationists, as compared to the 1.7 percent who defined themselves as atheists or of no religion.

87 *Vancouver Rationalist* 1, 1 (October 1914): 3, University of Manitoba Library; *Vancouver Sun,* May 9, 1914.

88 *Vancouver Province,* August 17, 1914, October 15, 1914. By 1915, both Spalding and Atkinson were listed as national lecturers with the Rationalist Association of North America.

89 Rationalist Association of North America, *Ten Rationalist Lectures at the Panama-Pacific Congress* (Chicago: Rationalist Association, 1915), 4.

90 *Vancouver Rationalist* 1, 1 (October 1914): 6.

91 Several of the associations were on the west coast (in Seattle, Portland, Los Angeles, and San Francisco), but there were others farther east – in Michigan, Illinois, and New York. There also appear to have been eighty-six associations affiliated through the Bohemian Freethought Association. Rationalist Association of North America, *Ten Rationalist Lectures,* 6–7. Although a secularist journal had been published out of Toronto from the 1880s to 1911, there did not appear to be a Toronto branch of this association.

92 For an extended discussion of Gauvin, see Elliot Hanowski, "A Godless Dominion: Unbelief and Religious Controversy in Interwar Canada" (PhD diss., Queen's University, 2015).

93 There was also a significant Vancouver free speech fight in 1912, but it does not appear to have involved the Salvation Army.

94 Mark Leier, *Where the Fraser River Flows: The Industrial Workers of the World in British Columbia* (Vancouver: New Star Books, 1990).

95 Ibid., 66. *Where the Fraser River Flows* includes a detailed discussion of the outcome of the free speech fights in Vancouver and Victoria.

96 *Vancouver Province,* May 28, 1909, 6.

97 Leier, *Where the Fraser River Flows,* 73.

98 *Victoria Times,* July 26, 1911, 9. Also see *Victoria Times,* July 26, 1911, 2.

99 *Vancouver Province,* May 27, 1909, 24.

100 James William Opp, *The Lord for the Body: Religion, Medicine, and Protestant Faith Healing in Canada, 1880-1930* (Montreal and Kingston: McGill-Queen's University Press, 2005), 105–20.

101 *Vancouver Province,* May 13, 1899, 7.

102 *Vancouver Province,* October 26, 1900, 8.

103 *Vancouver Province,* October 29, 1900, 5.

104 See McDonald, *Making Vancouver,* 193–96; and Reid, "Not So Secret Societies."

105 *Vancouver Province,* October 26, 1900, 4, October 29, 1900, 2.

106 *Victoria Times,* August 22, 1900, 5.

Chapter 6

1 See Introduction and Chapter 5.

2 More precisely, Jews comprised 0.7 percent of Vancouver's population in 1901 and 0.8 percent in 1911 (190 people and 905 respectively). They composed 0.6 percent of Victoria's population in 1901 and 0.5 percent in 1911 (141 and 140 people respectively). Canadian

Families Project (CFP), Victoria and Vancouver 100 percent databases 1901 manuscript census, Canada; Canada Century Research Infrastructure Project (CCRI), Victoria and Vancouver 100 percent databases 1911 manuscript census, Canada.

3 For further discussion of the BC Jewish community, see Cyril E. Leonoff, "The Rise of Jewish Life and Religion in British Columbia, 1858-1948," *Scribe: Journal of the Jewish Historical Society of British Columbia* 28 (2008): 1–204; Sarah H. Tobe, "Lured North of the 49th: Jewish Colonial Roots: Victoria, Vancouver Island, Canada," *Western States Jewish History Association* 46 (Winter-Spring 2014 special issue); and Lynne Marks, "'Not Being Religious Didn't Take Away from Their Jewishness': The Complexities of Lived Religion among Late 19th and Early 20th Century B.C. Jews," *BC Studies* 181 (Spring 2014): 63–82.

4 *Victoria Times,* October 4, 1900, 5. Also see *Victoria Times,* September 5, 1904, 6; *Victoria Colonist,* September 9, 1896, 5; and *Victoria Colonist,* March 15, 1908, 6.

5 Andrew Reid, "Not So Secret Societies: Fraternities and Masculine Identity in Victorian Victoria, 1860-1890" (major research paper, Department of History, University of Victoria, 2012), 32–34. See Tobe, "Lured North of the 49th," for further discussion of Jewish acceptance and integration in Victoria in this period.

6 Josephine Lancaster (Davis) and Daisy Minchin (née Salmon) interview, interviewed by Cyril Leonoff, July 23, 1972, BC Archives, Victoria, Jewish Historical Society of BC Oral History Collection (JHSBC Collection), T3883:75; Gertrude Weinrobe and Violet Franklin interview, interviewed by Clare Auerbach and Cyril Leonoff, July 25, 1972, BC Archives, JHSBC Collection, T3883:11.

7 Rena Robinson Phillips interview, interviewed by Cyril Leonoff, 1983, Jewish Museum and Archives of BC (JMABC), Vancouver, JHSBC Collection; Gloria Harris interview, interviewed by Carole Itter and Daphne Marlatt, 1977, BC Archives, Strathcona Project, T2800:0001; Anne and Jack Black interview, interviewed by Irene Dodek and Sally Tobe, October 24, 1989, BC Archives, JHSBC Collection, T4384:5-side 1. Also see Lillooet Nordlinger McDonnell, "In the Company of Gentiles: Exploring the History of Integrated Jews in British Columbia, 1858-1971" (PhD diss., University of Ottawa, 2011), 86.

8 Gerald Tulchinsky, *Taking Root: The Origins of the Canadian Jewish Community* (Toronto: Lester, 1992); Gerald Tulchinsky, *Branching Out: The Transformation of the Canadian Jewish Community* (Toronto: Stoddart, 1998).

9 Anti-Semitism increased throughout Canada during the 1920s. Tulchinsky, *Branching Out.*

10 For the ways in which American Jews came to be less racialized and increasingly perceived as white over the twentieth century, see Karen Brodkin, *How Jews Became White Folks and What That Says about Race in America* (New Brunswick, NJ: Rutgers University Press, 1998); and Eric L. Goldstein, *The Price of Whiteness: Jews, Race and American Identity* (Princeton: Princeton University Press, 2008).

11 Josephine Lancaster (Davis) and Daisy Minchin (née Salmon) interview, interviewed by Cyril Leonoff, July 23, 1972, BC Archives, JHSBC Collection, T3883:75.

12 Gertrude Weinrobe and Violet Franklin interview, interviewed by Clare Auerbach and Cyril Leonoff, July 25, 1972, BC Archives, JHSBC Collection, T3883:11.

13 The 1901 census listed almost a fifth of Jewish men as lodgers or boarders, fewer than the provincial average of 25 percent but nonetheless suggesting that a sizable number of Jews were far from home and family. For stories about single Jewish men making a living on British Columbia's late-nineteenth-century resource frontier, also see Esmond Lando interview, interviewed by Irene Dodek, April 30, 1986, BC Archives, JHSBC Collection, T19.86–05.

14 *Canadian Jewish Times,* September 10, 1909, 12, 39, quoted in Leonoff, "The Rise of Jewish Life," 84–85.
15 Leonoff, "The Rise of Jewish Life," 85.
16 *Canadian Jewish News,* November 25, 1910, 2, 14, quoted in ibid., 31.
17 Dora Roseman interview, interviewed by Sandy Fuchs and M. Katz, 1972, BC Archives, Reynoldston Research and Studies, T0053:0001.
18 Rena Robinson Phillips interview, interviewed by Cyril Leonoff, 1983, JMABC, JHSBC Collection. Despite efforts at ethnic connection some Jews did assimilate into the larger Christian community. In *Raincoast Jews: Integration in British Columbia,* (Vancouver: Midtown Press, 2014) Lillooet McDonnell notes that some members of the next generation of the small Victoria Jewish community inter-married with white Christians. *Raincoast Jews,* 47-48.
19 The first Vancouver gurdwara was built in 1908. In 1912, gurdwaras were founded in Victoria, Fraser Mills, and Abbotsford. The 1911 census identified 2,342 Sikhs in British Columbia.
20 Hugh Johnston, "Group Identity in an Emigrant Worker Community: The Example of Sikhs in Early Twentieth-Century British Columbia," *BC Studies* 148 (Winter 2005–06): 3–23. Also see Larry DeVries, "Hindu and Other South Asian Religious Groups," in *Asian Religions in British Columbia,* ed. Larry DeVries, Don Baker, and Dan Overmyer (Vancouver: UBC Press, 2010), 20.
21 Indo-Canadian interview no. 52, interviewed by G.S. Basran and B. Singh Bolaria, 1985, Multicultural Canada, Indo-Canadian Oral History Collection, http://www.multicultural canada.ca/node/62601.
22 Seema Sohi, *Echoes of Mutiny: Race, Surveillance and Indian Anticolonialism in North America* (Oxford: Oxford University Press, 2014), 58–59, 172.
23 Peter Campbell, "East Meets Left: South Asian Militants and the Socialist Party of Canada in British Columbia, 1904-1914," *International Journal of Canadian Studies/Revue internationale d'études canadiennes* 20 (Fall 1999): 35–65.
24 The Chinese population of Victoria was 2,942 in 1901 and 3,418 in 1911. That of Vancouver was 2,003 in 1901 and 3,764 in 1911. CFP, Victoria and Vancouver 100 percent databases 1901 manuscript census, Canada; CCRI, Victoria and Vancouver 100 percent databases 1911 manuscript census, Canada.
25 See Kay Anderson, *Vancouver's Chinatown: Racial Discourse in Canada, 1875-1980* (Montreal and Kingston: McGill-Queen's University Press, 1995). Not all Chinese immigrants lived in Chinatown. As Patrick Dunae and his colleagues note, Chinese domestics, laundrymen, and market gardeners lived well outside Victoria's Chinatown. The authors also suggest that there was more interaction between Chinese immigrants and Euro-Canadians in Victoria than was previously thought. Patrick A. Dunae et al., "Making the Inscrutable, Scrutable: Race and Space in Victoria's Chinatown, 1891," *BC Studies* 169 (Spring 2011): 51–81.
26 See Jordan Paper and Laurence G. Thompson, eds., *The Chinese Way in Religion* (Belmont, CA: Wadsworth, 1998); and Don Baker, Daniel L. Overmyer, and Larry DeVries, eds., *Asian Religions in British Columbia* (Vancouver: UBC Press, 2010).
27 Enakshi Dua, "Exclusion through Inclusion: Female Asian Migration in the Making of Canada as a White Settler Nation," *Gender, Place and Culture* 14, 4 (August 2007): 445–66; Enakshi Dua, "The Hindu Woman's Question," *Canadian Woman Studies* 20, 2 (Summer 2000): 108–16.
28 J.C. Speer, *The Story of China in Canada* (Toronto: Department of Missionary Literature, Methodist Church of Canada, 1900), 28.

29 However, the 1908 "Gentlemen's Agreement" between the Japanese and Canadian governments limited the immigration of Japanese men but did not mention women. As a result, an increasing number of Japanese women did enter Canada, the majority as picture brides of Japanese men who had already emigrated. Michiko Midge Ayukawa, *Hiroshima Immigrants in Canada, 1891-1941* (Vancouver: UBC Press, 2008).
30 *Vancouver Province,* January 20, 1899, 5.
31 The condescending and racist descriptions of Asian religious practices extend to the nature of photographs of these religious practices in BC in this period. There are a number of such photographs available, but they also "other" or render Asian religious practices as alien or exotic. As a result I chose not to include photographs in the book which included Asian individuals in religious contexts.
32 Speer, *The Story of China in Canada,* 34, 37.
33 *Vancouver Province,* February 20, 1899, 6. For similar comments, also see *Victoria Times,* September 19, 1900, 5; and *Victoria Colonist,* February 6, 1894, 5.
34 Dunae et al., "Making the Inscrutable, Scrutable." Also see Patricia Roy, *A White Man's Province: British Columbia Politicians and Chinese and Japanese Immigrants, 1858-1914* (Vancouver: UBC Press, 1989), 29–30.
35 *Victoria Colonist,* January 18, 1900, 5; *Victoria Times,* September 11, 1907, 1. For a discussion of white attitudes regarding Vancouver's Chinatown, see Anderson, *Vancouver's Chinatown;* and for anti-Asian racism in British Columbia more generally, see Timothy Stanley, *Contesting White Supremacy: School Segregation, Anti-racism, and the Making of Chinese Canadians* (Vancouver: UBC Press, 2011); Roy, *A White Man's Province;* and Peter Ward, *White Canada Forever: Popular Attitudes and Public Policy toward Orientals in British Columbia* (Montreal and Kingston: McGill-Queen's University Press, 1990).
36 Patricia Roy, "Anglicans and Asians in British Columbia: An Ambiguous Relationship" (unpublished paper, n.d.); Peter Ward, "The Oriental Immigrant and Canada's Protestant Clergy, 1858-1925," *BC Studies* 22 (Summer 1974): 40–55.
37 A Conservative MP by 1914, Stevens was involved in government efforts to prevent the *Komagata Maru*'s passengers from disembarking in Vancouver. H.H. Stevens interview by John Munro, May 19, 1966, Library and Archives Canada, Ottawa, MG27.
38 *Report of the Royal Commission on Chinese and Japanese Immigration: Session 1902* (Ottawa: S.E. Dawson, 1902); *Vancouver Province,* December 7, 1907, quoted in Roy, "Anglicans and Asians," 5.
39 *Report of the Royal Commission on Chinese and Japanese Immigration,* 31.
40 Ward, "The Oriental Immigrant."
41 S.S. Osterhout, "Our Chinese Missions in British Columbia," *Missionary Bulletin* 13, 3 (July-September 1917): 499–500, quoted in Ward, "The Oriental Immigrant," 42.
42 Supplementary report by N. Lascelles Ward, "The Oriental Problem," with B.C. Freeman, Secretary, General Ministerial Association of Vancouver, to Charles Stewart, Minister of the Interior, January 24, 1922, Library and Archives Canada, Department of Immigration Records, file 815661, microfilm reel C-10652; *Canadian Churchman,* February 23, 1922, both cited in Roy, "Anglicans and Asians," 9.
43 Speer, *The Story of China in Canada*; Roy, "Anglicans and Asians"; Ward, "The Oriental Immigrant."
44 *Victoria Times,* August 2, 1900, 4.
45 Marshall, *Cultivating Connections,* 42-44.
46 Speer, *The Story of China in Canada,* 63–65.

47 For scholarly studies of the Chinese Rescue Home, see Liam O'Reilly, "Missionaries and Women in Victoria's Chinatown: The Establishment and Evolution of the Chinese Rescue Home, 1886-1900" (major research paper, Department of History, University of Victoria, 2011); Karen Van Dieren, "The Response of the WMS to the Immigration of Asian Women, 1888-1942," in *Not Just Pin Money,* ed. Barbara K. Latham and Roberta J. Pazdro (Victoria: Camosun College, 1984), 79–97; Marilyn F. Whiteley, "'Allee Samee Melican Lady': Imperialism and Negotiation at the Chinese Rescue Home (Women Missionary Societies Set Up the Chinese Rescue Home to Save Chinese Women from Prostitution)," *Resources for Feminist Research* 22, 3–4 (1992–93): 45–50; Shelly Ikebuchi, "Marriage, Morals and Men: Re/defining Victoria's Chinese Rescue Home," *BC Studies* 177 (Spring 2013): 65–84; and Shelly D. Ikebuchi, *From Slave Girls to Salvation: Gender, Race and Victoria's Chinese Rescue Home, 1886-1923* (Vancouver: UBC Press, 2015).

48 Whiteley, "'Allee Samee Melican Lady'"; Ikebuchi, *From Slave Girls to Salvation.*

49 *Victoria Times,* January 3, 1900, 5; O'Reilly, "Missionaries and Women."

50 Anglican Diocese of New Westminster, *Monthly Record,* May-June 1894, 8, Anglican Provincial Synod of British Columbia Archives, Vancouver, Anglican Provincial Synod of British Columbia and Yukon fonds; *Victoria Times,* June 28, 1900, 4, and June 30, 1900, 7. The lack of success in converting the Chinese was also mentioned by missionaries who testified in 1902 before the Royal Commission on Chinese and Japanese Immigration. *Report of the Royal Commission on Chinese and Japanese Immigration,* 26–27, 35. Also see Marshall, *Cultivating Connections,* 37.

51 "Report of the Chinese Mission in British Columbia," in Appendix 11, "Report of the Foreign Mission Committee," Presbyterian Church, in *Acts and Proceedings of the General Assembly of the Presbyterian Church in Canada* (1894), lxxiv, United Church of Canada Archives, Toronto; A.M. Sanford to Alexander Sutherland, January 27, 1910, United Church of Canada Archives, Sutherland Papers, file 82, quoted in Ward, "The Oriental Immigrant," 46.

52 Jiwu Wang, *"His Dominion" and the "Yellow Peril": Protestant Missions to Chinese Immigrants in Canada, 1859-1967* (Waterloo, ON: Wilfrid Laurier University Press, 2006), 56.

53 Norman Knowles, "Religious Affiliation, Demographic Change and Family Formation among British Columbia's Chinese and Japanese Communities: A Case Study of Church of England Missions, 1861-1942," *Canadian Ethnic Studies* 27, 2 (1995): 59–80. Knowles argues that after the First World War, when more Japanese men were able to bring in their wives, the missions achieved much greater success among them, as they provided a social and cultural space for Japanese Canadian families.

54 *Vancouver Province,* February 20, 1899, 6.

55 Wang, *"His Dominion,"* 24–25. Also see the discussion of the Palace of the Saints, situated on the third floor of Victoria's Chinese Consolidated Benevolent Association building from 1885 until 1966, in Victoria's Chinatown, "The Chinese Consolidated Benevolent Association," http://chinatown.library.uvic.ca/chinese_consolidated_benevolent_association; and James Chan interview, interview by Theresa Low, July and August 1980-07, BC Archives, Chinese Historical Wrongs Legacy Initiative Collection, T3721:0001-0005, translated from Chinese by Liang Han.

56 *Victoria Colonist,* October 12, 1909, 15. According to the article, the working-class men smashed the ballot boxes that had been provided so that the community could vote on whether to close the temples. It stated that the men relied on visiting the temples when seeking good fortune and saw their closure as an attack on the "gods of their fathers." In

the opinion of the middle-class men, who were Confucian, the temples were relics of superstition.

57 Alison R. Marshall, *The Way of the Bachelor: Early Chinese Settlement in Manitoba* (Vancouver: UBC Press, 2011), 157; Alison R. Marshall, *Cultivating Connections: The Making of Chinese Prairie Canada* (Vancouver: UBC Press, 2014), Chap. 8.

58 Hong Low interview, interviewed by Theresa Low, June 17, 1980 BC Archives, Chinese Historical Wrongs Legacy Initiative Collection, T3710:0001-0002, translated from Chinese by Liang Han.

59 Wang, "*His Dominion,*" 137. Among people of Chinese origin, over 65 percent defined themselves as Buddhist or Confucian in this census year.

60 Marshall, *The Way of the Bachelor*; Marshall, *Cultivating Connections.*

61 For example, the Vancouver Chinese community organized Chinese schools that taught English and Confucian values and were very anti-Christian. Marshall, *Cultivating Connections,* 37. A Chinese school was also founded in Victoria, although it became significant only in light of the Chinese student strike during the early 1920s. See Stanley, *Contesting White Supremacy.*

62 "Report of the Chinese Mission in British Columbia," in Appendix 11, "Report of the Foreign Mission Committee," Presbyterian Church, in *Acts and Proceedings of the General Assembly of the Presbyterian Church in Canada* (1894), 74, United Church of Canada Archives, Toronto.

63 A.E. Roberts box, Talks and Articles file, 1922, United Church of Canada, British Columbia Conference Archives, Vancouver (UC Archives, BC). Those who put up these posters may have been influenced by anti-Christian movements in China at that time. Zhongping Chen, pers. comm., May 26, 2013.

64 Wang, "*His Dominion,*" 125–35. Ministers also testified to the Royal Commission on Chinese and Japanese Immigration that Chinese converts experienced hostility from others in their community. *Report of the Royal Commission on Chinese and Japanese Immigration,* 23, 30.

65 This would also be true of their relative lack of success in converting the Japanese community.

66 See for example, Michael Harkin, "Engendering Discipline: Discourse and Counterdiscourse in the Methodist-Heiltsuk Dialogue," *Ethnohistory* 43, 4 (1996) 643-61; Susan Neylan, *The Heavens Are Changing: Nineteenth-Century Protestant Missions and Tsimshian Christianity* (Kingston and Montreal: McGill-Queen's University Press, 2002); Leslie A. Robertson with the Kwagu'l Gixsam Clan, *Standing Up with Ga'axsta'las: Jane Constance Cook and the Politics of Memory, Church and Custom* (Vancouver: UBC Press, 2012).

67 Of course, the numbers of committed Indigenous Christians varied across the province. James Teit, "Religion: Attitudes of Indians towards Missionaries (Spences Bridge Band)," in "Salish Ethnographic Notes," c. 1906-10, original ms. in American Philosophical Society Library, Philadelphia, BC Archives, no. 61, Boas Collection 372, roll 4, no. 1, microfilm reel A00239. Thanks to Wendy Wickwire for providing this source from her research notes. Paige Raibmon, *Authentic Indians: Episodes of Encounter from the Late-Nineteenth-Century Northwest Coast* (Durham: Duke University Press, 2005), 23. Also see "Work of the Methodist Mission Boat 'Udal,'" 1909, United Church of Canada, British Columbia Conference Archives, Home Mission Records of the BC Conference of the Methodist Church, box 2 78.099C, for a discussion of missionary visits to Indigenous groups along the coast, some of whom were at least nominally Christian, whereas others were not converted.

68 Minutes of the Vancouver Methodist Ministerial Association, October 19, 1914, 161–62, UC Archives, BC, Methodist Ministerial Association fonds.

69 Raibmon, *Authentic Indians,* Chapter 1; Douglas Cole and Ira Chaikin, *An Iron Hand upon the People: The Law against the Potlatch on the Northwest Coast* (Vancouver: Douglas and McIntyre, 1990); John Lutz, *Makúk: A New History of Aboriginal-White Relations* (Vancouver: UBC Press, 2008).

70 Renisa Mawani, *Colonial Proximities: Crossracial Encounters and Juridical Truths in British Columbia, 1871-1921* (Vancouver: UBC Press, 2009). The Methodist Ministerial Association complained about "Orientals" who illegally sold alcohol to Indigenous people, advocating that individuals who did so should be deported. Minutes of the Vancouver Methodist Ministerial Association, November 10, 1913, 138–39, United Church Archives, BC.

71 Lyn Gough, *As Wise as Serpents: Five Women and an Organization That Changed British Columbia, 1883-1939* (Victoria: Swan Lake, 1988), particularly Chapters 4, 5, and 13.

72 See ibid.; and Melanie Ihmels, "The Mischiefmakers: Women's Movement Development in Victoria, British Columbia, 1850-1910" (master's thesis, University of Victoria, 2014).

73 Women's Missionary Society Sherwood Avenue minutes, Belmont Avenue Methodist Church, Victoria, June 26, 1914, 25, April 20, 1915, 61, December 19, 1916, 112, November 1917, 137; Women's Missionary Society minutes, Centennial Methodist Church, Victoria, September 7, 1897, 93; Women's Missionary Society minutes, Cumberland United Church, June 1, 1915, 74–75. All records in the UC Archives, BC. Also see Ihmels, "The Mischiefmakers"; and Ikebuchi, *From Slave Girls to Salvation.*

74 Gillian Weiss, "Women and Reform in British Columbia: Some Preliminary Suggestions," in *In Her Own Right: Selected Essays on Women's History in B.C.,* ed. Barbara Latham and Cathy Kess (Victoria: Camosun College, 1980), 279–84; Chris Clarkson, *Domestic Reforms: Political Visions and Family Regulation in British Columbia, 1862-1940* (Vancouver: UBC Press, 2007).

75 Lutz, *Makúk;* Roy, *A White Man's Province.* British Columbia's anti-Asian immigration legislation was regularly disallowed by the federal government, but it remained politically popular in the province.

76 Under the Indian Act, federal legislation prohibited drunkenness and gambling on Indigenous reserves.

77 For a discussion of Methodist women's efforts to gain ecclesiastical suffrage, see Ruth Comton Brouwer, "The Canadian Methodist Church and Ecclesiastical Suffrage for Women, 1902-1914," *Canadian Methodist Historical Society Papers* 2 (n.d.): 1–27; and Cora Krommenhoek, "'The Church Should Have Championed the Woman's Cause': Women's Liberation and the Methodist Church in Canada, 1874–1925," *Canadian Methodist Historical Society Papers* 9 (1991-1992): 145–66.

78 Brouwer, "The Canadian Methodist Church," 12.

79 Ibid.

80 *Victoria Colonist,* May 4, 1878, 5; December 10, 1897, 6; June 3, 1899, 7; November 6, 1913, 1.

81 Marilyn F. Whiteley, "Modest, Unaffected, and Fully Consecrated: Lady Evangelists in Canadian Methodism," in *Changing Roles of Women within the Christian Church of Canada,* ed. Elizabeth Muir and Marilyn Whiteley (Toronto: University of Toronto Press, 1995), 183–200.

82 From later in the 1890s, Maritime, Prairie, and more rural Ontario representatives also advocated for women's rights to vote and be delegates in the Methodist Church, again

without success. Brouwer, "The Canadian Methodist Church." Brouwer also discusses the Methodist opposition to women's rights.

83 Ibid., 15.

84 *Western Methodist Recorder,* June 1918, 6. In connection with women's ecclesiastical suffrage, Canadian Methodists were years behind their British and American counterparts. See Brouwer, "The Canadian Methodist Church."

85 Margaret E. Thompson, *The Baptist Story in Western Canada* (Calgary: Baptist Union of Western Canada, 1975), 272, 280.

86 *Western Methodist Recorder,* June 1913, 4; Thompson, *The Baptist Story,* 286.

87 Rebecca J. Mead, *How the Vote Was Won: Woman Suffrage in the Western United States, 1868-1914* (New York: New York University Press, 2004), 6, 39–40.

88 Patricia Grimshaw, "Settler Anxieties, Indigenous Peoples and Women's Suffrage in the Colonies of Australia, New Zealand and Hawai'i, 1888-1902," *Pacific Historical Review* 69, 4 (2000): 553–72; Patricia Grimshaw, "Reading the Silences: Suffrage Activists and Race in Nineteenth Century Settler Societies," in *Women's Rights and Human Rights: International Historical Perspectives,* ed. Patricia Grimshaw, Katie Holmes, and Marilyn Lake (London: Palgrave, 2001), 31–48.

89 *Victoria Colonist,* June 3, 1899, 7.

90 *Victoria Colonist,* December 10, 1897, 6.

91 *Western Methodist Recorder,* June 1913, 4.

92 *Western Methodist Recorder*, July 1914, 19.

93 Thompson, The Baptist Story, 286.

94 *Champion,* April 1914, 6–7.

95 *Champion,* July 1913, 5 and 8, November 1913, 9.

96 *Champion,* November 1913, 9, 10.

97 Carol Bacchi, *Liberation Deferred: The Ideas of the English-Canadian Suffragists, 1877-1918* (Toronto: University of Toronto Press, 1983).

98 *Champion,* August 1912, 11.

99 Nancy Forestell with Maureen Moynagh, *Documenting First Wave Feminism* (Toronto: University of Toronto Press, 2014), 2:3–16; Mariana Valverde, "'When the Mother of the Race Is Free': Race, Reproduction and Sexuality in First-Wave Feminism," in *Gender Conflicts: New Essays in Women's History,* ed. Franca Iacovetta and Mariana Valverde (Toronto: University of Toronto Press, 1992), 3–26; Janice Fiamenco, "A Legacy of Ambivalence: Responses to Nellie McClung," in *Rethinking Canada: The Promise of Women's History,* ed. Veronica Strong-Boag, Mona Gleason, and Adele Perry (Toronto: Oxford University Press, 2002), 149–63.

100 See Ihmels, "Mischiefmakers," for a discussion of the Christian orientation of so many suffragists and their involvement in church organizations. Also see Linda Louise Hale, "Votes for Women: Profiles of Prominent British Columbia Suffragists and Social Reformers," in Latham and Kess, *In Her Own Right,* 287–302.

Chapter 7

1 *Victoria Colonist,* December 1, 1907, 23.

2 David Marshall, "Canadian Historians, Secularization and the Problem of the Nineteenth Century," *Historical Studies* (Canadian Catholic Historical Association) 60 (1993–94): 57–81.

3 Catherine Albanese, "Introduction: Awash in a Sea of Metaphysics," *Journal of the American Academy of Religion* 75, 3 (2007): 582-88; Catherine Albanese, *A Republic of Mind and Spirit: A Cultural History of American Metaphysical Religion* (New Haven, CT: Yale University Press, 2007). Also see Robert C. Fuller, *Spiritual but Not Religious: Understanding Unchurched America* (Oxford: Oxford University Press, 2001).

4 See, for example, Douglas Todd, ed., *Cascadia, the Elusive Utopia: Exploring the Spirit of the Pacific Northwest* (Vancouver: Ronsdale Press, 2008); and Patricia O'Connell Killen and Mark Silk, eds., *Religion and Public Life in the Pacific Northwest: The None Zone* (Walnut Creek, CA: AltaMira Press, 2004).

5 Alex Owen, *The Place of Enchantment: British Occultism and the Culture of the Modern* (Chicago: University of Chicago Press, 2004). According to Owen, these new approaches also allowed for a focus on the self that in some ways replicated that of the fledgling science of psychology. Thus, as she suggests, in their own way, the metaphysical religions both reflected and helped to usher in the modern.

6 In *Religion and Society in Frontier California* (New Haven, CT: Yale University Press, 1994), Laurie Maffly-Kipp argues that the availability of religious and irreligious options very much undermined mainstream spiritual practice and reinforced the less traditionally religious nature of gold-rush California.

7 For a discussion of alternative religions in Ontario, see Ramsay Cook, *The Regenerators: Social Criticism in Late Victorian English Canada* (Toronto: University of Toronto Press, 1985). For spiritualism in Ontario, see Stan McMullin, *Anatomy of a Seance: A History of Spirit Communication in Central Canada* (Montreal and Kingston: McGill-Queen's University Press, 2004); and for Toronto Theosophists, see Gillian McCann, *Vanguard of the New Age: The Toronto Theosophical Society, 1891-1945* (Montreal and Kingston: McGill-Queen's University Press, 2012).

8 There is very little historical work on alternative religions in British Columbia. Among the few examples are Samuel Eldon Charles Wagar, "Theosophical Socialists in the 1920s Okanagan: Jack Logie's Social Issues Summer Camps" (master's thesis, Simon Fraser University, 2005); and Amanda Klang, "'The Charlatan of the Gulf Islands': Brother XII and Progressive Occult Discourse in the History of British Columbia" (master's thesis, University of British Columbia, 2007), both of which examine a slightly later period, the 1920s and the 1930s.

9 See Alex Owen, *The Darkened Room: Women, Power and Spiritualism in Late Victorian England* (London: Virago Press, 1989); Ann Braude, *Radical Spirits: Spiritualism and Women's Rights in Nineteenth-Century America* (Boston: Beacon Press, 1989); and Walter J. Meyer Zu Erpen and Joy Lowe, "The Canadian Spiritualist Movement and Sources for Its Study," *Archivaria* 30 (Summer 1990): 71–84.

10 For a discussion of spiritualism in Ontario and Manitoba during the late nineteenth and early to mid-twentieth centuries, see McMullin, *Anatomy of a Seance*.

11 Meyer Zu Erpen and Lowe, "The Canadian Spiritualist Movement," 76.

12 Emily Carr notebook, BC Archives, Victoria, Edna Parnall Collection, Add. MSS 2763, box 1, file 4, cited in ibid., 78.

13 Meyer Zu Erpen and Lowe, "The Canadian Spiritualist Movement," 74.

14 See ViHistory 1901 census database.

15 *Nanaimo Free Press*, October 8, 1897, 1.

16 Edward Cridge, *"Spiritualism:" or Modern Necromancy: A Sermon, with Preface and Notes* (Victoria, BC: privately printed, 1870), 3, 4, 9, BC Archives, MS-0320.
17 See, for example, *Victoria Colonist,* July 9, 1899, 4; and *Ainsworth Hot Springs News,* April 6, 1892, 2.
18 *Vancouver Province,* July 14, 1900, 3. Also see *Victoria Times,* May 16, 1900, 5; and *Vancouver Province,* January 10, 1899, 3.
19 McMullin, *Anatomy of a Seance,* 17–18.
20 *Nanaimo Free Press,* July 6, 1897, 4.
21 *Nanaimo Free Press,* September 3, 1897 3.
22 Timothy R. Noddings, "What It Means to Be Modern: A Messy History of Mass-Media Revivals in the Gilded Age and Progressive Era, 1875-1920" (master's thesis, University of Victoria, 2013).
23 McMullin, *Anatomy of a Seance,* Chapter 3.
24 *Lowery's Claim* (Vancouver), May 1903, 9. For another Lowery attack on spiritualism, see the *Greenwood Ledge,* March 26, 1908, 4.
25 Owen, *The Darkened Room,* 22.
26 Among the spiritualists whose occupations are listed in the 1901 manuscript census for Victoria, nine can be defined as middle class and ten as working class. Very few spiritualists lived in Victoria in 1911 and in Vancouver in 1901. Among those whose occupations are recorded in the 1911 Vancouver manuscript census, five can be defined as middle class and twenty-two as working class. Canadian Families Project, 100 percent databases, Victoria and Vancouver, manuscript census, 1901; Canadian Century Research Infrastructure Project, 100 percent databases, Vancouver and Victoria, manuscript census, 1911.
27 Declaration forming the British Columbia Society of Spiritualists in Victoria, B.C., under the Charitable Associations Act, 1891, BC Archives, GR1438, microfilm reel B4406, society file S654. One other founding member, M. Maynard, was listed on the 1891 census as a freethinker, but in the absence of a complete first name this linkage is not firm. Most of the other founding members who could be linked to the 1891 or 1901 manuscript census gave their religious affiliation as spiritualist, except for V.E. Ottaway, who was absent from the 1891 census and was recorded in 1901 as an Anglican.
28 Diary of Bishop Hills, December 8, 1890, Anglican Synod of British Columbia Archives, Vancouver, Bishop George Hills sous-fonds, Anglican Synod of the Diocese of British Columbia fonds.
29 The 1901 and 1911 manuscript census for Victoria records forty-three and sixteen spiritualists, respectively. In Vancouver, the manuscript census lists fewer than ten in 1901 and seventy-one in 1911.
30 Declaration of Incorporation under the Benevolent Societies Act of the First Spiritualist Church of Vancouver, July 1918, Survival Research Institute of Canada, Victoria. Photocopy provided by Walter J. Meyer Zu Erpen.
31 Owen, *The Darkened Room*; Braude, *Radical Spirits.*
32 "Hannah Maynard," in Cathy Converse, *Mainstays: Women Who Shaped BC* (Victoria: Horsdal and Schubart, 1998), 70–72.
33 This analysis is based on the ViHistory database, and on the linkage of those who defined themselves as spiritualists for at least one year between 1881 and 1911, and could be linked between two censuses, based on name, age, place of birth, and occupation. It excludes

those who were twelve or younger for at least one of those years. ViHistory database, University of Vancouver Island and University of Victoria.

34 "Petition for Repeal of Tax on Astrologers, Etc.," *Journals of the Legislative Assembly of the Province of British Columbia,* Session 1894, 57 Vic., vol. 23, Survival Research Institute of Canada. Thanks to Walter J. Meyer Zu Erpen for a photocopy of this document.

35 Petitioners were linked to the ViHistory database.

36 Bent Sivertz, *The Sivertz Family,* Book 2, *Elinborg* (Canby, OR: Rudolph Reid Prael, 1982), 7.

37 Ibid.

38 The labour revolt involved a number of general strikes across Canada in 1919. The most famous occurred in Winnipeg, but Victoria also had a general strike that year. Benjamin Isitt, "Searching for Solidarity: The One Big Union and the Victoria General Strike of 1919," *Labour/Le travail* 60 (Fall 2007): 9–42.

39 Sivertz, *The Sivertz Family,* 14.

40 For a discussion of movement from spiritualism to Theosophy, see Albanese, *A Republic of Mind and Spirit;* and Owen, *The Place of Enchantment.*

41 Mark Leier, *Rebel Life: The Life and Times of Robert Gosden, Revolutionary, Mystic, Labour Spy* (Vancouver: New Star Books, 1999), 20; Mark Leier, "The Life and Times of Robert Raglan Gosden: Anarchist, Saboteur, Mystic and Labour Spy," *British Columbia Historical News* 33, 3 (Summer 2000): 2–7.

42 Emily Carr became very interested in Theosophy during the 1930s.

43 McCann, *Vanguard of the New Age,* Chapter 3.

44 Michele Lacombe, "Theosophy and the Canadian Idealist Tradition: A Preliminary Exploration," *Journal of Canadian Studies/Revue d'études canadiennes* 17, 2 (Summer 1982): 101. Also see McCann, *Vanguard of the New Age;* Ann Taves, *Fits, Trances and Visions: Experiencing Religion and Explaining Experience from Wesley to James* (Princeton: Princeton University Press, 1999), 219–22; Albanese, *A Republic of Mind and Spirit;* and Joy Dixon, *The Divine Feminine: Theosophy and Feminism in England* (Baltimore: Johns Hopkins University Press, 2001).

45 *Victoria Colonist,* October 7, 1892, 5, November 14, 1894, 6.

46 In 1897, the *Lamp,* the journal of the Toronto Theosophical Society, listed only three Theosophical Societies in Canada: in Toronto, Montreal, and Victoria.

47 *Victoria Colonist,* October 27, 1896, 7, October 10, 1898, 3.

48 *Victoria Colonist,* March 25, 1911, 3, April 4, 1911, 9.

49 *Victoria Colonist,* June 14, 1894, 7, October 7, 1902, 5.

50 *Victoria Colonist,* August 29, 1894, 6.

51 Lacombe, "Theosophy and the Canadian Idealist Tradition"; Dixon, *The Divine Feminine.*

52 In 1921, 62 of the 135 BC Theosophists were female (46 percent). Dominion Bureau of Statistics, *Census of Canada, 1921* (Ottawa: Acland, 1924), vol. 1, Table 37.

53 Of the ten Theosophists whose occupations are listed on the 1911 manuscript census, eight were middle class.

54 There may have been other Theosophical Societies in pre-war British Columbia, but I have found no evidence of them.

55 Minutes of the Kelowna Lodge Theosophical Society, April 20, 1913, Kelowna Public Archives (KPA), Kelowna, 2005.288.

56 Ibid., August 11, 1913.

57 Ibid., April 20, 1913, August 25, 1913, January 25, 1914.

58 Ibid., June 1, 1913.

59 Irene Howard, *The Struggle for Social Justice in British Columbia: Helena Gutteridge, the Unknown Reformer* (Vancouver: UBC Press, 1992), 31–35.

60 Sheila Nickols, "Up with the Petticoats! Down with the Trousers! From Suffragist to Political Candidate: Mary Graves of Victoria, B.C.," *British Columbia History* 34, 3 (Summer 2001): 2–7. Although the Unitarians were not over-represented in British Columbia during this period, they did have churches in Vancouver and Victoria, both of which struggled to survive. At least some Theosophists appear to have been attracted to Unitarian services. See Phillip Hewett, *Unitarians in Canada: How the Unitarians Have Exerted a Powerful Influence on Canadian Life for Over 150 Years* (Toronto: Fitzhenry and Whiteside, 1978), 136–40.

61 Howard, *The Struggle for Social Justice,* 54. For more on the connection between New Thought and Theosophy, see Taves, *Fits, Trances and Visions,* 213. The published census did not list New Thought adherents until 1921, but there is evidence from 1904 that a New Thought league held meetings in Victoria. See *Victoria Colonist,* May 26, 1904, 5, and August 5, 1905, 5.

62 Gloria Whelen, "Maria Grant, 1854-1937: The Life and Times of an Early Twentieth Century Christian," in *In Her Own Right: Selected Essays on Women's History in B.C.,* ed. Barbara Latham and Cathy Kess (Victoria: Camosun College, 1980), 139–42.

63 Data from Canadian Families Project, 100 percent census database, Victoria, 1901 manuscript census, were linked with St. Andrew's communion roll, held by St. Andrew's Presbyterian Church, Victoria, BC.

64 Roberta J. Pazdro, "Agnes Deans Cameron: Against the Current," in Latham and Kess, *In Her Own Right,* 121. For a discussion of the links between Theosophy and early cremation in Canada, see McCann, *Vanguard of the New Age,* 52–53.

65 McCann, *Vanguard of the New Age,* 107–8.

66 Hugh Johnston, *Jewels of the Qila: The Remarkable Story of an Indo-Canadian Family* (Vancouver: UBC Press, 2011), 31.

67 Hugh Johnston, "The Surveillance of Indian Nationalists in North America, 1908-1918," *BC Studies* 78 (Summer 1988): 9–10; Hugh Johnston, *The Voyage of the Komagata Maru: The Sikh Challenge to Canada's Colour Bar* (Vancouver: UBC Press, 1989), 12–13.

68 McCann, *Vanguard of the New Age,* 63–64.

69 Johnston, *Jewels of the Qila,* 53.

70 Ibid.; McCann, *Vanguard of the New Age,* Chapter 3.

71 McCann, *Vanguard of the New Age,* Chapter 3. McCann and other scholars of Theosophy have also demonstrated that despite the progressive and inclusive approach of most Theosophical beliefs, the Nazis used some elements of the religion to promote Aryan superiority.

72 It is not clear that any BC Theosophists combined feminism, anti-racism, and socialism, although Helena Gutteridge was both a socialist and a feminist.

73 Leier, *Rebel Life,* 38–39, 112.

74 Mikko Saikku, "Utopians and Utilitarians: Environment and Economy in the Finnish-Canadian Settlement of Sointula," *BC Studies* 154 (Summer 2007): 3–38; Ian McKay, *Reasoning Otherwise: Leftists and the People's Enlightenment in Canada, 1890-1920* (Toronto: Between the Lines, 2008), 264–65. A later BC utopian community very much influenced by Theosophy (and notoriously rent by a distortion of its free-love ideals) was founded just south of Nanaimo by Brother XII in 1928. For a detailed discussion, see Klang, "'The Charlatan of the Gulf Islands.'"

75 Arvo Tynjala interview, interviewed by Imbert Orchard, June 22, 1967, BC Archives, Imbert Orchard Collection, T1016:0006.

76 Future researchers may discover a connection between Logie and the earlier Kelowna Theosophical Lodge, but his name does not appear in its minutes.

77 Cook, *The Regenerators,* 157, 163, 166.

78 Phillips Thompson, "Socialism and Theosophy," *Western Socialist,* April 24, 1903, 1, quoted in Wagar, "Theosophical Socialists," 16–17.

79 Wagar, "Theosophical Socialists," 36, 18. A number of Theosophists, like Stephen, also seemed to be part of a Vancouver literary circle.

80 Albanese, *A Republic of Mind and Spirit*; Owen, *The Place of Enchantment.*

81 Albanese, *A Republic of Mind and Spirit*; Owen, *The Place of Enchantment.*

82 Raymond J. Cunningham, "The Impact of Christian Science on the American Churches, 1880-1910," *American Historical Review,* 72, 3 (1967), 885-905.

83 "The Fads of Faith," *Victoria Colonist,* March 27, 1900, 8. For an exchange between a local minister and Christian Scientists about the extent to which Christian Science abandoned orthodox Christian belief, see *Hedley Gazette and Similkameen Advertiser,* January 29, 1914, 4; August 12, 1915, 2; August 26, 1915, 3; September 2, 1915, 2; and September 9, 1915, 3.

84 "The Fads of Faith," *Victoria Colonist,* March 27, 1900, 8. Also see Noddings, "What It Means to Be Modern," for similarly gendered attacks in the American context.

85 "Historical Record of Christian Science Movement, British Columbia, Canada" (1932), Mary Baker Eddy Library, Boston, series RMFC-010-D, shelf ORM, folder ID/box ID 220183/530744; Edward K. Jones, "Christian Science," in *Circle of Voices: A History of the Religious Communities of British Columbia,* ed. Charles P. Anderson, Tirthankar Bose, and Joseph I. Richardson (Lantzville, BC: Oolichan Books, 1983), 72–73; "New Westminster Building Permits," *Daily Building Record,* June 26, 1912, 2.

86 *Victoria Colonist,* April 25, 1909, 3; Jones, "Christian Science," 74; "Historical Record of Christian Science Movement," Mary Baker Eddy Library.

87 Jones, "Christian Science," 74; "Historical Record of Christian Science Movement," Mary Baker Eddy Library.

88 James William Opp, *The Lord for the Body: Religion, Medicine, and Protestant Faith Healing in Canada, 1880-1930* (Montreal and Kingston: McGill-Queen's University Press, 2005), 119.

89 *Victoria Colonist,* December 1, 1904, 3.

90 *Victoria Times,* May 29, 1907, 1.

91 *Victoria Colonist,* March 13, 1909, 11; *Vancouver Province,* March 13, 1909, 7.

92 CCRI, 100 percent databases of Vancouver and Victoria, 1911 manuscript census.

93 Opp, *The Lord for the Body,* 48–63. For a discussion of the appeal of Christian Science to middle-class Australian women in this period see Jill Roe, "'Testimonies from the Field': The Coming of Christian Science to Australia, c. 1890-1910," *Journal of Religious History,* 22, 3 (1998), 304-19.

94 This number includes all BC practitioners who are recorded in the Index of Christian Science Practitioners, *Christian Science Journal,* Mary Baker Eddy Library. Only one of the women is not given as "Mrs." Two of the male practitioners are married to female practitioners, and one man is listed on his own.

95 These observations are derived from linking the Victorians who called themselves Christian Scientists in 1911 (in the ViHistory database), with information about the same Victorians

in the ViHistory database for 1901 (at the very beginning of Christian Science's introduction to Victoria).

96 *New Denver Ledge,* November 22, 1900, 4.

97 *Fernie Ledge,* May 3, 1905, 3, September 26, 1907, 2.

98 *Greenwood Ledge,* July 2, 1908, 4, February 29, 1912, 2.

99 *Greenwood Ledge,* August 3, 1911, 3.

100 *Greenwood Ledge,* July 24, 1913, 2, August 15, 1912, 2.

101 *Toronto Globe,* November 3, 1917, 12. Also see *Hedley Gazette and Similkameen Advertiser,* August 12, 1915, 2, for an article by a Reverend Stewart in which he argues that the war, and the popularity of socialism, spiritualism, and Christian Science, were evidence of the end times.

Conclusion

1 Even if a significant minority of these people are "spiritual but not religious," this would also hold true for residents of other provinces, making the greater willingness of British Columbians to abandon formal religious affiliations no less important.

2 Another group that challenged Christian hegemony in British Columbia was the Doukhobors, who lived communally and espoused a distinctive form of Christianity that was not accepted by the mainstream churches. They started arriving in the Kootenays in 1908 (from Russia by way of Saskatchewan), and although by 1912 Kootenay residents had become concerned about their refusal to send their children to school and their competition with local farmers and businesses, they did not pose a major challenge to church and state until the First World War and particularly in the 1920s and 1930s. See, for example, Andrew Donskov, John Woodsworth, and Chad Gaffield, eds., *The Doukhobor Centenary in Canada* (Ottawa: Slavic Research Group, University of Ottawa, 2000); Robert Bogdan Klymasz and Koozma J. Tarasoff, eds., *Spirit Wrestlers: Centennial Papers in Honour of Canada's Doukhobor Heritage* (Hull: Canadian Museum of Civilization, 1995); William Blakemore, *Report of the Royal Commission on Matters Relating to the Sect of Doukhobors in the Province of British Columbia* (Victoria: King's Printer, 1913).

3 In 1921, 1.5 percent of the BC population claimed to be atheists or to have no religion (as compared to 0.3 percent of Canadians generally), whereas in 1931 only 1.1 percent of British Columbians claimed this status (as compared to 0.2 percent of Canadians). In absolute numbers, 8,198 British Columbians claimed this status in 1911, 7,810 in 1921, and 7,855 in 1931.

4 Jean Barman, *The West beyond the West: A History of British Columbia* (Toronto: University of Toronto Press, 1993), 238–39. Quebec had repealed Prohibition the year before. Barman suggests that returned soldiers had a significant impact on the push for repeal in British Columbia. There is certainly evidence that many Canadian Christians who fought in the war became disillusioned with religion, or at least organized religion, as a result of their horrific experiences. For a summary of interpretations on this subject, see Elliot Hanowski, "A Godless Dominion: Unbelief and Religious Controversy in Interwar Canada" (PhD diss., Queen's University, 2015), 25–27.

5 By 1931, women composed almost 43 percent of the non-Indigenous population, and by 1941 they comprised 46 percent of it. Barman, *The West beyond the West,* 435.

6 Robert Burkinshaw, *Pilgrims in Lotus Land: Conservative Protestantism in British Columbia, 1917-1981* (Montreal and Kingston: McGill-Queen's University Press, 1995).

7 James William Opp, *The Lord for the Body: Religion, Medicine, and Protestant Faith Healing in Canada, 1880-1930* (Montreal and Kingston: McGill-Queen's University Press, 2005); Timothy R. Noddings, "What It Means to Be Modern: A Messy History of Mass-Media Revivals in the Gilded Age and Progressive Era, 1875-1920" (master's thesis, University of Victoria, 2013).

8 Opp, *The Lord for the Body*, 158.

9 Only 6.5 percent of Chinese British Columbians defined themselves as Christians in the 1931 census. Jiwu Wang, *"His Dominion" and the "Yellow Peril": Protestant Missions to Chinese Immigrants in Canada, 1859-1967* (Waterloo, ON: Wilfrid Laurier University Press, 2006), 137.

10 See Norman Knowles, "Religious Affiliation, Demographic Change and Family Formation among British Columbia's Chinese and Japanese Communities: A Case Study of Church of England Missions, 1861-1942," *Canadian Ethnic Studies* 27, 2 (1995): 59–80.

11 See Chapter 3; and Callum Brown, *The Death of Christian Britain: Understanding Secularisation, 1800-2000* (London: Routledge, 2001), 190.

12 Peter Campbell, *Canadian Marxists and the Search for a Third Way* (Montreal and Kingston: McGill-Queen's University Press, 2000), 81; Hanowski, "A Godless Dominion."

13 Hanowski provides an important analysis of the followers of Marshall Gauvin, a rationalist (atheist) speaker in Winnipeg during the interwar years, revealing that most were working class and that a number had connections to socialist organizations. Hanowski, "A Godless Dominion," Chapter 3.

14 Hanowski does not look at rationalist speakers in British Columbia, but it seems very likely that they would have been active in the province, given the pre-war situation and their popularity elsewhere in Canada during the interwar years. More research is needed on this subject.

15 Census data for the "no religion" category are not available for 1941 or 1961.

16 Tina Block, "Ungodly Grandmother": Marion Sherman and the Social Dimensions of Atheism in Postwar Canada," *Journal of Women's History* 28, 4 (2014): 132-54.

17 Callum Brown, *Religion and the Demographic Revolution: Women and Secularisation in Canada, Ireland, UK and USA since the 1960s* (Woodbridge, UK: Boydell Press, 2012); Tina Block, *The Secular Northwest: Religion and Irreligion in Everyday Postwar Life* (Vancouver: UBC Press, 2016).

18 Hanowski, "A Godless Dominion," Chapters 5 and 6.

Bibliography

NEWSPAPERS

Ainsworth Hot Springs News
Daily World Vancouver
Fernie Free Press
Hedley Gazette and Similkameen Advertiser
Kaslo Kootenaian
Ladysmith Ledger
Ledge (Fernie, Greenwood, Nakusp, New Denver)
Lowery's Claim (Nelson, New Denver, Vancouver)
Nanaimo Free Press
Nelson Tribune
Phoenix Pioneer
Revelstoke Herald
Rossland Evening World
Sandon Mining Review
Sandon Paystreak
Toronto Globe
Vancouver Province
Vancouver Sun
Victoria Colonist
Victoria Times
Victoria Week

RELIGIOUS NEWSPAPERS, JOURNALS, AND NEWSLETTERS

BC Western Catholic
Canadian Churchman
Canadian Epworth Era

Catholic Register
Lamp
Messenger and Visitor
Parish and Home
Presbyterian
Reflector
Religious Intelligencer
Wesleyan
Western Methodist Recorder
Westminster
Work for the Far West

Political/Labour/Rationalist Newspapers

BC Federationist
Champion
Rationalist
Secular Thought
Western Clarion
Western Socialist
Western Wage Earner

Archival Sources

Anglican Diocesan Archives, Diocese of Kootenay, Kelowna, BC
Nelson Parish fonds, Revelstoke Parish fonds
Rowan Ernest Grice-Hutchinson fonds, 1913–16 St. George's Parish (Rossland, BC) sous-fonds, St. Andrew's Parish (Trail, BC) fonds
Anglican Diocesan Archives, Diocese of Niagara, Hamilton
St. Paul's Anglican Church Records, Dunnville, Ontario
Anglican Diocesan Archives, Diocese of Toronto, Toronto
Christ Church Anglican Church Records, Campbellford, Ontario
Anglican Provincial Synod of British Columbia Archives, Vancouver
Anglican Diocese of New Westminster, *Monthly Record,* 1893–95
Diary of Bishop Hills, Bishop George Hills sous-fonds, Anglican Provincial Synod of the Diocese of British Columbia and Yukon fonds
Diocese of Kootenay, committee reports/resolutions, 1900–11
Atlantic Baptist Archives, Wolfville, NS
Amherst, NS, Baptist Church fonds
Kentville, NS, Baptist Church fonds
Atlantic Canada Virtual Archives, University of New Brunswick
McQueen Family Collection http://preserve.lib.unb.ca/wayback/20141205152203/http://atlanticportal.hil.unb.ca/acva/en/mcqueen/index.php
BC Archives, Victoria
Declaration forming the British Columbia Society of Spiritualists in Victoria, BC, under the Charitable Associations Act, 1891, GR1438, microfilm reel B4406, society file S654

Edward Cridge, "Spiritualism:" or Modern Necromancy: A Sermon, with Preface and Notes (Victoria: privately printed, 1870), MS-0320
Canadian Baptist Archives, Hamilton
Campbellford, Ontario Baptist Church fonds
Dunnville, Ontario Baptist Church fonds
Catholic Archdiocesan Archives, Vancouver (CAAV)
Chancery Office fonds, 1902–04, GR 1 box 4,
Mary Baker Eddy Library, Boston
"Historical Record of Christian Science Movement, British Columbia, Canada" (1932), series RMFC-010-D, shelf ORM, folder ID/box ID 220183/530744
Index of Christian Science Practitioners, *Christian Science Journal*
Presbyterian Church in Canada Archives, Toronto
Campbellford Presbyterian Church fonds
Dunnville, Ontario, Presbyterian Church fonds
First Presbyterian Victoria Records
Metropolitan Methodist Victoria Records
Public Archives of Nova Scotia, Halifax
Kentville Anglican Church fonds
Kentville Methodist Church fond
Kentville Presbyterian Church fonds
Rossland Museum and Archives, Rossland, BC
United Church anniversary collection
Letter, James Wilke to W.L. Nayler, May 27, 1900
St. Andrew's Presbyterian Church, Victoria
Church Records
Survival Research Institute of Canada, Victoria
"Petition for Repeal of Tax on Astrologers, Etc.," *Journals of the Legislative Assembly of the Province of British Columbia,* Session 1894, 57 Vic., vol. 23
Declaration of Incorporation under the Benevolent Societies Act of the First Spiritualist Church of Vancouver, July 1918
Photographs of Victoria spiritualists, late nineteenth century
United Church of Canada Archives, Toronto
Acts and Proceedings, Presbyterian Church
Campbellford United Church fonds, Methodist Church records
Dunnville United Church fonds, Methodist Church records
Methodist Church Missionary Society fonds (fonds 14), series 4: Home Mission Records, accession 78.099C
Thomas Green fonds (fonds 3110)
United Church of Canada, British Columbia Conference Archives, Vancouver (UC Archives, BC)
A.E. Roberts box
A.M. Sanford Scrapbooks, vol. 1, no. 22
Annual Reports, Central City Mission, Vancouver, BC, 1908–11
BC Conference of the Methodist Church of Canada, Records of Conference, 1887–1925
Belmont Avenue United Church fonds
Centennial United Church fonds

Correspondence of General Secretaries of Missions (after 1906, called Home Missions), BC Conference of the Methodist Church of Canada, box 2 78.099C
Cumberland United Church fonds
First United Church Institutional Mission (Vancouver, BC) fonds, 1885–1984
James Bay United (Victoria) fonds
Methodist Church (Canada) Missionary Society, British Columbia Conference Branch, 1893–1925
Methodist Ministerial Association fonds
Mount Pleasant Presbyterian Church records, St. Giles United Church fonds
Nelson United Church fonds – with Trinity Methodist Church records and Nelson Presbyterian Church records
Presbyterian Church in Canada, British Columbia Synod, Home Mission Committee fonds, 1902–19
Report of the Committee on Church Life and Work, of the Presbyterian Synod of B.C., Vancouver, 1908
Revelstoke United Church fonds – with Revelstoke Methodist and Presbyterian Church records
Rossland United Church fonds – with Rossland Methodist and Presbyterian Church records
St. Aidan's United Church (Victoria) fonds
Vancouver General Ministerial Association fonds
Vernon United Church fonds – with Vernon Methodist and Presbyterian Church records
Victoria West United Church fonds
United Church of Canada, Maritime Conference Archives, Sackville, NB
Trinity-St. Stephen's fonds, Amherst, NS – with both Methodist and Presbyterian Church records

Oral History

BC Archives, Victoria
BC Pioneer Series
Behind the Kitchen Door Collection
Chinese Historical Wrongs Legacy Initiative Collection
Coal Tyee Society Oral History Collection
Imbert Orchard Collection
Jewish Historical Society of BC Oral History Collection (JHSBC Collection)
Revelstoke and District Historical Association Aural History Collection
Rich Mole (Christmas in British Columbia) Collection
Strathcona Project
United Church History Seekers Collection
Library and Archives Canada, Ottawa
Interviews with H.H. Stevens, 1966, by John Munro, MG27
Multicultural Canada
Indo-Canadian Oral History Collection, http://www.multiculturalcanada.ca/node/62601

Census Material

Canada, National Household Survey, 2011 http://www12.statcan.gc.ca/census-recensement/index-eng.cfm

Canadian Century Research Infrastructure Project (CCRIP)

National 5 percent sample of manuscript census Canada, 1911

Vancouver 100 percent manuscript census database, 1911

Victoria 100 percent manuscript census database, 1911

Canadian Families Project (CFP), University of Victoria

Database of atheists/agnostics and those of "no religion" for BC and selected towns and counties of Ontario, 1901 manuscript census

Databases of 1901 manuscript census (100 percent) for Vernon, Nelson, and Revelstoke, British Columbia; Campbellford and Dunnville, Ontario; Amherst and Kentville, Nova Scotia

National 5 percent sample of manuscript census Canada, 1901

Vancouver 100 percent manuscript census database, 1901

Victoria 100 percent manuscript census database, 1901

Dominion Bureau of Statistics. *Census of Canada, 1901.* Ottawa: Census Office, 1902.

–. *Census of Canada, 1911.* Ottawa: C.H. Parmelee, 1913.

–. *Census of Canada, 1921.* Ottawa: F.A. Acland, 1924.

–. *Census of Canada, 1931.* Ottawa: J.O. Patenaude, 1935.

–. *Census of Canada, 1951.* Ottawa: E. Cloutier, 1956.

Rossland 1901 census database

Courtesy of Jeremy Mouat

Statistics Canada. *Census of Canada, 1971.* Ottawa: Information Canada, 1972.

–. *Census of Canada, 1981.* Ottawa: Statistics Canada, 1982.

–. *Census of Canada, 1991.* Ottawa: Statistics Canada 1992.

–. "Population by Religion, by Province and Territory (2001 Census)." In *Census of Canada, 2001.* Statistics Canada (online).

–. "Religion (108), Immigrant Status and Period of Immigration (11), Age Groups (10) and Sex (3) for the Population in Private Households of Canada, Provinces, Territories, Census Metropolitan Areas and Census Agglomerations." Catalogue no. 99-010-X2011032. In *2011 National Household Survey.* Statistics Canada (online).

ViHistory database, University of Vancouver Island and University of Victoria http://www.viHistory.ca

Other Sources

Abrams, Lynn. *Oral History Theory.* London: Routledge, 2010.

Albanese, Catherine. "Introduction: Awash in a Sea of Metaphysics." *Journal of the American Academy of Religion* 75, 3 (2007): 582–88. http://dx.doi.org/10.1093/jaarel/lfm035.

–. *A Republic of Mind and Spirit: A Cultural History of American Metaphysical Religion.* New Haven, CT: Yale University Press, 2007.

Ammerman, Nancy T. "Golden Rule Christianity: Lived Religion in the American Mainstream." In *Lived Religion in America: Toward a History of Practice*, ed. David D. Hall, 196–216. Princeton: Princeton University Press, 1997.

Anderson, Douglas Firth. "'We Have Here a Different Civilization': Protestant Identity in the San Francisco Bay Area, 1906–1909." *Western Historical Quarterly* 23, 2 (1992): 199–221. http://dx.doi.org/10.2307/970445.

Anderson, Kay. *Vancouver's Chinatown: Racial Discourse in Canada, 1875–1980*. Montreal and Kingston: McGill-Queen's University Press, 1995.

Anderson, Kevin. "'This Typical Old Canadian Form of Racial and Religious Hate': Anti-Catholicism and English Canadian Nationalism, 1905–1965." PhD diss., McMaster University, 2013.

Antak, Ivan E. "John Robson and His Faith: Church and State in Late Nineteenth-Century British Columbia." Master's thesis, Simon Fraser University, 2012.

Armstrong, Christopher, and H.V. Nelles. *The Revenge of the Methodist Bicycle Company: Sunday Streetcars and Municipal Reform in Toronto, 1888–1897*. Toronto: Peter Martin, 1977.

Ayukawa, Michiko Midge. *Hiroshima Immigrants in Canada, 1891–1941*. Vancouver: UBC Press, 2008.

Bacchi, Carol. *Liberation Deferred: The Ideas of the English-Canadian Suffragists, 1877–1918*. Toronto: University of Toronto Press, 1983.

Baker, Don, Daniel L. Overmyer, and Larry DeVries, eds. *Asian Religions in British Columbia*. Vancouver: UBC Press, 2010.

Barman, Jean. *Sojourning Sisters: The Lives and Letters of Jessie and Annie McQueen*. Toronto: University of Toronto Press, 2003.

–. *The West beyond the West: A History of British Columbia*. 3rd ed. Toronto: University of Toronto Press, 2007.

Barnard, Stuart. "The Kootenay Revival Campaign of 1909." Master's thesis, University of Calgary, 2010.

Baskerville, Peter. "Familiar Strangers: Urban Families with Boarders, Canada, 1901." *Social Science History* 25, 3 (Fall 2001): 321–46.

Baskerville, Peter, and Eric Sager. "Finding the Work Force in the 1901 Census of Canada." *Histoire sociale* 28, 56 (1995): 521–38.

–, eds. *Household Counts: Canadian Households and Families in 1901*. Toronto: University of Toronto Press, 2007.

–. *Unwilling Idlers: The Urban Unemployed and Their Families in Late Victorian Canada*. Toronto: University of Toronto Press, 1998.

Bederman, Gail. *Manliness and Civilization: A Cultural History of Gender and Race in the United States, 1880–1917*. Chicago: University of Chicago Press, 1995. http://dx.doi.org/10.7208/chicago/9780226041490.001.0001.

–. "'The Women Have Had Charge of the Church Work Long Enough': The Men and Religion Forward Movement of 1911–12 and the Masculinization of Middle-Class Protestantism." *American Quarterly* 41, 3 (September 1989): 432–65. http://dx.doi.org/10.2307/2713149.

Belshaw, John. *Becoming British Columbia: A Population History*. Vancouver: UBC Press, 2009.

–. "The British Collier in British Columbia: Another Archetype Reconsidered." *Labour/Le travail* 34 (Fall 1994): 11–36. http://dx.doi.org/10.2307/25143844.

–. *Colonization and Community: The Vancouver Island Coalfield and the Making of the British Columbian Working Class.* Montreal and Kingston: McGill-Queen's University Press, 2002.

–. "The West We Have Lost: British Columbia's Demographic Past and an Agenda for Population History." *Western Historical Quarterly* 29, 1 (1998): 25–47. http://dx.doi.org/10.2307/970805.

Beyer, Peter. "Modern Forms of the Religious Life: Denomination, Church, and Invisible Religion in Canada, the United States, and Europe." In *Rethinking Church, State, and Modernity: Canada between Europe and America,* ed. David Lyon and Marguerite Van Die, 189-210. Toronto: University of Toronto Press, 2000.

–. "Questioning the Secular/Religious Divide in a Post-Westphalian World." *International Sociology* 28, 6 (2013): 663–79.

Blaikie, W.G. *Summer Suns in the Far West: A Holiday Trip to the Pacific Slope.* London: Nelson and Sons, 1890.

Block, Tina. "Everyday Infidels: A Social History of Secularism in the Post-war Pacific Northwest." PhD diss., University of Victoria, 2001.

–. *The Secular Northwest: Religion and Irreligion in Everyday Postwar Life.* Vancouver: UBC Press, 2016.

–. "Ungodly Grandmother: Marion Sherman and the Social Dimensions of Atheism in Postwar Canada." *Journal of Women's History* 28, 4 (2014): 132-54.

Blum, Edward J. *Reforging the White Republic: Race, Religion and American Nationalism, 1865–1898.* Baton Rouge: Louisiana State University Press, 2005.

Blum, Edward J., Tracy Fessenden, Prema Kurien, and Judith Weisenfeld. "Forum: American Religion and 'Whiteness.'" *Religion and American Culture* 19, 1 (Winter 2009): 1–35. http://dx.doi.org/10.1525/rac.2009.19.1.1.

Board of Temperance and Moral Reform of the Methodist Church, and the Board of Social Service and Evangelism of the Presbyterian Church. *Vancouver, British Columbia: The Report of a Brief Investigation of Social Conditions in the City Which Indicate the Need of an Intensive Social Survey, the Lines of Which Are Herein Suggested.* Vancouver, 1913.

Bobcock, Robert. *Hegemony.* London: Tavistock, 1986.

Bonazzi, Tiziano. "Frederick Jackson Turner's Frontier Thesis and the Self-Consciousness of America." *Journal of American Studies* 27, 2 (August 1993): 14–171. http://dx.doi.org/10.1017/S0021875800031509.

Boudreau, Michael. "'There Is ... No Pernicious Dualism between Sacred and Secular': Nova Scotia Baptists and the Social Gospel, 1880–1914." *Nova Scotia Historical Review* 16, 1 (1996): 109–31.

Bowen, Lynne. *Boss Whistle: The Coal Miners of Vancouver Island Remember.* Nanaimo, BC: Rocky Point Books, 2002.

–. *Whoever Gives Us Bread: The Story of Italians in British Columbia.* Vancouver: Douglas and McIntyre, 2011.

Braude, Ann. *Radical Spirits: Spiritualism and Women's Rights in Nineteenth-Century America.* Boston: Beacon Press, 1989.

–. "Women's History *Is* American History." In *Retelling U.S. Religious History,* ed. Thomas A. Tweed, 87–107. Berkeley: University of California Press, 1997.

Bridge, Kathryn. "Being Young in the Country: Settler Children and Childhood in British Columbia and Alberta, 1860-1925." PhD diss., University of Victoria, 2012.

–, ed. *Henry and Self: The Private Life of Sarah Crease, 1826–1922*. Victoria: Sono Nis Press, 1996.

Brodkin, Karen. *How Jews Became White Folks and What That Says about Race in America*. New Brunswick, NJ: Rutgers University Press, 1998.

Brouwer, Ruth Comton. "The Canadian Methodist Church and Ecclesiastical Suffrage for Women, 1902-1914." *Canadian Methodist Historical Society Papers* 2 (n.d.): 1–27.

Brown, Callum. *The Death of Christian Britain: Understanding Secularisation, 1800–2000*. London: Routledge, 2001.

–. "The People of 'No Religion': The Demographics of Secularisation in the English-Speaking World since c. 1900." *Archiv fur Sozialgeschichte* 51 (2011): 37–61.

–. *Religion and the Demographic Revolution: Women and Secularisation in Canada, Ireland, UK and USA since the 1960s*. Woodbridge, UK: Boydell Press, 2012.

Brown, Lorraine. "Domestic Service in British Columbia, 1850-1914." Master's thesis, University of Victoria, 2007.

Buck, Ian. "The Integration Index: Using GIS to Interpret the Residential Structure of Vancouver, British Columbia." Master's thesis, University of Victoria, 2001.

Budd, Susan. *Varieties of Unbelief: Atheists and Agnostics in English Society, 1850–1960*. London: Heinemann, 1977.

Burkinshaw, Robert. *Pilgrims in Lotus Land: Conservative Protestantism in British Columbia, 1917–1981*. Montreal and Kingston: McGill-Queen's University Press, 1995.

Butler, Jon. "Jack-in-the-Box Faith: The Religion Problem in Modern American History." *Journal of American History* 90, 4 (March 2004): 1357–78. http://dx.doi.org/10.2307/3660356.

Campbell, Colin. "Irreligion." In *Encyclopedia of Religion and Society*, ed. William H. Swatos, Jr. Hartford Institute for Religion Research, Hartford Seminary. http://hirr.hartsem.edu/ency/irreligion.htm.

Campbell, Peter. *Canadian Marxists and the Search for a Third Way*. Montreal and Kingston: McGill-Queen's University Press, 2000.

–. "East Meets Left: South Asian Militants and the Socialist Party of Canada in British Columbia, 1904–1914." *International Journal of Canadian Studies/Revue internationale d'études canadiennes* 20 (Fall 1999): 35–65.

Carnes, Mark. *Secret Ritual and Manhood in Victorian America*. New Haven, CT: Yale University Press, 1989.

Carter, Kathryn, ed. *The Small Details of Life: Twenty Diaries by Women in Canada, 1830–1996*. Toronto: University of Toronto Press, 2002.

Carter, Sarah. "Categories and Terrains of Exclusion: Constructing the 'Indian Woman' in the Early Settlement Era in Western Canada." *Great Plains Quarterly* 13 (Summer 1993): 147-61.

Christie, Nancy, and Michael Gauvreau. *Christian Churches and Their Peoples, 1840–1965*. Toronto: University of Toronto Press, 2010.

–. *A Full-Orbed Christianity: The Protestant Churches and Social Welfare in Canada, 1900–1940*. Montreal and Kingston: McGill-Queen's University Press, 1996.

–. "Modalities of Social Authority: Suggesting an Interface for Religious and Social History." *Histoire sociale* 36, 71 (2003): 1–30.

–, eds. *The Sixties and Beyond: Dechristianization in North America and Western Europe, 1945–2000*. Toronto: University of Toronto Press, 2013.

Clarke, Brian. *Piety and Nationalism: Lay Voluntary Associations and the Creation of an Irish-Catholic Community in Toronto, 1850-1895*. Montreal and Kingston: McGill-Queen's University Press, 1993.

Clarkson, Chris. *Domestic Reforms: Political Visions and Family Regulation in British Columbia, 1862–1940*. Vancouver: UBC Press, 2007.

Clawson, Mary Ann. *Constructing Brotherhood: Class, Gender and Fraternalism*. Princeton: Princeton University Press, 1989. http://dx.doi.org/10.1515/9781400860500.

Clayton, Jenny. "Local Connections: Stories from Early Vernon." Honours essay, Department of History, University of Victoria, 1999.

Cole, Douglas, and Ira Chaikin. *An Iron Hand upon the People: The Law against the Potlatch on the Northwest Coast*. Vancouver: Douglas and McIntyre, 1990.

Coleman, Daniel. *White Civility: The Literary Project of English Canada*. Toronto: University of Toronto Press, 2008.

Connor, Ralph. *Black Rock: A Tale of the Selkirks*. Toronto: Westminster, 1898.

Converse, Cathy. *Mainstays: Women Who Shaped BC*. Victoria: Horsdal and Schubart, 1998.

Cook, Ramsay. *The Regenerators: Social Criticism in Late Victorian English Canada*. Toronto: University of Toronto Press, 1985.

Cott, Nancy. *The Bonds of Womanhood: "Woman's Sphere" in New England, 1780–1835*. New Haven, CT: Yale University Press, 1997.

Crouse, Eric. *Revival in the City: The Impact of American Evangelists in Canada, 1884–1914*. Montreal and Kingston: McGill-Queen's University Press, 2005.

Cumbo, Enrico Carlson. "Salvation in Indifference: Gendered Expressions of Italian-Canadian Immigrant Catholicity, 1900-1940." In *Households of Faith: Family, Gender, and Community in Canada, 1760–1969*, ed. Nancy Christie, 203–33. Montreal and Kingston: McGill-Queen's University Press, 2002.

Cunningham, Raymond J. "The Impact of Christian Science on the American Churches, 1880-1910." *American Historical Review* 72, 3 (April 1967): 885-905.

Curtis, Bruce. *The Politics of Population: State Formation, Statistics, and the Census of Canada, 1840–1875*. Toronto: University of Toronto Press, 2006.

Davie, Grace. *Religion in Britain since 1945: Believing without Belonging*. Making Contemporary Britain. Cambridge, MA: Blackwell, 1994.

Delap, Lucy. "'Be Strong and Play the Man': Anglican Masculinities in the Twentieth Century." In *Men, Masculinities and Religious Change in Twentieth-Century Britain*, ed. Lucy Delap and Sue Morgan, 119–45. London: Palgrave Macmillan, 2013. http://dx.doi.org/10.1057/9781137281753.

DeVries, Larry. "Hindu and Other South Asian Religious Groups." In *Asian Religions in British Columbia*, ed. Larry DeVries, Don Baker, and Dan Overmyer, 17–42. Vancouver: UBC Press, 2010.

Dua, Enakshi. "Exclusion through Inclusion: Female Asian Migration in the Making of Canada as a White Settler Nation." *Gender, Place and Culture* 14, 4 (August 2007): 445–66. http://dx.doi.org/10.1080/09663690701439751.

–. "The Hindu Woman's Question." *Canadian Woman Studies* 20, 2 (Summer 2000): 108–16.

Dunae, Patrick. "Geographies of Sexual Commerce and the Production of Prostitutional Space: Victoria, British Columbia, 1860-1914." *Journal of the Canadian Historical Association* 19, 1 (2008): 115–42. http://dx.doi.org/10.7202/037428ar.

–. "Sex, Charades, and Census Records: Locating Female Sex Trade Workers in a Victorian City." *Histoire sociale* 42, 84 (November 2009): 267–97. http://dx.doi.org/10.1353/his.0.0092.

Dunae, Patrick A., John S. Lutz, Donald J. Lafreniere, and Jason A. Gilliland. "Making the Inscrutable, Scrutable: Race and Space in Victoria's Chinatown, 1891." *BC Studies* 169 (Spring 2011): 51–81.

Edmonds, Penelope. *Urbanizing Frontiers: Indigenous Peoples and Settlers in Nineteenth-Century Pacific Rim Cities.* Vancouver: UBC Press, 2010.

Emery, George. *The Methodist Church on the Prairies, 1896–1914.* Montreal and Kingston: McGill-Queen's University Press, 2001.

Epp, Marlene. "The Memory of Violence: Soviet and East European Mennonite Refugees and Rape in the Second World War." *Journal of Women's History* 9, 1 (Spring 1997): 58–87. http://dx.doi.org/10.1353/jowh.2010.0217.

Erickson, Lesley. *Westward Bound: Sex, Violence, the Law and the Making of a Settler Society.* Vancouver: UBC Press, 2011.

Ferguson, George V. "Queen of the Kootenays." *Beaver* 19 (March 1960): 18-22.

Fessenden, Tracy. *Culture and Redemption: Religion, the Secular, and American Literature.* Princeton: Princeton University Press, 2007.

Fiamenco, Janice. "A Legacy of Ambivalence: Responses to Nellie McClung." In *Rethinking Canada: The Promise of Women's History,* ed. Veronica Strong-Boag, Mona Gleason, and Adele Perry, 149–63. Toronto: Oxford University Press, 2002.

Fones-Wolf, Kenneth. *Trade Union Gospel: Christianity and Labor in Industrial Philadelphia, 1865–1915.* Philadelphia: Temple University Press, 1989.

Forestell, Nancy. "Bachelors, Boarding-Houses, and Blind Pigs: Gender Construction in a Multi-ethnic Mining Camp, 1909-1920." In *A Nation of Immigrants: Women, Workers, and Communities in Canadian History, 1840s-1960s,* ed. Franca Iacovetta, Paula Draper, and Robert Ventresca, 251–90. Toronto: University of Toronto Press, 1998.

Forestell, Nancy, with Maureen Moynagh. *Documenting First Wave Feminism.* Vol. 2. Toronto: University of Toronto Press, 2014.

Forseille, Ashley. "Reading Love between the Lines: Religion, Courtship and Correspondence in the Salvation Army, 1906-1910." Master's thesis, University of Victoria, 2012.

Frankiel, Sandra Sizer. *California's Spiritual Frontiers: Religious Alternatives to Anglo-Protestantism, 1850–1910.* Berkeley: University of California Press, 1988.

Furniss, Elizabeth. *The Burden of History: Colonialism and the Frontier Myth in a Rural Canadian Community.* Vancouver: UBC Press, 1999.

Gaffield, Chad. "Language, Ancestry and the Competing Constructions of Identity in Turn-of-the-Century Canada." In *Household Counts: Canadian Households and Families in 1901,* ed. Eric W. Sager and Peter Baskerville, 423–40. Toronto: University of Toronto Press, 2006.

Gagan, David. *Hopeful Travellers: Families, Land, and Social Change in Mid-Victorian Peel County, Canada West.* Toronto: University of Toronto Press, 1981.

Gauvreau, Michael. "Factories and Foreigners: Church Life in Working-Class Neighbourhoods in Hamilton and Montreal, 1890-1930." In *The Churches and Social Order in Nineteenth- and Twentieth-Century Canada,* ed. Michael Gauvreau and Ollivier Hubert, 225–73. Montreal and Kingston: McGill-Queen's University Press, 2006.

Gidney, Catherine. *A Long Eclipse: The Liberal Protestant Establishment and the Canadian University, 1920–1970.* Montreal and Kingston: McGill-Queen's University Press, 2004.

Goldstein, Eric L. *The Price of Whiteness: Jews, Race and American Identity.* Princeton: Princeton University Press, 2008.

Goodman, Lee-Anne. "Religion Marks a Divergent Path in Canadian-US History." *Global News,* May 8, 2013. http://globalnews.ca/news/544455/religion-marks-a-divergent-path-in-canadian-us-history/.

Gough, Lyn. *As Wise as Serpents: Five Women and an Organization That Changed British Columbia, 1883–1939.* Victoria, BC: Swan Lake, 1988.

Goutor, David. *Guarding the Gates: The Canadian Labour Movement and Immigration, 1872–1934.* Vancouver: UBC Press, 2007.

Greer, Karla. "Race, Riot and Rail: The Process of Racialisation in Prince Rupert, B.C., 1906-1919." Master's thesis, University of Victoria, 1999.

Grimshaw, Patricia. "Reading the Silences: Suffrage Activists and Race in Nineteenth Century Settler Societies." In *Women's Rights and Human Rights: International Historical Perspectives,* ed. Patricia Grimshaw, Katie Holmes, and Marilyn Lake, 31–48. London: Palgrave, 2001. http://dx.doi.org/10.1057/9780333977644.

–. "Settler Anxieties, Indigenous Peoples and Women's Suffrage in the Colonies of Australia, New Zealand and Hawai'i, 1888-1902." *Pacific Historical Review* 69, 4 (2000): 553–72. http://dx.doi.org/10.2307/3641224.

Gutman, Herbert. *Work, Culture, and Society in Industrializing America: Essays in American Working-Class and Social History.* New York: Vintage Books 1977.

Hale, Linda Louise. "Votes for Women: Profiles of Prominent British Columbia Suffragists and Social Reformers." In *In Her Own Right: Selected Essays on Women's History in B.C.,* ed. Barbara Latham and Cathy Kess, 287–302. Victoria: Camosun College, 1980.

Halliday, C.W. *The Valley of Youth.* Caldwell, ID: Caxton Printers, 1948.

Hanowski, Elliot. "A Godless Dominion: Unbelief and Religious Controversy in Interwar Canada." PhD diss., Queen's University, 2015.

Hare, Jan, and Jean Barman. *Good Intentions Gone Awry: Emma Crosby and the Methodist Mission on the Northwest Coast.* Vancouver: UBC Press, 2006.

Harkin, Michael. "Power and Progress: The Evangelic Dialogue among the Heiltsuk." *Ethnohistory* (Columbus, OH) 40, 1 (Winter 1993): 1–33. http://dx.doi.org/10.2307/482157.

–. "Engendering Discipline: Discourse and Counterdiscourse in the Methodist-Heiltsuk Dialogue." *Ethnohistory* 43, 4 (1996): 643–61.

Harris, R. Cole. *The Resettlement of British Columbia: Essays on Colonialism and Geographical Change.* Vancouver: UBC Press, 1997.

Henderson, Jennifer. *Settler Feminism and Race Making in Canada.* Toronto: University of Toronto Press, 2003.

Hinde, John R. *When Coal Was King: Ladysmith and the Coal-Mining Industry on Vancouver Island.* Vancouver: UBC Press, 2003.

Hogg, Robert. *Men and Manliness on the Frontier: Queensland and British Columbia in the Mid-nineteenth Century.* London: Palgrave Macmillan, 2012. http://dx.doi.org/10.1057/9781137284259.

Howard, Irene. *The Struggle for Social Justice in British Columbia: Helena Gutteridge, the Unknown Reformer.* Vancouver: UBC Press, 1992.

Hunt, Alan. "Measuring Morals: The Beginnings of the Social Survey Movement in Canada, 1913-1917." *Histoire sociale* 35, 69 (2002): 171–94.

Ihmels, Melanie. "The Mischiefmakers: Women's Movement Development in Victoria, British Columbia, 1850-1910." Master's thesis, University of Victoria, 2014.

Ikebuchi, Shelly. *From Slave Girls to Salvation: Gender, Race and Victoria's Chinese Rescue Home, 1886–1923*. Vancouver: UBC Press, 2015.

–. "Marriage, Morals and Men: Re/defining Victoria's Chinese Rescue Home." *BC Studies* 177 (Spring 2013): 65–84.

Isitt, Benjamin. "Searching for Solidarity: The One Big Union and the Victoria General Strike of 1919." *Labour/Le travail* 60 (Fall 2007): 9–42.

Jacoby, Susan. *Freethinkers: A History of American Secularism.* New York: Metropolitan Books, 2004.

Johnson, Susan Lee. "Bulls, Bears and Dancing Boys: Race, Gender and Leisure in the California Gold Rush." *Radical History Review* 60 (Fall 1994): 4–37.

Johnston, Hugh. "Group Identity in an Emigrant Worker Community: The Example of Sikhs in Early Twentieth-Century British Columbia." *BC Studies* 148 (Winter 2005–06): 3–23.

–. *Jewels of the Qila: The Remarkable Story of an Indo-Canadian Family.* Vancouver: UBC Press, 2011.

–. "The Surveillance of Indian Nationalists in North America, 1908-1918." *BC Studies* 78 (Summer 1988): 3–28.

–. *The Voyage of the Komagata Maru: The Sikh Challenge to Canada's Colour Bar.* Vancouver: UBC Press, 1989.

Jones, Edward K. "Christian Science." In *Circle of Voices: A History of the Religious Communities of British Columbia,* ed. Charles P. Anderson, Tirthankar Bose, and Joseph I. Richardson, 72-73. Lantzville, BC: Oolichan Books, 1983.

Jones, Jo Fraser, ed. *Hobnobbing with a Countess and Other Okanagan Adventures: The Diaries of Alice Barrett Parke, 1891–1900.* Vancouver: UBC Press, 2001.

Kan, Sergei. "Shamanism and Christianity: Modern Day Tlingit Elders Look at the Past." *Ethnohistory* (Columbus, OH) 38, 4 (Fall 1991): 363–87. http://dx.doi.org/10.2307/482478.

Katz, Michael. *The People of Hamilton, Canada West: Family and Class in a Mid-nineteenth-century City.* Cambridge, MA: Harvard University Press, 1975. http://dx.doi.org/10.4159/harvard.9780674494213.

Kealey, Gregory. "1919: The Canadian Labour Revolt." *Labour/Le travail* 13 (Spring 1984): 11–44. http://dx.doi.org/10.2307/25140399.

Kee, Kevin. *Revivalists: Marketing the Gospel in English Canada, 1884–1957.* Montreal and Kingston: McGill-Queen's University Press, 2006.

Kelm, Mary Ellen, ed. *The Letters of Margaret Butcher: Missionary-Imperialism on the North Pacific Coast.* Calgary: University of Calgary Press, 2007.

Kendall, Adam G. "The Whitewash Committee of 1914: The Knights of Columbus, Freemasonry and Anti-Catholicism in California." *European Journal of American Culture* 33, 1 (2014): 49–60. http://dx.doi.org/10.1386/ejac.33.1.49_1.

Kirkley, Evelyn. *Rational Mothers and Infidel Gentlemen: Gender and American Atheism, 1865–1915.* Syracuse: Syracuse University Press, 1999.

Klang, Amanda. "'The Charlatan of the Gulf Islands': Brother XII and Progressive Occult Discourse in the History of British Columbia." Master's thesis, University of British Columbia, 2007.

Knowles, Norman. "'Christ in the Crowsnest': Religion and the Anglo-Protestant Working Class in the Crowsnest Pass, 1898–1918." In *Nation, Ideas, Identities: Essays in Honour of Ramsay Cook,* ed. Michael D. Behiels and Marcel Martel, 52–72. Toronto: Oxford University Press, 2000.

–. "Religious Affiliation, Demographic Change and Family Formation among British Columbia's Chinese and Japanese Communities: A Case Study of Church of England Missions, 1861-1942." *Canadian Ethnic Studies* 27, 2 (1995): 59–80.

Korneski, Kurt. "Britishness, Canadianness, Class, and Race: Winnipeg and the British World, 1880s–1910s." *Journal of Canadian Studies* 41, 2 (2007): 161-84.

Krommenhoek, Cora. "'The Church Should Have Championed the Woman's Cause': Women's Liberation and the Methodist Church in Canada, 1874–1925." *Canadian Methodist Historical Society Papers* 9 (1991–92): 145–66.

Lacombe, Michele. "Theosophy and the Canadian Idealist Tradition: A Preliminary Exploration." *Journal of Canadian Studies/Revue d'études canadiennes* 17, 2 (Summer 1982): 100–18.

Lake, Marilyn. "Frontier Feminism and the Marauding White Man." *Journal of Australian Studies* 20, 49 (1996): 12–20. http://dx.doi.org/10.1080/14443059609391738.

Lane, Hannah. "Evangelicals, Church Finance, and Wealth-Holding in Mid-nineteenth Century St. Stephen, New Brunswick, and Calais, Maine." In *The Churches and Social Order in Nineteenth- and Twentieth-Century Canada,* ed. Michael Gauvreau and Ollivier Hubert, 109–50. Montreal and Kingston: McGill-Queen's University Press, 2006.

–. "Tribalism, Proselytism, and Pluralism: Protestants, Family, and Denominational Identity in Mid-nineteenth-century St. Stephen, New Brunswick." In *Households of Faith: Family, Gender, and Community in Canada, 1760–1969,* ed. Nancy Christie, 103–37. Montreal and Kingston: McGill-Queen's University Press, 2002.

–. "'Wife, Mother, Sister, Friend': Methodist Women in St. Stephen, New Brunswick, 1861–1881." In *Separate Spheres: Women's Worlds in the 19th Century Maritimes,* ed. Janet Guildford and Suzanne Morton, 93–117. Fredericton: Acadiensis Press, 1994.

Leier, Mark. "The Life and Times of Robert Raglan Gosden: Anarchist, Saboteur, Mystic and Labour Spy." *British Columbia Historical News* 33, 3 (Summer 2000): 2–7.

–. *Rebel Life: The Life and Times of Robert Gosden, Revolutionary, Mystic, Labour Spy.* Vancouver: New Star Books, 1999.

–. *Red Flags and Red Tape: The Making of a Labour Bureaucracy.* Toronto: University of Toronto Press, 1995.

–. *Where the Fraser River Flows: The Industrial Workers of the World in British Columbia.* Vancouver: New Star Books, 1990.

Leonoff, Cyril E. "The Rise of Jewish Life and Religion in British Columbia, 1858-1948." *Scribe: Journal of the Jewish Historical Society of British Columbia* 28 (2008): 1–204.

Lutz, John. *Makúk: A New History of Aboriginal-White Relations.* Vancouver: UBC Press, 2008.

Maffly-Kipp, Laurie. *Religion and Society in Frontier California.* New Haven, CT: Yale University Press, 1994.

Marks, Lynne. "'A Fragment of Heaven on Earth?': Religion, Gender and Family in Turn-of-the-Century Canadian Church Periodicals." *Journal of Family History* 26, 2 (April 2001): 251–71. http://dx.doi.org/10.1177/036319900102600205.

–. "Irreligion, Immigration, Racialization and Ethnicity in British Columbia at the Turn of the Nineteenth Century." Paper presented at the annual meeting of the Social Science History Association, Vancouver, November 3, 2012.

–. "'Not Being Religious Didn't Take Away from Their Jewishness': The Complexities of Lived Religion among Late 19th and Early 20th Century B.C. Jews." *BC Studies* 181 (Spring 2014): 63–82.

–. *Revivals and Roller Rinks: Religion, Leisure, and Identity in Late-Nineteenth-Century Small-Town Ontario.* Toronto: University of Toronto Press, 1996.

Marshall, Alison R. *Cultivating Connections: The Making of Chinese Prairie Canada.* Vancouver: UBC Press, 2014.

–. *The Way of the Bachelor: Early Chinese Settlement in Manitoba.* Vancouver: UBC Press, 2011.

Marshall, David. "Canadian Historians, Secularization and the Problem of the Nineteenth Century." *Historical Studies* (Canadian Catholic Historical Association) 60 (1993–94): 57–81.

–. *Secularizing the Faith: Canadian Protestant Clergy and the Crisis of Belief, 1850–1940.* Toronto: University of Toronto Press, 1992.

Mawani, Renisa. *Colonial Proximities: Crossracial Encounters and Juridical Truths in British Columbia, 1871–1921.* Vancouver: UBC Press, 2009.

McAllister, Clare. "Women of the West Kootenay." *B.C. Historical News* 10, 3 (April 1977): 13-17.

McCann, Gillian. *Vanguard of the New Age: The Toronto Theosophical Society, 1891–1945.* Montreal and Kingston: McGill-Queen's University Press, 2012.

McCormack, A. Ross. *Reformers, Rebels, and Revolutionaries: The Western Canadian Radical Movement, 1899–1919.* Toronto: University of Toronto Press, 1991.

McDonnell, Lillooet Nordlinger. "In the Company of Gentiles: Exploring the History of Integrated Jews in British Columbia, 1858-1971." PhD diss., University of Ottawa, 2011.

–. *Raincoast Jews: Integration in British Columbia.* Vancouver: Midtown Press, 2014.

McIntosh, W.R., ed. *Canadian Problems.* Toronto: R. Douglas Fraser, Presbyterian Publications, 1910.

McKay, Ian. *Reasoning Otherwise: Leftists and the People's Enlightenment in Canada, 1890–1920.* Toronto: Between the Lines, 2008.

McLeod, Hugh. *Piety and Poverty: Working-Class Religion in Berlin, London and New York, 1870–1914.* New York: Holmes and Meier, 1996.

McLeod, Hugh, and Werner Ustorf, eds. *The Decline of Christendom in Western Europe, 1750–2000.* Cambridge: Cambridge University Press, 2003. http://dx.doi.org/10.1017/CBO9780511496783.

McManus, Sheila. "Their Own Country: Race, Gender, Landscape, and Colonization around the Forty-Ninth Parallel, 1862-1900." In *The Borderlands of the American and Canadian Wests: Essays on Regional History of the Forty-Ninth Parallel*, ed. Sterling Evans. Lincoln: University of Nebraska Press, 2006.

McMullin, Stan. *Anatomy of a Seance: A History of Spirit Communication in Central Canada.* Montreal and Kingston: McGill-Queen's University Press, 2004.

McNally, Vincent J. "Challenging the Status Quo: An Examination of the History of Catholic Education in British Columbia." *Historical Studies* (Canadian Catholic Historical Association) 65 (1999): 71–91.

–. "Church-State Relations and American Influence in British Columbia before Confederation." *Journal of Church and State* 34, 1 (Winter 1992): 93–110. http://dx.doi.org/10.1093/jcs/34.1.93.

–. *The Lord's Distant Vineyard: A History of the Oblates and the Catholic Community in British Columbia.* Edmonton: University of Alberta Press, 2000.

Mead, Rebecca J. *How the Vote Was Won: Woman Suffrage in the Western United States, 1868–1914.* New York: New York University Press, 2004.

Mercier, Anne. *Father Pat: A Hero of the Far West.* Gloucester, MA: Minchin and Gibbs, 1909.

Meyer Zu Erpen, Walter J., and Joy Lowe. "The Canadian Spiritualist Movement and Sources for Its Study." *Archivaria* 30 (Summer 1990): 71–84.

Miller, J.R. "Anti-Catholic Thought in Victorian Canada." *Canadian Historical Review* 65, 4 (December 1985): 474–94. http://dx.doi.org/10.3138/CHR-066-04-03.

Mitchell, David, and Dennis Duffy, eds. *Bright Sunshine and a Brand New Country: Reflections on the Okanagan Valley, 1890–1914.* Sound Heritage 7, 3. Victoria: Province of British Columbia, 1979.

Moir, George T. *Sinners and Saints: A True Story of Early Days in the Farthest West by an Old Timer, Written and Told by Himself.* Victoria: n.p., 1948.

Morgan, Bonnie. "Conceiving Christianity: Anglican Women and Lived Religion in Mid-20th Century Conception Bay, Newfoundland." PhD diss., University of New Brunswick, 2014.

Morgan, Sue. "'Iron Strength and Infinite Tenderness': Herbert Gray and the Making of Christian Masculinities at War and at Home, 1900–40." In *Men, Masculinities and Religious Change in Twentieth-Century Britain,* ed. Lucy Delap and Sue Morgan, 168–96. London: Palgrave Macmillan, 2013.

Morgan, Sue, and Jacqueline de Vries, eds. *Women and Religious Cultures in Britain, 1800–1940.* London: Routledge, 2010.

"The Most Sacred of Hearts." *B.C. Catholic,* December 22, 2003, 12.

Mouat, Jeremy. "The Genesis of Western Exceptionalism: British Columbia's Hard-Rock Miners, 1895-1903." *Canadian Historical Review* 71, 3 (1990): 317–45. http://dx.doi.org/10.3138/CHR-071-03-01.

–. *Roaring Days: Rossland's Mines and the History of British Columbia.* Vancouver: UBC Press, 1995.

Moyles, R.G. *The Blood and Fire in Canada: A History of the Salvation Army in the Dominion, 1882–1976.* Toronto: Peter Martin, 1977.

Muise, Del. "'The Great Transformation': Changing the Urban Face of Nova Scotia, 1871–1921." *Nova Scotia Historical Review* 11, 2 (1991): 1–42.

Murphy, Mary. *Mining Cultures: Men, Women and Leisure in Butte, 1914–41.* Urbana: University of Illinois Press, 1997.

Nash, David. "Reconnecting Religion with Social and Cultural History: Secularisation's Failure as a Master Narrative." *Cultural and Social History* 1, 3 (2004): 302–25. http://dx.doi.org/10.1191/1478003804cs0017oa.

Nelson History Theatre Society. "A History of John Houston." http://www.johntruthhouston.com.

Newton, Janice. *The Feminist Challenge to the Canadian Left, 1900–1918.* Montreal and Kingston: McGill-Queen's University Press, 1995.

Neylan, Susan. "Encountering Spirits: Evangelical and Holiness Revivals in Victoria, B.C., and the 'Colonial Project.'" *Histoire sociale* 36, 71 (May 2003): 175–204.

–. *The Heavens Are Changing: Nineteenth-Century Protestant Missions and Tsimshian Christianity.* Montreal and Kingston: McGill-Queen's University Press, 2002.

Nickols, Sheila. "Up with the Petticoats! Down with the Trousers! From Suffragist to Political Candidate: Mary Graves of Victoria, B.C." *British Columbia History* 34, 3 (Summer 2001): 2–7.

Noddings, Timothy R. "What It Means to Be Modern: A Messy History of Mass-Media Revivals in the Gilded Age and Progressive Era, 1875-1920." Master's thesis, University of Victoria, 2013.

O'Connell Killen, Patricia, and Mark Silk, eds. *Religion and Public Life in the Pacific Northwest: The None Zone.* Walnut Creek, CA: AltaMira Press, 2004.

Opp, James William. *The Lord for the Body: Religion, Medicine, and Protestant Faith Healing in Canada, 1880–1930.* Montreal and Kingston: McGill-Queen's University Press, 2005.

O'Reilly, Liam. "Missionaries and Women in Victoria's Chinatown: The Establishment and Evolution of the Chinese Rescue Home, 1886-1900." Major research paper, Department of History, University of Victoria, 2011.

Orsi, Robert. "Everyday Miracles: The Study of Lived Religion." In *Lived Religion in America: Toward a History of Practice,* ed. David D. Hall, 3–21. Princeton: Princeton University Press, 1997.

–. *The Madonna of 115th Street: Faith and Community in Italian Harlem, 1880–1950.* New Haven, CT: Yale University Press, 1985.

–. "Who Cares about Religion? The Blind Spot in Contemporary Historiography." Paper presented at Qualicum History Conference, Parksville, BC, January 30, 2003.

Owen, Alex. *The Darkened Room: Women, Power and Spiritualism in Late Victorian England.* London: Virago Press, 1989.

–. *The Place of Enchantment: British Occultism and the Culture of the Modern.* Chicago: University of Chicago Press, 2004. http://dx.doi.org/10.7208/chicago/9780226642031.001.0001.

Palmer, Bryan. "Historiographical Hassles: Class and Gender, Evidence and Interpretation." *Histoire sociale* 33, 65 (May 2000): 105–44.

Paper, Jordan, and Laurence G. Thompson, eds. *The Chinese Way in Religion.* Belmont, CA: Wadsworth, 1998.

Pazdro, Roberta J. "Agnes Deans Cameron: Against the Current." In *In Her Own Right: Selected Essays on Women's History in B.C.,* ed. Barbara Latham and Cathy Kess, 101–23. Victoria: Camosun College, 1980.

Peers, Laura. "'The Guardian of All': Jesuit Missionary and Salish Perceptions of the Virgin Mary." In *Reading beyond Words: Contexts for Native History,* 2nd ed., ed. Jennifer Brown and Elizabeth Vibert, 284–303. Peterborough, ON: Broadview Press, 2003.

Perrin, Roberto. "Churches and Immigrant Integration in Toronto, 1947-65." In *The Churches and Social Order in Nineteenth- and Twentieth-Century Canada,* ed. Michael Gauvreau and Ollivier Hubert, 274–91. Montreal and Kingston: McGill-Queen's University Press, 2006.

–. *The Immigrants' Church: The Third Force in Canadian Catholicism, 1880–1920.* Canada's Ethnic Group Series Booklet 25. Ottawa: Canadian Historical Association, 1998.

Perry, Adele. *On the Edge of Empire: Gender, Race and the Making of British Columbia, 1849–1871.* Toronto: University of Toronto Press, 2001.

Raibmon, Paige. *Authentic Indians: Episodes of Encounter from the Late-Nineteenth-Century Northwest Coast.* Durham: Duke University Press, 2005. http://dx.doi.org/10.1215/9780822386773.

Rationalist Association of North America. *Ten Rationalist Lectures at the Panama-Pacific Congress.* Chicago: Rationalist Association, 1915. University of Manitoba Library.

Reid, Andrew. "Not So Secret Societies: Fraternities and Masculine Identity in Victorian Victoria, 1860-1890." Major research paper, Department of History, University of Victoria, 2012.

Reimer, Samuel. "A Look at Cultural Effects on Religiosity: A Comparison between the United States and Canada." *Journal for the Scientific Study of Religion* 34, 4 (1995): 445–57. http://dx.doi.org/10.2307/1387338.

Report of the Royal Commission on Chinese and Japanese Immigration: Session 1902. Ottawa: S.2E. Dawson, 1902.

Robertson, Leslie A. with the Kwagu'l Gixsam Clan. *Standing Up with Ga'axsta'las: Jane Constance Cook and the Politics of Memory, Church and Custom*. Vancouver: UBC Press, 2012.

Roe, Jill. "'Testimonies from the Field': The Coming of Christian Science to Australia, c. 1890-1910." *Journal of Religious History* 22, 3 (1998): 304-19.

Roediger, David. *The Wages of Whiteness: Race and the Making of the American Working Class*. London: Verso, 1991.

Rosenfeld, Mark. "'She Was a Hard Life': Work, Family, Community, Politics and Ideology in the Railway Ward of a Central Ontario Town, 1900–1960." PhD diss., York University, 1990.

Roy, Patricia. "Anglicans and Asians in British Columbia: An Ambiguous Relationship." Unpublished paper, n.d.

–. *Boundless Optimism: Richard McBride's British Columbia*. Vancouver: UBC Press, 2012.

–. *A White Man's Province: British Columbia Politicians and Chinese and Japanese Immigrants, 1858–1914*. Vancouver: UBC Press, 1989.

Royle, Edward. *Radicals, Secularists and Republicans: Popular Freethought in Britain, 1886–1915*. Manchester: Manchester University Press, 1980.

Rutherdale, Myra. *Women and the White Man's God: Gender and Race in the Canadian Mission Field*. Vancouver: UBC Press, 2002.

Ryan, Mary. *Cradle of the Middle Class: The Family in Oneida County, New York, 1790–1865*. Cambridge: Cambridge University Press, 1981.

Sager, Eric. "The National Sample of the 1901 Census of Canada: A New Source for the Study of the Working Class." Paper presented at the Social Science History conference, Amsterdam, March 1998. http://web.uvic.ca/hrd/cfp/publications/Eric%20W.%20Sager.pdf.

Saikku, Mikko. "Utopians and Utilitarians: Environment and Economy in the Finnish-Canadian Settlement of Sointula." *BC Studies* 154 (Summer 2007): 3–38.

Sandon Historical Society. "'Knights of the Green Cloth': Gamblers, Card Sharks and Sandon's Saloons." Sandon Museum, February 23, 2011. http://www.sandonmuseum.ca/characters/74-knights-of-the-green-cloth.

–. "The 'Soiled Doves' of 'Lower Sandon': Madames, Brothels and the Infamous Red Light District." Sandon Museum, February 23, 2011. http://www.sandonmuseum.ca/characters/76-the-soiled-doves-of-lower-sandon.

Sangster, Joan. "Telling Our Stories: Feminist Debates and the Use of Oral History." *Women's History Review* 3, 1 (1994): 5–28. http://dx.doi.org/10.1080/09612029400200046.

Sawyer, Bonnie. "A Critical History of Social Work, the Canadian Salvation Army, and Female Sexual 'Deviance' in Canada, 1886–1940." Master's thesis, University of Victoria, 2014.

Schmidt, Leigh Eric. *Village Atheists: How America's Unbelievers Made Their Way in a Godly Nation.* Princeton, NJ: Princeton University Press, 2016.

Schwantes, Carlos A. "The Churches of the Disinherited: The Culture of Radicalism on the North Pacific Industrial Frontier." *Pacific Historian* 25 (Winter 1981): 54–65.

–. *Radical Heritage: Labor, Socialism, and Reform in Washington and British Columbia, 1885–1917.* Vancouver: Douglas and McIntyre, 1979.

Schwartz, Laura. *Infidel Feminism: Secularism, Religion and Women's Emancipation, England, 1830–1914.* Manchester: Manchester University Press, 2013. http://dx.doi.org/10.7228/manchester/9780719085826.001.0001.

Scott, David, and Edna H. Hanie. *Nelson: Queen City of the Kootenays.* Vancouver: Mitchell Press, 1972.

Seager, Allen. "Socialists and Workers: The Western Canadian Coal Miners, 1900-1921." *Labour/Le travail* 16 (Fall 1985): 23–59.

Seager, Allen, and Adele Perry. "Mining the Connections: Class, Ethnicity, and Gender in Nanaimo, B.C., 1891." *Histoire sociale* 30, 59 (May 1997): 55–76.

Shaw, Christine. "'Sitting at the Feet of Jesus, Clothed and in Their Right Mind': The Convergence of Religion, Culture, and Race in Missionary Discourse in Halkomelem Territory, Southern Coastal British Columbia, 1850–1900." Master's thesis, University of Victoria, 2001.

Shearer, Ronald A. "The Chinese and Chinatown of Rossland: Fragments from Their Early History." http://spiritofred.ca/wp-content/uploads/chinese-in-rossland.pdf.

Shelvey, Bruce, and June Bull, eds. *The Archival Directory of Religious Organizations in the Greater Victoria Region.* Victoria: Centre for Studies in Religion and Society and the Department of History, University of Victoria, 1998.

Sivertz, Bent. *The Sivertz Family.* Book 2, *Elinborg.* Canby, OR: Rudolph Reid Prael, 1982.

Smith, Edward. "Working-Class Anglicans: Religion and Identity in Victorian and Edwardian Hamilton, Ontario." *Histoire sociale* 36, 71 (May 2003): 123–44.

Sohi, Seema. *Echoes of Mutiny: Race, Surveillance and Indian Anticolonialism in North America.* Oxford: Oxford University Press, 2014. http://dx.doi.org/10.1093/acprof:oso/9780199376247.001.0001.

Speer, J.C. *The Story of China in Canada.* Toronto: Department of Missionary Literature, Methodist Church of Canada, 1900.

Stanley, Timothy. *Contesting White Supremacy: School Segregation, Anti-racism, and the Making of Chinese Canadians.* Vancouver: UBC Press, 2011.

Stark, Rodney, and William Sims Bainbridge. *The Future of Religion: Secularization, Revival and Cult Formation.* Berkeley: University of California Press, 1985.

Steele, David M. *Going Abroad Overland: Studies of Places and People in the Far West.* New York: G.P. Putnam's Sons, 1917.

Stenhouse, John. "Imperialism, Atheism, and Race: Charles Southwell, Old Corruption, and the Maori." *Journal of British Studies* 44, 4 (2005): 754–74.

Stewart, Bob. "That's the B.C. Spirit! Religion and Secularity in Lotus Land." *Canadian Society of Church History Papers* (1983): 22–35.

Stob, Paul. "Religious Conflict and Intellectual Agency: Robert Ingersoll's Contributions to American Thought and Culture." *Rhetoric and Public Affairs* 16, 4 (Winter 2013): 719–51. http://dx.doi.org/10.1353/rap.2013.0046.

Storm, Ingrid. "Halfway to Heaven: Four Types of Fuzzy Fidelity in Europe." *Journal for the Scientific Study of Religion* 48, 4 (2009): 702–18. http://dx.doi.org/10.1111/j.1468-5906.2009.01474.x.

Taves, Ann. *Fits, Trances and Visions: Experiencing Religion and Explaining Experience from Wesley to James.* Princeton: Princeton University Press, 1999.

Taylor, Charles. *A Secular Age.* Cambridge, MA: Harvard University Press, 2007.

Thompson, E.P. *The Making of the English Working Class.* New York: Pantheon Books, 1964.

Thompson, Margaret E. *The Baptist Story in Western Canada.* Calgary: Baptist Union of Western Canada, 1975.

Tobe, Sarah H. "Lured North of the 49th: Jewish Colonial Roots: Victoria, Vancouver Island, Canada." *Western States Jewish History Association* 46, 2/3 (2014).

Todd, Douglas, ed. *Cascadia, the Elusive Utopia: Exploring the Spirit of the Pacific Northwest.* Vancouver: Ronsdale Press, 2008.

Tosh, John. *A Man's Place: Masculinity and the Middle-Class Home in Victorian England.* New Haven, CT: Yale University Press, 1999.

Townsend, Joan Helen. "Protestant Christian Morality and the Nineteenth Century Secular and Non-sectarian British Columbia Public School System." Master's thesis, University of British Columbia, 1974.

Tulchinsky, Gerald. *Branching Out: The Transformation of the Canadian Jewish Community.* Toronto: Stoddart, 1998.

–. *Taking Root: The Origins of the Canadian Jewish Community.* Toronto: Lester, 1992.

Turkstra, Melissa. "Working-Class Churches in Early Twentieth Century Hamilton: Fostering a Distinctive Working-Class Identity and Culture." *Histoire sociale* 41, 82 (2008): 459–503. http://dx.doi.org/10.1353/his.0.0026.

Turnbull, Elsie G. *Church in the Kootenays: The Story of the United Church of Canada in Kootenay Presbytery.* Trail, BC: Trail Times, for Kootenay Presbyterial United Church Women, 1965.

Turner, James. *Without God, without Creed: The Origins of Unbelief in America.* Baltimore: Johns Hopkins University Press, 1985.

Valverde, Mariana. *The Age of Light, Soap and Water: Moral Reform in English Canada, 1885–1925.* Toronto: McClelland and Stewart, 1991.

–. "'When the Mother of the Race Is Free': Race, Reproduction and Sexuality in First-Wave Feminism." In *Gender Conflicts: New Essays in Women's History,* ed. Franca Iacovetta and Mariana Valverde, 3–26. Toronto: University of Toronto Press, 1992.

Van Die, Marguerite. *Religion, Family and Community in Victorian Canada: The Colbys of Carrollcroft.* Montreal and Kingston: McGill-Queen's University Press, 2005.

–. "'A Woman's Awakening': Evangelical Belief and Female Spirituality in Mid-nineteenth-century Canada." In *Canadian Women: A Reader,* ed. Wendy Mitchinson, Paula Bourne, Alison Prentice, Gail Cuthbert Brandt, Beth Light, and Naomi Black, 49–68. Toronto: Harcourt Brace, 1996.

Van Dieren, Karen. "The Response of the WMS to the Immigration of Asian Women, 1888-1942." In *Not Just Pin Money,* ed. Barbara K. Latham and Roberta J. Pazdro, 79–97. Victoria: Camosun College, 1984.

Van Kirk, Sylvia. *Many Tender Ties: Women in Fur-Trade Society, 1670–1870.* Winnipeg: Watson and Dwyer, 1998.

–. "Tracing the Fortunes of Five Founding Families of Victoria." *BC Studies* 115–16 (Autumn-Winter 1997–98): 149–80.

Vibert, Elizabeth. *Traders' Tales: Narratives of Cultural Encounters in the Columbia Plateau, 1807-1846.* Norman: University of Oklahoma Press, 1997.

Victoria's Chinatown. "The Chinese Consolidated Benevolent Association." http://chinatown.library.uvic.ca/chinese_consolidated_benevolent_association.

Voas, David. "The Rise and Fall of Fuzzy Fidelity in Europe." *European Sociological Review* 25, 2 (2009): 155–68. http://dx.doi.org/10.1093/esr/jcn044.

Voisey, Paul. *Vulcan: The Making of a Prairie Community.* Toronto: University of Toronto Press, 1988.

Wagar, Samuel Eldon Charles. "Theosophical Socialists in the 1920s Okanagan: Jack Logie's Social Issues Summer Camps." Master's thesis, Simon Fraser University, 2005.

Wang, Jiwu. *"His Dominion" and the "Yellow Peril": Protestant Missions to Chinese Immigrants in Canada, 1859–1967.* Waterloo, ON: Wilfrid Laurier University Press, 2006.

Warburton, Rennie. "Race and Class in British Columbia: A Comment." *BC Studies* 49 (Spring 1981): 79–85.

Ward, Peter. "Class and Race in the Social Structure of British Columbia, 1870-1939." *BC Studies* 45 (Spring 1980): 17–35.

–. "The Oriental Immigrant and Canada's Protestant Clergy, 1858-1925." *BC Studies* 22 (Summer 1974): 40–55.

–. *White Canada Forever: Popular Attitudes and Public Policy toward Orientals in British Columbia.* Montreal and Kingston: McGill-Queen's University Press, 1978.

Welwood, R.J. "Lowery, Robert Thornton." *Dictionary of Canadian Biography Online.* http://www.biographi.ca/EN/009004-119.01-e.php?id_nbr=8251.

Whelen, Gloria. "Maria Grant, 1854-1937: The Life and Times of an Early Twentieth Century Christian." In *In Her Own Right: Selected Essays on Women's History in B.C.*, ed. Barbara Latham and Cathy Kess, 125–46. Victoria: Camosun College, 1980.

Whiteley, Marilyn F. "'Allee Samee Melican Lady': Imperialism and Negotiation at the Chinese Rescue Home (Women Missionary Societies Set Up the Chinese Rescue Home to Save Chinese Women from Prostitution)." *Resources for Feminist Research* 22, 3–4 (1992-93): 45–50.

–. "Modest, Unaffected, and Fully Consecrated: Lady Evangelists in Canadian Methodism." In *Changing Roles of Women within the Christian Church of Canada,* ed. Elizabeth Muir and Marilyn Whiteley, 183–200. Toronto: University of Toronto Press, 1995.

Wilkins-Laflamme, Sarah. "Religious-Secular Polarization Compared: The Cases of Quebec and British Columbia." *Studies in Religion/Sciences religieuses* (forthcoming).

Williams, S.C. *Religious Belief and Popular Culture in Southwark, c. 1880–1939.* Oxford: Oxford University Press, 1999. http://dx.doi.org/10.1093/acprof:oso/9780198207696.001.0001.

Winters, Donald E., Jr. *The Soul of the Wobblies: The I.W.W., Religion, and American Culture in the Progressive Era, 1905–1917.* Westport, CT: Greenwood Press, 1985.

Wolfe, Patrick. "Tramp Printer Extraordinary: British Columbia's John 'Truth' Houston." *BC Studies* 40 (Winter 1978–79): 5–31.

Index

Note: "(i)" after a page number indicates an illustration; "f" after a page number indicates a figure; "(t)" after a page number indicates a table

Abrahamson, Doug, 116, 120
Ackerman, Duke, 136
Acland, Paddy, 127
adherents: as census category, 33, 244*n*19, 263*n*17; ratio of communicants to total adherents, 33–34, 36, 49, 112, 145, 190, 222(t), 225–33(t), 244*n*20, 245*n*21
adult, definition of, 8, 236*n*17
Adult Bible Class Federation, 142
African Canadians, 102–3, 122–23, 237*n*23, 262*n*9
age and irreligion, 38, 43, 246*n*36
agnostics: census declaration as, 4, 22, 30, 243*n*11; definition of, 30–31; as proportion of population, 5(f), 29–30, 46(f), 223(t)
Albanese, Catherine, 187
alcohol: as masculine leisure activity, 16, 21, 25, 37, 68, 69–70, 70(i), 73–74, 82, 84, 85(i), 90, 113, 124, 152, 158, 160; Prohibition, 57, 136, 141, 142, 218, 271*n*33, 289*n*4; sale to Indigenous people, 178, 282*n*70
Americans, 48, 67, 258*n*22, 275*n*73; and church involvement, 5–6, 36, 110, 268*n*93; demographics of in British Columbia, 236*n*19, 250*n*83, 251*n*89, 268*n*92, 269*n*95; irreligious, 52–53, 70–71, 128, 151, 155, 214, 217–18, 250*n*84, 264*n*42
Amherst (Nova Scotia), 110; African Nova Scotian church in, 103; church involvement in, 108, 124, 129, 131, 132, 226(t), 228–31(t), 262*n*9, 264*n*27; demographics of, 102, 264*n*41
Ammerman, Nancy T., 258*n*22
Anglicans, 42, 50, 89–90, 90(i), 91–92, 101, 102–3, 105(i), 127(i), 135, 245*n*22; and Asian people, 170, 171, 172, 174; church involvement, 226–31(t), 244*n*18, 259*n*36, 263*nn*25–26, 265*n*43, 272*n*44; clergy, 6, 73, 79–80, 80(i), 81, 85–86, 87–88, 96, 148, 193, 210; percentage of communicants to total adherents, 222(t), 225(t), 232(t); women, 111, 115, 117, 121, 180, 182, 184
anti-Asian racism, 9, 216, 236*n*22, 254*n*57, 282*n*75; against Chinese, 66–67, 71–72, 75–76, 121–22, 164, 257*n*95; against Japanese, 167, 170–71, 219; against

South Asians, 99, 155, 161, 166–68, 188, 198, 203–4
anti-Catholicism, 3, 25, 79, 92, 93, 94–95, 95(i), 120, 216, 237*n*25, 239*n*40, 260*n*48
anti-clericalism, 45, 65, 76, 78, 140
Armstrong, Christopher, 140
Asians, population of in British Columbia, 10(f), 236*n*21. *See also* Chinese; Japanese; South Asians
Asiatic Exclusion League, 170–71
atheists: census declaration as, 4, 22, 223(t), 242*n*3, 243*n*11; definition of, 30–31; as proportion of population, 5(f), 46(f), 99, 224(t), 274*n*69; as proportion of the irreligious, 255*n*75
Atkinson, Sam, 154, 155, 276*n*88
Austin, Rev. B.F., 192

baptism, 87–89, 106, 264*n*29
Baptist Ladies Aid, 117
Baptist Young People's Union, 129
Baptists, 50, 58–59, 74, 75–76, 102–3, 226(t), 228–31(t), 252*n*35; African Nova Scotians, 103; and church involvement, 102, 103–4, 105, 108, 127, 129, 144, 263*n*25, 264*n*27; percentage of communicants to total adherents, 222(t), 232(t); and revivals, 218; women, 111, 117, 197; and women's suffrage, 181, 183
Barman, Jean, 117, 119, 121, 289*n*4
Barnard, Stuart, 13, 82, 269*n*100
B.C. Federation of Labour, 197
BC Federationist, 64, 254*n*57
BC Western Catholic, 64
Bedard, Fr. J.A., 92–93
Belshaw, John, 49–50, 51, 61, 69, 239*n*40
Bennett, R.B., 61
Besant, Annie, 199, 203
Beyer, Peter, 6, 235*n*11
Biggs, Herschel, 84
birthplace and irreligion, 52–54, 246*nn*43–44
Block, Tina, 13, 220
Board of Social Service and Evangelism (Presbyterian Church), 141
Board of Temperance and Moral Reform (Methodist Church), 141
boarders, 38–39, 110–11, 149, 151, 264*nn*40–41, 273*n*61, 274*n*70, 275*n*85, 277*n*13. *See also* lodgers
Bolton, Lorraine, 136
Bowen, Lynne, 49, 88
Bridge, Kathryn, 131, 135
British, 51, 128, 236*n*19, 268*nn*92–93
British Columbia Society of Spiritualists, 192–93, 285*n*27
Brooks, Eugene, 158–59
Brouwer, Ruth, 180
Brown, Callum, 13, 219, 220
Brown, Lorraine, 121–22
Buchner, Ludwig, 59
Buck, Ian, 147, 274*n*70
Buddhists, 52, 167, 171, 281*n*59
Bunoz, Rev. Emile-Marie, 177(i)
Burkinshaw, Robert, 218
Buttrum, Rev. St. George, 170

Cameron, Agnes Deans, 202
Campbell, Rev. Duncan, 184
Campbell, George, 190
Campbell, Muriel, 119
Campbell, Peter, 60, 167, 219
Campbellford (Ontario), 103, 108, 111–12, 123–24, 129, 131, 226(t), 228–31(t), 263*n*25, 264*n*27
Canadian Humanist Association, 220
Canadian Presbyterian Board of Moral and Social Reform, 82
Cariboo, 7, 8, 247*n*57; Americans in, 52–53, 251*n*89; demographics of, 247*n*57, 251*n*90; irreligious in, 44, 45–46, 49, 52–54, 108, 146, 224(t), 244*n*20, 251*n*90, 274*n*62; percentage of communicants to total adherents, 225(t). *See also* Nelson; Revelstoke; Rossland; Vernon
Carr, Emily, 189–90, 286*n*42
Carson, Rev., 184
Catholic Order of Foresters, 145–46
Catholics. *See* Roman Catholics
censuses, taking of, 21–23, 31, 244*n*19
Central City Mission, Vancouver, 152–54, 275*n*76, 275*n*78
Chilcotin, 8

children: age of communicant status, 36, 105; baptism of, 21, 87–88; Chinese, 168, 173(i); church involvement of, 131–32, 135–36; death of, 15, 106, 158, 194, 201; Doukhobor, 289*n*2; Japanese, 219; mixed-race, 121; religious affiliation of, 40–41, 42, 195, 247*n*49; and Sunday School, 21, 30, 88–89, 89(i), 119, 144. *See also* schools
Chinese, 9, 23, 95, 216, 250*n*82, 260*n*51, 281*n*63; and anti-Asian racism, 9, 66–67, 71–72, 75–76, 96, 121–22, 164, 170–71, 257*n*95; Chinatowns, 167, 168, 169, 169(i), 170, 173, 175, 176, 278*n*25, 280*nn*55–56; Christians, 175–76, 218–19, 281*n*64, 290*n*9; demographics of in British Columbia, 104, 167, 236*n*19, 262*n*14, 278*n*24; and Indigenous people, 178, 282*n*70; and irreligion, 20, 184–85, 274*n*63; loss of franchise, 236*n*22; and missionaries, 28, 75–76, 122, 171–74, 272*n*49, 280*n*50, 281*n*63; religious practices, 52, 161, 167, 168–70, 169(i), 175, 250*n*81, 280*n*56, 281*n*59, 281*n*61; rescue homes, 173(i), 179; women, 121, 167–68
Chinese Rescue Home, Victoria, 173(i), 179
Christadelphians, 186
Christian Science, 16, 27, 186, 188, 205–12, 215, 233(t), 288*nn*94–95, 289*n*101
Christie, Nancy, 6, 235*n*11, 239*n*45
Clarkson, Chris, 179
class: Catholics and, 60, 64, 85, 95–96; definition of, 268*n*84, 18, 45, 241*n*58, 248*n*62, 248*n*64, 249*n*70, 272*n*51, 285*n*26; Methodists and, 50, 58, 60, 61, 124–25, 252*n*35, 272*n*51, 273*n*52, 273*nn*60–61; Presbyterians and, 50, 58, 59–60, 124, 125, 147, 148, 272*n*51, 273*nn*52–54; and revivals, 269*n*100; spiritualism and, 190, 192–93, 285*n*26. *See also* Marxists; socialists; strikes; unions
Clayton, Jenny, 126
coal mining, 7, 8, 27, 46, 49, 50, 58, 61–62, 249*n*–72, 250*n*77. *See also* miners
Coccola, Fr. Nicholas, 73, 177(i)
Colby, George P., 190, 192
communicants: as census category, 33, 263*n*17; ratio of communicants to total adherents, 33–34, 36, 49, 112, 145, 190, 222(t), 225–33(t), 244*n*20, 245*n*21
Confucianism, 52, 161, 167, 250*n*81, 280*n*56, 281*n*59, 281*n*61
Congregationalists, 104, 184
Connelly, Fr., 184
Connor, Ralph. *See* Gordon, Charles
Continental Europeans: population of in British Columbia, 8, 236*n*19; in Saskatchewan, 237*n*24
Cox, Annie, 43, 247*n*55
Crease, Henry, 115
Crease, Sarah, 115
Cridge, Edward, 190–91
Crossley, Hugh, 136–37
Crowsnest Pass, 46, 47–48, 49, 57, 79, 82, 95, 249*n*71; coal mining in, 8
Curtis, Bruce, 21

Darwinism, 44, 187
Deists, 42, 43
Denison, Flora Macdonald, 202
Dixon, Lillian, 131
Dontenwill, Bishop Augustin, 72, 92, 93, 94, 96
Doukhobors, 289*n*2
Doull, Bishop, 210–11, 218
Dow, Rev. J.A., 111
drinking. *See* alcohol
Dua, Enakshi, 167–68
Dubinsky, Karen, 137
Dunae, Patrick, 151, 275*nn*72–73, 278*n*25
Dunnville (Ontario), 103, 108, 123, 124, 129, 130, 131, 132, 226(t), 228–31(t), 263*n*25, 264*n*27

Early, Nellie, 151, 275*n*72
eastern Europeans, 237*n*24, 256*n*81; Slav, 9, 72–73, 96, 104, 145, 262*n*16
Eddy, Mary Baker, 205, 206
Edwards, George, 118, 128
Edwards, Mrs., 118–19
Ellison, Price, 131

Emery, George, 110
employees and irreligion, 45, 248*nn*62–64, 249*n*70
employers and irreligion, 45, 248*nn*62–64
Episcopalians, 42, 103, 189, 190
ethnicity, 10(f); Catholics, 145–46, 272*n*48; and church involvement, 128, 146; and identity, 30, 43–44, 51–54, 94, 124, 197; and irreligion, 51–54, 243*n*13; Jewish, 162–66, 278*n*18; Presbyterians, 124, 146. *See also* fraternal orders
evangelicals, 26, 105, 114, 120, 128, 146; and revivals, 82, 136, 218–19; and Sabbatarianism, 70, 73; and the social gospel, 141, 152–54. *See also* Woman's Christian Temperance Union (WCTU)

Fell, James, 193
feminists, 181–84, 198, 201–2, 212, 287*n*72. *See also* suffrage
Ferguson, George, 73, 128
Fernie, 57, 58, 63, 72–73, 82, 87, 88, 96
Finns, 98, 131, 204
First Spiritualist Church of Vancouver, 193
fishing industry, 7
Forbes, Rev., 94
Foreshaw, Mrs., 148
Fraser, W.J., 94
Fraser Valley, 177(i); agriculture in, 7–8
fraternal orders, 89–96, 125, 144, 149, 158–59, 163–64, 260*n*51; female auxiliaries of, 91, 125; and funerals, 97, 260*n*59
Freeman, Rev., 177, 279*n*42
Freemasons, 90, 91, 163–64; Chinese, 260*n*51
freethinkers, 44, 57, 66, 174, 276*n*91, 285*n*27, 253*n*50; census declaration as, 30, 31, 42, 43, 45, 71, 74, 151, 196, 243*n*11, 248*n*64, 275*n*72; and anti-Sabbatarianism, 140–41. *See also* agnostics; atheists; infidels; Lowery, Colonel Robert Thornton; no religion; secularists; skeptics; unbelievers
frontier, concept of, 17, 240*n*50
Fuller, Robert, 187
funerals, 96–98, 97(i), 260*n*59, 261*n*61; Chinese, 122; and cremation, 198, 202

gambling, 16, 21, 37, 68–69, 70, 82, 149; Chinese men and, 172; Christian efforts to control, 25, 73, 74, 136, 137, 141, 160, 170, 178, 182; Indigenous peoples and, 178, 282*n*76
Gardom, Esther, 119
Gauvin, Marshall, 155, 290*n*13
Gauvreau, Michael, 6, 235*n*11, 239*n*45
gender, and church involvement, 15–18, 111–19, 215, 228–30(t); and class, 123–28; and irreligion, 16, 36–44, 51, 53, 65–66, 224(t), 243*n*13, 245*n*34, 246*n*38, 246*n*40, 247*n*45, 253*n*50, 255*n*74, 255*n*75; ratio, 7, 8, 15, 46, 71, 132, 147, 211, 218, 247*n*57; and secularization, 219, 238*n*37. *See also* marital status; marriage; masculinity; women
Germans, 88, 96, 146, 164, 250*n*83, 272*n*48
gold, 7, 8, 9, 113(i), 143, 163
Good Government League, 142
Gordon, Annie McQueen. *See* McQueen, Annie
Gordon, Rev. Charles, 79
Gosden, Robert, 198, 201, 204
Goutor, David, 67
Gow, H., 148
Graham, Lydia, 116, 120
Graham, Thomas, 148
Grant, Maria, 183, 202
Graves, Mary, 201–2
Green, Thomas, 81, 87
Greene, Canon Alan, 80, 87, 261*n*62
Greene, Rev. Thomas, 85–86
Greenwood (Kootenays), 73, 74, 81, 93, 119, 207
Greenwood, Nancy, 207
Greenwood, Samuel, 207, 208
Greenwood Ledge, 210, 260*n*59
Grice-Hutchinson, Rev. Rowan Ernest, 81, 87–88, 96, 259*n*31
Griffith, Dr., 199
Grimshaw, Patricia, 17, 181
Gutteridge, Helena, 201, 287*n*72

Hall, Florence, 180, 181, 182
Hall, Rev. L.W., 168
Halliday, C.W., 126

Hamilton (Ontario), 146, 232(t), 272*n*50
Hanowski, Elliot, 219, 221, 290*nn*13–14
hardrock mining, 8, 46, 103. *See also* miners
Hardy, Mary Ann, 194
Hardy, Thomas, 194
Hawthornthwaite, James, 62, 86
Hayward, Minister, 138
heathen, 88, 162, 259*n*31; applied to Asian people, 9, 52, 67, 77, 169, 170, 174, 178, 185, 216; applied to Indigenous people, 52
Hills, George (Bishop), 6, 96, 148, 193
Hinde, John, 61
Hinduism, as an influence on theosophy, 188, 198, 203
Hindus, 155, 166, 167, 199
Hirst, Margaret, 43, 247*n*56
Houston, John, 74–75, 75(i), 76, 77, 95, 97–98, 256*n*90, 257*n*95
humanists. *See* secularists
Hunter, John, 136–37

immigrants, 237*n*24, 246*n*44; time of immigration as factor in irreligion, 39, 52, 110, 149, 227(t), 273*n*60. *See also* Americans; British; Chinese; Eastern Europeans; Italians; Japanese; Jews; South Asians
Indigenous peoples, 7, 109, 179; and alcohol, 282*n*70, 282*n*76; conversion to Christianity, 19, 20, 28, 162, 176–78, 177(i), 185, 281*n*67, 275*n*84; defined as heathen, 52; defined as pagan, 20, 51–52, 177; and interracial relationships, 254*n*63, 266*n*67; and irreligious census category, 51; population, 8, 9, 104, 215, 236*n*18, 237*n*24; racism toward, 56, 68, 93–94, 121, 122–23, 138, 267*n*80
Industrial Worker, 63, 64
Industrial Workers of the World (IWW), 63–64, 76, 98, 156–57, 198, 214, 253*n*40
infidels, census declaration as, 6, 14, 22, 49, 193, 196, 243*n*11. *See also* agnostics; atheists; freethinkers; infidels; no religion; secularists; skeptics; unbelievers
intermarriage. *See under* marriage
Irish, 124, 145, 146, 272*n*48
irreligion, definition of, 6–7, 31, 236*n*12; percentage of population, 223–24(t), 234*n*3, 274*n*69, 289*n*3. *See also* agnostics; atheists; freethinkers; infidels; no religion; secularists; skeptics; unbelievers
Italians, 9, 68, 72, 73, 95, 96, 104, 145–46, 256*n*81, 257*n*95, 262*n*16, 272*n*48
Iverson, Louise, 121

Japanese, 9, 96, 121, 161, 174, 216, 250*n*82, 279*n*29; and anti-Asian racism, 170–71, 219; demographics of in British Columbia, 167–68; loss of franchise, 236*n*22; and missionaries, 20, 28, 172–73, 272*n*49, 280*n*53, 281*n*65
Jews, 9, 14, 26, 93, 161, 162–66, 185, 216, 276*n*2, 277*n*13, 278*n*18; experience of anti-Semitism, 164, 277*n*9; and irreligion, 164–66; in Quebec, 237*n*25; Temple Emmanu-El, Victoria Synagogue, 163–64, 163(i), 271*n*36
Jinarajadasa, Mr. C., 199
Johnston, Hugh, 166, 203
Johnston, Tom, 86, 131–32

Kamloops, 115, 207
Kaslo (Kootenays), 40, 118(i)
Kaslo Methodist Ladies Aid Society, 118(i)
Kelowna (Okanagan Valley), 200–1, 207
Kelowna Theosophical Society, 200–1, 288*n*76
Kentville (Nova Scotia), 102–3, 108, 123, 124, 129, 131, 132, 226(t), 228–31(t), 262*n*9
Ketlo, Allan, 177(i)
Ketlo, Leon, 177(i)
Kipp, James, 88
Klinkenstein, Rabbi, 163
Kneeshaw, Robert H., 186, 189
Knights of Pythias, 90, 92
Knowles, Norman, 13, 79, 87, 174, 280*n*53
Komagata Maru, 99, 166, 279*n*37
Kootenay Revival Campaign 1909, 82
Kootenays, 47(i), 103, 145; anti-Sabbatarianism in, 73–74; demographics

of, 8, 53; Father Pat (Henry Irwin) in, 79–80, 80(i), 105(i); irreligious in, 18–19, 27, 45, 46–49, 46(f), 111, 274*n*68; Protestant-Catholic tensions in, 93–94, 95. *See also* Greenwood; Kaslo; Nakusp; Nelson; Revelstoke; Rossland; Sandon
Kurikka, Matti, 204

labour activism. *See* Marxists; socialists; strikes; unions
Lacombe, Michele, 198–99
Ladies Aid Societies, 106, 117–18, 118(i), 136
Ladysmith, 47, 50(i)
Lake, Marilyn, 17
Lancaster, Josephine, 164
Lane, Hannah, 41, 43–44, 247*n*54
Lang, Muriel, 119
Laverdure, Paul, 141
Ledge, The (newspaper, Fernie, Greenwood, Nakusp, Nelson, New Denver). See under Lowery, Colonel Robert Thornton
Leier, Mark, 67, 156, 198
leisure: church activities, 128; Sabbatarianism as limiting, 73, 76. *See also* alcohol; gambling; opium smoking; sex trade
Lockwood, Mabel, 151, 275*n*72
lodgers, 38–40, 110–11, 151, 246*n*41, 264*nn*38–41, 274*n*70, 275*n*85, 277*n*13. *See also* boarders
lodges. *See* fraternal orders
logging camps, 7, 36, 37, 61, 71, 73, 81, 82, 97(i), 98, 122, 168, 261*n*62
Logie, Jack, 204, 205, 288*n*76
London (England), 11, 83, 86, 87, 88, 89, 153
London (Ontario), 146, 232(t), 272*n*50
London Theosophical Society, 201
Low, Hong, 175
Lowery, Colonel Robert Thornton, 57(i), 69, 84, 87, 192, 251*n*5; and Christian Science, 209–10; and gender, 65–66, 79; *The Ledge*, 58, 209, 210, 260*n*59; *Lowery's Claim*, 55, 57, 58–59, 65, 76, 220–21, 257*n*99; and racism, 66–67, 76, 77; and *Sandon Paystreak*, 251*n*15
Lowery's Claim. See under Lowery, Colonel Robert Thornton
Lutherans, 131, 146, 197

Maccabees, 93
MacLeod, Rev. P.M., 199–200
Maffly-Kipp, Laurie, 17, 143, 187–88, 284*n*6
marital status and irreligion, 18, 38, 46–47, 49, 128–33, 149–56, 214, 223(t), 230(t), 243*n*13, 246*n*35. *See also* marriage
marriage: effect on male church involvement, 15, 107, 131; equality within, 65; and religious affiliation, 40–44; mixed marriages between denominations, 40, 50, 239*n*40; spousal cohabitation and irreligion, 246*n*38
married men. *See* marital status and irreligion
married women. *See* marital status and irreligion
Marshall, Alison, 172, 175, 260*n*51
Marxists, 21, 45, 48, 60–62, 65, 204–5, 217. *See also* Socialist Party of British Columbia
masculinity, Christian domestic, 15, 65–66, 77; and the clergy, 17, 79–80; and fraternal orders, 90, 144, 149, 160. *See also* alcohol; gender; gambling; sex trade
Mawani, Renisa, 19, 67, 68, 178, 254*n*63
Maynard, Hannah, 194, 195(i), 196(i)
Maynard, M., 285*n*27
McAdams, William, 59–60, 65, 66, 76, 251*n*15
McBride, Richard, 142, 271*n*33
McCann, Gillian, 198, 203, 287*n*71
McCormack, Ross, 61
McDonald, Bob, 148–49, 150
McDonald, Dave, 85
McDonnell, Lillooet, 278*n*18
McInnes, Phoebe, 114
McKay, Ian, 60
McLaren, Rev. E.D., 6, 14, 100
McLeod, Hugh, 83, 86, 235*n*10

McMullin, Stan, 192
McNally, Vincent, 13
McQueen, Annie, 112–14, 119, 120, 131
McQueen, Jessie, 40, 100, 112, 114–15, 116(i), 116–17, 119, 121, 131, 247*n*46
Mead, Rebecca, 181
metaphysical religions, 27, 187–89, 190, 192, 217, 284*n*5. *See also* Christian Science; spiritualism; Theosophy
Methodist Women's Missionary Society, 172, 179; conference delegates, 183(i)
Methodists, 6, 102–3, 109(i), 192, 264*n*37, 266*n*61, 270*n*4; and Asian people, 168, 170, 171, 172, 174, 179, 282*n*70; census declaration as, 21, 22, 30, 42, 43; church involvement, 21, 34, 50, 105, 108–9, 110, 111–15, 127, 131, 135, 136, 144, 146–47, 149, 225–31(t), 242*n*73, 244*nn*18–19, 263*n*25, 264*n*27, 265*n*43, 272*n*51, 273*n*52, 273*n*55; and class, 50, 58, 60, 61, 124–25, 252*n*35, 272*n*51, 273*n*52, 273*nn*60–61; and Indigenous peoples, 121, 122, 138; and metaphysical religions, 196, 197, 202, 203, 206; missionaries, 81, 98–99; percentage of communicants to total adherents, 33–34, 222(t), 232(t); and Catholic-Protestant tensions, 94–95; and Sabbatarianism, 74; and the social gospel, 81, 141; and Sunday School, 88, 144; women, 111–15, 117–18, 118(i), 120, 125, 127, 136; and women's rights, 180–81, 182–84, 183(i), 282*n*82, 283*n*84
mining. *See* coal; gold; hardrock; silver
miners, 47(i), 50(i); and alcohol, 69–70, 71, 73, 257*n*94; and church involvement, 84–85, 86, 87, 97, 99, 111–12, 118, 123, 125, 128, 260*n*59, 265*n*43; and irreligion, 40, 42, 43, 45–46, 49–50, 62, 76, 84, 224(t), 249*n*71, 264*n*42; and labour militancy, 48, 50, 51, 52–53, 58–59, 61, 63, 252*n*35, 256*n*81; and metaphysical religions, 190, 192, 194; missionaries to, 79–82, 80(i)
missionaries, 20, 29, 36, 37, 53, 70–71, 73, 75, 80–81, 82, 98, 152, 216; and Asian people, 28, 104, 122, 168–69, 171–74, 176, 198, 203, 219, 280*n*50; female missionary societies, 106, 118, 121, 172, 179, 183(i); and Indigenous peoples, 28, 122, 176–78, 177(i), 216, 267*n*80, 281*n*67
Moffat, Miss, 40, 247*n*46
Moir, George, 58–59, 74–75, 257*n*94
moral reformers, 14, 68–69, 135, 137–42, 152, 160, 178–79, 182, 184, 216–17. *See also* alcohol; gambling; Sabbatarianism; Sabbath legislation; sex trade; social gospel; suffrage
Morgan, Rev., 75–76
Mouat, Jeremy, 48, 69
Muslims, 166, 167

Nakusp (Kootenays), 57, 260*n*59
Nanaimo, 7, 42, 43, 49, 51, 63–63, 69–70, 92, 224(t); Chinese people in, 72, 122, 172; Christian Science in, 207; church involvement in, 86, 88, 91, 118, 128, 131–32; demographics of, 8, 249*n*73; irreligious in, 84, 85; spiritualism in, 190, 191, 192, 193, 194, 195–96; strike in, 47, 252*n*35
National Rationalist Association. *See* Rationalist Association of North America
Nelles, H.V., 140
Nelson (Kootenays), 69, 70(i), 89(i), 91(i), 104(i), 109(i), 207; Chinese community in, 72, 75–76, 172; church involvement in, 108–9, 115, 122, 123, 125, 128, 129–30, 226–31(t), 263*n*26, 264*n*27, 265*n*43, 268*n*93; demographics of, 8, 103, 110, 236*n*15, 262*n*14, 262*n*16, 264*n*41, 269*n*95; irreligious in, 82, 111, 112, 224(t); newspaperman and mayor John Houston, 74–75, 75(i), 76, 77, 95, 97–98, 256*n*90, 257*n*95; women, 112, 115, 116, 117–18
Nelson Baptist Ladies Aid, 117
Nelson Catholic Ladies Aid, 117
Nelson Methodist Ladies Aid, 117
New Brunswick, 41, 247*n*54
New Denver, 57, 96, 209, 260*n*59
New Thought. *See under* Theosophy
New Westminster, 207, 247*n*57, 272n44

Nicola Valley, 6, 112
Nipissing (Ontario), 244*n*20
no religion: census declaration of, 4–5, 242*n*3, 243*n*11; definition of, 30–31; as proportion of population, 5(f), 29–30, 46(f), 99, 223–24(t), 234*n*3, 274*n*69
Noddings, Timothy, 192
North-West Territories, 34, 237*n*24
Norwegians, 250*n*83
Nova Scotia, 60, 107, 110, 117, 123, 125, 264*n*36; church involvement in, 226(t), 228–30(t), 261*n*3; percentage of communicants to total adherents, 222(t), 264*n*27. *See also* Amherst; Kentville

Oddfellows, 90, 91(i), 97
Ogle, Frank, 62, 252*n*31
Okanagan Valley, 8, 103, 131, 236*n*14. *See also* Kelowna; Vernon
Ontario, 39, 117, 123, 124–25, 175, 188–89, 235*n*11, 264*n*36, 282*n*82; church involvement in, 33, 34, 92, 107, 108, 132, 148, 226(t), 228–30(t), 244*n*20, 261*n*3, 272*n*50; communicants in, 222(t), 232(t), 245*n*21, 264*n*27; irreligious in, 223(t), 247*n*45; and metaphysical religions, 188–89, 191, 202, 203, 204, 205. *See also* Campbellford; Dunnville
opium smoking, 170, 172
Opp, James, 158, 207–8, 218
Orange Order, 90, 92, 94, 95(i). *See also* fraternal orders
O'Reilly, Kathleen, 135
Orchard, Imbert, 24
Orsi, Robert, 11–12, 83
Osterhout, S.S., 171
Ottaway, V.E., 285*n*27
Owen, Alex, 187, 192, 194, 284*n*5

Pacific Coast Rationalist Association, 154–56
pagan: applied to Asian people, 52; applied to Indigenous people, 20, 51–52, 177; census category, 22
Parke, Alice Barrett, 86–87, 122
Pat, Fr. (Henry Irwin), 79–80, 80(i), 105(i)
Pentacostals, 218
Perry, Adele, 16, 37, 68, 71, 115, 254*n*63
Pettipiece, Parmeter (Parm), 64, 274*n*66
Political Equality League, 183, 197
practical Christians, 21, 25, 78–99, 258*n*22
Prairies, 9, 110, 127–28, 275*n*84
preachers, 81, 82, 120, 127–28, 144, 153, 197, 202, 257*n*99; opposition to, 58, 60, 64–67; revivalist, 82, 136; Salvation Army, 153–54, 156–57, 253*n*40; Zionites, 157–59
Presbyterian Christian Endeavour Society, 117, 118
Presbyterian Young People's Society, 119
Presbyterians, 102–3, 210; and Asian immigration, 67, 75, 168, 171, 172, 174, 176, 254*n*57; census declaration, 21, 22, 30; and church involvement, 33, 37, 105, 108–9, 110, 146–47, 149, 226–32(t), 242*n*73, 244*nn*18–19, 263*n*25, 264*n*27, 264*n*39, 265*n*43, 272*n*51, 273*nn*52–55, 273*nn*60–61; and class, 50, 58, 59–60, 124, 125, 147, 148, 272*n*51, 273*nn*52–54; and ethnicity, 124, 146; and irreligion, 79, 82, 144; and marriage, 42, 43, 273*n*55; ministers, 265*n*45; missionaries, 29, 37, 53, 70, 75, 82, 175; percentage of communicants to total adherents, 222(t), 225(t), 232(t); and religious education, 14; and the social gospel, 141; and spiritualism, 196; and Sunday School, 88–89, 144; and Theosophy, 199–200, 202; women, 40, 111–16, 114(i), 116(i), 117, 118, 119, 120, 125, 147, 179, 180, 202, 247*n*46
Price, Charles, 218–19
Prohibition, 57, 136, 141, 142, 218, 271*n*33, 289*n*4
prostitution. *See* sex trade
Protestant Protective Association, 260*n*48
Protestants: and church involvement, 23, 33–36, 34(f), 49, 85, 88, 96, 102, 107, 114, 117, 127, 145, 244*nn*19–20, 263*nn*22–26, 264*n*27; and ethnicity, 146; and fraternal orders, 91–92, 94–95, 95(i), 260*n*48; and irreligion, 20, 41, 72–73, 151, 152; and metaphysical religions, 190–91, 192–93; and moral reform, 21,

26; and Protestant-Catholic tensions, 25, 79, 93, 94–95, 95(i), 120, 216, 237*n*25, 239*n*40, 260*n*48; and schools, 13–14; and whiteness, 56. *See also* Anglicans; Methodists; Presbyterians; Prohibition; suffrage; Woman's Christian Temperance Union

Quebec, 33, 34, 34(f), 221, 222(t), 237*n*25, 245*n*22, 289*n*4

racial origin, census enumeration of, 9, 10(t), 23, 51–52, 237*n*24, 250*n*82
racialization, 8–10, 19–21, 30, 51–52, 68, 237*n*24, 250*n*82. *See also* African Canadians; anti-Asian racism; eastern Europeans; Indigenous peoples, racism toward; Italians; whiteness
Raibmon, Paige, 177
Rationalist Association of North America, 155
Rationalists, 154–56, 276*n*88, 276*n*91, 290*nn*13–14
Reid, Andrew, 93, 144, 163–64, 259*n*37
Reimer, Samuel, 5–6
rescue homes, 154, 172, 173(i), 178–79
resource extraction. *See* gold; fishing; logging; mining
Revelstoke (Kootenays), 94–95, 95(i), 116, 117, 118, 122, 123, 224(t), 264*n*33; church involvement in, 108–9, 111, 112, 115, 125, 129–30, 226–31(t), 268*n*93; demographics of, 103, 110, 262*n*14, 262*n*16, 264*n*35
revivals, 82, 114, 135–37, 218–19, 269*n*100. *See also* Salvation Army
Robbins, Rev. A., 73, 81
Robinson, Rev. J. Millen, 112, 265*n*45
Robson, John, 140, 269*n*106, 271*n*24
Roman Catholics, 20, 22, 43, 50, 102–3, 104, 141, 245*n*22; and Catholic-Protestant tensions, 3, 25, 79, 92, 93, 94–95, 95(i), 120, 216, 237*n*25, 239*n*40, 260*n*48; and class, 60, 64, 85, 95–96; church involvement, 33–34, 34(f), 35(f), 49, 72–73, 85, 107–8, 108–9, 135, 143, 145, 225(t), 245*n*21; and ethnicity, 145–46, 272*n*48; and fraternal orders, 92–93, 95–96, 145–46, 163–64, 260*n*48; and funerals, 96; and Indigenous people, 177(i); and irreligion, 72–73, 85; and metaphysical religions, 191, 201, 210; percentage of communicants to total adherents, 222(t), 232(t); and schools, 13, 239*n*41, 239*n*44; and socialism, 60, 64; women, 117, 120
Roseman, Dora, 165
Rossland (Kootenays), 48(i), 69, 90(i), 105(i), 123, 127(i), 265*n*44, 266*n*61; Christian Science in, 207; church involvement in, 89–90, 91, 108, 110, 111, 115–17, 118, 125–26, 128, 129, 130, 226–31(t), 264*n*27, 264*n*39, 265*n*43, 268*n*93; demographics of, 8, 103, 104, 110, 236*n*15, 262*n*14, 262*n*16, 264*n*41, 269*n*95; irreligious in, 45–47, 46(f), 53, 82, 224(t), 264*n*42; women, 112, 115–17
Roy, Patricia, 19, 142, 170, 171
Royal Commission on Chinese and Japanese Immigration, 1902, 170, 171, 280*n*50, 281*n*64

Sabbatarianism, 57, 73, 76, 128, 121, 138, 139–42, 155. *See also* Sabbath legislation
Sabbath legislation, 14, 68, 76, 140–41, 142, 155, 270*n*23. *See also* Sabbatarianism
Salvation Army, 104, 114, 152, 275*nn*84–85, 276*n*86; and the Industrial Workers of the World (IWW), 63–64, 156, 253*n*40; and street preaching, 153–54, 156–57
Sandon (Kootenays), 57, 69, 260*n*59
Sandon Paystreak, 59, 65, 251*n*15
Sanford, Rev. A.M., 266*n*61
Saskatchewan, 35, 175, 237*n*24; percentage of communicants to total adherents in, 222(t)
Scandinavians, 104, 261*n*62, 262*n*16; Finns, 98, 131, 204
schools: Catholic, 13, 239*n*41; Chinese, 281*n*61; public, 161; religious instruction in public schools, 13–14, 239*nn*43–44, 243*n*7; residential, 178; Sunday Schools, 21, 30, 37, 59, 87–89, 89(i), 117, 119, 128, 136, 144, 207, 271*n*36
Scott, Ann, 43, 247*n*55

Scott, Edwin, 171
Scottish ancestry, 124, 146, 272*n*48
secularists, 40, 154, 155, 192, 211, 220, 223(t), 236*n*12, 243*n*11, 276*n*91
secularization, theories of, 11–13, 238*n*37, 268*n*91
sex trade, 14, 25, 37, 68, 69, 73, 76, 128, 141, 214, 257*n*94
sex trade workers, 40, 69, 120, 154, 170, 173, 173(i), 215, 265*n*55; and church involvement, 115–16, 151–52, 265*n*54; and freethought, 151, 275*nn*72–73
Shaw, Charlie, 126–27
Sikhs, 9, 161, 166–67, 199, 203, 278*n*19
silver mining, 8, 69. *See also* miners
Simmons, Elder, 158
Singh, Kapoor, 203
Singh, Kartar, 203
Singh, Teja, 203
single men. *See* marital status
single women. *See* marital status
Sivertz, Bent, 196–97
Sivertz, Christian, 197
Sivertz, Elinborg, 197
skeptics, census declaration as, 22, 243*n*11
Slavs, 9, 72–73, 96, 104, 145, 262*n*16
Slocan, 57, 84, 257*n*94; irreligious in, 45–47, 46(f), 224(t), 274*n*68
Smythe, A.S., 203
social gospel, 60, 81, 141, 152–54, 203, 204, 219, 275*n*76, 275*n*78
socialism, 4, 8, 17, 18, 22, 47, 53, 60, 61, 62, 143, 144, 204–5, 287*n*72, 289*n*101. *See also* Marxism; Socialist Party of Canada
Socialist Party of British Columbia. *See* Socialist Party of Canada
Socialist Party of Canada, 19, 62, 65, 78, 143–44, 156, 157, 167, 205, 252*n*24, 252*n*31; radical atheism of, 19; *Western Clarion*, 60–61, 63, 64, 65, 76, 77, 125, 252*n*28; *Western Socialist*, 204
Sohi, Seema, 167
South Asians, 9, 20, 28, 99, 161, 168, 216; and anti-Asian racism, 99, 155, 161, 166–68, 188, 198, 203–4; demographics of in British Columbia, 166; Hindus, 155, 161, 166, 167, 199; loss of franchise, 236*n*22; Muslims, 166, 167; Sikhs, 9, 161, 166–67, 199, 203, 278*n*19; and Theosophists, 188, 198, 203–4
southern Europeans. *See* Italians
Spalding, C.T., 154–55, 276*n*88
Speer, Rev. J.C., 138, 139(i), 168, 169, 206–7
spiritualists, 16, 22, 27, 97, 186, 188, 189–98, 285*n*27; and class, 190, 192–93, 285*n*26; clerical attitudes toward, 190–91, 210–11, 289*n*101; combining Christianity with, 191–92, 194–95, 195(i), 196(i), 200, 206; number of, 211, 233(t), 285*n*29, 285*n*33; socialists and, 204; women and, 189, 193–94, 195(i), 197, 201, 215
Springhill (Nova Scotia), 60
Stephen, A.M., 205, 288*n*79
Stevens, H.H., 61, 170, 252*n*29, 279*n*37
Stewart, Bob, 13, 109
Stewart, Margaret, 127
Stowe, Emily, 202
strikes: Chinese school student, 281*n*61; labour, 47–48, 50, 51, 60, 63, 64, 103, 126, 252*n*35, 256*n*81, 286*n*38
suffrage, 27, 141–42, 162, 180–84, 185, 197, 201–2, 282*n*82, 283*n*84
Sunday Schools. *See under* schools
Swedes, 146, 250*n*83
syndicalism, 63–64

Taoism, 167
Taylor, Charles, 237*n*31
Taylor, James, 205
Thayer, Fr., 94, 118
Theosophy, 16, 211, 212, 221, 233(t), 286*n*53, 287*n*60, 287*n*71, 287*n*74, 288*n*76, 288*n*79; clerical attitudes toward, 27, 199–200, 206; New Thought off-shoot of, 202, 211, 287*n*61; origins of, 198–99; and socialism, 204–5; and South Asians, 188, 198, 203–4; Theosophical Societies in Canada, 186, 199, 201–2, 286*n*46; women and, 200–1, 201–2, 215, 286*n*42, 286*n*52, 287*n*72
Thomas, Ernest, 81

Thompson, Phillips, 204
Tickle, Albert, 86
Toronto Theosophical Society, 198, 203, 286*n*46
transiency, 8; and irreligion, 15, 17, 36, 39–40, 41, 46, 49, 53, 71, 99, 109–11, 118, 125, 132, 214, 247*n*52
Trinity Methodist Church, Nelson
Tsadias, Chief George, 177(i)
Tugwell, Cora, 275*n*72

unbelievers, census declaration as, 197, 243*n*11, 274*n*63. *See also* agnostics; atheists; freethinkers; infidels; no religion; secularists; skeptics
unions, 8, 18, 45, 51, 58, 74, 91, 97, 124, 125, 149, 157, 256*n*81, 260*n*59, 286*n*38; Industrial Workers of the World (IWW), 63–64, 76, 98, 156–57, 198, 214, 253*n*40; Western Federation of Miners, 48, 53, 61
Unitarians, 194, 287*n*60
United States, 17, 143, 187–88, 92, 244*n*19, 284*n*6; Christian Science in, 205, 206, 209; church involvement in, 143; freethought in, 44, 66; irreligion in, 5–6, 16, 36, 53, 143, 187, 217–18, 234*n*3, 235*n*4; labour radicalism in, 45, 214; Rationalists, 155, 276*n*88, 276*n*91; spiritualism in, 189, 191; and suffrage, 181; Theosophy in, 198, 200, 201; unions in, 45, 63. *See also* Americans
Universal Brotherhood. *See* Theosophy

Van Die, Marguerite, 238*n*37
Vancouver, 150(i), 260*n*48; Chinese community, 99, 167, 168, 170–71, 172, 174–75, 176, 272*n*49, 278*nn*24–25, 281*n*61; church involvement in, 100, 135–36, 142, 144, 145–49, 232(t), 272*n*44, 273*nn*53–54; demographics of, 8, 135, 247*n*57, 272*n*48; Indigenous peoples, 177; irreligious in, 6, 26, 27, 40, 44, 64, 134–35, 141–42, 149–60, 214, 274*nn*64–67, 274*n*70, 275*n*76, 275*n*78, 276*n*86; Japanese community, 99, 167, 170–71, 172, 272*n*49; Jewish community, 162, 163–65, 276*n*2; and metaphysical religions, 191, 192, 193, 200, 203–4, 205, 207, 208, 209, 285*n*26, 285*n*29, 287*n*60, 288*n*79; revivals in, 218; and Sabbatarianism, 88, 139–41; Salvation Army in, 114, 152, 153–54, 156–57, 253*n*40, 275*n*85, 276*n*86, 276*n*93; schools, 13–14, 239*n*44; South Asian community, 99, 166, 278*n*19, 279*n*37
Vancouver General Ministerial Association, 152, 275*n*76
Vancouver Island, 7, 8, 247*n*51, 247*n*57; church involvement, 49–50, 146, 225(t), 244*n*20; and irreligion, 41, 50–51, 223–24(t), 243*n*13, 245*n*34, 246*n*35, 246*n*44, 249*n*71; and labour radicalism, 47–48, 50, 61–62. *See also* Ladysmith; Nanaimo; Victoria
Vancouver Social Survey 1913, 141–42, 154, 271*n*30
Vancouver Theosophical Society, 205
Varey, Carrie, 207
Varey, Charles, 207, 208
Veale, W.S., 157
Vernon (Okanagan Valley), 91, 127(i), 264*n*33, 264*n*35, 264*n*41, 269*n*99; church involvement in, 108–9, 111, 115, 117, 126, 127–28, 129, 133, 226–28(t), 229(t), 230–31(t); demographics of, 103, 104, 110, 262*n*14, 264*n*41, 268*n*92; Indigenous people in, 104, 123
Victoria, 7, 62, 73, 93; Chinese community, 23, 52, 72, 75, 138, 167, 168, 169(i), 171–74, 173(i), 175, 179, 218–19, 272*n*49, 274*n*63, 278*nn*24–25, 280*nn*55–56, 281*n*61; church involvement in, 43, 115, 123, 135–36, 142–49, 232(t), 271*n*36, 272*n*51, 273*n*52, 273*n*55, 273*nn*60–61; demographics of, 8, 272*n*48, 273*n*61; Indigenous peoples, 138; irreligious in, 23, 26, 27, 37, 40, 41, 96, 134–35, 149–60, 214, 220, 223(t), 274*nn*63–65, 274*n*67; Japanese community, 171–72, 173, 272*n*49; Jewish community, 162–64, 163(i), 165–66, 276*n*2, 278*n*18; labour radicalism in, 143, 156, 157, 286*n*38; metaphysical religions in, 186,

189–91, 192–93, 194, 195–97, 196(i), 199–200, 201–2, 206, 207–8, 209, 285*nn*26–27, 285*n*29, 285*n*33, 286*n*46, 287*nn*60–61, 288*n*95; revivals in, 136–37, 218; and Sabbatarianism, 139–40; Salvation Army in, 153–54, 156, 157, 275*n*85; South Asian community, 166, 278*n*19
Victoria Theosophical Society, 186, 199, 201–2, 286*n*46
Victoria Trades and Labour Council, 157
Voisey, Paul, 127

Wagar, Samuel, 204, 205
Wang, Jiwu, 174, 176
Ward, Rev. Neville, 171
Ward, Peter, 19, 170, 171
Weinrobe, Gertrude, 164
Weiss, Gillian, 179
Wellington, Vancouver Island, 85(i)
Western Clarion, 60–61, 63, 64, 65, 76, 77, 125
Western Federation of Miners, 48, 53, 61
Western Wage Earner, 64. *See also BC Federationist*
White, Rev. J.H., 98–99, 219
White, Jimmy, 112, 113(i), 265*n*46
Whiteley, Marilyn Fardig, 173
whiteness, 25, 56, 67–68, 78–79, 84, 93–94, 95–96, 99, 101, 122, 132, 149; Christian settler women and, 17; Jews and, 162–66. *See also* racialization
Wilkins-Laflamme, Sarah, 234n3
Williams, Sarah C., 11, 83, 86, 87, 88, 89
Wilson, Rev. G.H., 170
Winchester, Rev. A.B., 75, 176
Winnipeg, 146, 155, 232(t), 286*n*38, 290*n*13
Winslow, Rev. J.W., 6
Winters, Donald E., 63
Woman's Christian Temperance Union, 37, 136, 141–42, 152, 178–79, 181
women: as proportion of population, 7, 8, 15, 46, 71, 132, 147, 211, 218, 247*n*57, 249*n*73, 289*n*5; rights of, 27, 141–42, 162, 180–84, 183(i), 185, 197, 201–2, 282*n*82, 283*n*84. *See also* gender; marriage; marital status; sex trade workers; suffrage

Yale, 247*n*57; Americans in, 52–53, 251*n*89; irreligious in, 44, 45–46, 49, 52–54, 108, 146, 224(t), 244*n*20, 251*n*90, 274*n*62; percentage of communicants to total adherents, 225(t); population, 247*n*57. *See also* Nelson; Revelstoke; Rossland; Vernon
Young Men's Hebrew Association (YMHA), 164–65

Zionites, 157–59, 160